Oswald Talked

OSWALD TALKED

The New Evidence in the

JFK

ASSASSINATION

Ray and Mary La Fontaine

PELICAN PUBLISHING COMPANY

Gretna 1996

To Bill Adams
and
in memory of Al Dooley

The word "Pelican" and the depiction of a pelican are trademarks of Pelican Publishing Company, Inc., and are registered in the U.S. Patent and Trademark Office.

Library of Congress Cataloging-in-Publication Data

La Fontaine, Ray.
    Oswald talked : the new evidence in the JFK assassination / Ray and Mary La Fontaine.
        p.   cm.
    Includes bibliographical references and index.
    ISBN 1-56554-029-8 (hc)
    1. Kennedy, John F. (John Fitzgerald), 1917-1963—Assassination.
2. Oswald, Lee Harvey. I. La Fontaine, Mary. II. Title.
E842.9.L24   1995
364.1'524'0973—dc20   94-45945
                                                    CIP

Manufactured in the United States of America
Published by Pelican Publishing Company, Inc.
1101 Monroe Street, Gretna, Louisiana 70053

Contents

Preface

In 1992, following the furor created by the Oliver Stone film *JFK*, Dallas became the first city in the nation to release files on the assassination of President John F. Kennedy. As Dallas-based journalists looking into this story, we had yet to write on the Dealey Plaza tragedy, about which we held only one preconceived notion: Lee Harvey Oswald had acted alone. Indeed, our first story on the newly declassified files (for the *Houston Post*) conclusively debunked one of the most enduring assassination conspiracy myths. This was the legend of the "three tramps"—whose arrest records, we discovered, were among the thousands of papers released by the Dallas Police Department. Prior to this discovery, conspiracy fans had long suspected the three hitherto anonymous men, arrested in a downtown rail yard during the confused moments after the shooting, of being disguised government hitmen prematurely (or intentionally) let out of jail by a bumbling DPD. They weren't, it turned out. They were "tramps" after all.

Ironically, the debunking of this conspiratorial myth was not the end of the story. It was the beginning—the genesis of *Oswald Talked*.

As we would gradually realize, the legend of the tramps masked the key to the case. In the same file with the arrest records identifying the tramps were two *other* arrest records dated November 22, 1963. Appearing innocuous at first, the latter documents would prove to be among the most significant ever withheld from the American public. They were the records of two more men, who, like the hapless tramps, had been caught in the hectic police sweep of that day. Both were eventually released. Before they were, however, both were placed, for at least several hours on the Friday of the assassination, in the same tiny cellblock with Lee Harvey Oswald.

During this interval—documented with a full arsenal of telephone logs and other records—the men overheard Oswald "talk." Oswald talked about Jack Ruby, about a secret motel-room meeting where money and guns changed hands, and about another prisoner already

5

held in the Dallas jail (and whom Oswald identified to unknown
authorities in the corridor outside the cell, most likely the FBI, as
having been present at the motel meeting). One of the inmates over-
hearing this exchange, John F. Elrod, described it nine months later,
in August 1964, to the Memphis sheriff's office and the Memphis
FBI. The FBI responded by attempting to discredit Elrod, lying about
his Dallas incarceration, and burying his report for three decades.

As we pursued the documentation for this startling disclosure
(with the inestimable help of Freedom of Information Act expert Bill
Adams, who discovered the long-forgotten 1964 Elrod FBI report),
the newly released records from the FBI, CIA, and U.S. Army began
to tell the true story of Lee Harvey Oswald and the assassins of President Kennedy. It soon became clear that the Bureau of J. Edgar
Hoover, far from investigating the assassination, had participated in
a massive cover-up about Oswald. It also became clear why: conducting a real investigation would have disclosed the embarrassing fact
that Oswald, the accused assassin of the president and Dallas police
officer J. D. Tippit, had been recruited in March 1963 as an FBI informant (picking him up from the CIA, the likely agency that had earlier sent the ex-Marine, complete with a telltale intelligence ID, on
a mission to Russia). It was in the role of FBI informant that Oswald
visited New Orleans later that year, returned to Dallas in early October, and, on November 16, warned the Bureau of an impending
assassination attempt on the president by a "Cuban faction." The
warning was communicated to the FBI's Washington headquarters,
and relayed from there to other Bureau offices.

In 1967, during the investigation of New Orleans D.A. Jim Garrison, word began to leak about the 1963 warning. An FBI clerk who
had received the warning Teletype in the New Orleans office was
then issued his own warning by the Bureau: "Shut up." Though he
made no attempt to publicize his story, the former FBI clerk (by then
senior vice-president of a Louisiana bank) gave sworn testimony
about the incident to the House Select Committee on Assassinations.
That testimony was not released until 1993, by which time it had
become obvious that HSCA counsel Robert Blakey distorted the testimony in the HSCA's *Report* issued in 1979. It included the clerk's
revelation that he had seen Oswald's FBI informant folder in the files
of New Orleans agent Warren deBrueys.

On one point HSCA counsel Blakey was not mistaken or disingenuous. As he noted in a television appearance, a conspiracy to assassinate President Kennedy required that the conspirators be *associated with Oswald*—whether he served as a coconspirator or (as he claimed) a "patsy."

Only one group conspicuously fills this bill. It happens to be the same virulently anti-Castro group known through recently released FBI and CIA files to have been holding clandestine meetings in Dallas only weeks before the assassination, seeking to set up an armed invasion of Cuba in the last week of November 1963. It was also this exile group that was involved in the gunrunning operation Oswald described in the Dallas jail, and with whom he had been intimately associated in New Orleans during the summer of 1963. The same Cuban group, moreover, was on the CIA payroll (per newly available agency documents, which reveal that the group was so out of control that the CIA dubbed it their enfants terribles) and demonstrably tied to mobsters, one of whom would confess a role in the assassination prior to his death—John Martino. (Martino himself traveled twice to Dallas in October 1963, first to meet with Cuban exiles and later, under an alias, with Ruby's friend, a gunrunning Fort Hood army officer. The officer was an FBI asset who was officially authorized to provide arms for the planned invasion of Cuba in the last week of November.) Finally, it was this group of anti-Castro Cubans that Oswald infiltrated as an FBI informant, and they knew it. He became their perfect patsy.

Suspicions of Oswald intelligence involvements have been with us for more than thirty years. *Oswald Talked* documents the story for the first time. But—of course—heaven is in the details. The details of Oswald's conversation in the presence of Elrod, and of the FBI's attempts to suppress the account, may be found in chapter 1 and Appendix B ("The Case Against Oswald"); of Oswald's DoD card suggesting an intelligence assignment to Russia, in chapter 3; of Oswald's FBI recruitment and services for the Bureau, in chapters 6, 8, and 10; and of Oswald's close involvement with the anti-Castro "Cuban faction" on which he was spying, in chapters 5, 6, and 10. In addition, Appendix A ("Countdown to the Assassination") provides a chronology of events leading to November 22, 1963, and beyond.

Chapter 2 contains pertinent background on Oswald's childhood and Marine service, and chapter 4, on his CIA handler in Dallas, the inimitable Baron George de Mohrenschildt.

Chapter 9 explodes Silvia Odio's celebrated tale of a meeting with Oswald in the company of members of the Bobby Kennedy-backed exile socialist group, JURE. Ms. Odio's account, a transparent hoax as the chapter demonstrates, may be best understood not only as a cover story, but as an attempt to shift the identity of Oswald's true associates. (Still more such attempts to develop this fallback position may follow release of this book; ignore them.)

Finally, if you insist on the lamentable practice of turning to the "conclusion" first, try chapter 10 (or perhaps the chronology of Appendix A)—not 11. The latter, designed precisely to discourage such shortcuts to wisdom, is an epilogue. Read it as dessert—a snack of media chicanery and Dallas impresarios who prey on gullible assassination tourists—*after* the first ten chapters.

Acknowledgments

If American life were a Greek drama, or maybe a play by Shake-speare, it would be tempting to blame our present hellish social ills (if not also the floods, fires, and earthquakes) on a grave unatoned sin now more than three decades old, the ghost of which is still rattling chains and demanding retribution. Who will come forward as sweet Hamlet to satisfy the aggrieved father, or better yet, as Oedipus, to cleanse the pollution his own guilt created? Though sadly, such full-service tormented heroes are no longer in vogue, it has been reassuring to find their noble spirit intact in a hardy band of eminently sane Kennedy assassination investigators. If anyone can get to the bottom of this lingering mystery, it is researchers like Bill Adams, Paul Hoch, Hershel Womack, and Peter Dale Scott. Without any of them, this book would not have been possible.

Bill Adams, the man who started it all with his discovery of the August 11, 1964 FBI report on John Franklin Elrod. (Courtesy Bill Adams)

Paul Hoch, Berkeley computer analyst, physicist, and JFK assassination researchers' researcher. (Courtesy Paul Hoch)

9

Above all, we have relied on Bill Adams' superb skills as a researcher and analyst almost since the day he first contacted us, in the fall of 1992, about his retrieval of an FBI report on a man whose arrest record Mary had found, John Elrod. Bill, a cyberspace warrior from Silicon Valley, provided assistance on almost every phase of the project. He helped locate a number of the witnesses interviewed, and obtained most of the major documents presented in this book through his Freedom of Information Act requests and other research. These included not only the original FBI report on John Elrod, but also other FBI reports on the Elrod incident, a Memphis sheriff's department wire to J. Edgar Hoover confirming that Elrod had come in to give information on the murder of Lee Harvey Oswald, House Select Committee depositions from John Thomas Masen and Frank Ellsworth, FBI reports showing an apparently authorized military operation supplying guns to Cuban exiles through a middleman, inquest records on the suicide of George de Mohrenschildt, FBI and other reports on Thomas E. Davis, and file releases on John Thomas Masen. Finally, Bill obtained the documents revealing the full extent of the plan to invade Cuba in November 1963.

Paul Hoch's name has appeared in acknowledgment sections in virtually every major book on the assassination of President Kennedy, from Sylvia Meagher's *Accessories After the Fact* in 1967 to Gerald Posner's *Case Closed* in 1993. In addition to maintaining one of the largest private libraries in the U.S. of government documents on the Kennedy assassination, Paul reviews current literature and keeps readers of his "Echoes of Conspiracy" newsletter abreast of the latest publications and developments. As a Harvard-trained physicist and information analyst, he has written his own careful studies of government documents, and is in a unique position to analyze new work in its historical and scientific context; and he is almost unmatched among assassination critics in his ability to apply simple logic to the facts. We are happy to acknowledge him for his invaluable advice and assistance.

We are also deeply indebted to the expert assistance and support of Hershel Womack throughout this project. A professor of photography at Texas Tech University and former Smithsonian staffer, Hershel has contributed his photographic expertise in the analysis of the backyard photos of Lee Harvey Oswald. Without his wisdom and late-night faxes, we would not have been able to determine that the authenticity of some of these photographs is still very much open to question, and would have missed out on many other insights as well across the gamut of Kennedy research.

Although we had not even met Peter Dale Scott prior to completing the original manuscript of this book, we and everyone seriously interested in the history of the case owe Peter an enormous debt of gratitude—first, for his several books on the subject, and secondly because he continues unselfishly to provide colleagues with leads and analysis from his own vast store of documents and knowledge. In particular, the leads Peter provided on Oswald's long-forgotten November 16, 1963 meeting with the Dallas FBI, as well as on the DRE press release of December 9, 1963 from Mexico City, were key components of this story.

We thank Brian Sirgo for his role in bringing the mysteries of the Kennedy assassination to a new generation of Americans including ourselves, as well as for his friendship and commitment to the truth.

We are also grateful to Professor Larry Haapanen of Idaho for providing generous assistance on a crucial document related to the arrest of Donnell Whitter; for insights on the November 22, 1963 meeting of agents of the FBI, ATF, and military intelligence; for informed analysis of George de Mohrenschildt and the planned Haitian invasion of May-June 1963; and for other information on Oswald and military matters in general.

For fine prints of many important photographs and other generous assistance, and for his scholarship in producing *JFK Assassination Photographs: A Comprehensive Listing of the Photographic Evidence Relating to the Assassination of President John F. Kennedy,* we thank John Woods II.

For his commitment to bringing the new evidence on Lee Harvey Oswald and Jack Ruby to the attention of the congressional oversight committee on the release of the JFK files, and for his work on the new CIA releases and other areas of our history, we thank John Newman.

Dallas researchers Joe and Greg Lowrey have been generous in their support and research in uncovering key elements of the Oswald puzzle. We look forward to Greg's book on the murder of Officer J. D. Tippit.

We thank Jack White for his analysis of the Oswald photograph on the Department of Defense ID card, and for bringing the assassination truly home to us for the first time in an all-night videotaping session of his massive slide collection. Jack's presentation makes the assassination come horrifyingly alive as no written word can do.

We are grateful to Gaeton Fonzi for contributing to our understanding of the circumstances of George de Mohrenschildt's death, as well as of the inner workings of the HSCA.

We thank Anthony Summers for providing helpful documents on Nancy Perrin Rich, and for his still important work on the assassination, *Conspiracy*.

We thank Dallas archivist Mary Ferrell for providing the information on Francis Gary Powers, including his Department of Defense ID card; for the arrest records of Lawrence Reginald Miller and Donnell Whitter; and for her devilish sense of humor.

We thank Roger Feinman and David Lifton for their interest in the Oswald DoD card story, and for generously volunteering to disseminate the news story through the major on-line services when the wire services did not run it.

Two media organizations were also major contributors to this project. The *Houston Post,* and particularly our editor, Jim Jennings, provided a serious outlet for stories on the new evidence emerging from recently released files on the assassination. Over a period of a year and a half, the *Post* devoted valuable space to this work despite a virtual blackout by the regional office of the Associated Press in Dallas. Jim Jennings also contributed world-class volumes to our understanding of profanity. We hope this book provides a few answers to his favorite rejoinder: "So *what?*" The recent closing of the *Post* is a loss to Texas and the nation.

The second media contributor to the project is the Paramount Television tabloid, "Hard Copy." When we were unable to obtain funding for a PBS affiliate-sponsored project on the new evidence, "Hard Copy" and its executive producer Linda Bell Blue and supervising producer Ron Vandor picked up the project. With their commitment, we were able to videotape interviews with John Elrod, his brother Lindy, retired ATF agent Frank Ellsworth, and Oswald's best Marine buddy Jim Botelho, among others.

We thank Jefferson Morley for his thoughtful analysis of the new evidence in his November 18, 1993 story for the *Washington Post,* and for his invaluable assistance as an editor in bringing "The Fourth Tramp," our story of John Elrod, to his paper's national audience.

Eric Hamburg contributed to this project in numerous ways—from his staff work for Cong. Lee Hamilton on the release of the JFK files, to his work at Ixtlan Productions, where he obtained and provided information on the newly released Cuban files and their documentation, and worked to bring the new evidence to the widest possible audience. The latter sections of this book could not have been written without Eric's help. He represents the best of both our working government and the American film industry.

The sensitive and intelligent hand of Nina Kooij, our editor at Pelican, is evident on every page of this book—more to us than the reader perhaps, transparency being one of the notable angelic virtues. Nina's wings are probably a bit more frazzled today than two years ago, when she innocently believed we were capable of meeting deadlines. She knows better now, of course, but has maintained her serenity intact. We thank her for her patience and rigorous skills (reassuring in an age when language standards are déclassé), and the publisher for the maverick courage to take on a story that the national media tried to ignore.

Like all others writing on the assassination today, we are also indebted to Oliver Stone. In the aftermath of the tragic bombing of the federal building in Oklahoma City, Stone detractors have a new refrain: he is now, in addition to his other sins, the archetypal author of antigovernment hate. It appears to have gone unnoticed that his *JFK* was the genesis of the release of long-classified government documents on the uninvestigated murder of a U.S. president.

Other persons who are a part of our lives, and of this and other projects, are David and Deborah Sawyer; Sandra, Nathan, and Jeremy Fiel; Phil and Lunell Isett; Kenny Likis; Virginia, Bill, and Joe Transue; Joe and Jewell Mogan; Jim and Pat Barber; David Sawyer, Jr., and Didi Coker; Jimmy and Pat Lunney; Dr. Josep M. Solà-Solé of the Catholic University of America; and the merciless arbiter of all social and aesthetic values, Tom Wright.

We thank Phil and Evelyn, Ralph and Teresa, Gary, Mike, Sandy, and their families.

We also thank Raymond for actually sending letters and postcards on his world travels, and David, who would rather be in Philadelphia, for his continuing accomplishments. We keep up with him in the *New York Times*.

We thank James and Charlotte Lunney, Frances and Serafín Carvajal, and Papi and his beautiful sisters, whom we hope to see again.

Finally, we thank Charlotte and Eugenia for putting up with weird parents. We hope they'll stick around a little longer to see what happens next.

CHAPTER ONE

Follow the Guns

John Elrod was having trouble again. The thirty-one-year-old sometime cook had separated from his wife, Jackie, and was trying to dry out in Harbor House, a Memphis home for alcoholics. Late one Monday night, after drinking an unknown amount of beer and vodka, he picked up a sawed-off twelve-gauge shotgun and dwelled for some time on the possibility of killing Jackie. Suddenly realizing what he was contemplating, the shaken Elrod headed out the door and took the gun with him, not stopping until he reached the Shelby County Sheriff's Office in downtown Memphis in the early hours of Tuesday morning. A Memphis FBI report dated that day—August 11, 1964—gamely summed up the woozy situation: "Inasmuch as he had the sawed-off shotgun and the desire to kill her was known to him, he decided he should come to the Sheriff's Office and talk, which he did."[1]

In the course of this talk, Elrod volunteered to the Shelby County authorities that fear of what he might do to his wife had been only one matter preying on him that morning. There was something else, something he couldn't quite put out of his mind. It had happened almost a year back, in the less stormy days when he and Jackie lived in Dallas and he had steady work at a Mexican restaurant owned by his brother-in-law—though even then his drinking landed him in scrapes. He had been arrested twice by Dallas police for driving drunk, and the second DWI, in 1962, cost him three days in the city jail.

The event haunting Elrod had occurred late the following year, during a second stay in the jail. This one had nothing to do with his drinking problem, he said. On the Friday afternoon of November 22, 1963, Elrod had been walking near a railroad track by Harry Hines Boulevard. He had just learned that the United States had had a new president for several hours, and that the one until that morning, John Fitzgerald Kennedy, had been mortally shot at half past noon on Elm Street in downtown Dallas, two and a half miles away. But Elrod was unaware that Dallas police, having hastily rounded up hobos and other vagrants from the downtown rail yards in the moments after the shooting, were now casting their nets everywhere. They had already been alerted, minutes before, that a man "carrying a rifle" had been spotted walking along the tracks near Harry Hines. When the squad cars pulled up, the surprised Elrod, who did not have a rifle, was the only man in sight. He soon ended up in a cell on the fifth floor of the Dallas jail "for investigation of conspiracy to commit murder," the same all-purpose charge police had used to round up other suspicious characters that day. When finally released, he fled Dallas without ever returning to his job. He took refuge in the more familiar territory of Memphis, not far from his small hometown in east Arkansas, and ten months later, after a night of crisis with a sawed-off shotgun, had walked into the Shelby County Sheriff's Office to talk to someone.[2]

Elrod informed the deputies on that August morning that what he hadn't been able to get out of his head were some remarks his Dallas cellmate had made shortly after they were locked in together. A man with a gruesomely battered face had been led through the corridor outside their cell.[3] He was an inmate with an escort of guards. Elrod heard his cellmate say he recognized the injured inmate despite his "smashed up" face. He had met him previously in a motel room with four other men, he said. The men in the room had been advanced money under some type of contract, and the man with the injured face received some of the money. He wasn't injured then and drove a car loaded with guns, a Thunderbird. That was what Elrod could remember his cellmate saying, except for the most important thing: that one of the men in the motel room had been Jack Ruby.

When Elrod got to this part, Shelby County called in the FBI. The Memphis Bureau office responded the same day, sending Agents Norman L. Casey and Francis B. Cole to talk to the man the sheriff was holding. That Ruby's name attracted the quick attention of the FBI was hardly surprising. The Dallas bar owner had gone on trial in March of that year for his role in the final catastrophe of the Dallas tragedy. Two days after a deadly fusillade robbed the country of its president and seriously wounded Texas governor John Connally, Ruby, not to be outdone, committed the most public murder in history. In full view of millions watching on television, and in the packed basement of a citadel of authority, the Dallas police station, he had stepped up and shot the president's accused assassin, Lee Harvey Oswald, in the abdomen at point-blank range.

This incredible event—occurring while Elrod was confined in a cell five floors overhead, according to his statements in Memphis—had sparked immediate speculation and rumors about Ruby's possible involvement with the death of the president. Newspapers around the land delved into such matters as the bar owner's curious relationship with the Dallas police, his seemingly glaring ties to underworld figures, and some mysterious trips he was said to have taken to Castro's Cuba. The most spectacular yarns were claimed preassassination sightings (usually secondhand) of Ruby and Oswald huddled in conversation somewhere, often at a table at Ruby's own bar and strip joint, the Carousel.

By mid-1964, two months before Elrod talked with the FBI in Memphis, the questions surrounding the now-convicted assassin of Oswald had caused division even among the ranks of the Warren Commission, which President Lyndon Johnson had appointed to investigate the assassination. When Commission members traveled to Dallas early in June to pay their only visit to Ruby, the delegation included sitting U.S. Supreme Court Chief Justice Earl Warren, future president Gerald Ford, and a crew of Commission attorneys, among them later Pennsylvania senator Arlen Specter. Conspicuously absent were the two Warren attorneys most aggressively looking into Ruby's past, Leon D. Hubert, Jr., and Burt W. Griffin. Hubert had already effectively resigned in frustration, believing his work was being ignored, and returned to New Orleans; and Griffin, like Hubert, was not informed beforehand of the important meeting with Ruby in Dallas. Records of the June 7 interview show that Ruby pleaded repeatedly with his visitors to take him with them back to Washington, where he would feel more free to talk. Warren, whose Commission Report three months later would absolve Ruby of any

connection with organized crime or the assassination of President
Kennedy, denied the request.

FBI agents Casey and Cole closeted themselves with Elrod in the
Shelby County Sheriff's Office for an unspecified length of time. Finishing the interview, in which Elrod repeated his story of having been
jailed by Dallas police on the day of the assassination, and of what the
cellmate had told him about a motel room meeting with Jack Ruby,
the agents dictated a two-page report dated the same Tuesday afternoon, August 11, 1964. The FBI report summarized what Elrod had
told the agents, but took note of his alcoholism and an admission
he was said to have made of being "confused at the time concerning
the events which occurred." The report also noted that Elrod did not
know, or claim to know, anything about the presidential assassination
or Ruby of his own knowledge. Thus the value of what he had to say
was essentially nil: "hearsay information he had received from his
unknown cellmate."

If the agents were intially unimpressed by the potential significance of Elrod's tidings, any remaining possibility of taking him seriously was laid to rest the following day, when they received the FBI
identification record on John Franklin Elrod from the Bureau computer. The printout showed five offenses, ranging in time from the
first Dallas DWI in 1961 to the previous day's arrest and detention
in the sheriff's office. It included Elrod's three days in the Dallas jail
for the repeat DWI in 1962, but showed no arrest or jail time for
him during the critical days on and around November 22, 1963. The
only offense noted for that year was a charge of simple assault in
Quitman, Texas back in March. After Quitman, there was only the
entry for his last stunt at the Memphis sheriff's office almost seventeen months later.[4]

According to the FBI record, Elrod had invented the story of his
troubles in Dallas following the assassination. He may have been an
alcoholic with hallucinations, or a disturbed attention seeker of the
type who complicate lawmen's lives by confessing to crimes they
never committed. Who knew? It wasn't the agents' job to fathom
the countless possible reasons for such a lie. They appended the
printout to their previous report with a final, definitive notation:
"The identification record of JOHN FRANKIN ELROD, FBI number
91 666 E, dated August 12, 1964, which follows, does not reflect
incarceration of ELROD in the Dallas City Jail, as claimed."

Their job done, either Casey or Cole dropped the pages into the labyrinth of FBI files. The report remained undetected for nearly thirty more years, until a computer programmer from San Jose, California found a copy in the National Archives in August 1992.

It was late afternoon on the still-normal Monday of the last week of President Kennedy's life, and Joe Abernathy's knees were getting stiff. The fortyish FBI agent had been in nearly the same crouched position for a half-hour, hiding behind an unmarked car alongside two Dallas detectives in a warehouse district not far from downtown.

The lawmen were eyeing a small empty lot on the other side of Trunk Street, where their car was parked. They had taken the space closest to the corner with Main Street, then piled out to begin their stakeout. Another unmarked car was parked slightly closer to the lot, and behind it crouched two more Dallas detectives. Finally, a sleek white '63 Dodge rounded the corner from Main in the gathering dusk. It glided slowly on Trunk past the out-of-sight Abernathy and his partners of that evening, and pulled into the small lot across the street, in front of a warehouse. The driver, the only occupant of the newly arrived vehicle, made no attempt to get out. He stayed impassively behind the wheel, as if waiting. Fifty feet away, Agent Abernathy and the four detectives waited with him.

Not many blocks from Trunk and Main that same evening— November 18, 1963—Frank Ellsworth also waited. Ellsworth was an agent of another federal agency, the Internal Revenue Service's Division of Alcohol and Tobacco Tax (now the Bureau of Alcohol, Tobacco and Firearms). Working undercover, the ATF revenuer had arranged with a crooked gun-shop owner, on whom he was gathering evidence, to make a big buy of stolen guns—military rifles and automatic weapons, the latest and best stuff. The gun-shop owner had told Ellsworth where to be waiting on Monday; a car would meet him there with the merchandise, he said. But though the ATF agent and another undercover partner stayed at the appointed spot well into the night, the promised weapons never showed up.

The two ATF men were unaware that hours before they called off their sting, the weapons they awaited had been en route to them in the back of the white Dodge that had pulled into the lot off Trunk Street. The four city detectives watching the Dodge, members of the Division of Burglary and Theft, had received a tip from a police informant, FBI agent Abernathy would later explain. Some or all of the weapons stolen the previous week from a Texas National Guard armory in Terrell, twenty miles from Dallas, would be brought to that location on Trunk Street around this time on Monday. Capt. Walt Fannin of the B&T Division had passed the word on to Abernathy, who had been working the Terrell armory case for the Bureau since the theft was discovered four days earlier, on the Thursday morning of November 14. In some respects, the armory burglary had disturbing earmarks of an inside job. According to the armory employee charged with protecting the weapons stolen on the night of the 13th, they had been stored in a vault awaiting repairs, not their normal location. The burglars had known where to look, apparently.

At 6:45 P.M., some ten minutes after the arrival of the white Dodge, another car rounded the corner onto Trunk Street. There was still enough daylight, aided by a nearby lamppost which was already on, as well as by flashes of passing car lights on two-way Main Street, for Abernathy and the Dallas detectives to make out the vehicle's pale blue color. It was an impressive late-model sports car, a 1962 Thunderbird convertible, and, like the gleaming, chrome-laden Dodge, appeared to be in mobster creampuff condition. Two men were inside the T-Bird, which pulled up alongside the Dodge and stopped.

The five crouching lawmen watched the two arrivals get out of the sports car, open the nearest rear door of the Dodge, and start passing weapons from the white car to the adjacent convertible. The impassive man in the Dodge stared straight ahead. He did not move to help, and did not talk to the pair unloading the arms from his car. The cache of guns transferred from one vehicle to the other, it was found later, consisted of two .30 caliber Browning automatic rifles, two air-cooled .30 caliber Browning machine guns, and one .45 caliber M-3 submachine gun.

When the two men finished their task, they got back in the Thunderbird. Both cars cranked up and their lights came on.

The group who had been observing this scene from a distance had to move quickly. Not only were the suspects getting ready to pull away, they would most likely be splitting off in different directions. Of the shady trio, the impassive man in the white Dodge presumably held the most interest for Agent Abernathy, since the driver of this car appeared to be one link closer in the chain to the Terrell armory break-in than the two men receiving the contraband weapons. But

Abernathy wasn't making the calls this night. The stakeout was a Division of B&T operation, and the tipped-off detectives had invited the agent along—he had ridden in one of their cars—in view of his ongoing investigation of the recent armory burglary.

Having now missed or declined the option of an on-the-spot arrest, the Dallas Police Department detectives made a seemingly curious choice. Despite being capable of pursuing both cars with the two unmarked police vehicles at the site, they decided to follow only the guns. Whether they chose this path from excitement or by calculation—not wanting to risk losing the evidence, or maybe having some well-conceived plan to try to catch a bigger fish—has not been determined. It has also not been determined who the man in the white Dodge was (the license number was never recorded), who provided the B&T Division with the tip leading to the stakeout, or even who the detectives were who brought Agent Abernathy with them that Monday. They did not appear later in court and their names were successfully barred from the record. Today, Abernathy says he does not recall the identity of the four companions.

He remembers the ensuing car chase, however. After the Thunderbird pulled away—crossing Main and heading toward Elm—the FBI agent followed at an inconspicuous distance in the car of the two detectives with whom he had arrived at the stakeout. A few blocks later a Dallas patrolcar passed Abernathy's car, slipping into the space between it and the receding T-Bird. By now Agent Abernathy had lost track of the pair of detectives in the second unmarked vehicle. He assumed they were behind him, however, and that it had been they who had radioed for police support, since he knew the men in his car had not. One of the officers in the patrolcar that passed Abernathy's car, J. B. Allen, testified later that he had received radio instructions—presumably from the second detective car—to tail the blue Thunderbird, but not to arrest the occupants until they committed a traffic infraction. This tactic, which the patrolcar was to obey, would further veil the participation of the four B&T detectives in the events of that evening.

At the corner of Hall and Elm the patrolcar nudged in behind the Thunderbird, which was stopped at a light. The car, pointing north on Hall, appeared to be on the verge of making a wrong turn onto one-way Elm, and moreover, officer Allen would testify, started into the intersection before the light changed. When the patrolmen turned on their toplight and honked for the T-Bird to pull over, the suspect in the passenger's seat turned back and saw them. He immediately "said something to the driver," whereupon the convertible squealed across Elm, racing north on Hall with the police car in pursuit. The desperate chase through downtown traffic reached speeds of sixty miles an hour. Five blocks later, at Hall and Junius, the Thunderbird plowed between two cars stopped at a light, sideswiping both, and continued on to Gaston. There it tried to make a left, missed the turn, and crashed head-on into a utility pole.

Despite suffering a ruptured abdominal wall and the exposure of several internal organs, the driver of the totaled Thunderbird, identified as Donnell Darius Whitter, managed to run some thirty feet before being tackled by Allen's partner, Officer J. R. Sales. The groggy suspect was arrested, and "the next thing he recalled he was at Parkland Hospital [a week later] across the hall from Governor Connally who had been shot," according to a psychiatric report.

Whitter's passenger, the man who had looked back and warned him of the patrolcar behind them, was unable to leave the car. His face had smashed into the windshield. He was identified as Lawrence Reginald Miller and, like Whitter, was treated at Parkland Hospital emergency and charged with a long list of counts, including investigation of burglary and theft, of armed robbery, of auto theft, and of violation of the National Firearms Act. Unlike Whitter, however, Miller was able to leave the hospital after his face was stitched. He was remanded to the Dallas city jail at Main and Harwood, the same facility where John Elrod told FBI agents in Memphis he had been housed that month. According to his arrest report, Miller remained in city jail until November 25, when he was transferred to the sheriff's lockup in Kaufman County, where the Terrell armory break-in had occurred.

On the morning after the crash—Tuesday, November 19—Dallas-stationed ATF agent Frank Ellsworth read in the paper of the capture of two men in a car laden with contraband weapons, and realized why his planned undercover buy of guns the previous evening failed to materialize. It had been intercepted by Dallas police, foiling Ellsworth's bead on the gun-shop owner who set up the purchase, a young man named John Thomas Masen. The capture had blown the ATF agent's cover with Masen, who had also read the papers. Masen was livid, "crawling the walls," Ellsworth said thirty years later.

"He thought I'd set the whole thing up. He never spoke to me again."

Masen's illegal activities and the radical nature of his associations during this period were documented in Warren Commission papers that were kept classified for twelve years.[5] One recently released FBI Teletype characterizes the gun dealer as an "opportunist" willing to do anything for money short of involving himself in "white slavery or narcotics."[6] Kennedy conspiracy buffs would also come to know Masen (described in the same FBI document as a slightly built twenty-three-year-old with a sallow complexion, prominent nose, and receding hairline) as someone reputedly bearing an uncanny resemblance to Lee Harvey Oswald. It was Ellsworth himself who started up this line of thinking, when, as fate decreed, the agent was asked to participate in the interrogation of Oswald shortly after the suspect's arrest at the Texas Theater in Oak Cliff. Ellsworth's first impression, he would tell *Village Voice* writer Dick Russell in 1976, was that he had seen the accused assassin before. He soon realized, however, that it wasn't Oswald he had seen, but Masen, who resembled him. Conspiracy sleuths eventually took up the purported likeness between the two men to support theories that someone had gone around town in the days prior to the assassination impersonating Oswald, usually by involving himself in some conspicuous scene that could be remembered by onlookers later.

That Masen may have had an avocation as Oswald impersonator has never been conclusively proven. There's not much question he was modifying and selling illegal weapons around this time, however. The day after Ellsworth and Masen found out about the crash, the agent—who had been collecting evidence prior to the aborted weapons purchase—cashed in his chips and arrested the young gun vendor and reputed member of the right-wing Minutemen.[7] Masen was released on bond a day later, November 21, 1963, but was eventually convicted, lost his license, and paid a small fine. Ellsworth, who had a good working relationship with the DPD, passed off the interference with his sting as another unfortunate instance of insufficient coordination among law-enforcement agencies. He put the matter out of his mind, just as everyone else would soon forget the crash and arrest of two men in a Thunderbird in the mounting excitement of that week in Dallas. The president of the United States was coming to town.

A generation later, in the high-tech, post-cold war environment of Silicon Valley, Bill Adams found a small parcel in his mail. Adams, thirty-two, was a computer programmer and manager at a well-known communications company in San Jose and, on his own time, a seasoned researcher in the mazy world of Kennedy assassination investigation. Unlike more glamorous names in the same calling, David Lifton or Mark Lane, say, he hadn't written any books and was not much interested in the inner rewards of weaving elaborate assassination scenarios. Like the legendary Cap'n Crunch of San Francisco some years before, Adams had discovered the different exhilaration of spelunking the mysterious manmade caverns of complex information systems. The Cap'n explored telephone switching systems and learned to beat long-distance tolls with the tone of a plastic whistle found in a children's cereal, his namesake. Adams navigated more legal channels. He had developed a specialty accessing government information repositories through Freedom of Information Act requests (FOIAs, pronounced *foyahs* by the cognoscenti), a subtle art requiring just the right amount of technical specification and a jeweler's eye for finding the single valuable fact in reams of barely legible Xeroxes.

The thread Adams had been pursuing in early October of 1992 had begun the previous year, when the smash release of Oliver Stone's *JFK* provided young audiences with a crash course in assassinology. Its lexicon included such fauna as a "babushka lady," an "umbrella man," and the suspiciously natty "three tramps." The film, drawing on books by frequently pilloried former New Orleans D.A. Jim Garrison and Dallas-area researcher Jim Marrs, offered a text for the new consensual reality replacing the old Warren myths. More significantly for researchers like Adams, the brilliantly made *JFK,*called a "great movie" by Norman Mailer (albeit "one of the worst great movies ever made"), launched an irrepressible groundswell for the opening of sealed government files related to the Kennedy investigation. Most of the clamor focused on congressional and intelligence files in Washington, but Kennedy files were widely dispersed—in Lubbock, Austin, and Dallas, for example, as well as various presidential libraries throughout the country.

The Dallas police files, the first to be fully opened in the wake of *JFK*'s release, were especially interesting. The documents were freed by decree of the city council. They were transported in boxes by the

DPD to the Dallas city archives, and became available to the public on January 27, 1992. Almost as quickly, assassination buffs and the *Dallas Morning News* pronounced the materials a disappointment, and in truth, the newly released files contained nothing new. Everything in them, much of it Oswald trivia, duplicated documents available for many years in other archives or collections, such as the papers of former Texas attorney general Waggoner Carr at Texas Tech University, or even the twenty-six volumes of the Warren Commission.

There was, however, a *second* batch of Dallas police files at the Dallas city archives. These files the city had made available back in 1989, well before *JFK* mania set in. There had been no clamor to release assassination files then, and no need for self-congratulatory fanfare about dusty boxes of DPD papers added to the archives on some particular day. They had been put up quietly, without announcement.

One week after the city made its well-publicized opening of police files, Mary La Fontaine walked into the striking I. M. Pei-designed cantilevered fortress that is Dallas City Hall. It was a Monday, February 3, 1992, and she had tried to persuade her husband, Ray, at breakfast that morning that somehow, beyond reason and expectation, a significant scrap might have slipped past the career experts who had already looked at the files on the fifth floor.

"Yeah? Like what?" he said.

"Well, like the arrest records of the three tramps."

"Right."

"I told Paul Hoch last night I was going to find them. Just kidding, of course."

Ray grunted. "Who's Hoch again?"

The more Kennedy-challenged La Fontaine, who had been grumbling about Mary's recent fixation with the assassination and the long-distance phone calls this entailed, stayed home at the word processor. He was revising a translation of a fifteenth-century Catalan novel—stuff for the ages, he told himself, which was also about the length of time he'd been putting it off. Mary, who had more time to devote to the mere passing show of the present century, left by herself for city hall.

When she arrived at the archives, she discovered five minutes into her one-hour time allowance that the experts had been right all

The "three tramps," with Harold Doyle in foreground, followed by John Forrester Gedney and Gus W. Abrams. (Courtesy The Sixth Floor Museum Archives)

along. A list of the contents of the newly released materials plainly showed nothing not already found elsewhere, and eager researchers had gone all through the files during the previous week to make sure there were no surprises. She was gloomily pondering turning around and going back—a stop at Newhaus Chocolates in North Park Mall might be some consolation—when archivist Cindy Smolovik placed a second content list on her desk. This was for the batch of police materials released in 1989, she explained. Cindy hadn't had much luck interesting the recent wave of researchers in this earlier line of archival goods; they had spent most or all of their allotted hour on the main order of business, the new releases, which featured such information as Lee Harvey Oswald's elementary-school report cards. Mary glanced cursorily at the second content list, then stopped at an item.

"Let me try this one," she said, pointing out a file name on the list. It read: *Arrests, November 22, 1963.*

Of the scores of persons hauled in by Dallas police on the day of the assassination, only five men other than Oswald had actually been arrested. The single slender folder that Cindy placed on Mary's desk

"Tramp" Harold Doyle ca. 1985.

a few moments later contained the records of these five arrests. Mary, who had joked with Berkeley researcher Paul Hoch only the night before about finding the famous three tramps, was stunned to see that the top three arrest reports in the folder were for men picked up in or around boxcars behind Dealey Plaza minutes after the shooting. Incredibly, the tramps, whose anonymous images had been captured by news cameras as they were marched under police escort along the downtown sidewalks, and on whom arrest reports had not been kept, according to the Rockefeller Commission in 1975, the U.S. House Select Committee on Assassinations (HSCA) in 1979, and *Newsweek* magazine as recently as December 1991, had been rediscovered and christened with documented names. They were Harold Doyle, Gus Abrams, and John Forrester Gedney. The names would later prove to be genuine, and the men actual rail riders, dashing the

ARREST REPORT

ON

INVESTIGATIVE PRISONER

RT THUMB PRINT

| FIRST NAME | MIDDLE NAME | LAST NAME | DATE | TIME |
| John | Franklin | Elrod | 11-22-63 | 2:45 P M |

| RACE | | SEX | | AGE | DATE OF BIRTH | HOME ADDRESS |
| WHITE ☒ COLORED ☐ | | MALE ☒ FEMALE ☐ | | 31 | 1-12-32 | 3314 Knight |

ADDRESS WHERE ARREST MADE
3400 Blk Harry Hines

TYPE PREMISES (IF BUSINESS GIVE TRADE NAME ALSO)
. Railroad Tracks

CHARGE
Inv. Murder & Co. Vag

BUSINESS WHERE ARREST MADE HAS
BEER   LIQUOR   STATE
LICENSE ☐   LICENSE ☐   LIC. NO.

HOW ARREST MADE
ON VIEW ☒ CALL ☐ WARRANT ☐

LOCATION OF OFFENSE (IF OTHER THAN PLACE OF ARREST)
400 Block Elm St.

COMPLAINANT (NAME RACE SEX AGE)   HOME ADDRESS—PHONE NO   BUSINESS ADDRESS—PHONE NO.

WITNESS   HOME ADDRESS—PHONE NO   BUSINESS ADDRESS—PHONE NO

WITNESS   HOME ADDRESS—PHONE NO   BUSINESS ADDRESS—PHONE NO

PROPERTY PLACED IN POUND (MAKE. MODEL. LICENSE NO OF AUTO)   PROPERTY PLACED IN PROPERTY ROOM

NAMES OF OTHERS ARRESTED AT SAME TIME IN CONNECTION WITH THE SAME OR SIMILAR OFFENSE

NAME OF AND/OR INFORMATION CONCERNING OTHER SUSPECTS NOT APPREHENDED

OTHER DETAILS OF THE ARREST

This man was arrested on railroad tracks a few minutes after radio call was

dispatched that man was walking along railroad carrying a rifle. This man

was not carrying rifle at time of arrest. This suspect is unemployed,

states he has been in Dallas for two weeks. Lost his job last week at

El Fenix. States he has been arrested for theft and D.W.I. .

CHECK ALL ITEMS WHICH APPLY
DRUNK ☐ DRINKING ☐ CURSED ☐ RESISTED ☐ FOUGHT ☐

INJURED BEFORE ARREST ☐   INJURED DURING OR AFTER ARREST ☐   OFFICER(S) INJURED ☐   SPECIAL REPORT ☐

ARRESTING OFFICER	I. D. NO.	ARRESTING OFFICER		I. D. NO.
C.M.Barnhart	924	M.A.Rhodes	974	
OTHER OFFICER B.M. Hart	678	OTHER OFFICER F.A.Hellinhausen	1437	

| INVESTIGATION ASSIGNED TO | CHARGE FILED | FILED BY | DATE | DATE - TIME TO CO. JAIL |

| RELEASED BY | DATE - TIME | H.C. BOND BY | DATE - TIME | COURT | DATE | TIME |

DISTRIBUTION: (REMOVE CARBON—CHECK ORIGINAL FOR RECORDS BU.—CHECK COPY FOR EACH BUREAU CONCERNED)
RECORDS BUREAU ☐   SPEC. SER. BUREAU ☐   HOMICIDE ROBBERY ☐   AUTO THEFT ☐   BURGLARY THEFT ☐   FORGERY ☐   JUVENILE ☐   TRAFFIC ☐
USE REVERSE SIDE IF MORE SPACE NEEDED

The arrest record of John Franklin Elrod, "lost" for almost three decades (together with the arrest records of the "three tramps") until discovered by the authors in February 1992. Elrod's arrest record demonstrates the FBI did not tell the truth in a 1964 Memphis report that stated Elrod had not been incarcerated in Dallas on November 22, 1963, "as claimed."

spirits of some conspiracy sleuths who had based careers on tortured arguments that the "tramps," always with quotes, were really people like E. Howard Hunt, Frank Sturgis, Charles Harrelson, or any of a long additional string of usual suspects.

The two other arrest records Mary found in the slender folder were clearly less newsworthy, and not mentioned in a front-page story the La Fontaines wrote on the finds for the following Sunday's *Houston Post*. One of these reports was for a man named Daniel Wayne Douglas, who happened to walk into the downtown police station after the Kennedy maelstrom kicked in. He was intending to confess to a car theft in another state and ended up charged with suspicion of murder. The other report was for a man who (like Doyle, Abrams, and Gedney) was arrested near a railroad track on the Friday of the assassination, but too far from downtown to have been been one of the three tramps. His name was John Franklin Elrod.

The story of new finds in the Dallas files, first published February 9 in the *Post*, was picked up in other mainstream papers (including the *Washington Post* and *Boston Globe*, but not, remarkably, the *Dallas Morning News*) and the following month reached a supermarket tabloid, the *Globe*. The tabloid made a brief reference, in a sidebar to a story offering shocking evidence that JFK was murdered by his own limo driver, to the assassination-day arrest of John Elrod. Elrod's name, the *Globe* article said, had been found among "unearthed reports" in "secret Dallas police files." This passing mention in a tabloid had been enough for assassination researcher Bill Adams in San Jose. He located copies of all available Dallas police arrest records for November 22, 1963, and systematically sent out FOIA requests on the lot to the National Archives in Washington, D.C.

Some weeks later, the National Archives sent Adams a reply. They had information only on the man named Elrod, the letter said. By coincidence, the response from the Archives was dated August 11, 1992, exactly twenty-eight years after the date of the 1964 Memphis FBI report to which the letter referred—and which as yet Adams knew nothing of. He sent for the report. It was this document that had arrived in his mail—on microfilm, inside a small parcel—on the Monday afternoon of October 5, 1992.

It was an interesting fact that of the countless conspiracy-minded researchers, investigators, opportunists, disinformation artists, and ordinary nuts with typewriters who had been drawn over the decades to the vagaries of the Kennedy assassination, virtually all of whom had been men, the two most distinguished and universally admired were women. One was the late Sylvia Meagher of New York, a public-health writer whose pioneering *Accessories After the Fact*, published in 1967, was characterized eight years later by Pennsylvania senator Richard S. Schweiker as "by far the most meticulous and compelling indictment of the Warren Report" ever made. The other was alive and well, and lived in Dallas. Her name was Mary Ferrell, called by her detractors the "gatekeeper" and sometimes the "dragon lady," and she was reputed to have the most comprehensive knowledge— and library—of Kennediana in the country. She also had a sense of humor. "Anyone who would devote thirty years to this, neglecting husband and children, has got to be crazy," she liked to tell visitors making the pilgrimage to her Holland Street home. Unlike Sylvia Meagher, however, Mary had never published her findings, nor did she intend to. Her mission, as she saw it, was to collect information and make it available to those worthy of having it. Bill Adams was one such person.

When the San Jose researcher blew up the Washington microfilm at a library, he realized he had found something new. But he needed to check, and who better to check with than the scholarly doyenne in Dallas, Mary Ferrell? She had already done him a favor a few months back, when he called her to verify the existence of the tramp arrest records in the Dallas files. He had gotten hold of the La Fontaines' February story in the *Houston Post* and seen the March 17 *Globe* article, but needless to say he hardly believed everything that came out in the papers, and even less in the tabloid press. It had been Mary Ferrell who, having previously checked in the Dallas archives for herself, sent him copies of the arrest documents. Now he called her again.

"Do you know anything about an FBI report on Elrod back in Memphis in 1964?" he asked.

When she told him she didn't, Adams got about as excited as he gets. Usually, if Mary Ferrell didn't know something, it hadn't happened. This one she had missed, though, and probably so had everyone else.

"Well, get this," he said. "It says here Elrod was never arrested in Dallas."

"What? But I sent you his arrest record."

"I know, I'm holding it in my hand. But that's why the FBI never took his information seriously. That's what they said, anyway. There was nothing in the FBI computer about an Elrod arrest in Dallas in November 1963."

"What information are you talking about, dear?"

Adams described what the report said about the interrogation with Elrod—his claims of having been locked up with a cellmate, and how the cellmate had said that another inmate, who had an injured face, drove a car stashed with guns and had been in a motel room with Jack Ruby.

When he finished, Mary Ferrell stayed quiet for a moment, her wheels turning.

A few days later, Adams received a package from Dallas. In exchange for a photocopy of the FBI report on Elrod, which he had put in the mail to Mary Ferrell after finishing his conversation, she had sent him copies of several newspaper clippings from her voluminous holdings.

One story, by John Rutledge of the *Dallas Morning News,* dated November 19, 1963, told of a sixty-mile-an-hour chase through Dallas streets the evening before, ending in the capture of two ex-convicts when their "swank sports car" crashed into a utility pole. The car, also described as a "blue 1962 sports car," was found to be loaded with weapons stolen from a Texas National Guard armory in Terrell. The men were identified as Lawrence Reginald Miller, thirty-three, and a "5-time loser," Donnell Darius Whitter, forty-three. Miller suffered "deep face cuts," his face "hacked by glass when his head plunged through the windshield." He had been "treated at the Parkland Hospital emergency room, then jailed along with Whitter for burglary."[8]

In early fall of 1992, Bill Adams placed a call to another Dallas Mary, far less experienced in Kennedy research than Mary Ferrell. Journalist Mary La Fontaine knew the Kennedy literature well, however, and had had what Ray grousingly called "beginner's luck" with the finds in the Dallas police files. Bill, who had called to trade some documents, mentioned that he was planning an article on his Elrod findings, which he was thinking of publishing in a university newsletter. Mary suggested a wider audience for the story, and they agreed to work together exploring the further saga of John Elrod.

In January Mary inveigled a college friend, Deborah Sawyer, into accompanying her on the thirty-mile trek to Fort Worth, where she planned to visit the Federal Records Center, a branch of the National Archives. She wanted to examine the trial transcripts and other court records of the men named in the *Morning News* article, Miller and Whitter, and Deborah had obligingly agreed to spend a sunny afternoon inside a windowless warehouse, once an army storage depot, helping make the Xeroxes. It was from these transcripts and records, as well as interviews with retired federal agents Abernathy and Ellsworth, that the hectic events of November 18, 1963 were learned.

But the trial of Lawrence Miller—in Dallas Federal Court, on February 10, 1964—had interest in its own right as well. In some respects, it was a routine affair; the serial numbers of the five weapons found in the possession of Miller and Whitter were shown to match those of arms stolen from the Terrell armory, and Miller was quickly convicted. District Judge Joe Estes sentenced him to four years in the federal penitentiary in Texarkana.

Whitter, who appeared in court but was not tried with Miller, was sent for psychiatric examination to the U.S. Medical Center for Federal Prisoners in Springfield, Missouri, the same facility that had held such other troublesome figures in need of observation as Gen. Edwin Walker, and later, Albert Bolden and Richard Case Nagell.[9] The medical center found Whitter competent to stand trial. At his May trial in Dallas, though, Whitter was sent back to the Springfield institution to serve his four-year federal sentence by Judge Sarah T. Hughes, who six months earlier, aboard Air Force One, had sworn in President Johnson alongside a devastated Jacqueline Kennedy.

One curious aspect of Miller's trial in February was a motion filed by B. H. Timmins, Jr., assistant to U.S. Attorney (and later distinguished federal judge) Barefoot Sanders. Timmins' motion asked the court to limit defense cross-examination of FBI agent Joe Abernathy regarding the sources of information for his investigation. In essence, the motion would relieve Abernathy from having to explain how he knew to be at Trunk and Main on the evening the weapons were transferred. Such a limitation would not have been unusual under some circumstances—for example, if the source of information were a civilian informant whose safety or future services would be compromised by the revelation of his or her identity. It was, in fact, this safety-based argument that Assistant U.S. Attorney Timmins' motion made: "There is some indication," it stated, "that to reveal the identity of at least one of these sources would jeopardize the life of the person furnishing this information."

The motion also noted, however, that the source in question was not a common stool pigeon; the information had come "from the Alcohol and Tobacco Tax Unit of the Treasury Department and other sources." Assuming this to have been the case, there was little reason to have denied the court the names of such public employees as ATF personnel or the police detectives who had accompanied Abernathy on his investigative mission. They were expected to give evidence in court when necessary; that was part of their job, and paid for by public funds. This, at least, was the view of veteran defense counsel Lester May, who told the judge: "I have never run across this type of motion in a criminal case before, and I have tried a good deal of them." Even so, Agent Abernathy was not required to reveal the names of any other investigative persons connected with the case, including the four detectives.

But there was another mystery associated with Timmins' motion. As has already been noted, FBI agent Abernathy learned something was happening at Main and Trunk from the Burglary and Theft Division of the Dallas police, *not* the ATF. He is adamant on this point today, as is former ATF agent Ellsworth, who not only knew nothing about the planned criminal dealings on Trunk Street, but wasted a night waiting for an undercover buy of weapons, and lost his cover, as a result of it. Had Ellsworth been present at the stakeout (as he himself pointed out in reading the court records for the first time in 1993), all the parties to the gun transfer could have been arrested on the spot. Because the ATF had broader enforcement powers than the FBI in such cases, it would not have been necessary for Ellsworth to have called in traffic patrolmen to watch for a "probable cause" to stop the car, as was deemed necessary in the actual arrest of November 18.

Two months after Miller and Whitter faced Judge Estes in Dallas, a definitive memorandum denying ATF participation in their arrest was issued from Washington by Arnold Sagalyn, director of law-enforcement coordination for the U.S. Treasury Department, parent agency of the ATF. Sagalyn's memo, dated April 29, 1964, was directed to U.S. Secret Service inspector Thomas J. Kelley, who was conducting the service's investigation of the Kennedy assassination

and had been one of only a handful of people to interrogate Lee
Harvey Oswald.

"In response to your request" [emphasis added], Sagalyn informed
Kelley in the memo, "Alcohol & Tobacco Tax was not involved in
any way" in "the firearms case involving Donnell D. Whitter" [and
Lawrence Miller]. The ATF, he went on to explain, "only learned
about this [violation of the National Firearms Act] when it received a
telephone call from the U.S. Attorney concerned." Presumably this
U.S. attorney would have been Sanders' assistant, B. H. Timmins, Jr.
Why then did Timmins—who now says he remembers nothing about
the case—file a motion claiming that Abernathy's source of information was the ATF, and not, as Abernathy knew, the Dallas police?
Why did the B&T detectives not appear in court to testify to this
effect? More puzzling still, why had the Secret Service official investigating the Kennedy assassination taken an interest (never communicated to the Warren Commission, apparently) in the obscure
firearms case of two anonymous Dallas hoodlums, Larry Miller and
Don Whitter?[10]

A possible clue to such questions may be found in another memo,
dated just eight business days before Sagalyn's, on Wednesday, April
17, 1964. The memo was from a DPD deputy chief, M. W. Stevenson, to Texas attorney general Waggoner Carr, then conducting a
court of inquiry into the assassination concurrently with the Warren
Commission. The subject was "Check of Garages and Service Stations
Patronized by Jack Ruby." Deputy Chief Stevenson was reporting to
the state attorney general that "Donnell D. Whitter, named in the
enclosed report, formerly worked at the Texaco Service Station [at]
Clarenden and Ewing, [and] serviced Ruby's car when he came to
the station."[11] Similarly, a memo from Lt. E. L. Cunningham of the
DPD to Chief of Police Jesse Curry had reported the same information some two weeks earlier (April 5): Whitter worked for V. E.
Moralli, the man who owned the gas station at Clarenden and Ewing,
and Ruby traded at the station. ("Moralli states he does not know if
they [Ruby and Whitter] were friends or had relations other than
that of customer and station attendant or not," Cunningham
added.)[12]

The evidence strongly suggests, as it must have suggested to some
officials at the time, that Miller and Whitter, caught with a batch of
stolen military weapons, were lower-level operatives in Ruby's

gunrunning operation. That Ruby was involved in gunrunning has been well documented by respected journalist Seth Kantor and others, and was hardly a secret even in 1964—except, perhaps, to the Warren Commission, which had no ears to hear the questions being bruited about the former owner of the Carousel Club, or for what he might admit to them in a safer clime than Texas. (In fact, Ruby had already admitted to his gunrunning ways on at least two occasions prior to his trial, once to one of his attorneys and again to a jailer, to whom, Ruby later stated, "I broke down and said that I had sent guns to Cuba.")[13] Armory break-ins like the one in Terrell (and a more extensive string of inside thefts at the Fort Hood U.S. Army post in Killeen that ATF agent Ellsworth had been working on when Miller and Whitter were arrested) were a standard source of supply for gunrunners like Ruby, who flourished in the marriage of convenience between mobsters and the Central Intelligence Agency. The history of mob-CIA cooperation dated back to World War II, when Lucky Luciano's help was recruited in the campaign against Italian dictator Benito Mussolini. The more modern version of the strange alliance between underworld and patriotic interests was their common front against Fidel Castro, who had sinned against organized crime by shutting mob-controlled gambling out of Cuba. Weapons of the type found in Miller and Whitter's possession were typically earmarked for anti-Castro Cubans or other spunky freedom fighters of the proper denomination to advance American interests. As in Irangate years later, everyone profited and the right cause was served.

Whatever the fine points of Miller and Whitter's roles in Ruby's gunrunning enterprises may have been, Elrod's arrest report showed that he had told the truth to the FBI about his arrest in Dallas on the day the president was assassinated. But what about the rest of his claims? Were they also supported by the later evidence?

One claim was not, it would turn out, though the contradiction was relatively minor. According to the report of FBI agents Casey and Cole in Memphis, Elrod said that he and his Dallas cellmate had been held in a "cell 10." There was, however, no simple cell 10 in the Dallas city jail. Cells were grouped into blocks that were designated alphabetically and numerically. Douglas, for example, the man who walked into the station wanting to confess to car theft, had been placed in cellblock F. But the faulty cell address wasn't of great moment. A man sitting on the wrong side of jail bars may have more on his mind than musing on his exact cell number, or he can forget it a year later, or the person taking it down can hear it wrong.[14]

Available documents provide strong support for the remainder of Elrod's claims, and suggest Lawrence Miller—in the same jail at the same time as Elrod, and whose face had been seriously injured in a car accident a few days before—as the inmate Elrod described to the agents in Memphis as having a "smashed up" face. Elrod also informed them that his cellmate said the man "was reported to have been driving a Thunderbird with a large quantity of guns contained therein," according to the FBI report. The make of the car was a detail included in court and arrest records, but not in the graphic news account on the crash published in the *Dallas Morning News* of November 19, 1963. That story had only described the vehicle as a "swank sports car." The *Times Herald* of the same date had identified the car as a Thunderbird, but in a much smaller one-column article buried on page 20 that said nothing of the bloody injuries. If Elrod (or the cellmate) made up the story of the injured man in the corridor from the newspapers, he would have had to gather information from both of the accounts appearing on November 19, and then make an uncanny connection between the man and Jack Ruby—a connection not remotely suggested in the news articles, and neither known nor speculated about at that time. Ruby hadn't made his grand entrance yet and wasn't the subject of investigative memos reporting on his associations with "gas station employees" like Whitter. He was still just the obscure owner of a downtown Dallas dive.

The least contrived explanation to account for Elrod's claims regarding the man with the smashed face is that he simply passed on a story from his cellmate that was a true account. That it would be true can't be considered a remarkable development from our vantage point thirty years later. The cellmate's story would only corroborate what we now know, that Ruby was heavily involved in back-room gunrunning deals, and would have conducted at least some of those deals in face-to-face meetings with henchmen exactly like Miller and Whitter, who were tried and convicted of possessing stolen military weapons. But assuming, as the cellmate said, that Miller was one of the men in the room with Ruby, at least one other "identified" person had to be there as well: the cellmate who witnessed the gathering.

John Elrod ca. 1963.

Elrod today, on Mississippi River island north of Memphis. (Photo by Ray La Fontaine)

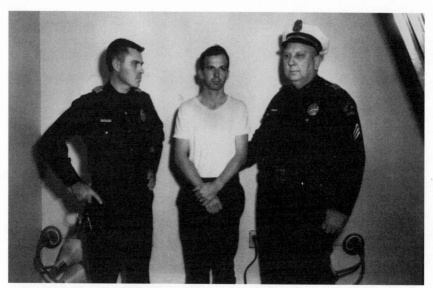

Lee Harvey Oswald in custody. (Courtesy Dallas Municipal Archives and Records Center, City of Dallas, Texas)

The car of Officer J. D. Tippit at the scene of his murder. (Courtesy Dallas Municipal Archives and Records Center, City of Dallas, Texas)

Who was the man who told former cook John Elrod a story that changed his life, affecting his behavior to this day?

The Memphis FBI report, in discounting the Elrod testimony as "hearsay," makes a point of noting that Elrod did not know the cellmate. But the same day Agents Casey and Cole prepared their report, a sergeant at the sheriff's office, Alton C. Gilless, Jr., issued a letter to FBI director J. Edgar Hoover. This letter, which wasn't shown to Warren investigators, made no mention of an anonymous cellmate. Instead, Sergeant Gilless (today sheriff of Shelby County) wrote simply:

"The subject walked into our office at approximately 12:30 A.M., this date [Aug. 11, 1964], and stated he had information concerning the murder of Lee Oswald."[15]

Similarly, it was Oswald whom Elrod had on his mind when his older brother Lindy, who managed the Oak Lawn El Fenix restaurant where John worked, picked him up from the Dallas jail in November 1963.

"John told me that day he was in the same cell with Lee Harvey Oswald, and that he knew Oswald didn't kill Kennedy," Lindy said in an interview in 1993.[16] "He was very scared about something that happened. He made a 180-degree turnaround and left me in the lurch—never came back to his job." John Elrod gave a similar account about his cellmate to brother-in-law and El Fenix owner Gilbert Martinez, sister-in-law Connie Elrod, and other members of his family more than three decades ago, following his release.

Eight months after walking out of the Dallas jail, he says today, he also revealed this identity to the two Memphis agents.[17] They responded by noting—three times in their brief two-page report—that the cellmate was "unknown."

To be sure, Elrod's account that he shared a cell with Lee Harvey Oswald would go a long way toward explaining some mysteries—why the Arkansas native fled Dallas after his release from jail, for example. But did his claim square with the known facts about Oswald's incarceration? Would the Dallas police really have put the accused presidential assassin in a cell close to another inmate?

The answer, it turns out, is yes.

When Oswald was overwhelmed in the Texas Theater, he was brought into the downtown Dallas police station not for assassinating the president, but for the murder of a policeman in Oak Cliff, J. D. Tippit.[18] While killing a cop was (and is today) about the worst thing a man could be accused of in Dallas, the catastrophe in Dealey Plaza two hours earlier had shattered all normal priorities. The main police business was processing the men being hauled in as potential assassination conspirators and storing them in the cells upstairs until they could be given a closer look. If Oswald was initially considered a suspect in the murder of the president, it was as another face in the crowd; *everyone* was a suspect at that frantic hour. Unlike the others, however, who were charged with suspicion of conspiracy in the assassination, Oswald was charged only with the murder of Officer Tippit. As late as his Friday night press conference, when he was presented to the world as the true probable assassin of Kennedy, he still maintained to reporters that he knew of no other charges against him.

Contrary to police reports in the Warren findings that Oswald was kept isolated while in confinement, phone documents show that he was placed just one cell apart from Douglas, the Tennessee car thief snagged by police when he arrived at the station in the midst of the Kennedy turmoil. Oswald occupied cell F-2, and Douglas, an adjoining cell.[19] This suggests that other, if not all, prisoners suspected of complicity in the assassination were kept in the same three-cell F block. In an interview in July 1993, Elrod accurately described Douglas as a "kid from Tennessee who had stolen a car in Memphis." The Douglas arrest record describes him as nineteen years of age, from Memphis, and a confessed car thief. What Elrod was calling a "cellmate" may have been that—the cells were filling up quickly that day—or he may have been an inmate in an adjacent cell, with whom Elrod, in F-3 perhaps, could talk through the bars. The fact that Elrod describes Oswald sitting on a toilet—because he and Douglas were on the beds—suggests the former interpretation.

No phone record exists for Elrod, who claims he wasn't allowed to make a call. According to John's brother Lindy, Dallas policeman H. R. Arnold—a personal friend who notified him by phone of his brother's incarceration, and again when John was released—came by to seem him shortly after John left Dallas. Arnold told Lindy that John was "only in the cell with Oswald about four hours." (John also says Arnold saw him at the jail and "pretended not to know me.") Although Arnold today denies remembering either Elrod brother or making either call to Lindy, he still answers to the nickname— "Hap"—they knew him by. The nickname is not listed in the phone book, or in the records of the Dallas police. It would appear that the Elrod brothers' memories are better than his.

It is certain, in any case, that Lee Harvey Oswald started the last forty-eight hours of his life in cell F-2. It is almost equally certain that once Oswald was recognized as the most important prisoner in DPD history, police would also realize (despite their later denials) that he had spent at least some of his hours in custody within talking distance of another inmate, either in the same F-2 or an adjacent cell. Such an inmate, within earshot of Oswald, would be a critical police asset and of acute interest to investigators. He may have gained some special information—perhaps of other possible "conspirators"—and would require special observation to determine what, if anything, he had found out. Elrod says today that he was put on a chain with Oswald, appeared in lineups, and was interrogated "around the clock" for forty-eight hours until Ruby shot Oswald. "Then, everything changed," he says. Elrod also relates that it was the FBI, not the Dallas police, who questioned him. Details of the interrogation, such as Elrod's claim that his interrogatiors knew the names of his parents' neighbors in Arkansas, support his story that the interrogators were federal rather than local. "They were suits," says Elrod, "with white shirts and black ties."[20]

There can be little doubt that Elrod understood, probably well before he left the Dallas city jail for the last time, that his cellmate had been the one who was supposed to have killed Kennedy—and that the very man Oswald had been talking about, and whom he wasn't supposed to have known beforehand, Jack Ruby, had shown up in the police station shortly afterwards and shot him dead with a pistol. It wasn't a comforting realization, and moreover the kind of thing a man could get killed for just for knowing. And so John Elrod dropped out, leaving the life and city he had known since he was seventeen, and returned to the safe obscurity of his mother's home. "He went home to mama," says his brother.

As noted earlier, tenuous claims (and outright lies) regarding "witnessed" meetings of Oswald and Ruby prior to the assassination have appeared ever since Ruby murdered Oswald two days after the president was assassinated. Some of the claims have more interest than others and will be taken up in later pages. What all of the claims to date have had in common is a lack of evidence. They have no support beyond the credibility of the person telling the story. The connection Elrod establishes between Oswald and Ruby is of a different type, depending not only on Elrod's slight oral testimony—he isn't saying much of anything these days—but on a paper trail of records, the most pertinent of which is the Memphis FBI report discovered by Bill Adams. The documentation of this Oswald-Ruby link by a handful of researchers, all employed at other occupations, is more than two full-scale investigations by the U.S. government, millions of pages of FBI and other agency reports, and a high-tech media industry lately occupied with tabloid journalism have done.

Today John Elrod lives in Tennessee, miles from even the smallest hamlet. He has no telephone. "I've told the FBI everything I know," he says. He adds, truthfully, "Everyone involved in this thing has ended up dead."

The man with the injured face, Miller, most of whose remaining time would be spent in a federal prison, was dead at forty-three, less than ten years after the wild car chase in Dallas.

His companion, Ruby-associate Whitter, served a four-year sentence under psychiatric scrutiny at the Medical Center for Federal Prisoners in Springfield, Missouri, and died in Temple, Texas in 1991. Despite his death (and the recent release of nearly a million pages of assassination-related materials), Whitter remained a restricted topic until very recently. The FBI would not grant the National Archives permission to make public a fourteen-page document on the obscure ex-convict. The remarkable reason for withholding the pages: national security related to the protection of the president of the United States.[21]

Ruby and the cellmate—who, realizing he was in serious trouble, talked about him—are dead these thirty years.

The only survivor is Elrod, the man who heard what he shouldn't have, and who then tried to tell the FBI; they did not listen.

But the documents that tell Elrod's story also survive, and they raise new questions. Was his Dallas arrest of November 22, 1963 intentionally withheld or purged from the FBI record, just as the paper records of all the vagrant arrests of that day vanished for thirty years, until uncovered by Mary in 1992?

Was fear of what Elrod might tell reporters the real reason the Dallas police—after the grotesque blunder of letting Ruby shoot Oswald in their own station—"admitted" to yet another stroke of apparent incompetence, that they kept no arrest records of the men rounded up after the assassination?

Had a federal agency or other high officials, in the month before Ruby went on trial, leaned on prosecutors in the court case of Lawrence Miller to suppress information linking Ruby to organized crime, and possibly to Oswald?

Most importantly, who was Lee Harvey Oswald and what was he really doing in Dallas?

CHAPTER TWO

Land of Oz

I never called him Lee or Harvey or Oswald. It was always Oz.

NELSON DELGADO, USMC
Testimony to Warren Commission

Anyone old enough to remember November 22, 1963 can usually recall exactly what he or she was doing when the news came. Most times it may have been nothing grander than ringing up another customer at an Abilene supermarket or petting the family cat in Dubuque. In New York City, however, where events occur on a bigger scale, the lightning hit in the midst of a weekly ritual that was "nothing more or less than a celebration of power," as former *Life Magazine* staffer Loudon Wainwright remembers.[1] It was the Luce publishing empire managing editors' lunch, held each Friday at 12:30 in Dining Room 1 on the forty-seventh floor of the Time & Life Building. The gathering, numbering no more than the twelve or fifteen main gods one might expect to find on Mount Olympus, included bushy-browed Henry Luce himself, who on this day was going to toss out some ideas on the state of the economy, and the men who ran his magazines on different floors of the towering T & L stronghold: Duncan Norton-Taylor of *Fortune*, Andre Laguerre of *Sports Illustrated*, George Hunt of *Life*, and Otto Fuerbringer of *Time*.

It was Fuerbringer who got the call, just before the final coffees and cigars. In a few seconds, his questions on the phone brought the remaining conversations to a halt. "Where? Is he dead? Who shot him?"

Before anyone could react with more than stunned silence, the incomprehensible news was seconded by a portly and normally cool maître d', who stuck his head in the dining-room door and shouted: "The president is going out!" *Life*'s Hunt would remember that Luce "put his elbows on the table, cupped his face in his hands and, looking pale and ill, stared straight ahead."

Of the somber editors and chief lieutenants hurrying back to their floors to begin coping with the event, Hunt and his crew faced the most formidable task. On that November 22, the *Life* issue of November 29, with navy star quarterback Roger Staubach on the cover, was already running on presses in Philadelphia, Chicago, and Los Angeles at a rate of 80,000 copies an hour. The decision to stop the giant machines was expensive, but made without hesitation by assistant publisher Jim Shepley even before told to do so by Hunt. The awesome occurrence in Dallas—and the magazine's tradition of excellence—demanded heroic measures.

Two *Life* reporters were immediately deployed to Dallas, Richard Stolley of the West Coast office, and an outgoing writer on his staff, Thomas Thompson. Incredibly, within hours and under the nose of hordes of local and out-of-town newsmen, each man scored a magnificent find.

To Stolley it fell to discover that a shockingly graphic 8-mm film of the assassination had been made by a Dallas dressmaker, Abraham Zapruder; by Saturday morning, November 23, over the squawks of other reporters locked out in an outside office, Stolley had obtained print rights to Zapruder's handiwork, as well as the original film and one copy. (Two other duplicates had already been made, one sent to the FBI and another given to the Dallas police.)

Thompson's coup was no less remarkable. Accompanied by *Life* photographer Allan Grant, he attended a hopelessly packed Friday night Dallas jailhouse press conference in which the accused assassin was paraded out to talk to reporters. Quickly sizing up the spectacle as useless photographically and storywise, the pair decided to bail out. Before leaving, however, Thompson deftly extracted from a chatty deputy sheriff the address of Lee Harvey Oswald's rooming house at 1026 N. Beckley in Oak Cliff.

At the Beckley house, which as yet hadn't been reached by other reporters, Thompson learned from his landlady that her tenant, known to her as "O. H. Lee," made frequent calls on the hall pay phone to the town of Irving. Knowing nothing more, the writer and photographer set out for Irving (not yet glamorized with the Studios at Las Colinas and the Cowboys' Texas Stadium), where Thompson unearthed another clue. A sheriff's dispatcher told the friendly reporter that feds had been nosing around the town earlier in connection with the assassination—"looking for some woman a few streets south."

A few minutes later, and still on that same first night, Thompson and Grant were knocking on the woman's door. She opened it, entering history as Ruth Paine, the person with whom Marina Oswald, frequently separated from Lee, had been staying in the days preceding the assassination. In the living room of the Paine house, watching the president's coffin arrive in Washington on TV, was Marguerite Oswald, the mother of the accused man. Popping up from another room on the way to the kitchen was Marina, his wife, cradling his new baby in her arms. Thompson and Grant had stumbled onto the world's greatest lair of Oswalds, four of them in all, by knocking on a door at random; Ruth's had been one of the few houses on the street with the lights burning.[2]

By noon of the 23rd, when the Secret Service relieved Thompson of his prize subjects (as consolation, he knew the agency would also keep them away from other reporters), the *Life* writer had gathered enough material to pound out some 2,100 words, which he filed to the magazine that same Saturday night. Working under an inhuman deadline, and on the wings of whatever gods had led him alone to this story, he turned out the first portrait of Lee Harvey Oswald. It was a remarkable and compelling account, stark and poetic in places, and not devoid of human sympathy for the man Thompson introduced to readers as a world-class American loser who did his drifting, and his terrible damage, on a global scale. The young ex-defector with the pretty hazel-eyed wife was a loner, a "strange and withdrawn" man consumed by Marxism and without (as one former fellow Marine stated) "any close friends that I can remember."

Despite the pathos of the women who still believed in his innocence, Marguerite and Marina, the police were "building their case" against Oswald "slowly, methodically," Thompson wrote. The case consisted of

> connecting Oswald with the mail-order purchase of a rifle like the one that fired the fatal bullet, placing him on the scene of

the shooting with a long parcel the size and shape of a rifle, comparing his palm-marks with the one found on the murder weapon, finding traces of burned powder on his hands. Then the police turned up the most damning evidence of all. It was a snapshot of Oswald showing him holding a rifle that apparently was identical with the one that killed the President.[3]

The story closed as it had started, with a sentence added at the last moment: "Before the district attorney of Dallas County could demand the death penalty, Lee Harvey Oswald, who had achieved such horrifying fame, himself was dead." This latest information, coming as if from nowhere, had the surprising finality of Ruby's bullet.

The *Life* issue of November 29 that carried Thomas Thompson's article, while representing an example of American journalism at its best (it would be followed by a less distinguished effort the very next week, as we'll see), also marked the beginning of the myth of Oswald—not only as unquestioned assassin of the president, but as lone-nut drifter and lifelong misfit. This version of the ex-Marine from New Orleans, further honed over the next several months, culminated in the famous *Life* cover of February 21, 1964, labeled "Lee Oswald with the weapons he used to kill President Kennedy and Officer Tippit." No one could mistake the menacing figure in front of a backyard fence one glaring afternoon, with an unbalanced leftward tilt and the eyes deep in shadows, as anything but an assassin. With a faint sneer, he brazenly invited the viewer to behold the Trotskyite newspaper in his right hand, his Bible, so to speak. Strapped on his hip was the cop-killing revolver, and grasped in his left hand, in grim present-arms parody of his hated Marine days, was the instrument of the greatest villainy of the century, the weapon "confirmed" by Dallas police as "the rifle found in the Texas Book Depository."[4] As Thompson had written three months earlier, the snapshot on this cover—retrieved from the Paine house garage the night of the assassination—was "the most damning evidence of all."

The centerpiece of the Oswald cover issue of February 21 was a long story by Donald Jackson titled "The Evolution of an Assassin." Jackson expanded on the quick study by Thompson, providing additional in-depth interviews and supporting details. His theme remained the same, however: Oswald, per the title still the unquestioned assassin, was damaged goods, a loner and misfit who even as a kid was largely remembered as a bit loopy and defective. The eccentricity only grew worse as he "evolved," Jackson reported. It was this *Life Magazine* vision of Oswald that fed the American psyche in the crucial opinion-forming days prior to the lumbering report (and evidence volumes) of the Warren Commission. The government findings, released to the public seven months after the sneering Oswald cover, only officially confirmed what had long been "known," thanks in good part to the Luce publication—that the murders of the president and his killer were two unconnected acts by two separately deranged men.

But even the tenacious *Life* take on the Dallas tragedy did not entirely dispel early doubts about the scenario. As early as the second issue after the assassination (December 6), which again contained an excellent piece by Thomas Thompson on the near-simultaneous burials of Oswald and police officer J. D. Tippit, an article appeared by Paul Mandel seeking (as the headline noted) to put an "End to Nagging Rumors"—among them, "Was it really Oswald who shot the President?" Mandel answered the disturbing question with a definite *yes*. He noted, however, that "a Dallas doctor" (unnamed, but probably Malcolm Perry) had complicated matters somewhat by reporting that one of the bullets hitting President Kennedy had entered his throat from the front. Since at the time of the shooting "the limousine was 50 yards past Oswald and the President's back was turned almost directly to the sniper, it has been hard to understand how the bullet could enter the front of his throat," Mandel pointed out. "Hence the recurring guess that there was a second sniper somewhere else."[5]

But the article provided an explanation for the seeming contradiction. The answer could be found in the 8-mm Zapruder film, which "shows the President turning his body far around to the right as he waves to somone in the crowd," Mandel wrote. "His throat is exposed—toward the sniper's nest [i.e., in the book depository]—just before he clutches it."[6] This was why the president could have been shot by Oswald from behind and still been hit in the throat from the front; he'd been turning around to wave at people behind him.

What readers wouldn't know from the Mandel piece was that the Zapruder film to which it referred (and which would only be seen publicly for the first time twelve years later, in 1975) showed no such turning around by President Kennedy prior to placing his hands on his neck. The rearward turn described in the issue of December 6 was a fabrication, presumably intended to help remove this particular "nagging rumor." The invention may have been perceived by the writer and editors as a civic-minded white lie with no great harm done, since the point it addressed had become moot: the publication now believed that the frontal neck entry was a mistaken assessment by rube Dallas doctors. (The assessment had been "corrected" to an exit wound in the Bethesda autopsy the evening of November 22.)

Yet, if such a journalistic lapse was possible in Mandel's article, what about the credibility of the case described by Thompson as "slowly, methodically" building against Oswald? Thompson's account of November 29 was not marred by such blatant distortions, however rationalized; he had reported unerringly what he saw, heard, and believed to be true, including the highest levels of police investigative reasoning on the evidence against the accused assassin. This evidence was essentially comprised of items summarized at the conclusion of his article: Oswald's mail-order purchase of a Carcano carbine, the "long parcel" he carried to the book depository the Friday of the assassination, his palm mark on the rifle, the traces of nitrate on his hands, and of course, the prophetic backyard photo. As we shall see with the hindsight of later discoveries, each of these points of evidence would prove seriously flawed. The case against Oswald was, from its inception, a house of cards.

Lee Harvey Oswald was Marguerite Claverie Oswald's third son, born in New Orleans October 18, 1939. Two months earlier, the twice-married young mother had unexpectedly become a widow. Her husband, Robert E. Lee Oswald, though a life-insurance salesman, hadn't left much to fall back on, and soon Marguerite took up waitressing to keep a roof over her family. For Lee and his older brothers, Robert and John, the roof was sometimes that of an orphanage, where the Oswald boys would stay on weekdays while their mother worked.

In some ways the resilient Marguerite resembled another staunch New Orleans mother with an unusual and sometimes burdensome son—the fictional Mrs. Riley of John Kennedy Toole's Pulitzer Prize winning novel, *A Confederacy of Dunces*. Like Mrs. Riley (and Toole's own mother), Marguerite was frequently frustrated by her youngest son's behavior, but appreciating his gifts, could rise to eloquent heights in his defense. Unlike Mrs. Riley, Marguerite didn't stay put in the Crescent City. Her days with Lee were a constant peregrination in search of a better life.

The changes of address started on a promising note when "Mr. Eckdahl" (as Marguerite would later refer to her older third husband) arrived from Boston. Edwin A. Eckdahl, an engineer, was smitten with the Widow Oswald, who by now had risen to manager of a hosiery store on Canal Street and gained an appreciation of the value of security. Even so, she made him wait a year for her hand. They married when Lee was five years old and resettled in Fort Worth, Texas. The two older brothers were put in a Mississippi military school, from which point on only Lee lived fulltime with his mother.

The youngest Oswald entered elementary school in January 1947 as a chubby, sweet-faced boy who brought home strong B report cards with a few As on the side. In March of the following year he was transferred to another school on the same South Side of Fort Worth, where he finished the second grade. Meanwhile, Mr. Eckdahl, who had proved a cunning adulterer, sued Marguerite for divorce, claiming she nagged and threw things at him. The divorce was granted for a bargain $1,500. Henceforth, Marguerite's life became, as one fiction writer noted, "a dwindling history of moving to cheaper places."[7]

The first such place was a small frame house on Ewing Avenue, where Lee spent the next four years, in the process being transferred to yet another Fort Worth elementary, Ridglea West. When he finished the sixth grade, Marguerite carried out a more ambitious move: a cross-country trek in a 1948 Dodge to New York City, where she expected to make more money and live closer to the son by her first marriage, Coast Guardsman John Pic. Lee quickly upset this notion when, wanting to whittle wood, he pulled out a penknife in the Pic apartment and waved it in front of John's new bride. Forced to vacate her older son's premises, the mother and almost thirteen-year-old boy found themselves no more prepared to cope with the Bronx than *The Glass Menagerie*'s fatherless family with the grim travails of St. Louis.

The pair took a single room in a basement and Lee continued changing schools. His first transfer in the Bronx (from a Lutheran school to P.S. 117) occurred after three weeks. The new junior high, where Lee was now a seventh grader, wasn't much to his liking, apparently. After six years as a satisfactory student, the Oswald boy suddenly turned truant, missing forty-seven school days between October 1952 and January 1953.

In March Marguerite moved again, inflicting on her son his third Bronx school in seven months. When he didn't show at P.S. 44, he became a case in New York Children's Court. According to *Life* reporter Donald Jackson, Lee told truant officer John Carro that "most of all he just liked to be by himself and do things by himself." The boy, Carro continued,

> would get up in the morning and watch television all day. There was no one else at home. The mother worked. He didn't have any friends, and he didn't seem to miss having any friends.[8]

Another man who examined the thirteen-year-old truant around this time, Youth House psychiatrist Renatus Hartogs (like Carro, a precursor of the storm of psycho-babblers to torment later decades), told the *Life* reporter that he was "not surprised" when Oswald was arrested for the assassination of the president, for "psychologically, he had all the qualifications of being a potential assassin."[9] A few months later, on April 16, 1964, Dr. Hartogs similarly testified to the Commission that he "had found him [Oswald] to have definite traits of dangerousness" and "a potential for explosive, aggressive, assaultive acting out."[10] As Sylvia Meagher would point out in 1967, however, this is not what Hartogs wrote in his report exactly eleven years earlier, on April 16, 1953. Young Oswald exhibited "no indication of psychotic changes; superior mental endowment; no retardation despite truancy; no psychotic mental changes," the psychiatrist had written then. He described Oswald as a "disturbed youngster who suffers under the impact of really existing emotional isolation and deprivation."[11]

(Typically, 1993 *Case Closed* author Gerald Posner would quote only the more damaging psychiatric assessment, taking no note of the disclosure by Sylvia Meagher twenty-six years earlier, or of the suggestion by Warren attorney Wesley J. Liebeler to Hartogs that his postassassination comments about Oswald were based on mistaken identity.)[12]

It was Carro's opinion that Oswald would benefit from "placement" at a children's facility where he could receive psychiatric treatment. "When you get a thirteen-year-old kid who withdraws into his own world, whose only company is fantasy, who wants no friends, who has no father figure, whose mother doesn't seem to relate either—then you've got trouble," he told Jackson. The boy's mother, Carro added, "was detached and noninvolved. She kept saying that Lee wasn't any problem, and she didn't understand what the fuss was all about."[13]

Marguerite, indeed, was adamant in rejecting the truant officer's alien sociology:

> Mr. John Carro told him, "Lee, you'll have to report to me every week." I said, "Mr. Carro, my son is not going to report to you. He's no criminal. He's given his word that it's not going to happen again. The first time he doesn't keep his word, then he'll report to you." I was not going to have a boy of that age and caliber going to a probation officer.[14]

Toole's Mrs. Riley couldn't have put it better.

When Marguerite's son wasn't staying home alone he rode the subway. On one of his truant wanderings he came across a frumpy, middle-aged woman handing out tracts at the entrance to the El steps. In Bible Belt Fort Worth, the tracts given out by such a determined soul might have asked, *Have You Been Saved?* In New York, the woman's said, *Save the Rosenbergs.*

The boy took her offering back to his room and read it. A connection was made, and he was never the same again; the ideological Oswald had been conceived, seeded by a single pamphlet under clearly just the right moon. "I can still remember that pamphlet," he said in later years. "Then I discovered one book in the library, Karl Marx's *Das Kapital*. It was what I'd been looking for. It was like a very religious man opening the Bible for the first time."[15]

For Marguerite, a more immediate and practical concern after sixteen hellacious months was extricating herself and her son from New York City. In 1954, the family finally limped back to New Orleans, and Oswald's eighth-grade attendance—at Beauregard Junior High—immediately jumped. He missed just nine days during the entire 1954-55 school year. That same year Lee was to meet a man who would become an inextricable part of his later life. Twice in the summer of 1955 he was photographed on camp-outs with Capt. David Ferrie of the Civil Air Patrol.[16]

Photograph released by Associated Press showing Lee Harvey Oswald (far right, white tee shirt) and David Ferrie (second from left) at a Civil Air Patrol camp near Alexandria, Louisiana in 1955. The photo belies arguments of Gerald Posner that Ferrie did not know Oswald and "was not even in the Civil Air Patrol when Oswald was a member in 1955" (Case Closed, 143).

The next fall Oswald enrolled at Warren Easton High School, did well on his achievement tests, but stayed in school less than a month. Unlike New York, where he played hookey to ride the rails, at Warren Easton he played hookey to read books in the city libraries. Oswald wanted books "more advanced than the school texts, books that put him at a distance from his classmates, closed the world around him," novelist Don DeLillo writes with fictional but on-target insight. "They had their civics and home economics. He wanted subjects and ideas of historic scope, ideas that touched his life, his true life, the whirl of time inside him."[17]

Was Lee a kind of Don Quixote, maddened by commie literature instead of chivalric romances? In her pragmatic wisdom, Marguerite didn't think so. "He brought home books on Marxism and social-ism," she told *Life*'s Jackson. "But I didn't worry. You can't protect children from everything, just try to help them see things in the right way. Besides, if those books are so bad, why are they there where any child can get hold of them?"[18]

But leftist writings weren't Oswald's only interest during these days. He'd already told caseworkers in the Bronx of his desire to become a Marine, like his older brother Robert. In October 1955 he wangled Marguerite into writing a letter to the New Orleans high school saying that the family was moving to California. The letter was a ruse designed to withdraw him from school so he could enlist in the USMC on his sixteenth birthday, which fell that same month. Everything went as planned, except for the Corps' cooperation; despite a false affidavit, Oswald was rejected on account of his age.

He stayed out of school for the rest of the year anyway, reading his Marx and Engels, the lore on Trotsky and Stalin (whose real name, he delighted in explaining, was Dzhugashvili), and alongside these, in preparation for his postponed day of enlistment, his brother Robert's Marine Corps manual. When he wasn't reading, the sixteen-year-old Oswald worked as a runner for a dental lab and carried messages to steamship lines on the docks of the Mississippi. (With his first paycheck, he bought Marguerite a thirty-five-dollar coat.)

Oswald made his last school transfer when, in late summer of 1956, Marguerite once again decided to try her luck in Fort Worth. There, at Arlington Heights High, he sleepwalked through another month of school, waiting for his seventeenth birthday in October. He also continued immersing himself in his books, all extraneous to the academic curriculum. A few years later Oswald would put some of his gained wisdom into a letter to his brother Robert. "Happiness is not based on oneself," he wrote. "It does not consist of a small home, of taking and getting. Happiness is taking part in the struggle, where there is no borderline between one's own personal world, and the world in general."

But the kid capable of entertaining these views didn't cut an impressive figure at Arlington Heights. If anything, he appeared sadly diminished to the ordinary eye—as one fellow high-school student noted who had known him back in grade school. He reported that when Oswald walked up to him in the halls,

> I remember I had to look down to talk to him, and it seemed strange, because he had been the tallest, the dominant member of our group in grammar school. [But now] he looked like he was

just lost. He was very different from the way I remembered him.
He seemed to have no personality at all. He couldn't express himself well. He just hadn't turned into somebody. He hadn't turned
into anybody.[19]

Perhaps sensing that her son was out of his element in this world—
perhaps in any world—Marguerite no longer tried to talk him out
of the Marines. The week after his seventeenth birthday he traveled
to Dallas and signed up for a three-year hitch. This time the enlistment stuck.

The skinny kid from New Orleans with the slightly squinty eyes
(and who could wiggle his ears, it turned out) needed a nickname;
every Marine does. At Atsugi Naval Air Station in Japan he became
Ozzie the Rabbit, or just Bugs. Later, after the thirteen-month Atsugi
stint ended, the guys at the new duty station in Santa Ana, California pinned another tag on the private, who was constantly practicing Russian: Oswaldskovich. He liked this name better.

The two main phases of Oswald's USMC career, Atsugi and Santa
Ana, are focal points of two contrasting interpretations of the
Marine. Both call for a more complex and socially competent Oswald
than the version presented by *Life Magazine* in the aftermath of the
assassination.

The first interpretation was forged by former Harvard faculty
member Edward Jay Epstein and countenanced by former CIA chief
of counterintelligence James Jesus Angleton, whom Epstein cites in
his epigraph. The interpretation stems from a question posed by
Warren attorneys W. David Slawson and William T. Coleman, Jr., in
a top-secret staff report to the Commission: "How are we to assess
whether or not what we know of Oswald's 'real life' is not just a 'legend' designed by the KGB and consistently lived out by Oswald thereafter?" Epstein, who called his book propounding this theory *Legend,*
argued that Oswald was "turned" while in Japan and thereafter acted
as a KGB operative.[20]

After boot camp in San Diego and combat training at Camp
Pendleton, Oswald attended classes in aviation electronics at the
Naval Air Technical Training Center in Jacksonville, Florida, fol-
lowed by more weeks of radar operations training at Keesler Air
Force Base in Biloxi, Mississippi. He received a MOS job title of 6741

(radar operator). According to another Marine radar operator who trained at the same locations as Oswald, Bud Simco, "we monitored radar scopes and worked behind the plotting boards, communicating by radio with air traffic . . . with the officers who actually directed the aircraft, and with other squadrons."[21] Because the work involved classified codes, call signs, and radar gear, Oswald, like Simco, was granted a confidential security clearance upon graduating from the Biloxi radar school.[22]

He arrived at Atsugi (on the same ship with another Marine whom we shall see later, Roscoe White) in September 1957, some eleven months after his enlistment. Oswald was assigned to Marine Air Control Squadron One, and it was while working the MACS-1 radar "bubble" that he first heard a mysterious pilot's voice requesting wind information for a then-officially impossible altitude of 90,000 feet. The pilot, he discovered, was aboard the base's greatest secret, the dark, long-winged U-2, prosaically called a "utility plane" by the Americans, and by the Russians, the "Black Lady of Espionage." Stowed at the remotest hangar of the base, the plane, when unleashed, could climb beyond the range of any ground-to-air missile and penetrate the air spaces of China and Russia with impunity— had been doing so for years, in fact. Except to the radar operators, the U-2's operational altitudes were top secret, as indeed was everything else about it. Even so, Oz and his buddies would occasionally catch glimpses of the exotic craft as it was towed by tractor out of a hangar surrounded by armed guards, and later, as it would return with a prolonged shriek from yet another mission laden with high-altitude photos.

Proficient at his radar work, Oswald was also a less isolated figure in Epstein's account than the Marine "oddball" rendered by *Life*'s Donald Jackson. Though still disliked for his standoffish ways by some of the "rougher" jarheads (who would throw him in the showers fully dressed and call him "Mrs. Oswald"), others apparently felt a genuine appreciation for him. Thus one Atsugi barracks mate told Epstein that "Ozzie would read deep stuff," seemed "to think about what he was going to say," and "was absolutely truthful, the kind of guy I'd trust completely."[23] Another Marine volunteered that Oswald "used to do me favors, like lending me money until payday," and that he was "the sort of friend I could count on if I needed a pint of blood."[24] And despite the fact that Oswald was frequently unable to get along with men—to be "one of the boys," whether at P.S. 44 or Atsugi—he was surprisingly luckier in his relations with women.

Epstein relates, for example, that Oswald, though making less than eighty-five dollars a month in take-home pay, developed a relationship with a "hostess" of one of the most expensive nightclubs in Tokyo, the Queen Bee. He took her out with "surprising regularity," thereby arousing the envy of other Marines who professed astonishment that "someone of her 'class' would go out with Oswald at all."[25] One of Oswald's Marine friends also recalled meeting him at a house in Yamato with a handsome Japanese man and a girlfriend who impressively "was not a bar girl or prostitute."[26] Similarly, another Marine, Owen Dejanovich (who is no longer talking about Oswald), claimed to see "Bugs" occasionally talking to an attractive Eurasian woman who apparently was teaching him Russian. "She was much too good looking for Bugs," he told Epstein, and he "wondered why such an attractive 'roundeye,' who was obviously not a common bar girl, would waste her time with a Marine private."[27]

To Epstein, such instances of Oswald's unlikely "success" with women supported the writer's contention that the young Marine had made a connection with a communist cell while in Japan. It was this connection that either supplemented Oswald's finances enough to allow him the services of expensive girls from the Queen Bee, or made him the ideological compatriot of such alluring females as the half-Russian "roundeye"—or both. Epstein's argument was further bolstered by Oswald's study of the Russian language, which he indeed began while in the Far East, as well as by his supposed bitterness over spending several weeks in the brig following a hostile run-in in a bar with a military superior (his second court-martial offense).[28] In sum, according to this interpretation, the Atsugi tour of duty was the defining period of Lee Harvey Oswald's life, for "unknown to his fellow Marines, Oswald was during this period in Japan making careful plans and preparations to defect to the Soviet Union."[29]

While the theory of Oswald as Soviet spy isn't without interest, and would "explain" some of Oswald's behavior (e.g., his devoted study of Russian), it doesn't explain all of it, nor has it been proven by post-Soviet collapse revelations. Similarly, it isn't necessary to see women's attraction to Oswald as unusual or as evidence of conspiracy. The record shows he routinely elicited a certain sympathy from the opposite sex, starting with his protective mother, continuing with then-Moscow-based American reporter Priscilla Johnson McMillan[30] (and a circle of female friends in Minsk), and including, several years later, reported affairs with Japanese "spy" Yaeko Okui and Mexico City Cuban embassy secretary Sylvia Duran.[31] Epstein also omits some significant details contradicting his theory. He notes, for example, that Oswald "apparently contracted a mild case of gonorrhea" in Japan, without taking into account that Oswald's military *Chronological Record of Medical Care* shows the disease's "origin" to be "in [the] line of duty, not due to own misconduct."[32] The medical entry clearly suggests that if the Marine was involved in intelligence work, it was on the U.S. side. (Epstein would cut even more spectacular corners in treating Oswald's later days in New Orleans, never mentioning the suspicious ties to the Camp Street Newman Building, headquarters of ex-FBI agent Guy Banister [chapter 5]—another matter unsupportive of the writer's KGB agent hypothesis.) Not entirely surprisingly, one of the Oswald Marine roommates Epstein talked to, Jim Botelho, received the impression his interviewer "had an agenda."[33]

On November 2, 1958 Oswald completed his Japanese tour of duty and traveled to the U.S. aboard the USS *Barrett*. He visited Fort Worth by bus on a one-month leave, spending time with his brother Robert hunting squirrels and rabbits with .22 rifles.[34] On December 21 Oswald boarded a bus and returned to the Marines. Just before Christmas he reported to his new unit, Marine Air Control Squadron Nine (MACS-9), in Santa Ana, California.

An alternate version of Oswald's activities may be gleaned from the companions who knew him best at MACS-9. The weight of their observation is that he was neither the lone Marxist rube of *Life Magazine* nor the KGB operative of Epstein; the MACS-9 Oswald, rather, was fixated on Cuba, but seemingly as an intelligence agent (who occasionally tried to recruit other Marines) for some U.S. federal agency.

According to MACS-9 Marine Bud Simco, Oswald was generally sloppy, wore his hat down over his eyes "Beetle Bailey style," kept his boots scuffed, and "almost seemed to cultivate [an] unkempt appearance." As a result, says Simco, "anytime a work detail was formed, he was usually the first to be selected. He would take everything in stride with a cocky 'so what' attitude," and was never seen to lose his cool or "be particularly upset by anything." Among Oswald's fellow MACS-9 radar operators was an aspiring writer, Kerry Thornley. Thornley was so impressed by the unusual Marine that he started writing a novel on him *before* the assassination—a fact that later so discombobulated New Orleans district attorney Jim Garrison that he threatened to subpoena the young novelist as a material witness.[35]

Perhaps the oddest aspect of Oswald was his preoccupation with the "study of all things Russian," Simco recalls. "[But] most people, including myself, really didn't take Oswald all that seriously. For that matter, most didn't really take anything that seriously. Oswald himself was probably more sober than any of us." Simco remembers one occasion in which a not-too-bright lieutenant walked into the mail room and saw a Russian publication addressed to Oswald. The officer went around asking why anyone would subscribe to such a paper, and "when I heard this account from others in the recreation hut, those present just laughed, because that was 'just Oswald.'"[36]

Interestingly, Russian was not the only language Private Oswald was studying during this period. His first Quonset hut roommate at MACS-9 was Nelson Delgado, a Brooklyn-born Puerto Rican who gave Oz Spanish lessons.

As Delgado told the story to the FBI, and later, on April 16, 1964, to Warren legal staffer Wesley J. Liebeler, Oswald's interest in learning Spanish was intertwined with his interest in the then-recent Cuban revolution. The exciting events in the Carribean country had been the topic of many a bull session between the two young Marines, both of whom initially admired Fidel Castro (who had not yet declared himself a Marxist) as well as the swashbuckling antics of William Morgan, a former army sergeant who had gone to Cuba and become a military hero. "We talked how we would like to go to Cuba," Delgado told Liebeler. "We could go over there and become officers and lead an expedition to some of these other islands and free them too."[37]

For Delgado, such conversations with Oswald were frankly "barracks talk,"[38] as Liebeler surmised. If the Puerto Rican Marine ever seriously considered an adventure in Cuba, his interest quickly waned after Castro "turned around and started to purge." Oswald was another story, however.

He [Oswald] started actually making plans, he wanted to know, you know, how to get to Cuba and things like that. I was shying away from him. He kept on asking me questions like "how can a person in his category, an English person . . . be part of that [Cuban] revolution movement?"[39]

The slightly rattled Delgado suggested to the intense roommate that he might try getting in touch with the Cuban embassy. Sometime later, Oswald informed him he had done just that—an assertion Delgado at first believed to be mere bravado, "one of his, you know, lies." The Brooklyn native found out differently when, in the time-honored custom of roommates, he went rummaging through Oswald's belongings looking to borrow a tie and came across an envelope addressed to Oswald and bearing "an official seal" from the Cuban consulate in Los Angeles. More letters from the consulate were to follow, Delgado testified, "little pamphlets and newspapers" that Oswald began receiving in addition to his staple of Russian papers.

Delgado also recalled two other apparent Oswald-Cuban connections during this period. One was an unusual visit to Oswald by a civilian whom Delgado associated with the Cuban consulate. The visitor arrived at the base after nine o'clock at night and talked privately with Oswald for some two hours. Another connection involved a Friday-night train trip Oswald took "to see some people in Los Angeles,"[40] as Oz explained to Delgado when they ran into one another at the Santa Ana station. Delgado too was on his way to L.A., and they rode together on the same train.

This trip was doubly unusual for Oswald. First, he seldom left the base (unlike Delgado, who traveled to Los Angeles almost every weekend), and secondly, despite being a casual dresser, he was on this occasion "all suited up; white shirt, dark suit, dark tie."[41] When the two Marines reached L.A., they went their separate ways; Oswald didn't elaborate further on the reason for his trip, and Delgado didn't ask.

"I came to find out later on he had come back Saturday," Delgado told Liebeler. "He didn't stay like we did, you know, come back Sunday night [on] the last train." Again, Delgado associated Oswald's brief and seemingly purposeful visit to the city with the Cuban consulate. (Indeed, Oswald later confirmed to Delgado that his trip had been for the purpose of going to the consulate, though as before the Puerto Rican thought "it was just his, you know, bragging of some sort.")[42]

As was the fate of numerous other witnesses testifying to events related to the assassination, Delgado's recollections were not all welcomed by his official listeners (notably the FBI) or were selectively rendered by writers seeking to promote a particular interpretation of Oswald's life.[43] Thus, for example, what was perhaps Delgado's most famous piece of testimony—that Oswald's shooting skills were mediocre, and indeed often "a pretty big joke, because he got a lot of 'Maggie's drawers'" (complete misses of the target)—did not sit well with a Bureau intent on supporting the Warren thesis of Oswald as a lone gunman capable of assassinating a president with a weapon far inferior to an M-1 rifle:[44]

> Mr. DELGADO. Am I allowed to say what I want to say?
>
> Mr. LIEBELER. Yes; I want you to say exactly what you want to say.
>
> Mr. DELGADO. I want to believe that Oswald did what he was supposed to have done [i.e., assassinate Kennedy], but I had the impression they [the FBI] weren't satisfied with my testimony of him not being an expert shot.
>
> Mr. LIEBELER. You say you got the impression that the FBI agents that talked to you didn't like the statement that you made about Oswald's inability to use the rifle well; is that right?
>
> Mr. DELGADO. Right.[45]

Likewise, Delgado's testimony to the FBI that he had seen Oswald make only one trip to Los Angeles (presumably to visit the Cuban consulate) did not please the agents. In this instance they did more than badger him to change his statement; they changed it for him, as Liebeler discovered.

> Mr. LIEBELER. There are two of these FBI reports here that tell me that you told the FBI that Oswald used to go to Los Angeles every other week.
>
> Mr. DELGADO. I used to go to Los Angeles every other week.[46]
>
> Mr. LIEBELER. But not Oswald?
>
> Mr. DELGADO. No.
>
> Mr. LIEBELER. And you are sure that you told that to the FBI?
>
> Mr. DELGADO. Positive.

Mr. LIEBELER. You have no question about that at all?

Mr. DELGADO. No question about that at all. Otherwise I wouldn't have made the statement that he had been with me one time. It would have been common to see him in the train station. But it wasn't.[47]

After Oswald and Delgado started to have their differences, Delgado left and was replaced by another roomy, future judge Jim Anthony Botelho of San Juan Bautista, California. The two new roommates got along well, and on one occasion Botelho invited the New Orleans Marine home to San Juan Bautista. Oswald accepted and met Botelho's family.

Later, when Oswald hastily applied for an early discharge on grounds of family hardship, Jim and everyone else in the company were surprised to learn that the request was granted so quickly, according to Simco. During the days that Oswald awaited the discharge, he made "quite a few trips" back to MACS-9 to visit his friend Botelho,[48] repeatedly telling him and others about going to Cuba, where he'd be paid to train troops. Oswald seemed to be trying to recruit his listeners to volunteer for such a venture. Botelho begged off, saying he knew nothing about training troops and anyway "was a lover, not a fighter."[49] To such objections Oswald reportedly replied that they could "fake it." Oswald "made this suggestion more than once and was serious, but no one was interested."[50]

Later, when the MACS-9 Marines finally learned of Oswald's defection to Russia, several of those who knew him, including Simco and Botelho, speculated that he was on a "mission" for the U.S. government and not a genuine defector.

Today a justice of the peace, Botelho still believes strongly that Oswald traveled to the Soviet Union as a U.S. agent—and moreover, that he was essentially a "gentle man," a "pacifist" who would not have murdered the president. "I will never believe that," he says. "If he was involved, it was as an informant of some kind, someone who was probably trying to stop the assassination, not participate in it. He was a hero of our time, not a killer."[51]

Which was it? Was Oswald a KGB agent as Epstein surmised? Was he an agent of U.S. intelligence with an infiltrator's interest in Cuba and a later Soviet mission, as his MACS-9 buddies believed? Was he perhaps neither . . . "just Oswald," as Simco once said? The historical record through Oswald's military career doesn't provide a definitive answer. It does, however, offer a clue—as we'll see—in the form of a long-overlooked Department of Defense ID.

CHAPTER THREE

House of Cards

It isn't surprising that the erratic turns in Lee Harvey Oswald's life caused some Kennedy investigators to surmise that there was more than one Oswald. The mixed-up kid from New Orleans had the ambiguity of a quantum particle whose trajectory couldn't be predicted, even theoretically. He was first a good student, then a delinquent, then a convert to Marxist thought, then a U.S. Marine, then a defector to Russia with a radically improved social life, then an impoverished husband and father in Texas, then a leftist militant or leftist-militant impersonator passing out pro-Castro pamphlets and hanging out with anti-Kennedy fanatics in New Orleans, then a guy looking to defect to Cuba from Mexico—all this before launching into a spectacular two-part closer as both alleged presidential assassin and assassin's victim. In typical Oswald fashion, his final two acts were self-contradictory.

At the heart of the Oswald puzzle is the ambiguous nature of his behavior, or at least of the evidence of this behavior. We know, for example, that he started learning Russian while at Atsugi; but did he do this as a Marxist enthusiast, a patriotic recruit of the CIA, or a turncoat already conspiring with the KGB? His study of Russian has been used to support all three theories.[1] Similarly, Delgado tells us Oswald visited the Cuban consulate during the MACS-9 phase of his Marine career. But did he go as the barracks Castrophile Oswald-skovich or as an intelligence operative establishing a cover? Again, the same act supports both interpretations.

Fortunately, not all of the evidence regarding Oswald has been equally double edged. One decidedly *un*ambiguous clue is a Department of Defense ID card found in Oswald's possession following his arrest for the murder of Dallas police officer J. D. Tippit. In this instance there's no question either of what the document suggests (the card is of the same type found on known CIA contract agent Francis Gary Powers when his U-2 plane went down over the Soviet Union) or of its authenticity; the USMC has admitted issuing the ID to Oswald prior to his discharge in 1959. Yet in all probability the Warren investigators were not even shown the card by the FBI, as will be seen. Like the Bureau's report on John Elrod, the card's significance was overlooked for more than thirty years.

In the fall of 1992 the La Fontaine clan rented an oversized van and set out on one of life's major passages—dropping the kid off at college. In this case the kid was Eugenia, who, mouthy from birth, had written in the essay portion of her application that she couldn't decide whether her mom was "a candidate for the Pulitzer or the loony bin." It must have been taken well; she was accepted.

One evening not long after the van had been returned, Mary was repacking a box of documents and photographs. The materials had come from the effects of a deceased Dallas police officer whose sons now lived in West Texas. It turned out, however, that the photos were identical to negatives and prints she'd seen before in the Dallas police files released earlier that year to the city archives. But as Mary boxed the last papers to drop at the local Fed Ex kiosk (the owners were getting antsy for their return), she lingered a moment over a contact sheet. It showed two actual-size prints of items the police had found in Lee Harvey Oswald's wallet. One was a photo of young Marina, pensive and alluring amidst flowers on a sunlit day in Minsk; easy enough to see why this was the shot of his wife that the ex-Marine had chosen to carry. The other print on the sheet was more prosaic, an ID card of Oswald with the number N 4,271,617.

The card had been photographed on the front side only. It bore a mug shot of Oswald and an impressive circular seal, in the center of which was an eagle radiating stars and clutching three mean-looking arrows—or were they rockets? Mary's contacts, which she still had on, weren't great for close-up. One thing she could see clearly enough, though. Rimming the seal were the words *Department of Defense, United States of America.*

Looking more closely, she also noted what appeared to be a postmark, or perhaps two postmarks, one superimposed over the other, overlapping both the Department of Defense seal and the lower right-hand corner of the ID photo. The most visible postmark was dated October 23, 1963, less than a month before the assassination and some ten months after the card's expiration date of December 7, 1962.

There was something vaguely familiar about this curious card. But Mary, who had a good memory, couldn't remember having seen it before—except in the archives fairly recently, and now, in this batch of documents. Surely, though, it had to be referenced *somewhere.* She went to the bookcase and pulled out the one-volume *Report of the Warren Commission on the Assassination of President Kennedy.*

Looking through the photos accompanying the volume, Mary quickly discovered what it was about the card with the DoD seal that struck her as familiar. It was the picture of Oswald. His photo on the Defense card was the same as that on another ID he had notoriously carried: a phony Selective Service card bearing his picture but the name Alek James Hidell. But though the phony Hidell card was included (and duly identified as a forgery) in the photo exhibits of the *Report,* the Defense ID on the contact sheet was nowhere pictured in the book's pages.

The omission was annoying, but not entirely remarkable. In addition to the *Report* in her hand—the Warren conclusions conveniently summarized in a single book—there were of course twenty-six *more* Warren volumes of "evidence" stashed in the city library. Somewhere in those fat and chaotic volumes the Defense card could probably be found.

For the time being, Mary turned to Appendix XI of the *Report* and located the statement dictated by FBI special agent Manning C. Clements the day after the assassination. This agent's report, though containing no pictures as Mary knew, listed the contents of Oswald's wallet. Sure enough, the Department of Defense card was on the list—definitely identified by number, N 4,271,617—as was the fake draft card with the name Alek James Hidell.

The Hidell card was described by Clements as "Photo of Selective

Service System card," about which he noted that it bore a picture of Oswald, contained "erasures and retyping of the information," had on the reverse side the address of the draft board (which the agent provided), and showed an "indistinct" signature by the board member or clerk issuing the card; Clements guessed the signer's name could be "Good" something, like Goodson or Goodman. The agent's description was comprehensive, presenting factual data from both sides of the draft card, volunteering a partial interpretation for a hard-to-make-out signature, and conveying quick recognition that the card was probably fraudulent.

About the Defense ID, Clements was more reserved. He did provide the card's number and expiration date, as well as information it contained regarding such matters as Oswald's Marine status, birthdate, and color of eyes (gray). But he failed to remark the place or date of issue, or who the issuing officer was, all shown on the card's reverse side. Clements also left unmentioned the seemingly unavoidable fact that, on the front side, the card had a photograph—the same photo as on the phony Hidell card, which he had just described. Why would the otherwise competent and conscientious agent have omitted such an obvious, and possibly relevant, observation? This had been the first thing Mary noticed about the two cards, that they had the same picture of Oswald.

Still puzzled, but out of time if she wanted to get her box of documents to Fed Ex before the kiosk snapped shut, Mary chugged the battered family Subaru out of the driveway. She stopped at a Kinko's Copy Center just long enough to make a Xerox of the Defense card, and rolled on.

That evening she got in touch with Paul Hoch in Berkeley.

Hoch published an annotated newsletter and bibliography of Kennedy literature, and was widely considered the researcher's researcher, prominently acknowledged in almost every serious book on the assassination. As wary of undocumented "conspiracy theories" as the Catholic hierarchy was about claims of miraculous visitations, he had, in recent years, sounded more like a Warren defender than a critic. But he kept an open mind.

"Oh, yes," he said when Mary brought up the ID she'd photocopied. "That's the DD 1173."

"The *what?*"

"It's the type of card it is, a DD Form 1173," he explained blandly. "It says so on the reverse side."

"Where did you see it?" she asked.

"I have a copy that was published in Jesse Curry's book. That's the only place I can recall."

"You mean the card wasn't published in the evidence volumes of the Warren Commission?"

"Nooo—," he said. "I remember I was surprised by the card myself when the Curry book came out. That was around 1969, I think."

Hoch explained that shortly after seeing a picture of the ID in this book (*JFK Assassination File: Retired Dallas Police Chief Jesse Curry Reveals His Personal File*), he attempted to discover the significance of the seldom-mentioned card. But preoccupied with other lines of investigation—and not receiving a great deal of meaningful response to his letters—he'd finally let the matter drop sometime in the early 1970s. He still had this old correspondence, however, and before hanging up agreed to send Mary everything he had in his files on the card.

When Paul Hoch's package arrived, it included a copy of the page in the now-out-of-print Jesse Curry book that showed the Oswald Department of Defense card. Unlike the contact sheet on which Mary had first seen the card, the Curry page displayed the ID's reverse side as well as the front.

The back of the card provided information left out by FBI special agent Manning Clements in his otherwise informative Warren description. It identified the card as a "Uniformed Services Identification and Privilege Card," and, as Hoch had remembered, a DD Form 1173. The card's reverse side also showed it had been issued September 11, 1959 at El Toro Air Station in Santa Ana, where Oswald completed his Marine service as a member of MACS-9. It was on that same date that Oswald was discharged; five weeks later, he crossed the Finnish-Soviet border on his way to Moscow, where he would announce his intention to defect.

The Defense card had been signed on the back by the issuing officer, Marine 1st Lt. A. G. Ayers, Jr., who had also prepared and signed the discharge entry on Oswald's military record. Ayers' entry in this record (dated September 11, 1959) showed that Oswald was released from active duty "by reason of hardship" and that a card with the number N 4,271,617 was "issued this date . . . in accordance with paragraph 3014.5 PRAM [Personnel Records and Accounting Manual]."

Unlike the Hidell draft card, which was fraudulent in every aspect (including the fact that it had a photo at all), the DoD card cross-referenced with military records and was an authentic issue of the USMC.

The reverse side also provided a possible clue to the postmark or postmarks on the front. "If found, drop in any mail box," the card instructed; it then told the postmaster: "Return to Department of Defense, Washington 25, D.C." Had the card been lost, then found by someone who dropped it in a mail box? If so, that might account for the postmarks on the front side. The ID had been treated like a piece of mail and eventually returned to Oswald.

But the card raised other questions. Mary wondered if everyone getting an honorable discharge from the Marines received such a privilege card, for example. It specifically granted Oswald access not only to the PX, commissary, and post theater, but to medical care facilities. She was under the impression—not from Ray, whose military career was almost as disgraceful as Bill Clinton's, but her brother, who had gone to Vietnam—that such military privileges stopped when a soldier left active duty. This was so, she believed, even if the soldier went into the reserves after his or her discharge. Her brother had been a reserve when he returned from the army, and she remembered he had complained a couple of times about how high everything at Kroger's and Albertson's was compared to the commissary. Knowing Jimmy, she figured that's where he would've shopped if he had his choice; but he never did. Was it that they'd stopped giving out the privilege card by the time of Vietnam?

Mary was also curious about the postmark. If the card was put in a mail box and sent to the Department of Defense, as the reverse side instructed the postmaster to do, why had Defense returned it to Oswald as late as October 1963, a month before the assassination? Someone in the Pentagon had taken the trouble to look up Oswald's address and get it back to him. The logistics of this feat alone were impressive; how would the returner know where Oswald lived in October 1963? And if the person knew this, how could he or she fail to know the most basic fact of Oswald's file to date, that he was a defector? Or to notice that the card hadn't been good for almost a year? Wouldn't sending such an obviously dead card back to its "owner" just encourage possible misuse of the ID to obtain no-longer permissible privileges?

Later, Robert Blakey, former general counsel of the House Select Committee on Assassinations, would also ponder the question of the postmark when the Defense ID was brought to his attention. If the card was mailed to the Pentagon, he told Mary for a story in the *Houston Post,* "Defense would have had to have given it *back* to Oswald . . . interesting."

But the military was notorious for doing things its own way, and ordinary logic wasn't always the presiding concern. There could be obscure technical reasons that would account for the original issuance of the card, and perhaps even for its being returned, a year after expiration, to an untrustworthy defector suspected of having passed military secrets to the Soviets. There *could* be. Mary decided to check.

She started with the old correspondence sent to her in the last package from Paul Hoch. In 1974, Hoch too had wondered about the DoD card, and had written a letter to USMC captain L. D. Orlando, assistant head of the Marine publications and printing office in Washington. Hoch's letter requested Captain Orlando's office to "locate the section of PRAM (1959 version) which deals with the issuance of the Uniformed Services Identification and Privilege Card to a member of the Marine Reserve."

The letter also reminded Captain Orlando that Hoch had requested this section of the PRAM before, but had been sent the wrong information, possibly because of a "typographical error." What the Marines had sent him was a different section of the 1959 PRAM, namely paragraph 3014.5. This, to be sure, was the paragraph number cited in Oswald's military record as containing the regulation authorizing and governing the issuance of the Defense ID. But paragraph 3014.5 had turned out to refer "only to the issuance of the USMC identification cards 2MC, 2MC(RET), and 2MC(RES)," Hoch complained. What he was looking for, he repeated, was the section of the PRAM applying to the Defense Department's DD Form 1173 card.

"If you cannot readily locate the relevant section," he added politely, "please let me know how I can arrange to inspect all of this [1959] version of PRAM personally. I will be in the Washington area late in September."

Two weeks later Captain Orlando had sent an answer:

Dear Mr. Hoch:

In reply to your letter of 26 August 1974 to which you attached your check for $2 in payment for a copy of the section of PRAM (1959 version) dealing with the issuance of the Uniformed Services Identification and Privilege Card (DD Form 1173) to a member of the Marine Corps Reserve is enclosed.

Sincerely,

L. D. ORLANDO
Captain, U. S. Marine Corps
Assistant Head, Publications and Printing Branch
Headquarters Support Division
By direction of the Commandant

The captain's letter was missing more than a little attention to syntax. Its only enclosure, in return for the researcher's two-dollar check, was another copy of paragraph 3014.5.

In 1959, as Mary would learn, three types of ID cards were routinely issued by the USMC. Active-duty officers and enlisted men received a green 2MC card, retired Marines received a gray 2MC(RET), and members of the reserve a red 2MC(RES). This scheme, which exhausts all the normal modes of being a Marine, is still in place today. Of the three types of Marine IDs, it was the last-named 2MC(RES) that Oswald should have received in September 1959 when he was discharged into inactive reserve. The 2MC(RES) was, for example, the card issued to Oswald's MACS-9 roommate, Jim Botelho, when he left the Marines a few months after Oswald, in early January of 1960. It was also a 2MC(RES) the other guys in MACS-9 received when they were discharged and placed on reserve. "What I got was a pink or red ID," said Bud Simco. "The active card [2MC] was green."

The long and short of it was that in Oswald's circle, only he—the Russian-studying oddball, career private, and seemingly least likely candidate for advancement—had received a buff-colored Department of

Defense ID; and that the Marine PRAM under which the card was said to have been issued did not check out. Hoch knew or suspected much of this back in 1974. He also realized the Marines could continue to "misunderstand" his inquiries on the Defense card forever, if they wished. After a while, he stopped writing letters.

Now, some twenty years later, in October 1992, Mary cranked the search back up. By this go-round, the cold war had vanished and the La Fontaines had the advantage of encountering a new generation of Marines and other military employees, many media-wise, courteous, and themselves curious about that event of long ago, the assassination of President Kennedy. They'd seen *JFK* too.

But Mary wasn't leading with Lee Harvey Oswald. She started by looking for someone in the Department of Defense who could explain the purpose of a DoD identification and privilege card. She didn't relate her inquiry to the assassination in any way. Her story was that she was doing an investigative article on a "person" and was told he'd carried such a card. It wasn't a major point, but she'd like to know what the card meant.

Surprisingly, given the Pentagon's no-doubt deserved reputation as a maze of stupefying proportions, it didn't take long to locate a DoD employee who was the precise expert to answer her question. His name was Steve Gammons, and his specialty was defense history.

"That's a dependent's ID," Gammons said after listening to Mary's description.

"A what, now?"

"A military dependent's card. You know, children, wives of military personnel. It allows them to use the PX, commissary, stuff like that."

"But it wasn't his dependents who got the card," she said. "It was this person, *he* got the card, when he was leaving the military."

"No, couldn't happen," Gammons assured her. "He wouldn't have received any card when he left, unless he was in the reserve."

"He *was* a reservist," she said. "Maybe that explains it."

"No," said Gammons again. "If he was a reservist, he would've gotten a Marine reservist's card."

"How do you tell the difference?"

"Well, you said the picture on the card was flush left; that's like a dependent's card. A reservist has a card with a picture in the center; that card is red. The card you're describing is buff."

"So he shouldn't have had the card?" Mary said dubiously.

"That's right. The card should've gone to a dependent. That's why it's called a dependent's card."

Mary sighed. She thought the conversation was effectively over—and without a clear conclusion.

But Gammons added an afterthought.

"Well, there's one exception," he said.

"What's that?" she asked.

"Well, those buff ID cards are sometimes issued to civilian personnel requiring military identification overseas."

Mary took this in for a moment. It suddenly struck her as almost too eerily perfect. Oswald had been on the verge of becoming just that, an overseas American civilian, when he was issued the card. And the card could explain an abiding mystery. When Oswald defected to Russia, he flew from London to Helsinki, apparently aware that he could get a quick visa in the Finnish capital for travel in the Soviet Union. But there was a glitch—no commercial flights were scheduled at the time he made his trip. For this reason, some persons had speculated he had taken a military transport. With the DoD card, he could have done exactly that.

Oswald had received a discharge on grounds of family hardship, but it wasn't a secret around the MACS-9 barracks that he was planning on enrolling in some sort of Swiss university. Some Marines, like Botelho, knew. Who else knew, and how high up?

"Was that regulation in effect in the late fifties?" she finally managed.

"That I can't tell you," said Gammons. "You need to contact the National Archives, to pull up the manual. I'll give you the number."

She wrote it on an envelope and thanked him for the information. The receiver was warm when she set it down.

It turned out that the military section of the National Archives, though able to find some documentation on the DoD card, had trouble deciphering it. From what he could make out, an archivist told Mary, the Defense card appeared to have been discontinued in 1957. Did that sound about right? he asked. No, she said, the card she was talking about had an issue date in the fall of 1959. It had to have been issued at least through that year. The archivist suggested she try the U.S. Army Military History Institute, people who were specialists in these things. The institute was at the War College in Carlisle, Pennsylvania. He gave her the number.

In Carlisle, Mary located a Defense historian, Dennis Vetock, who agreed to check on the circa 1959 regulations that governed issue of the DoD card. He would check historically, from the beginning, and call her back, he said. A few days later, he did.

He told her that as she had suspected, the man from the National Archives had indeed misread the data he'd found on the card. The card's usage didn't end in 1957. That was when it *started.*

"What about who got the card?" Mary asked.

"Mostly dependents," said Vetock. He itemized the permitted categories of DoD ID recipients. In addition to military dependents, the card could be issued to disabled veterans, reservists, foreign military personnel and their families, and the overseas civilians in need of ID that Gammons had mentioned.

Reservists. "Did you say reservists could get the card too?"

"That's right. They've been getting it from the very beginning. I found a directive on this dated 16 July '57. It says military personnel on active duty get the green card, DD Form 2MC, and that *all other personnel*—and it specifically names the reserve in this category—are supposed to be issued DD Form 1173, the uniformed services identification and privilege card."[2]

Mary tried to get this straight. If the buff DoD card was the street-legal ID for reservists back then, why did Botelho and all the rest get a red 2MC(RES) card at the end of active duty? Was it that the PRAM on the Marine IDs was changed in the few months between Oswald's discharge and Botelho's? If so, that would account for the difference in the card issues. But of course she wasn't sure when this PRAM had been revised. She just knew that at some point it *had* been, since reservists were no longer given the Defense card.

"But not later, right?" she verified. "Later the reservists didn't get the DD 1173s, right?"

"No, that's *not* right," said Vetock. "They're still issued the card today, so far as I know."

"That's got to be wrong," Mary insisted. "I was told at the DoD that the card isn't given to reserves."

"Just because someone's in DoD doesn't mean he can't make a

simple mistake," he observed with maddening calm. "I've got the facts right here in front of me."

That was Friday.

Monday, he called back.

"You were right," Vetock said, "the reservists *don't* get that card."

He'd done a bit more hunting over the weekend and found a 1959 manual that cleared up the matter, he explained. Originally, members of the reserve—along with everyone else not on active duty—did get the DD Form 1173. But as he'd found out, this practice was changed two years later, in 1959, when the three-card ID system went into effect.

All *right*. But *when* in 1959?

"Was that change made before the fall?" she asked innocently.

"Yes," he confirmed. "It was in place as of the manual of July 1959."

Two months, thought Mary. The DoD card was supposed to have stopped being issued to reservists two months before Oswald received his. Then why hadn't the Marines followed the regulation in his case?

"I guess if someone didn't read the manual the card could still have been issued to a reservist by mistake," she posed.

"Not hardly," said Vetock. "The military *runs* on these manuals; they're like bibles. Besides, long before a manual is issued there are directives that come out, putting the new changes into effect. That would have been the case on this changeover to a three-card ID system. They were issuing officers and enlisted men the green, gray, and red cards, not the DD Form 1173, for some time before the manual was distributed."[3]

"But still"—she couldn't help throwing in—"you did say anyone could make a simple mistake, didn't you?"

"This wouldn't be a *simple mistake*," he shot back. "Only a harebrain in some far outpost would give that Defense card to someone in contradiction to the manual, and in that case it would be immediately revoked."

Vetock's findings were not contradicted by the Marines. Lt. Kim Miller, a USMC public affairs officer in Washington, acknowledged that the Corps hadn't given the DD Form 1173 to Oswald in conformance to PRAM "paragraph 3014.5," as the military record indicated. The card may have been issued, she hazarded, either because

Oswald had suffered an injury while on active duty that entitled him to medical privileges, or because he was a civilian employee overseas needing a military ID. She also noted, however, that the military records didn't show an injury to Oswald, and that civilian employment "would not have been annotated to his military book."

Ray, who by now had finally sent off his endless Catalan project, had been catching up on his Kennedy homework. He thought the 1959 regulations uncovered by historian Dennis Vetock, coupled with the USMC's inability to explain why the card had been issued to Oswald, provided the clincher to Mary's card story. The *Houston Post* agreed, and slated the story for the Sunday front page of November 22, 1992, the twenty-ninth anniversary of the assassination.

But this date was still two weeks away, and there were still some loose ends to tie up. One was the tracking down of Lieutenant Ayers, who issued the card. The Marines' Lieutenant Miller had promised to see what she could find on Ayers after Mary, armed with the historical background on procedures, called to get an official statement from USMC headquarters as to why Oswald had been given the ID. When Ray called the lieutenant once again to see what she might have turned up, she told him that the search for the Ayers record—one of millions in the personnel computers—had been hopeless without a social-security record or so much as a first name. She also noted, not unreasonably, that even if Ayers could be found, the chances were he wouldn't remember anything about the Oswald card. "When you get an ID, you know, somebody just signs off on it. Lieutenant Ayers didn't probably even take it up [i.e., the processing of the card]. Some administrative clerk did and then Ayers just signed it."

Ray told Lieutenant Miller he'd probably see what he could come up with on Ayers under FOIA.

"If you find a reason for the card, please let us know," she said. "We're just as puzzled by this as you guys are."

When the Corps finally responded to Ray's detailed FOIA on the Oswald card, the regulations simply raised more doubts about its origin. They provided, for example, that the negative and one print of the photograph taken for the card should be retained in the permanent file of the recipient. However, Oswald's clearly was not—at least, not by the Marine Corps. On October 10, 1963, the CIA in Mexico City had cabled the Office of Naval Intelligence, requesting the navy's most recent picture of Lee Henry [*sic*] Oswald. ONI never sent the picture, but after the assassination of President Kennedy, it produced an envelope addressed to the CIA and containing Oswald's 1956 induction photo. Had the Marine Corps followed its own procedure in issuing the DD Form 1173 to Oswald, it would have had a print and negative of the photograph on the card in its files. None has ever been produced and the photo on the card appears not to have been taken when he was in the Marines—he certainly doesn't have a Marine-style haircut in the photo, even though his passport photo, taken the same week the card was issued, shows a decidedly short-haired Oswald. Nor was the DoD card laminated as it should have been, per 1959 Marine Corps regulations. Like the Powers card, Oswald's is unlaminated. From these inconsistencies with normal Marine procedure, it would appear that the Oswald card, like Powers', may have been issued by another U.S. government agency.

Another loose end was the role of the FBI in the Oswald Defense-card affair. As noted earlier, FBI special agent Manning Clements had low-balled the significance of the Defense ID in his report to the Warren Commission by omitting not only the fact that it had a picture, but that it was the same Oswald picture as on the phony Hidell Selective Service card. But the Bureau also misled (or cooperated in an unspoken alliance with) the Commission by mishandling another copy of the same Oswald photograph. The latter appeared in the *Report* and evidence volumes as Exhibit 2892 and was labeled (from data provided by the FBI) "Photo taken in Minsk." This photo was identical to the "Hidell" and DoD photo, and even showed a white circular cutout in the lower right-hand corner corresponding to the overlapping postmark(s) on the Defense ID card.

The Minsk contradiction—the fact that Oswald's trip to Russia occurred *after* the issuance of the DoD card—was not evident to the Commission, which felt confident enough to include the "Minsk" photo among its exhibits. The most benign explanation for this misstep on the part of the Warren investigators is that the FBI withheld the Defense card from their direct examination.

But the Bureau's apparent skullduggery in this affair was not limited to misleading the Commission. The Hoover agency went on to destroy the original, quite literally, as archivist Sue McDonough of the National Archives (Civil Reference branch) would report to the La Fontaines. In December 1966, when the Bureau finally released the Oswald Defense card to the Archives, it arrived "nearly obliterated by FBI testing," McDonough said. "The color, the image, the printing, everything is gone; you couldn't use it to show anything." The archivist repeated the gist of these assertions in a letter to Ray dated November 16, 1992, a week before the DoD card story would appear in the *Post*. The card, she noted there, had "undergone extensive chemical forensic testing," was "significantly discolored and stained," and had "no visible date stamp [postmark]."

Informed that the National Archives had blown the whistle, FBI spokesperson Bill Carter of the Bureau's public affairs office in Washington effectively denied that his agency would stoop to such tactics as "testing" the card into oblivion, or indeed that it had tested the card at all. "How does she [archivist McDonough] *know* it was tested by the FBI?" he challenged. "Does she have a report?"

"Who else but the FBI could have done it?" McDonough responded. She added that there were no pictures of the card in its unobliterated state at the Archives.

On Sunday, November 22, 1992 the Oswald card story ran in the *Houston Post* as expected. Word of the Defense ID and its implications reached an impressive audience of assassination researchers and buffs both in and outside of Texas, and became an "inside" subject of interest in Kennedy conferences and on computer networks like CompuServe and Prodigy.

Unfortunately, the news never made it to the general public beyond the reading range of the *Post*. As had happened previously with the Dallas police files series, the Associated Press chose not to move the story of the Oswald DoD ID on its national wire, despite the fact that the account was documented and carried on the front page of a mainstream, major-market newspaper.

The *Post* story quoted Oswald expert Wesley J. Liebeler, the Warren Commission associate counsel who had taken Delgado's testimony, and Robert Blakey, general counsel for the later investigation by the House Select Committee on Assassinations, on their reactions to the Department of Defense card. Both men expressed surprise at the Defense ID, which hadn't been considered in either of the two major investigations of the Kennedy assassination conducted by the U.S. government.

"This is all new to me," Liebeler remarked. "Two things seem odd.

The picture identified as Oswald in Minsk, and the postmark on the Defense card. The postmark implies the Defense Department either mailed it back to him [Oswald] or gave it to him at some time." Blakey too had found it "interesting," at least at the time of his interview, that the DoD would have given such a card "*back* to Oswald."

After publication, however, former HSCA counsel Blakey's surprise over this odd circumstance diminished considerably. No longer "interesting," the matter was now "much ado about nothing," a phrase the now-Notre Dame law prof repeated seven times in the course of a brief follow-up interview with Ray. Blakey's irritation with the story as published was caused by his perception that it "was slanted toward a particular perspective that there was something sinister in the card." The Oswald DD Form 1173, he believed, had a benign explanation: "The officer that issued it to him [Oswald] ran out of the recent Marine card and used the other card. If you ran out of the other cards and issued that one, it is clearly much ado about nothing."

"But the card gave him *privileges*," said Ray. "You don't issue a card granting privileges to a person not entitled to them just because you run out of the right form."

"I don't want to argue with you," Blakey snapped. "It's been thirty years. Will you let the man lay in his grave?"

The solicitous former counsel had granted JFK eighteen years of peace before issuing his own conspiracy book in 1981. He had reissued the book eleven years later, in the same 1992 that he expressed his concern to Ray. Blakey's work, *The Plot to Kill the President* (written with Richard N. Billings and published by Time Books), promoted the thesis, somewhat unusual among the conspiracy-minded, that the mob had murdered Kennedy *without* government involvement.[4] The intrusion of new evidence in the form of the Oswald DoD card undermined that lone-mob speculation, as well as the dignity of Blakey's HSCA investigation, which over its two-year span had never taken up the question of the government ID.

Still, though ever prepared to think the worst of anyone disagreeing with him, Ray considered the slim possibility that Blakey might have a point. Could the DD Form 1173 have been issued by mistake, simply because the issuing officer ran out of the right card? Military historian Vetock had contended that "only a harebrain" would pull a stunt like that; but what did the Marines themselves have to say? Ray decided to call back Lt. Kim Miller.

"Oh, no," she informed him emphatically; the DD Form 1173 *wouldn't* have been used as an impromptu "substitute" for a reservist's card. "It would have given him privileges. He'd be authorized to use the commissary, the exchange, the base theater, medical facilities, all of which are things an inactive reserve wouldn't have the authority to use."

"OK," said Ray, "just checking."

"I thought we went through this the last time," the lieutenant said quizzically.

"That was probably with Mary," he mumbled, hanging up.

Meanwhile, Mary was zeroing in on the mysterious Lt. A. G. Ayers who had signed the back of the Oswald card and whom the USMC hadn't been able to help locate. The absence of Ayers from the La Fontaines' *Houston Post* article had been another "weakness" on which Blakey had seized. "You published the story without talking to Ayers or telling me why you haven't been able to talk to him, to wit, he's dead," he'd told Ray. "Until you talk to the guy who issued the card, I don't think you have a story."

A few weeks after the card story ran, the La Fontaines got some help. Hershel Womack, a photography expert at Texas Tech University, had a friend post a note on a national genealogy bulletin board requesting any information on "A. G. Ayers." Remarkably, two hours later, the former Marine officer had been traced. He was Alexander G. Ayers, alive and well half a continent away in Portland, Oregon.

Reached at home the next day, Ayers was surprised to learn from Mary that the Oswald DD Form 1173 had been the subject of news. He agreed, as did everyone else by now, that a reservist-to-be should never have been issued this card; not in the fall of 1959.

"Is my name on the back of it?" he asked.

"Yes," she said.

"Oh, wonderful."

As Marine spokesperson Miller anticipated, Ayers had no recollection of the specific card issue: "I just signed all of his [Oswald's] separation papers; I'm sure I never consciously set eyes on the man." The processing of such paperwork, including decisions on which IDs to give out, he explained, was done by administrative assistants under the supervision of the senior noncommissioned officer. When the papers were ready, they were brought en masse to Lieutenant Ayers for his signature—in essence, an anonymous process by anonymous personnel.

Had a bizarre mistake been made by a faceless office minion? Or had someone taken advantage of the impersonal procedure to slip a DoD privilege card into the separation papers of a man, nicknamed Private Oswaldskovich, embarking on an undercover assignment?

Ayers didn't know. Nor was he aware that his name appeared on yet another curious document, Oswald's passport application.

Within hours of the publication of the DoD card story, an account of the article was posted by L.A. conspiracy writer David Lifton on the Prodigy network JFK assassination bulletin board, and by New York attorney Roger Feinman on the CompuServe journalism forum.

The twin postings generated immediate responses. On CompuServe, for example, a writer identifying himself as an irate ex-Marine officer surfaced from the Washington, D.C. area to excoriate the mild-mannered Feinman "and your friends, the La Fontaines." Pumping in messages to the journalism forum at a manic 13,000 bytes per clip (slightly more than eight double-spaced pages), the former Marine—retired since 1942—charged the writers with having a probable "agenda" in their *Houston Post* story. This agenda was revealed by certain La Fontaine slipups, which fortunately had been caught and exposed by the keen-eyed retiree. Among these (there were many more), he noted the following: 1) the *Post* story suggested the Hidell draft card was authentic; 2) the story also suggested the U.S. Marines had issued the card to Oswald *in the Soviet Union*; 3) a laminated card (as the DD Form 1173 should've been) could not possibly hold a postmark; 4) Lt. Kim Miller had been misquoted; and 5) the La Fontaine article quoted a "conspiracy buff" (i.e., Paul Hoch).

As a closing zinger, the aging but indefatigable ex-Marine would ask: "By the way, are you one of those who promote the government conspiracy ideas? Is that the reason for your interest?"

Beleaguered by the constant loony attacks, and probably regretting ever having posted the story, Feinman requested a supporting response from Ray (whom he had never met). Ray complied by e-mailing a message to the attorney to be posted on the forum. The message provided the full text of Lieutenant Miller's comments, thereby countering the criticism that the Marine spokesperson had been misquoted in the *Houston Post* story. Ray also answered some of the more lurid accusations, which were piling up daily. In response to the charge that the writers were unaware that the Hidell card was a phony (a fact known by everyone for the last thirty years), he wrote:

> It would be interesting to know what gave [the retired Marine] the first clue that a card with Oswald's picture and the name Alek James Hidell was probably fraudulent, as well as what point he is making with this revelation. We did of course mention the draft card (introduced in the story by the phrase "a phony Selective Service classification card"). This mention occurred in the context of noting that the pictures on the phony card and DD 1173 were the same, a fact never mentioned by the FBI to the Warren Commission or ever previously stated in print. What about it?

Alas, Ray's sarcasm was as ineffective on the hardy retiree as it usually was on his own wife and daughters. Within a few days, the former Marine had put the finishing touches on yet another killer message—in length, if not acuity—and was back on the CompuServe journalism forum. "Let me correct a few of your comments and those of your friends, the La Fontaines," he began. Ray sighed, searching for the escape key.

A few weeks later, Ray checked in on the j-forum again. The row between defenders and critics of the card had now reached such a pitch that the fastidious SysOp had stepped in (whether for the first or umpteenth time Ray wasn't sure) to warn participants not to resort to personal violence. The ex-Marine was still leading the *anti*-crowd, apparently having found in this pursuit a new, life-fulfilling occupation.[5]

Still, not every criticism from this obsessed nemesis was equally clownish, Ray pondered. By regulation, the DD Form 1173 should have been laminated. Oswald's wasn't, as the postmark and later FBI chemical testing suggested. The crusty jarhead with the CompuServe habit had latched onto this inconsistency among his avalanche of otherwise nutty complaints. If the card had been issued laminated per USMC regulations, and Oswald later removed the lamination to update his photo, this alteration would—as the critic had noted— "require equipment more sophisticated than available to Oswald, but not the KGB." Damn . . . the old guy *would* have to make sense about one thing, Ray grumbled (or at least as much sense as he made). He stored away the loose end in Mary's to-explain file.

In the meantime, David Lifton had attracted a more substantive response to the card story. In his green days in the conspiracy business, the L.A. author was rumored to have speculated that the chauffeur of JFK's limo had somehow pulled off a Houdini-like marvel by assassinating the president (and presumably wounding the late Governor Connally) without the knowledge of the very occupants of the car, or, of course, anyone else. If Lifton once considered this daring notion, his more sober *Best Evidence,* containing the first graphic photos of Kennedy's mutilated body, had become one of the best-selling assassination books of all time. Now he struck gold again, not in dollars, but in the form of a Prodigy note from an old aquaintance, Mary Ferrell of Dallas.

The Defense card, she pointed out to him, was referenced by number—N 4,271,617—on the passport application Oswald made out on September 4, 1959, a full week *before* the card was issued. Oswald had used it as his identification on that date in signing the passport before the deputy clerk of the Superior Court of Santa Ana, as noted in Warren Commission Exhibit 1114. As a supporting attachment to the application was a brief note, also dated September 4:

TO WHOM IT MAY CONCERN:

> This is to certify that PFC (E-2) Lee Harvey OSWALD, 1653230, U.S. Marine Corps is scheduled to be released from Active Duty and Transferred to the Marine Corps Reserve (Inactive) on 11 September 1959.

The note was signed by a Sergeant Stout—over the typed signature block of Lt. A. G. Ayers, the officer who had signed Oswald's Defense card.

When Ayers was located in 1993, the now-Portland businessman couldn't explain the contradiction noted by Mary Ferrell: why the DoD card was already in Oswald's possession a week before its issuance date of September 11, 1959. He was similarly surprised to learn that his name was on the application attachment, and wasn't sure of this document's purpose.

The note, he admitted, was bland enough. He probably would've signed it if it had been presented to him; but it wasn't. The paper instead had been signed in his name by a subordinate, not an unusual circumstance in bureaucratic routines. Problem was, Ayers couldn't remember ever hearing of a "Sergeant Stout." This lack of recollection, if true—and he seemed candid enough otherwise— struck Mary as a bit odd. The sergeant wouldn't have been just another uniform on the base, not for Ayers, at least; Stout had the authority to sign off on documents on behalf of the lieutenant. Whether Ayers granted him this authority himself or had no hand in the arrangement, and whether he liked or loathed the underling, he surely must have been well aware of a person whose discretion could directly affect his own military career. After three decades, the ex-lieutenant might not be able to bring Stout's name readily to mind; that was understandable. But would Ayers, a competent man who played tennis and ran his own successful business, forget him so completely that he couldn't even recognize his name when it was called out to him? Mary couldn't quite see it, not unless he was lying, and her hunch was he wasn't. Her hunch—which she would need to check out—was that "Stout" might be an invention, a fictional name scribbled in by someone over Ayers' signature block to expedite the processing of a passport application riddled with contradictions.

Ayers was at a loss to account for yet another paradox related to Oswald's application. To the former lieutenant's knowledge, Oswald was discharged from the Marines for reasons of family hardship; this was the reason entered by Ayers on Oswald's military record on the same September 11 of both Oswald's discharge and the card's ostensible "issuance."

Why, then, did the passport application, dated a week earlier by the witnessing deputy clerk of the Santa Ana court (and filled out with full USMC knowledge and support, as attested by the mysteriously signed "To whom it may concern"), state that the purpose of the trip was to attend colleges in Switzerland and Finland, and to "visit" eight countries, including Cuba and Russia? Again, Ayers didn't know. Indeed, no one today in the USMC or DoD, from drudge researcher to nuevo-wavo friendlier and gentler spokesperson, claims to be able to explain this extraordinary discrepancy, nor another: to Ayers' knowledge, the USMC never issued ID cards earlier than the effective date. Yet the Santa Ana court clerk listed the Oswald card, dated September 11, as an ID for an affidavit dated one week earlier, September 4.[6]

This was additional stuff for the to-explain file, obviously. There were so many questions, so few answers, and all from a single card. . . .

Ah, but wait. There's more.

Shortly after notifying David Lifton of the reference to the Defense card on the Oswald passport application, Mary Ferrell faxed the conspiracy writer a stunning new message. Once again she'd been rummaging through her bottomless hoard of Kennediana; and again, as with her news clippings of the bloody smashup involving a "swank sports car" full of contraband weapons, she'd made precisely the right find.

This time the Dallas researcher had pulled from her shelves an obscure and dusty book, *The Trial of the U2*. The title page described it as the "exclusive authorized account of the court proceedings of Francis Gary Powers heard before the Military Division of the Supreme Court of the USSR." The book had been rushed into print in September 1960, the month after Powers' Moscow trial, by a Chicago firm no longer in business, Translation World Publishers. Its introduction, by Harvard academic Harold J. Berman, dwelled on the vagaries of spying, international law, and Soviet trial procedure. The remainder (and vast bulk) of the book was an English-version transcript of the three-day trial of the Kentucky native who startled the world by falling out of the blue onto Russian soil on the early morning of a Soviet patriotic holiday, May Day 1959, his American spy plane punched from the sky by an anti-aircraft rocket. Powers would have other surprises to offer as well, taking bold early steps toward the loopy Era of Oprah. Unlike other tight-lipped spooks of his day, such as KGB colonel Rudolph Ivanovich Abel (who leaked not a word despite merciless grilling by the FBI), the U-2 pilot and CIA contract agent "pleaded guilty, took the stand, described his activities in detail, and admitted that he was a spy."[7]

Still, as any kid knows, a book's real interest is in the pictures. *The Trial of the U2* had plenty, and they provided a refreshing (and in some instances, hilarious) counterpoint to the book's solemn anti-American moralizing. One photo was of a silk cloth poster found in Powers' possession. The poster had a U.S. flag at the top and "I am an American. . . . I need food, shelter. . . . I will not harm you. . . .

You will be rewarded," translated into fourteen languages; no U.S. spy should leave home without it.

Other pictures in the U-2 book showed additional items in Powers' stranded-spy survival kit: a snazzily long-barrelled handgun, compass, cartridges, hunting knife, kindling, signal flares, morphine, wads of high-denomination banknotes and gobs of watches and rings to disperse to the peasantry ("you will be rewarded . . ."), and of course, most morbidly fascinating of all (and in Powers' case, most naïvely optimistic), the saltshaker-size glass cartridge containing a needle dipped in curare—"most deadly known poison to man," according to a mournful accompanying text, ever saddened and shocked by American perfidy.

But for all of their riveting appeal, none of these pictured items were what Mary Ferrell had in mind as she thumbed through the little-known account of the Powers trial. The researcher was looking for something else, an object she remembered seeing years before, or thought she'd seen, when she first brought the bargain-priced volume home from a secondhand bookstore. She recalled the item as a U.S. government ID card that the Russians had stripped from Powers, along with the curare needle, watches, rings, and fourteen-language silk cloth poster. The ID had been partly torn and mangled in the harrowing ordeal, but still perfectly recognizable, both sides of the card presented on a single page. But had it been a page of the Powers trial book or of something else?

Well, it *was* the Powers book, it turned out. The card, once found, was so prominently displayed—opposite a photo of a diagonally soaring Lockheed U-2—that you didn't see how you could have missed it. The side-by-side layout suggested that to the Russians, at least, the card was as important as the plane itself, and with good reason: it was foolproof evidence that the pilot was an agent of the U.S. government.

Mary Ferrell focused on the lower left-hand corner of the government card's reverse side.

It read: *DD Form 1173.*

In Russia, the DD Form 1173 may have been irrefutable proof that its bearer was a CIA contract operative. In America, and in particular when the bearer was Oswald, the card was no such thing; it must have been issued "mistakenly," fraudulently, or in some other way

Oswald's Department of Defense ID card, DD Form 1173, was the same type of
ID carried by U-2 pilot Francis Gary Powers. Powers was a "civilian employee
of the government requiring military identification," a CIA contract agent.
(Oswald card courtesy Dallas Municipal Archives and Records Center,
City of Dallas, Texas; Powers card from out-of-print *The Trial of the U2*)

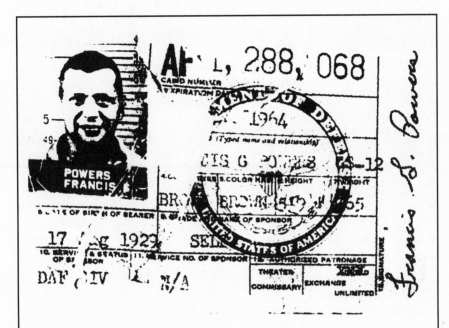

AF L, 288, 068

CARD NUMBER
EXPIRATION DATE
1964

DEPARTMENT OF DEFENSE
UNITED STATES OF AMERICA

CIS G POWERS 7S-12

EYES 5. COLOR HAIR 6. HEIGHT 7. WEIGHT
BROW BROWN 5'9" 165

POWERS
FRANCIS

5
49

8. PLACE OF BIRTH OF BEARER   9. GRADE OR RANK OF SPONSOR

17 Aug 1929

10. SERVICE OF SPONSOR   11. STATUS   11. SERVICE NO. OF SPONSOR   12. AUTHORIZED PATRONAGE

DAF CIV   N/A

THEATER
COMMISSARY   EXCHANGE
UNLIMITED

Francis G. Powers

14. MEDICAL CARE FACILITIES AUTHORIZED   DATE OF ISSUE

CIVILIAN   UNIFORMED SERVICE   17 JULY 1958

16. PLACE OF ISSUE

Detachment 10 TUSLOG, APO 259, N.Y.

SIGNATURE

TYPED GRADE AND NAME

RAY A. SOELBERG, Capt, USAF, PM

NON-TRANSFERABLE · VOID IF ALTERED

ISSUING OFFICER

WARNING: USE OF THIS AUTHORIZATION BY OTHER
THAN PERSON NAMED THEREON, OR ANY USE IN
VIOLATION OF PROVISIONS OF DEPENDENTS' MEDI-
CAL CARE ACT OF 1956 RENDERS USER LIABLE FOR
PROSECUTION UNDER APPLICABLE FEDERAL LAWS
PERTAINING TO FALSE STATEMENTS (18 USC 1001)

IF FOUND
DROP IN ANY MAILBOX

POSTMASTER: RETURN TO
DEPARTMENT OF DEFENSE
WASHINGTON 25 D. C.

PROPERTY OF UNITED STATES GOVERNMENT

DD FORM
1 JAN 57   UNIFORMED SERVICES IDENTIFICATION AND PRIVILEGE CARD

that denied its obvious implications. We will, however, retain these implications, however contradictory they may be in light of another undeniable facet of Oswald's existence: his Marxist leanings (more on this later).

Is it possible to be both a good Marxist and a temporary asset of some U.S. government intelligence agency? In the Platonic world, perhaps not. In the real world, however, where contracting syphilis in the "line of duty" is an unsurprising matter duly noted in official reports, it would appear that almost anything is possible—except, perhaps, discerning what Oswald had in mind, when, as he apparently did, he accepted an assignment to tour the world, courtesy of the U.S. government. Was he putting one over on the American intelligence experts who smoothed the way for his acquisition of a card he shouldn't have had, taking their bucks and logistics assistance, but privately keeping his own options open as to what he would really do once he arrived in the socialist paradise? It's as good a guess as any, and consistent with Oswald's temperament; it worked for him, in any case.

He stayed in Russia close to three years, not necessarily gathering information for the people who sent him, but having a good time (and befuddling the KGB in the bargain), checking out the girls, and finally marrying the prettiest one he could find. He also checked out the Soviet socialist system and discovered it to be intolerable—rejecting it, as the Russians themselves would do a few decades later. Unfortunately, in deals with American intelligence, as with the Mafia, it isn't so easy to pick up and go home once the party's over. When Oswald returned, he would find the FBI waiting. He had been marked, and, as we'll see beginning in chapter 6, was forced to undergo yet a second adventure as an "operative." (Again, he would prove nuttily capable of maintaining a consistent ideological stance—Marxism—while working in a government capacity that did not conflict with that stance.)

Meanwhile, there is something perhaps as interesting to consider: the domestic life of Lee and Marina in Dallas, and the "best friend" he ever had—the remarkable Russian baron, George de Mohrenschildt.

CHAPTER FOUR

The New Old Story
of George de Mohrenschildt

George de Mohrenschildt, working on his fourth marriage by the time Lee Oswald met him, had never passed himself off as a model of bourgeois respectability. A titled European cosmopolite with an exotically shady past, a free spirit with a touch of the roué and the sophisticated charm of Cary Grant, he spoke six languages, belonged to such heady organizations as the Dallas Petroleum Club and World Affairs Council, and traveled so extensively that "it was absolutely impossible to remember everywhere he went."[1] Acquaintances of the Russian-born baron included virtually every known plutocrat from H. L. Hunt to then-Zapata Oil chieftain George Bush, the innermost circle of the Lyndon Johnson presidency, and perhaps most notably, Janet Auchincloss, mother of Jacqueline Kennedy. Jackie herself broke off all ties to de Mohrenschildt following the assassination, when his "friendship" with Oswald came to light. Though moved by her plight, the baron was hardly abashed by the social snub. Jackie's second husband, Aristotle Onassis (de Mohrenschildt would write in an unpublished manuscript), was a murderous tub of guts with no more education than Oswald and an ill-made fortune stemming from the proceeds of overinsured old tankers callously put in the path of Nazi submarines. "If you believe in just punishment," he added, "Aristotle's rotten soul will remain forever in the Greek-Orthodox hell."[2]

After the assassination, de Mohrenschildt was called back from Haiti (where he was supposedly conducting a "geological survey")

by a letter from Warren chief counsel J. Lee Rankin. The Russian was
to provide testimony concerning the only role in his glitteringly mul-
tifaceted career for which cruel history would remember him: his
seven-month association with the impoverished Oswald between
1962 and 1963. The Warren investigators had taken a strong interest in de Mohrenschildt after Marina Oswald testified to the Commission that he had burst into the Oswald household a couple of
days after the attempted shooting of Gen. Edwin Walker, shouting,
"Lee, how did you miss General Walker?"

Flown expenses-paid to Washington, D.C. with his wife, Jeanne
(who also testified), and two Manchester terriers, the baron
explained to the Commission that his remark to Oswald on Easter
Sunday 1963 was a poor spontaneous joke; the attempt on Walker's
life had played prominently in the papers, and de Mohrenschildt
had just been shown a rifle in Oswald's closet. Later, in one of her
many reversals before the Commission, Marina acknowledged that
she did not believe de Mohrenschildt had prior knowledge of
Oswald's alleged potshot at the right-wing general.

But there was far more to de Mohrenschildt's testimony than a
rebuttal of Marina's original statements. During almost three days
of questioning by Chicago attorney and former Northwestern law
professor Albert E. Jenner, Jr. (later minority counsel for the House
Judiciary Committee's impeachment proceedings against President
Richard M. Nixon), de Mohrenschildt heaped remarkable and devastating scorn on the man he had once insisted on befriending (frequently much to the bafflement and annoyance of other members of
the conservative Dallas White Russian community), Lee Harvey
Oswald. For the better part of a year prior to the assassination he had
shepherded and defended the prickly former defector to the Soviet
Union; now he could give only the *Life Magazine* version of the lone
nut assassin.

"I would never believe that any government would be stupid
enough to trust Lee with anything important," he told Jenner.[3] He
called the ex-Marine a "semieducated hillbilly,"[4] a "crazy lunatic" who
killed Kennedy because "it made him a hero in his own mind," and
a man "insanely jealous" of JFK,

> who was young, attractive, had a beautiful wife, and had all the
> money in the world and was a world figure. And poor Oswald.

He had nothing. He had a bitchy wife, had no money, [and] was a miserable failure in everything he did.[5]

De Mohrenschildt also described Oswald as "an unstable individual, mixed-up individual, uneducated individual, without background," a man so worthless that "even the government of Ghana would not give him any job of any type." He was a malcontent; his whole life was "an example of his instability."

> He switched allegiance from one country to another, and then back again, disappointed in this, disappointed in that, tried various jobs. But he did it, you see, without the enjoyment of adventure—like some people would do in the United States, a new job is a new adventure, new opportunities. For him it was a gruesome deal. He hated his jobs. He switched all the time.[6]

There was more, almost all of it bad.

Twelve years later, however, in the summer of 1976 and continuing into the fall, de Mohrenschildt again told a different story. He did so in a manuscript he wrote during the last months of his life, when presumably he'd have little left to gain or lose by telling anything other than the truth as he knew it. This truth, recounted in a surprisingly well crafted first (and only) draft of 246 double-spaced typed pages,[7] was that Oswald had *not* shot Kennedy; he was a patsy, a "convenient" assassin for both the U.S. government and the friends and family of the late president. As the Russian perceived, virtually everyone preferred to think, "maybe unconsciously, that the assassin was a crazy, semi-literate ex-Marine, [a] screwed-up Marxist lunatic, with an undesirable discharge and a poverty-stricken childhood, unsuccessful in his pursuits both in the USSR and in [the] USA," rather than discover "that the assassination was a devilishly clever act of revenge caused by the Bay of Pigs disaster. . . ."[8] Far from the deranged nonentity of de Mohrenschildt's Warren testimony, the Oswald of the manuscript was a striving idealist "always groping for truth, for a light."[9]

In all,

> Lee was not a harmful person, [but] on the contrary a rather inspiring individual. His deep desire [was] to improve relations between the United States and the Soviet Union. . . . He hoped that these two powerful countries would become friends and he

[strived] to achieve it in a naïve and maybe foolish, but sincere way. It is clear now that [a] war between these two countries would end in a holocaust. And so, Lee Harvey Oswald had dreamed and hoped for a detente and for friendship, not so bad for a high school dropout from a New Orleans slum.[10]

And incidentally, "Marina was not such a bitch, while Jacqueline was not so beautiful."[11]

Why, then, had de Mohrenschildt said what he did to Warren interrogator Albert E. Jenner in 1964? The manuscript explained that too—colorfully, if not entirely adequately.

De Mohrenschildt was, he wrote, done in by the fatiguing three-day ordeal (which he compared to the psychological torture of Soviet show trials), and particularly by Jenner, a "sneaky bastard" who "played with me as if I were a baby"[12] and whose sleazy manipulations made the Russian feel like the "star of a pornographic movie."[13] In reality, de Mohrenschildt said, Jenner spoke much more at the hearing than he did—wheedling, flattering, putting words in his mouth—but the Warren report, "so well doctored," didn't show it.[14] The Warren witness, moreover, worried about an "insignificant, small skeleton" in his closet that might jeopardize his business arrangement in Haiti.[15] (The skeleton, it would turn out, was a Mann Act violation with a nubile Mexican girlfriend.) Though de Mohrenschildt omitted from his list of excuses a still more substantial reason for betraying Oswald before the Warren Commission—his likely role as CIA "handler" of the ex-Marine—his sense of guilt for his misleading testimony of 1964 seems sincere enough.

> How the oppressive weight influenced my testimony can be seen so clearly by me now, looking at it after several years, as if it were somebody else['s] deposition, deprived of a warm feeling for Lee, full of my own stupid jokes, which makes me sad now. I was not expressing myself really, I didn't defend Lee vigorously and passionately enough, which I am sure he would have done if he had to defend me in a similar situation. I was cleverly led by the Warren Committee counsel, Albert Jenner, into saying some things I had not really want[ed] to say, to admit certain faults in Lee, which I wasn't sure were his; in other words I consider myself a coward and a slob who did not stand up to defend proudly a dead friend, whatever odds were against him.[16]

As will be seen, de Mohrenschildt's manuscript, though incorporated into the report of the House Select Committee on Assassinations after the Russian's death in 1977, has been largely neglected or mis-read even by such researchers as Jim Marrs, whose *Crossfire* was a pri-mary resource for Oliver Stone's *JFK*. One reason for this lack of attention may be the general suspicion of de Mohrenschildt as a CIA operative, which indeed we shall see he almost certainly was, as he may also have been an intelligence agent on both the Allied and German sides during World War II. It was probably in his last vestige as CIA handler that de Mohrenschildt shredded Oswald (who had thought of the influential Russian as his "best friend") with his damn-ing testimony before the Warren Commission. As already noted, however, de Mohrenschildt emphatically recanted this testimony, and his unpublished manuscript—which he titled *I Am a Patsy! I Am a Patsy!*, perhaps with a bitter glance at his own role as well as Oswald's—is the means by which he recanted; that is precisely its most obvious value. But the document has additional value: it is not only the most important eyewitness record of Oswald during his time in Dallas, but quite possibly the most perceptive interpretation of the accused assassin ever written.

Not the least of the work's appeal is a self-deprecating humor, which in itself provides a refreshing respite from the dry bureau-cratic memos and sappy conspiratorial tomes of much Kennedy lit-erature. One of de Mohrenschildt's anecdotes relates a picaresque adventure during WWII, from which he was exempted from Ameri-can service for high blood pressure. His blood pressure did not pre-vent him, however, from getting in a flashy convertible in New York with a young Mexican widow (his Warren "skeleton") and setting out on a motel-hopping cross-country tour. The party came to an abrupt halt near a Texas beach, where the pair had spent "a delight-ful day," de Mohrenschildt painting "water-color landscapes" among other recreations. "Driving back from the beach," he tells us, "we were stopped on a deserted road by a bunch of people who we thought were plain American gangsters. We had little money with us, the car was insured, so we stopped without too much fright. The characters identified themselves: they were FBI agents who had taken us for German spies observing United States fortifications. . . ."[17]

After inspecting the couple's luggage and enduring the "angry Spanish shrieks" of the Mexican girlfriend, the agents "realized they had made a foolish mistake." Whether such a realization actually occurred, and whether de Mohrenschildt was indeed innocently sketching seascapes—in the vicinity of a U.S. naval installation—remains conjectural; he was later deported from Mexico (where he and the young señora were headed), suspected of committing espionage for the German side. The foiled Texas agents salvaged some satisfaction, in any event, by slapping Mann Act charges on de Mohrenschildt for crossing state borders in pursuit of licentious acts.

"Of that," he adds, "we were certainly guilty, we had crossed dozens of borders on the way to Mexico and committed dozens, maybe hundreds, of licentious acts. However, we were not put in jail, just had to sign some papers that we were not married and proceeded all the way to the Mexican border. We felt as if someone dirty put his filthy hands in our very personal lives."[18]

Capable of telling a good story on himself (and on the federal agency he loathed), de Mohrenschildt clearly had a writer's flair—no matter that he misspelled each and every time (as "Osvald") the subject of his manuscript. He understood paradox, the underlying principle of Oswald's life, and like Oswald had a sympathy for the underclass; he ended his own glamorous career as a teacher at a black college.

Who better to introduce us to the inner workings of that other complicated figure at the opposite end of the social spectrum?

As de Mohrenschildt tells it, early in the summer of 1962—the same summer Oswald returned from Russia—he heard "rumors" of "an unusual couple" living in Fort Worth. They'd come from Minsk, de Mohrenschildt's native city. Strictly curious, wanting only "to find out what had happened to Minsk," he set out unannounced with a businessman of Russian descent, Col. Lawrence Orlov, to look up the pair.

> We drove over the dreary, sewage-smelling miles separating the two cities. Texas does have some lovely open spaces, but here they were degraded and polluted. After some searching, we found a shack on Mercedes Street in a semi-industrial, slummy area, near Montgomery Ward.
> I knocked and a tawdry but clean young woman opened the door.[19]

This was Marina, of course. The baron introduced himself and his companion, the colonel, who found her beautiful: "so charming and so young!"

De Mohrenschildt, noting Marina's "bad teeth and mousy blond hair," was less impressed:

> I did not find her very attractive although she had a certain charm and she spoke beautiful, melodious Russian, so different from the language used by us who anglicized our language and bastardized it by foreign intonations and words.
>
> Marina offered us some sherry and said that Lee would be over soon. . . . She had a pretty good sense of humor but the opinions she expressed seemed trite to me.[20]

Finally, Oswald entered. He, our observer recognized at once, was a different story.

> He wore overalls and [had] clean workingman's shoes on. Only someone who had never met Lee could have called him insignificant. "There is something outstanding about this man," I told myself. One could detect immediately a very sincere and [straight]forward man. Although he was average-looking, with no outstanding features and of medium size, he showed in his conversation all the elements of concentration, thought and toughness. This man had the courage of his convictions and did not hesitate to discuss them. I was glad to meet such a person and was carried away back to the days of my youth in Europe, where as students, we discussed world affairs and our own ideas over many beers and without caring about time.[21]

As would later prove typical of other members of the emigré community, Orlov did not share de Mohrenschildt's enthusiasm for Oswald. The colonel sympathized with Marina, "the poor Russian refugee," but "resented Lee, his offhandedness, his ironic smiles and especially his ferocious spirit of independence."[22]

A few days after this meeting, Oswald and Marina arrived by bus from Fort Worth with baby June in tow to visit de Mohrenschildt and his wife, Jeanne, at their home in ritzy University Park. Oswald and the baron sat on a comfortable sofa and "talked all evening," the conversation running predictably (and ironically) to the subject of class differences and the exploitation of the poor by the rich. The two men also swapped jokes on the foibles of both the socialist and capitalist systems. "What I liked about him [Oswald]," observes de Mohrenschildt in his manuscript, "was that he was a seeker for justice—he had highly developed social instincts." And he adds: "I was disappointed in my own children for the lack of such instincts."

Despite the consistent (and unmistakable) regard for Oswald shown by de Mohrenschildt in these and later pages of the work, assassination writer-*JFK* consultant Jim Marrs would assert as late as 1991 that the Russian's book painted a direly negative picture of the accused assassin. According to Marrs' unaccountable interpretation in *Crossfire,* de Mohrenschildt, while in an "unbalanced mental state," depicted Oswald in the manuscript "as a cursing, uncouth man with assassination on his mind, a totally opposite picture from his descriptions of Oswald through the years."[23]

On the contrary, of course, it was Marrs with the "totally opposite picture" of the matter. About the "cursing" Oswald, for example, de Mohrenschildt actually wrote in his late-life manuscript, "Incidentally, I never heard Lee use any four-letter Anglo-Saxon words, no profane language in English or in Russian. This was most unusual for a man of his background, I mean New Orleans and Fort Worth slums and the United States Marine Corps."[24]

And if, as Marrs mistakenly indicated, the unpublished book was a reversal of the Russian's previous descriptions of Oswald, it reversed only those descriptions that de Mohrenschildt had given—under duress, and with a hidden agenda—to his Warren interrogator Albert Jenner. "I hope," he says in clarifying the purpose of the manuscript, "that this book will correct the generally low opinion people in this country have had on Lee"[25]—the same low opinion that he himself was guilty of promoting with his false testimony of 1964. As for how the frequently informative Marrs could have been so wrong, the kindest explanation may be that in his preconceived notion of the "unbalanced" baron, he skipped the chore of reading (but of course not of reviewing) the unpublished pages.

It should be noted, however, that if the Russian admitted in spades the shabbiness of his Warren performance—a performance that, to the Commission's relief, administered the coup de grâce to Oswald—he was less candid elsewhere in his manuscript.

His sins in this regard were of omission, particularly concerning his probable reporting relationship to the CIA. As has been noted by other authors attracted to the enigma of the silver-tongued, six-foot-two M. de Mohrenschildt, nothing about his life is lucid; and considering his multiple self-inventions and the tangled ties to intelligence agencies on several continents, it would only be surprising if he *weren't* a CIA operative. The "gangster"-looking FBI agents who descended on the sleek European near a Galveston beach in 1942 found him in possession of two personal résumés, one identifying him as a Greek national and the other as a gentleman "of Swedish origin."[26]

The best present-day guess is that he was born in Minsk, served as a lieutenant in the Polish cavalry in the early 1930s, and continued his allegiance to Poland until that country was divided in 1939 between Nazi Germany and the Soviet Union. During the early years of World War II, he appears to have traveled across the U.S. in the service of the French counterintelligence front of Schumacher & Company, while simultaneously cooperating in projects with a distant cousin, Nazi agent Baron Konstantin Von Maydell, at least until Maydell was apprehended in September 1942 and rudely shipped to the hinterlands of North Dakota.

De Mohrenschildt spent the next several war years in neutral Mexico as a "film producer."[27] Following his forced departure when the land of Montezuma and Frieda Kahlo had its fill of the noble snooper, he surfaced in Austin as a UT petroleum engineering grad student with suspected communist leanings and a heart-fluttering non-Longhorn accent. His new degree in hand, the world traveler worked in Cuba, Venezuela, and the Rangely oil field in Colorado. During his Rangely years he was naturalized as an American citizen despite the attempted interference of his bête noire, the FBI, which brought up his Mann Act past as a reason for denying his application. "The judge laughed at the FBI story" (de Mohrenschildt's manuscript tells us) and he became an American, "maybe not first class, because naturalized, but a citizen still."[28] By 1952 we find the Russian in Dallas with his most lucrative venture yet, his third marriage, to oil heiress Winifred Sharples. The first two marriages had lasted less than a year; this one lasted four, until 1956.

His first known CIA association began the following year, in 1957, when he traveled as a geologist to Yugoslavia for the U.S. government. An investigation of his background, summarized by the CIA, noted that he appeared to be "a dubious character."[29] But to paraphrase the later Billy Joel tune, it just may have been a dubious character the agency was looking for; no objection was made to de Mohrenschildt's government employment as a "consulting geologist" in the country of Marshal Tito. When he returned to Dallas after eight months of peeking at coastlines and fortifications, he was debriefed by a man whose name we shall hear again, CIA agent J. Walton Moore of the Domestic Contact Service. ("Looks like it's a specialty of these government agents to have a capital letter instead of the first name," de Mohrenschildt noted in passing in his unpublished pages.)

In the following years the Russian continued his mind-numbing whirl of suspicious adventures. He traveled to such African countries as Togoland and Dahomey (as a "stamp collector"), married his fourth and equally adventuresome wife, Jeanne—who was born in China, spoke Russian, and was a successful clothes designer—and promptly departed with the new bride on a long trip to Mexico. The next year, in mid-1960, George and Jeanne set out on a still more ambitious outing, billed to friends in Dallas as a year-long "walking tour" from Mexico to South America. In fact, the de Mohrenschildts seem to have camped out in Guatemala for some four months within observing distance of secret CIA training bases for Cubans preparing to embark on the ill-fated Bay of Pigs invasion. Later they traveled to Haiti for two months—if they walked, it would've been the first known such event since the days of Galilee—and finally returned to Dallas in fall of 1961, a few months before the arrival in Texas of that other voyaging couple, the Oswalds of Minsk.

What de Mohrenschildt omitted from his manuscript was precisely this backdrop of subterfuge. By the time he sat down to write his story in the U.S. Bicentennial year of 1976, more than a decade after his Warren testimony, his good fortune had deserted him, and he was quite possibly sick at heart of his life of dissembling—a life whose values and inevitable momentum had led him to sacrifice the one friendship by which history, as he surely suspected, would judge him. (The last time he stayed with his daughter Alexandra, not long after completion of the manuscript, he "seemed to be unhappy with the way he'd run his life," she told Ray.)[30]

The baron's dilemma in putting together his final written account was that he could not atone for his Warren sins without further dissembling. The friendship with Oswald, however sincere, had grown unexpectedly from the seed of an intelligence "assignment," one of de Mohrenschildt's many informal favors for his helpful government contacts. To tell the whole story would make him that much more of a knave in his and everyone else's eyes, or so he appeared to believe; like Elrod, he could only get himself to say part of what happened. The part de Mohrenschildt tells in his unpublished pages is informative, however. So, indeed, are the omissions, which may be ascribed to shame, guilt, or even (far more tortuously) CIA innocence. The one possibility we may safely rule out is that he was compelled to write a manuscript recanting his Warren testimony (though repressing certain matters) in order to further some conspiratorial government purpose; he did it on his own.

What the baron keeps from his narrative, or gives only the slightest hints of, are his intelligence involvements, in particular his CIA relationship with Moore, the man who he would later admit set him up as Oswald's baby-sitter. In the manuscript, Moore is a jolly and urbane sometime companion, "a very nice fellow" who had "interviewed me upon my return from a government mission in Yugoslavia" and who "got along fabulously well with Jeanne."[31] More significantly, the matter of Oswald is supposedly broached with Moore only *after* de Mohrenschildt has met the ex-Marine, on his own initiative and out of simple curiosity.

> A short time after meeting Lee Harvey Oswald, before we became friends, I was a little worried about his opinions and his background. And so I went to see Mr. J. Walton Moore [at] his office . . . and asked him point blank: "I met this young ex-Marine, Lee Harvey Oswald, is it safe to associate with him?" And Mr. Moore's answer was: "He is OK. He is just a harmless lunatic."
>
> That he was harmless was good enough for me. I would decide for myself whether Lee was a lunatic. . . .[32]

It might be added that even this insufficient admission of a preassassination CIA contact on the subject of Oswald—an admission de Mohrenschildt had previously made both in his Warren testimony and to an FBI agent who visited him in Haiti—had brought pressure to bear on the Russian, especially from the "brutal and naive" federal agency he most detested. W. James Wood, the FBI man who interviewed de Mohrenschildt in Haiti, was "more than disturbed" by the statement, he tells us. Wood

tried to make me deny this statement. And so we were sitting in
a luxurious Embassy room [in Haiti], staring with animosity at
each other, and this repulsive, replete bureaucrat dared to tell
me: "You will have to change your statement."

"What do you mean?" I asked incredulously.

"That false statement of yours that a government man told
you that our President's assassin was a harmless lunatic."

"False statement! Man, you are out of your mind!" I answered
sharply.

And so the gray-suited man in no uncertain terms threatened
me: "Unless you change your statement, life will be tough for you
in the States."

"Nuts!" was the only answer I could make.

After meeting Mr. W. James Wood, I immediately began having doubts of Lee's guilt. And while I was talking to him—the
conversation lasted quite some time—he constantly tried to
intimidate me [by] reminding me [of] a lot of undesirable people I had met in my life and puritanically challenging me on
the grounds of moral turpitude, i.e. too many women.[33]

But of course what de Mohrenschildt had told Jenner and Wood,
and incorporated into his manuscript shortly before his death, was
only the tip of the Oswald-CIA iceberg.

The notion that at the height of the cold war, Oswald, ostensibly
a Russian defector and even a possible factor in the downing of the
U-2, could return from his unpatriotic sojourn without the agency's
notice or interest stretches credibility to the breaking point; so does
the de Mohrenschildt manuscript's version of a disinterested friendship with the ex-Marine, begun by happenstance prior to a merely
cursory check with Moore, a man whom he allows was "probably a
CIA agent."[34]

It's true that this account of the relationship is still largely held by
de Mohrenschildt's daughter (by first wife Dorothy Romagne Pier-
son), Alexandra, as Ray discovered when he interviewed her in July
1993. The basis for the friendship between her father and the
Oswalds was "very simple," she told him: the de Mohrenschildts felt
sorry for Marina.

My stepmother [Jeanne] felt sorry for her; my father did too—
he just wanted to help out. That's exactly what the deal was. She
was Russian and my father was Russian; it really didn't have a lot
to do with Lee Harvey Oswald. It didn't have anything to do with

him at all, really. It had to do with Marina. That was what it was all about.

Alexandra noted further that though de Mohrenschildt may have appeared to favor Oswald over Marina (whose opinions he found commonplace) by the lights of the manuscript, her father was in fact quite changeable; he was fond of intellectual arguments and "could like you one day and dislike you the next, depending on whether he found your responses intelligent enough for him." Perhaps, she suggested, Marina

> wasn't bright enough for him when he really got to know her; and maybe he felt that Lee was basically a brighter person— maybe he gave him a better argument. Because my father loved to argue about everything you shouldn't argue about—religion, politics—that's all he liked to talk about, things that would cause dissension. And then he'd sit back and just see what would happen.

Granting the core of truth to Alexandra's recollection—there can be little question that the de Mohrenschildts wanted to help Marina, and even less that her father enjoyed "arguing" with the intelligent Oswald—the manuscript's explanation of how the relationship started contradicts all common sense, the testimony of contemporary observers, and the baron's own admissions in the final days of his life.

To begin with, de Mohrenschildt's intelligence connections were an open secret guessed by many of his White Russian friends and well known to his own Dallas lawyer, Patrick Russell.[35] Secondly, Moore was no casual acquaintance but a man with whom the de Mohrenschildts dined once a fortnight, according to Jeanne.[36] (The association between the two men went back to the CIA agent's 1957 debriefing of de Mohrenschildt after the baron's government trip to Yugoslavia—a debriefing that generated at least "ten separate intelligence reports," according to a CIA document.)[37] The Dallas-based Moore, though telling a reporter he'd "never heard" of the ex-Marine defector prior to the assassination and couldn't imagine "where George got the idea that I cleared Oswald for him," later testified to the HSCA that he "had 'periodic' contact with de Mohrenschildt for 'debriefing purposes'" over the years."[38]

The agent's admission was only a step short of what the baron would tell his final interviewer in 1977: that it was Moore himself who suggested to him that he strike up an acquaintance with Oswald prior to the alleged first meeting at a Fort Worth "shack on Mercedes" in the company of Colonel Orlov.[39] In the same session, de Mohren-schildt admitted to other omissions from his manuscript finished the previous year. It was no accident, he explained, that Marina was the one who greeted him on his first visit to the Oswald house. Seeking to conduct an "unwitting debriefing" in Moore's behalf—and having been told that she spoke no English—de Mohrenschildt chose

> a time when Oswald was not at home to introduce himself to Marina and converse with her in Russian about his hometown of Minsk. By the time Oswald returned, he had already charmed her, and offered to introduce them both to the Russian community in the Dallas area. Since the Oswalds did not have a car, he offered to chauffeur them around the city.[40]

That was how the friendship started.

Baron de Mohrenschildt had given us some of the facts in his manuscript; just not all of them.

He left out, for example, that he encouraged Oswald to write a "detailed memoir" of his days in Minsk, supposedly for possible publication; and that upon receiving it, he'd quickly passed a copy of the typescript on to Moore.[41] What the Russian left *in* was how he probably (and rather cruelly) broke the news to his protégé that the solicited Minsk account (which in this version was voluntarily "brought to me") would go nowhere. It was "very poorly written," he told him, "deprived of any sensational revelations," and "really point-less."[42]

The baron's assistance to Oswald on the matter of jobs was another point on which the pages of the manuscript are silent—though not entirely.

On the same first night he and Oswald sat on a comfortable sofa in University Park and "talked all evening," de Mohrenschildt tells us, Marina announced

> that Lee was going to be laid off from his job in Fort Worth at Leslie Welding Company, if I remember correctly. It was a poor job anyway, minimal wages, long hours, unhealthy conditions but Lee did not complain, he never complained, it was Marina who was constantly dissatisfied. The air of American prosperity bothered her, she was envious of other people's wealth or

wellbeing. Lee's mind was of a stoical, philosophical type, that's why, I guessed, he had gotten along so well with the other Russians he met in the Soviet Union.[43]

(This is again a significant revision of de Mohrenschildt's damning Warren testimony twelve years earlier, which then described Oswald as a whining malcontent, "disappointed in this, disappointed in that," and who "hated his jobs.")

On a later visit by Oswald and Marina to the de Mohrenschildts, the baron says he promised to give the ex-Marine introductions to "a few influential people," members of the White Russian community in Dallas, since he wanted to see the Oswalds move from their "gruesome" Fort Worth slum. To this offer Oswald reportedly responded with typical graciousness: "Thanks a lot, I can take care of myself, I don't need those creeps." The reply didn't offend de Mohrenschildt; it won his admiration. "This was an example of Lee's independence, he refused help, even my help. Rather than to be indebted to someone, he would rather starve on his own."[44]

In time, de Mohrenschildt notes, "Lee finally found a job at Taggart's [Jaggars-Chiles-Stovall] Reproduction Company [in Dallas] through the Texas Employment Agency without help from anyone."[45]

Actually, as he himself later observes, this wasn't quite the case. Before Oswald got the job at Jaggars,

> I asked my daughter Alex and my son-in-law Gary Taylor to help the Oswalds [move] to Dallas. The Taylors went to visit the Oswalds in Fort Worth and right there they offered Marina to stay with them and to keep the baby. Whatever furniture they had would be stored in their garage. This generous proposition was accepted, Marina moved to Dallas. Lee stayed for a short time in the apartment in Fort Worth and then moved to a small room at [the] YMCA in Dallas, close to his work at Taggart's [Jaggars]. During Marina's stay at my daughter's place, my wife helped her, drove her to the Baylor Hospital where they pulled out her rotten teeth.[46]

As we learn from other sources, when, on Sunday, October 7, 1962, the Taylors arrived at the threadbare Oswald quarters at the request of Alexandra's father, they found the living room packed with a motley gathering that had the air of an emergency session of the Security Council. The "emergency" was Oswald himself, who had announced to the group that he had been fired by Leslie Welding—a lie, as investigators would later discover. The ex-Marine sat silently in a tee shirt, looking "slightly contemptuously at the others who were discussing his future."[47] Present were the surprisingly beautiful Marina, Oswald's befuddled mother, Marguerite (who appeared to believe that de Mohrenschildt had already fixed her son up with a job in Dallas), and "creeps" from the Russian community—Elena Hall and Anna Meller,[48] among others. And of course there was the baron, whom Gary Taylor saw as the obvious leader of the Oswald relocation mission.

A subplot of the melodrama in the cramped Cow Town apartment was the emotional distress and possible physical beatings the stranded refugee Marina was believed (by some, at least) to be suffering at the hands of her boorish American husband—a rumor de Mohrenschildt himself may have been covertly promoting in his campaign for a change of locale. If so, his rumor mongering was not necessarily malicious. More likely, it was a tactic aimed at achieving his probable intelligence "assignment" from frequent dinner pal J. Walton Moore of the CIA Domestic Contact Service; the baron wanted the couple in Dallas, where he could more conveniently keep an eye on Oswald. More conjecturally, he may also have been seeking to separate the couple, as he supposedly had already attempted to do just the previous Monday with a trumped-up story to Frances Bruton, wife of retired navy admiral and Collins Radio vice-president Henry C. Bruton.

Mrs. Bruton was another unsuspecting wife at whose door the crafty nobleman reportedly knocked while her husband was away. De Mohrenschildt had done so at his first appearance at her lavish Farmer's Branch estate, when he introduced himself as having been "drawn to her house by fond memories of the good times he had had there when it was owned by a friend of his—Colonel Schurger."[49] With that opening gambit and his always impeccable aristocratic bearing and amusing banter, he had gained the confidence of the Brutons, at whose large swimming pool he and Jeanne became frequent fixtures. The admiral, coincidentally, had been a director of top-secret naval communications systems, and continued in a corresponding capacity with the Collins firm. On one occasion, de Mohrenschildt told interviewer Epstein, he had tried to get the admiral to place

Oswald in an electronics job with the company; Bruton "abruptly changed the subject" and the baron took the hint.[50]

On the Monday before the Fort Worth job crisis brainstorming session, de Mohrenschildt had tried another—perhaps fall-back—tack. With the admiral in Europe, the Russian arrived at the Bruton home with Jeanne as usual, but this time with Marina and baby June in tow. De Mohrenschildt introduced the young mother to Frances Bruton as the suffering victim of fate and a runaway husband. She was penniless, spoke no English, and had no place for her and her baby to live, except with the de Mohrenschildts, with whom she was presently ensconced; but sad to say, even that shelter could only be temporary, for the gallant nobleman didn't have enough room to keep the new additions indefinitely. Mrs. Bruton, touched by the tale, which was a total lie (Marina and baby June were still living with Lee in Fort Worth), was on the verge of opening her palatial home to the mother and child—when who should appear at the Bruton gate but the supposedly runaway cad himself, slightly disheveled from his hard day's work at Leslie Welding, and looking for his wife and daughter. This obviously unexpected and grating arrival of Oswald, in addition to embarrassing the baron, utterly devastated whatever devious scheme he had been cooking up. Was he intending, as some believe, to "plant" Marina as a kind of mole amidst the communications secrets of the Collins vice-president? Or was the plan less ambitious, and perhaps more sincerely humane—simply to expedite the separation of Marina and Oswald? That it was the latter is suggested by the fact that in the following weeks de Mohrenschildt was again telling the story of Marina's abandonment and mistreatment to others, apparently in hopes of securing her a permanent home away from Oswald.[51]

If de Mohrenschildt *was* prematurely seeking to separate the Oswalds (as the Bruton incident implies), his manuscript suppresses the information—not surprisingly, perhaps—and indeed strikes an apologetic tone for a separation he admits having caused, though unintentionally. As he tells us ruefully, the plan to place Marina and the baby with his daughter and son-in-law in Dallas while Oswald made new work and living arrangements had "unpleasant results."

First, it turned out that the Taylors and Oswalds did not get on. Gary Taylor, who had started off on the wrong foot with de Mohrenschildt by eloping with his daughter Alexandra, was a "scatter-brained, simple-minded but pleasant young man" whose "fondest ambition consisted of becoming rapidly another Clint Murchison or H. L. Hunt." Taylor looked down on Oswald as "a supercilious, unpractical lunatic with revolutionary ideas," and Alexandra had a similarly low opinion of Marina, who was "slovenly," slept till noon, and "didn't know anything about baby-care." Alexandra was also unimpressed with Oswald, her father notes, for "he was not good-looking, did not care about his appearance, neither was he inclined to make money."

"As for me," he continues, "I regretted that Alex did not see any qualities I liked in Lee—the fact that he was socially motivated, was a dreamer and a seeker of truth. But such people have a very hard time in life and that's why so many people considered him a 'failure' and a 'loser.'"[52]

In any case, the practical consequences of "introducing people of such different backgrounds" as the Oswalds and Taylors were unfortunate:

> First of all we caused a separation between Marina and Lee. We did understand that it was not the first separation between them, but we actually caused this one. It amazed my daughter that Lee called Marina on the phone unfrequently and did not express much desire to be with her. But he missed baby June. It was peculiar for a young husband but I already suspected that he was pleased being alone at [the] YMCA and was already bored with Marina's company."[53]

This October 1962 separation, during which Marina and June stayed first briefly with the Taylors in Dallas, then in the Fort Worth home of Elena Hall, is usually treated by assassination writers as a month-long "missing Oswald" period. He was in Dallas during that time, but where, exactly? He was not at the YMCA (except perhaps one or two nights), not, as he let on, at the Carleton Boarding House, and not at the Taylors', whose phone number he gave out if he needed to be reached and whose address he used in applying for a post office box. Some five months later, the box would serve as his return address for the Mannlicher-Carcano rifle he reportedly ordered under an assumed name from a Chicago sporting-goods store. The riddle of Oswald's whereabouts during most of October (he would surface only on weekends for Sunday visits to Marina in

Fort Worth) is normally bundled with another complex of questions related to his new employment at a Dallas company not thought likely to hire a former defector to Russia with an undesirable discharge.

Two days after the October 7 Sunday gathering at which Oswald announced his "firing," the young job seeker appeared in coat and tie at the Dallas office of the Texas Employment Commission. Recommended by Mrs. Meller's husband (who had never met him), he made a successful personal presentation in which he claimed to have photographic experience. On Thursday, October 11, he was sent for an interview at the graphic-arts firm of Jaggars-Chiles-Stovall. The interview was brief, and again successful. That same afternoon, Oswald was informed he had the job of photo-print trainee with the company and would start the next day at the downtown print shop at $1.35 an hour, or ten cents more than he made at Leslie Welding.

Much has been made by Oswald watchers of the "suspicious" aspects of his employment at Jaggars. It is inevitably pointed out, for example, that in addition to the routine preparation of glossy advertising materials—catalogues, brochures, and the like—the company had contracts with the U.S. Map Service. The latter work involved the typesetting of place names for maps made by secret aerial reconnaissance methods such as U-2 overflights, as well as processing and analyzing photos taken by the spy planes. Though Oswald neither worked directly with these sensitive materials nor had the security clearance required to do so (presumably he would have been unable to obtain one), the very thought that a man with his past could have been easily hired by a company in this line of work sets off alarms in the minds of assassination investigators. That's for starters.

Then there's the frequently noted fact that regardless of Oswald's official lack of access to classified materials, the cramped working conditions at Jaggars made secrecy impossible as a practical matter. He could have sneaked lots of peeks if he wanted to, and probably did. (What red-blooded American boy wouldn't, given the chance?) And there's the troublesome recurring motif of the U-2. As one writer reminds us, Oswald

> was near the U-2 in Atsugi, Japan; he was in the Soviet Union when it was shot down; now, back in Texas, he was working at a firm that did U-2 photo analysis. It is not as if the U-2s were like

McDonalds restaurants—so ubiquitous one expects to run into them everywhere. It is more likely that Oswald and the spy plane kept crossing paths because they were programmed by the same source.[54]

At Jaggars, moreover, the ex-Marine could put his hands on dreamy photographic hardware, stuff New York mail-order salons like Spiratone, Cambridge, and 47th Street Camera hadn't even heard of. He was taught how to work ultraspecialized gear like Robertson vertical cameras, and how to distort, reduce, and do blowups and miniaturizations. It was with this knowledge, and with the sophisticated equipment at his disposal, that he was thought by the Warren Commission to have created a phony Selective Service card with the name Alek James Hidell, a cornerstone of the case against him as presidential assassin. But the crowning point of the suspicious employment scenario can be summarized in two simple words, "micro dots," found next to the Jaggars entry in Oswald's address book following the assassination.

A microdot is the grown-up version of secret message code rings and other neat gizmos kids used to love to order from the backs of comic books. It is the stuff of spy novels and movies like *I Was a Communist for the FBI*. Flash Gordon probably wrote letters home to his mother from Pluto on microdots. And somewhere along the line, voracious reader Lee Harvey Oswald heard about them and made a famous two-word notation (spelling never being his strong suit) alongside his place of employment. What did it mean?

Microdotting, we learn (as co-worker Dennis Ofstein learned from Oswald, who brought up the topic one day), is an espionage technique by which a large volume of information is reduced to a tiny "dot," hence the name. The dot can then pass for a period at the end of a sentence in an otherwise innocuous letter, or, as Oswald apparently suggested to the puzzled Ofstein (who had never heard of the process), hidden "under a postage stamp." One author tells us that, as Ofstein knew, "Jaggars-Chiles-Stovall certainly did not have any facilities for doing microdot photography."[55] Another writer—the same man who believed Oswald and the U-2 were "programmed by the same source"—explains that "indications are that Jaggars had equipment sophisticated enough to do microdotting."[56]

But like Ofstein, none of the other employees at Jaggars knew what a microdot was, as they later testified to the Warren Commission.

Only Oswald, the American original, was familiar with the process. Was he using company equipment to send nifty microdot messages to Cuba or Russia? If so, would the deft spy have left us a handy clue by writing out "micro dot" in his address book (hell, why didn't he *microdot* it?) and casually expounding on the topic to a workmate? De Mohrenschildt, the Oswald student *par excellence*, reminds us that his subject enjoyed discussing esoteric ideas, and that unlike Marina, who "was a practical one,"[57] he liked "to play with his own life."[58] That he also liked playing with the fascinating possibilities of miniature secret messages is a given. On balance, however, the prosaic conclusion is probably best: the "micro dot" Oswald entered in his address book did not represent a Jaggars fact of life, but a childhood wish for a better and more interesting game.

Similarly, other prosaic considerations tarnish the conspiratorial picture of Oswald as job-hopping spy. Given what we know of de Mohrenschildt's nimble ways and his need to keep tabs on Oswald, it doesn't take much imagination to figure out that it was the baron who suggested to the young proletarian that he should walk out of his backbreaking assembly job in Fort Worth. The Russian had a small battalion of overheated volunteers at his disposal to help Oswald find something better in Dallas (especially if they thought he had been "laid off," another de Mohrenschildt inspiration, no doubt), and Oswald was eager to get away from Marguerite, who at one point threatened to write a book about her son, the government agent. All in all, the suggestion to head thirty miles east wasn't a bad idea. Compared to Leslie Welding, Jaggars offered Oswald a cushy "brain" job and even slightly better pay. The position also involved photography, something many persons gladly do for nothing, as a recreational hobby. As for the astonishing fact that a company loosely involved with "classified" work would employ a former defector to Russia, consider that Jaggars was no uptight General Dynamics or TRW, major government contractors with beady-eyed security armies whose only job is to keep "uncleared" employees away from sensitive compartments. Jaggars was a good-ole-boy Dallas company with no secured areas, and willing to believe Oswald's simple interview lie that he had an honorable military discharge. And if it was odd that management allowed a one-time defector to roam the premises, what can one say about another Jaggars employee-in-good-standing, John Caesar Grossi, alias "Jack Bowen," who was a convicted bank robber?[59]

It was this bank-robber Jaggars employee, by the way, who later claimed Oswald brought to work, and showed him, the Mannlicher-Carcano rifle he had supposedly ordered by mail under the alias "A. Hidell."[60]

On Sunday, October 28, 1962, Oswald made his weekly trek to Fort Worth to visit Marina and June at the house of Elena Hall. He announced on this occasion that the time was coming to end the separation (and thereby his October "disappearance"); he was already looking for a place for them.

The following Sunday, November 4, the Taylors moved Marina and the baby from Elena's house to the three-room Dallas apartment he had found in the old Oak Cliff section south of the Trinity River. This was still not exactly convenient for de Mohrenschildt, who grumbled that the new location was ten miles away from his own upscale neighborhood, but better that than Fort Worth.

Anyway, Oswald had a street address again, on Elsbeth.

If the baron was previously apologetic in his manuscript for the month-long separation he had caused, his tone became less so as he increasingly focused on the havoc of the Oswalds' marital life.

One day, he tells us, he and Jeanne stopped by Oswald's ground-floor apartment on Elsbeth Street. The building was a dreary red brick, and the neighborhood atmosphere "conducive to suicide." Still, Oswald was proud of having his own place and had spruced it up with "lovely photographs" of Russian countryside he had taken himself and enlarged at Jaggars, where "he was happy to have access to elaborate photographic equipment."[61]

But the baron goes on:

> While Lee and I were chatting on that moth-eaten sofa of his in the living-room, Marina invited Jeanne to come to the kitchen. There she cried and showed an infected spot on her shoulder. "The son of a bitch caught me smoking and he grabbed the cigarette and put it out on my bare flesh," she cried.
>
> "This is terrible, this is terrible," shouted Jeanne, coming out of the kitchen. "Lee, what have you done to your wife?"
>
> "Well, she smoked against my orders," he said sullenly.
>
> "You lived abroad only two years and picked up those customs," Jeanne attacked him. "You could not have picked up this brutality in Russia where women are independent. And here you

have no right to brutalize a woman just because she smokes occasionally."

Right there we discussed with them very frankly their growing antagonism and tried to find a solution to it. We came up with an idea of a temporary separation but [left] it up to them. "Take it easy," I told Lee, "and stop abusing your wife."

"But she enjoys brutality," he answered calmly. "Look at me, I am all scratched up." Indeed, even in the darkish room we could see long red marks on his face—traces of Marina's fingernails. "She is provoking me," he added sadly.

"Still, it's no excuse," I said. "Your temperaments obviously clash—it's another reason for separation."

The Oswalds remained silent, wrapped up in their misery.

"Do it," said Jeanne, "before you really hurt each other. And you, Lee, are responsible because you are stronger."[62]

As we've already noted, de Mohrenschildt is not averse to suppressing information. He didn't fully report the circumstances of his first meeting with the Oswalds, for example (except in an interview during his last hours), evidently because he was reluctant to embarrass himself further; possibly he still harbored some hopes for social redemption. He therefore withheld admitting that in addition to betraying the innocent ex-Marine (so he viewed him) with his Warren testimony, he had also initially sought him out as part of a CIA "debriefing" assignment. Whether his reluctance to go this last mile was rational or well advised—would the world really have thought less of him for such an admission, or merely breathed a sigh of gratitude?—is another matter; it is the choice he made.

In scenes such as the above, however, there is no apparent ulterior need to suppress or distort anything. The Russian simply reports Oswald's home life—a "dysfunctional" mess, as we'd say today—and the report matches accounts from other observers (none as close or perceptive as de Mohrenschildt), is internally consistent with other descriptions in the manuscript, and not unimportantly, has the ring of truth. In a later age, perhaps, Lee would be considered a candidate for a twelve-step program, and the couple might be seen by everyone on Montel Williams with electronic letters across their chests, Oswald's reading "Beats his wife," and Marina's, "Sleeps till noon." (In the end, they would be advised to "take up counseling.") De Mohrenschildt did not live in a later age. He and his wife told them, sanely enough—and three times in the space of a brief sequence—to consider separating for their own good.

And separate they would, repeatedly, not because (as Gary Taylor later told Summers and the Warren Commission) Oswald did whatever George told him, "whether it was what time to go to bed or where to stay,"[63] but because the situation was frankly hopeless. Marina was everything the intense, ascetic party-pooper Oswald wasn't—carefree, fun-loving, sexual, lazy, mundane, shallow, and of course materialistic. She annoyed Jeanne de Mohrenschildt with her complaints about "'that idiot Lee who does not make enough money,'"[64] and was "really destined by nature for the mediocre, middle class American life: new clothes, new buildings, plastic, neutral surroundings, tall, well-dressed men."[65]

Marina liked to smoke and drink; Oswald did neither. He "respected education and knowledge"; she bragged about having cheated to pass her pharmacist examinations in Russia. Whereas Oswald somberly identified with the plight of minorities, his wife's version of social consciousness was to make Jeanne slow down the car to drool at a "tall, muscled, black youngster standing proudly at the corner."[66] And she enraged her proud and impoverished husband by throwing up to him the lavish gifts given to her and baby June by the affluent White Russians, some of whom, the baron suggests, did so maliciously, precisely to get Oswald's goat. If so, Marina played her part perfectly. "She foolishly bragged [to Lee]: 'Look at this, look at that. They gave it to me. They can afford it.'"[67]

On November 5, the very night after the Taylors moved Marina and June into the Elsbeth Street apartment, "Anna Meller received a telephone call from Marina, asking whether she could stay at her apartment that evening," according to *Legend* author Epstein. "She said that she had just had a fight with Oswald. Mrs. Meller told her to come right over."[68]

De Mohrenschildt tells the matter somewhat differently.

One day later that fall, he says, Marina showed up at his apartment "without announcement, crying, badly bruised all over and carrying baby June along."[69] Deciding it would be dangerous for her to continue living with Oswald, the de Mohrenschildts consulted with Teofil and Anna Meller. This elderly and childless refugee couple, having already assisted Lee in finding his present job at Jaggars-Chiles-Stovall, now agreed to help again by taking in his wife and child. "Little did they suspect," the manuscript later notes, "that this kindly action would cause them so much trouble . . . and that their gentle life would be disturbed by the insane suspicions and crazy publicity following Kennedy's assassination."[70]

With the Mellers' agreement in hand, the de Mohrenschildts called Oswald over. When he arrived, Jeanne explained their proposal. The couple needed to separate as quickly as possible, she told him matter-of-factly; they had to stay away from one another. This could best be worked out if he didn't know where Marina and the baby would be living. Later he'd be informed, but not before some time passed.

"At that Lee became indignant," we're told. He shouted:

> "I shall tear up all of June and Marina's clothes and break the furniture." He was incoherent and violent. We never saw him in this condition before.
>
> "If you do this, you will never see June and Marina again. You are ridiculous," she [Jeanne] said quietly. "There is a law here against abuse."
>
> "By the time you calm down, I shall promise you will be in contact with baby June again," I interceded, knowing that Lee was afraid that someone would take the child away from him. And so he calmed down, promised to think the situation over, assured us that there would be no more violence and after a while we drove the couple back to the dreary Elsbeth Street apartment.[71]

Two days later, after Oswald had reluctantly consented to the arrangement, George and Jeanne returned to Elsbeth to move Marina and little June. They found Oswald gloomy and taciturn. He did not move from the sofa to help with the crib or the baby's belongings, but when it came to Marina's "innumerable" clothes—which were starting to fill up the de Mohrenschildts' large Ford Galaxie convertible—"he became infuriated."

> Lee grabbed a bundle of them and shouted: "I will not permit it! I will not permit it! I shall burn all this garbage!" And so we went back into the apartment following Lee and the bundle of Marina's clothes.[72]

The operetta continued, Jeanne shouting for Oswald to calm down, George debating whether to call the police. He decided against it.

Lee looked so desperate that I sat on the sofa again, grabbed him by the arm and tried to reason with him. "Brutality won't help you, Lee," I said. "If you keep on with these tantrums, Marina and the baby will be gone anyway and you won't see them again. So better submit and keep your word."

He sat gloomily, not sure of what he was going to do.[73]

After a while, Oswald resigned himself and "agreed to everything."

He even helped carrying Marina's clothes acquired from the hateful Russian-American benefactors, and put them on top of our overloaded car. With all this junk, our convertible sank almost to the ground and groaned.

And so we departed, Jeanne holding up all that stuff to prevent it from falling out, Marina holding on to baby June. As I was driving I laughed because we looked so obviously ridiculous.[74]

After all this, the separation was short-lived. Oswald called or visited the de Mohrenschildts daily, begging for Marina's number. Finally, the couple broke down and gave it to him "against Marina's will."[75] She, meanwhile (as she'd done previously to Jeanne and Alexandra), had been trying the patience of saintly Anna and Teofil with her slothful ways, not helping with the household chores and behaving "like a primadonna."[76] When Oswald got hold of their number and "began calling his wife at all times of day and night, disturbing everybody," they threw in the towel and asked Marina to move out.[77]

In time, after an intervening stay at the house of another Russian refugee, Katya Ford, she returned to Oswald and the Elsbeth apartment—temporarily.

By now, de Mohrenschildt was starting to have second thoughts about the wisdom of his interventions in Oswald's marital affairs. Besides, "life was catching up with us," he says. "Jeanne had to finish some urgent designing jobs and my long awaited project of a geological survey of Haiti was coming to fruition."[78] About this next "project" we will see more later; it is another matter with significant intelligence implications about which the baron withholds information. He does not, however, hold back on Oswald.

One night, he says, when "we were seeing the Oswalds rather seldom," Lee showed up at the door. He "came alone and seemed very depressed."

"Lee, my friend," I told him. "You like Tolstoy, don't you? He said many clever things, but this one applies to you: 'Man must be happy. If not, he has to work on himself to correct this misunderstanding which makes him unhappy.' I think I know what your 'misunderstanding' is."

Lee nodded sadly. "My tragedy is," he said, "that my suffering is inflicted on me by a person close to whom I want to be, and from whom I would want to find protection and consolation."

These words, which I remember distinctly, touched me greatly.

"You try to change Marina into your image. It's difficult, if not impossible. You should like her for what she is, not for what you would want her to be. Do you [see] my point?"

"But she is becoming like an American middle-class wife," Lee fought [back] feebly. "She thinks only of foolish comforts. She is becoming like the rest of them, talking of washers, driers and other gadgets as if they were the most important things in life."

"Lee, you are too demanding. She is new in this country and is affected by it. Take it easy. Try to be friends with her. Somebody said: 'Friendship is a quiet and exquisite servant, while love is a ferocious and demanding master.'"

"I am a fool and I am very unhappy," said Lee quietly. "But thanks for advice anyway. You are a very good friend."

When he left I thought: Here is a good fellow whose tragedy is a complete misunderstanding of himself. He wants love from a woman who does not understand him. And he himself does not face squarely the issues. What is the most important to him? In the meantime the despair is like an organism which destroys him. He begins to lose hope.[79]

This is slightly artificial dialogue for a quiet conversation between friends, perhaps. But the evident regard for Oswald is not artificial, nor is the understanding of a friend's dilemma (and of Marina's). It is this, in the last analysis—despite the occasional suppressions and self-serving turns—that redeems the baron's unpublished work.

At the end, of course, he was no longer suppressing information.

He told his last interviewer, at The Breakers Hotel in Palm Beach, that indeed he had "done favors" for the CIA since the 1950s, and had been rewarded in turn with business contracts such as his 1957 survey of the Yugoslav coast. On that occasion de Mohrenschildt had provided reports "on Yugoslave officials in whom they had

expressed interest." He said more. He said that "in late 1961," while
Oswald was still in Minsk, he had met in downtown Dallas with CIA
agent J. Walton Moore. Initially, they discussed the Central American
"walking trip" from which de Mohrenschildt had just returned.
Moore had gone on to tell him, however, of "an ex-American
Marine" who was presently working in an electronics factory in Minsk
and "in whom there was 'interest,' since he was returning to the Dallas area." Later, in the summer of 1962, it had been "one of Moore's
associates" who had provided de Mohrenschildt with Oswald's
address in Fort Worth and suggested he "might like to meet him."[80]

Though long suspected, these admissions had never been made by
the baron before.

On the same day he made them, he was dead.

On the Tuesday afternoon of March 29, 1977, the skull of George
de Mohrenschildt "exploded, in a sense."[81] Immediately, a large volume of gases and blood spurted from his mouth and nose, soaking
the Persian carpet in front of him and splattering the walls and door
of his bedroom. He, or someone, had inserted the barrel of a 20-
gauge shotgun between his lips and pulled the trigger.

A coroner's inquest a week later ruled the death a suicide. In the
Kennedy annals, however, few if any persons related to the assassination are ever admitted to have met a purely spontaneous or non-
controversial death, and the baron is no exception. To be sure, the
circumstances surrounding de Mohrenschildt's demise are suspicious, and his own wife, now deceased, did not believe he shot himself. "No one that knew him does,"[82] Jeanne told writer Dick Russell
the year after Alexandra returned from shopping and discovered her
father's body in the Manalapan, Florida mansion (near West Palm
Beach) of her aunt and adoptive mother, Nancy Sands Tilton.

Before looking further into the question, however, it is necessary
to reach into the grab bag of Kennedy oddities and pull out one of
the finest specimens of its genre, a Dutch Yalie by the name of
Willem Oltmans. Inextricably mingled with de Mohrenschildt's last
decade (and last days, especially), Oltmans' near-indescribable antics
resemble nothing so much as those of the "men in black" who are
said to haunt the lives of UFO witnesses.

Four years after the death of President Kennedy, Oltmans, a journalist, journeyed to the U.S. for the express purpose of interviewing

de Mohrenschildt for a Netherlands-TV film on the assassination. In time, the Dutchman became a "very personal friend" who "visited us every year," the baron wrote in his manuscript.[83] As it happened, the film produced by the Dutch journalist would disappear "mysteriously," as author Russell noted—although in the quicksand of questions related to Oltmans, one mysterious disappearance more or less could hardly be expected to get anyone too alarmed.

Russell announced another seeming Oltmans surprise in his generous 824-page *The Man Who Knew Too Much* (focusing on purported conspiracy figure Richard Case Nagell), published in 1992. He discovered, after de Mohrenschildt's death, "an FBI file reporting that Oltmans had contacted its New York office on April 3, 1967—around the time the Dutch journalist first met de Mohrenschildt. It had Oltmans saying he 'had received information from an informant in Western Europe that de Mohrenschildt was the principal organizer of the assassination of President Kennedy.' A curious thing for a 'friend' to do to the baron."

But another glance at de Mohrenschildt's own manuscript, available for fifteen years at the time of Russell's writing, shows that the matter was both less—and more—curious than the conspiracy author suggests. It wasn't surprising that Oltmans would tattle on de Mohrenschildt to the federal agency on April 3, 1967, assuming the journalist believed he had something world-shaking to announce, since as of that date the two men had yet to meet face-to-face; they couldn't very well be considered acquaintances then, much less friends.

What *was* strange was the nature of the "informant" in the FBI report. As de Mohrenschildt reveals (in a manuscript chapter fittingly titled "Willem Oltmans and His Clairvoyant"), this person was Gerard Croiset, an "amazing Dutchman who has been solving crimes and murders all over the world."[84]

De Mohrenschildt's chapter explains that as he was told by Oltmans, the U.S.-educated journalist became interested in the Kennedy assassination in 1964, when, on a speaking trip to Texas, he ran into Marguerite Oswald at an airport ticket counter. The two "sat together during the following dinner-flight and it was during this journey that Oltmans first began to doubt the truth as to Lee Oswald being the killer of President Kennedy all by himself and miserably alone."[85]

When Oltmans returned to the Netherlands, he discussed his mind-expanding American encounter (Marguerite had told him the Dallas police interrogated her son for forty-eight hours without making a tape recording or even keeping notes) with another mind-bender, the clairvoyant Croiset. As psychics are wont to, Croiset experienced a flash; he revealed to the journalist "that I existed," says de Mohrenschildt. "Croiset told Oltmans that Lee had a friend in Dallas, in his fifties. He described some of my physical features, including that my name held the letters *sch* and the word *de*."[86]

More significantly, the clairvoyant informed Oltmans that this partly spelled out friend of Oswald, whom he also described as of noble descent and a geologist, was "the architect of the ambush in which Kennedy had been killed." Oswald, he said, "was only the fall guy."[87]

Oltmans carried this news bulletin to the chief of programs at the Hilversum-based television network. It may be worth considering that whereas in America it was a gaffe for a First Lady to consult an astrologer, Dutch authorities didn't blush at employing "paranormal" avenues—men like Croiset and Peter Hurkos—in searching for bodies and lost children. At any rate, on the basis of Croiset's pronouncement, we're told, the Hilversum management sent Oltmans back to the other side of the world, Texas, USA, to check out the story.

Again he visited with Oswald's mother. This time Marguerite pointed to a volume "of a complete set of the Warren Report and indicated our name and existence to the Dutch journalist."[88] Discovering (amazing!) what he was looking for, Oltmans placed a call in April 1967 to the Oswald friend who fitted so precisely the clairvoyant's description, George de Mohrenschildt, and asked for a TV interview. This was three years after the publication of the twenty-six volumes of evidence of the Warren Commission, when one of the longest testimonies in the entire collection had been given by a man with a *sch* and *de* in his name, identified as being of noble birth and a geologist, and quizzed intensely on his puzzling relationship with Lee Harvey Oswald.

Though not initially successful, Oltmans may have asked for his TV interview at just the right time. De Mohrenschildt had been stewing quietly for several years over his performance in the Washington hearings, where he'd been strongly encouraged to brand Oswald as a nut. Always before, he had flourished with his social glibness, which had been his strongest suit. His undeniable intellectual brilliance was a bit vagrant, like Oswald's; one man told him, he claimed, that he was too openly critical and talked too much to do well in the espionage game.[89] De Mohrenschildt knew this to be true about himself, he says, and relied on his shallow side, the cosmopolitan charm, to forge his way. But the habit of "live and let live" (as he called his guiding philosophy) and swapping of informal favors hadn't served him well at the Warren ordeal, which marked a turning point in his life: his emergence as a public—and notorious—figure. Despite his company-man-like betrayal of Oswald (and his own conscience), he hadn't benefited from this final "favor." The bad press had been disastrous to his sensitive business; he and Jeanne had already been chased out of Haiti. Things would continue on a downhill slope (as he probably already suspected), thanks to his now well known association with the accused assassin of the president. All of his cautious preliminary checks had been for naught, and the assurances he'd been given that the ex-Marine was "safe" had proved as reliable as many later such assurances, sworn on motel-room Gideon bibles, in the age of AIDS. Oswald had ruined his life.

These weren't matters that the baron had any great urgency to talk about, but he had been played for a chump, and it rankled him. He put off Oltmans, saying he needed to attend the World Petroleum Congress in Mexico City. But he told him to call back in a couple of weeks.[90]

When the journalist "reported to Hilversum that he had contacted me," de Mohrenschildt tells us, "the Dutch television presidium felt Oltmans was in grave danger. They reasoned that so many people, directly or indirectly connected with trying to unravel the Kennedy assassination had been killed or mysteriously disappeared, that Oltmans was immediately instructed to contact the office of Robert F. Kennedy, at the time the Senator of the State of New York."[91]

Oltmans wasted little time traveling to Bobby Kennedy's New York City office and explaining his "endangered" situation. It was then that the FBI got in the act. A Kennedy aide, press assistant Tim Hogan, reportedly assured the Dutchman that RFK "personally picked up the phone and talked to J. Edgar Hoover"[92]—presumably without informing the gruff Bureau chief (and notorious Kennedy hater) that the whole matter had originated with a psychic vision on another continent.

Two hours later, a pair of FBI agents appeared at Oltmans' door. They let him know that "from that moment on he would be 24-hours a day under surveillance of the FBI and there would be nothing to worry about," de Mohrenschildt says Oltmans told him.[93]

Well, the next night Oltmans decided to pay a call on a friend in Greenwich Village. As he hummed along in his car at about sixty miles per hour, he noticed that he

> was being overtaken by a cab with a passenger riding in the back seat. The cab cruised for a while next to Oltmans' car until the 53rd Street exit was reached. Then the cab made a fast move, in which Oltmans was cut off in such a way that he crashed in the rails. His car was a total loss. His head was bleeding. He was brought to the Kew-Gardens hospital, where he was examined, bandaged, and sent home. The insurance awarded him within ten days a new car, which Oltmans quickly shipped to the Netherlands. He himself left a few days afterwards.[94]

Oltmans left the country, de Mohrenschildt might have added, still not having met the man he came to America to find. He did, however, have a New York City car accident under his belt, which, though not exactly an unprecedented occurrence, served the purpose of providing the journalist with an article, a few months later, in the Dutch weekly magazine *Haagae Post*. On the cover of the issue recounting the fortuitous smashup was a photo of JFK and George de Mohrenschildt.

It was after publication of this 1967 article that frequent-flyer Oltmans returned to the New World, in October of that year, to tape interviews of (and meet for the first time) the Dallas baron from Minsk for a Netherlands-TV program. The edited version of the interview footage would ultimately disappear eight years later from the television corporation's archives, according to the Dutchman.

But the October encounter with Oltmans "was a very pleasant meeting for us," says de Mohrenschildt. He notes:

> From that moment on, this Dutch journalist, who initially approached us because he had received indications that we might be involved indirectly through Oswald with the Kennedy

assassination, became a very personal friend. He has visited us every year since 1967. He will by now be convinced that we had nothing to do whatsoever with the JFK assassination.[95]

This sanguine assessment of Oltmans, however, was not shared by Jeanne—or even by de Mohrenschildt himself in the days shortly before his death.

By the fall of 1976, when the baron completed his manuscript, his wife had grown increasingly wary of the motives of the strange Hollander, as well as of the effects of his repeated visitations on George, who she sensed was being worn down by the assault. De Mohrenschildt had suffered a wicked bronchitis attack earlier that year and endured an enervating series of drug treatments by a man whom Jeanne suspected of being a quack or worse. "I have become convinced," she later told writer Jim Marrs, "that this doctor, in some way, lies behind the nervous breakdown George suffered in his final months."[96]

But the brunt of her suspicions was apparently reserved for Oltmans. By December 1976 she went so far as to commit her husband to Parkland Hospital for observation largely to keep him away from the ubiquitous Dutchman, who that month was once again nosing around town. "We knew that one more interview, and he would have had it," she admitted to the Euro-journalist, if we can believe an article he published in a girlie magazine a year after the burial of the baron.[97] If her husband's death was "engineered," she also reportedly told him, it was because Oltmans "focused such attention on [de Mohrenschildt] that the real conspirators decided to eliminate him just in case George actually knew something."[98]

Putting Jeanne's well-grounded fears of the obsessed visitor to one side temporarily, another question arises: the Russian's state of mind at the time he worked on his manuscript. We may recall *Crossfire* author Marrs as the writer with a mistaken idea that de Mohrenschildt's manuscript depicted Oswald "as a cursing, uncouth man with assassination on his mind." While everyone should be granted an occasional error, Marrs unfortunately compounded his by seeking to demonstrate, over several pages, that the baron could only have held such a wrong-headed view if he'd written the manuscript while in an "unbalanced mental state."[99] Toward this end, Marrs notes that de Mohrenschildt attempted suicide with tranquilizers on the fall night he finished the work, and that while at Parkland later, where he was given electroshock, he told a roommate: "I know damn well Oswald didn't kill Kennedy—because Oswald and I were together at the time."[100] This statement, Marrs explains, "is untrue since both George and Jeanne were at a reception at the Bulgarian embassy in Haiti the day Kennedy was killed. But the incident serves to illustrate George de Mohrenschildt's mental condition at the time."[101]

The "incident" does nothing of the kind. Apart from the fact that de Mohrenschildt's alleged remark could have been invented by the roommate, who told the story to a supermarket tabloid, a man undergoing electroshock and drug treatments may be expected to say anything. He can suddenly realize he is Rita Hayworth or God's unknown Second Son, and nothing can, or should, be made of it; he is temporarily addled, and the condition is not retroactive to the earlier seasons when he worked on his pages.

As for the observation that de Mohrenschildt attempted suicide the night he completed the manuscript, this may well be true, but what does it illustrate? Did Hemingway invalidate his previous writing when he decided to reach for the shotgun? Passages from the baron's manuscript, cited in abundance earlier, are lucid and frequently elegant, hardly what one would consider the work of a deranged mind. And a suicide try after finishing the long draft may as easily be interpreted to mean that he had completed his last purpose: to set his Warren testimony straight by showing who Oswald really was, a "patsy." Having accomplished that, nothing was left for de Mohrenschildt except to battle with old age (and demons like Oltmans), or go straightway to the Big Question. That he decided on the latter course is a bit unusual statistically maybe, but not utterly irrational.

(Incidentally, it was the Syrian, not Bulgarian, embassy at which the baron claimed to be on the day of the assassination.)[102]

None of this is to say that 1976 wasn't a very bad year for de Mohrenschildt, or that he didn't suffer tremendous mental strain. Marrs gets it right when he says the baron was both ailing and "distrustful of hospitals," and that he was convinced, in the early part of the following year, that "evil forces" were after him.[103] (With Oltmans around, the conviction wasn't necessarily delusional.) There were also financial woes. De Mohrenschildt was now teaching in mostly black Bishop College in Oak Cliff. The high-flying days of lucrative government-assisted "surveys" and schmoozing with the rich and powerful were a thing of the past. And there was no pension; he'd done his spy work, recall, on the basis of "informal" quid pro quo favors, never as "a paid employee of the CIA."[104] With winter coming on, the once carefree grasshopper from Minsk was age sixty-five, mostly broke, and his fourth marriage—the only one that had lasted—was starting to unravel.

When writer Dick Russell showed up unannounced at the de Mohrenschildts' Travis Street apartment earlier that year, the baron answered the door in tee shirt and cutoffs, and a headband around his forehead. Jeanne, taking a page from Marina, was "still in her dressing gown as the noon hour approached." The apartment was "small and rather unkempt," though with paintings and houseplants. When Russell asked about the taped interviews Oltmans had made with the couple nine years earlier, in 1967, Jeanne was "adamant" that she didn't want them released. De Mohrenschildt, however, "wondered aloud how much money they might bring."[105]

Times were tough. The baron was now driving a thirteen-year-old Jaguar.

By January of 1977, hard upon de Mohrenschildt's release from the Parkland Hospital commitment by Jeanne, she decamped for California. The marriage was over. She'd had enough. Alexandra today doesn't have much nice to say about Jeanne. She told Ray that originally she liked her stepmother, but that Jeanne had become a "hideous, hideous woman," an "opinionated alcoholic shrew," and that she'd call her something worse if she could find the right words. Alexandra stated that the dress designer, the woman de Mohrenschildt affectionately said in his manuscript he'd finally found who could stand him, had driven her first husband into an insane asylum, and "I'm not real surprised that she drove my father right along." Whatever Jeanne's faults may have been toward the end, though, she guarded the door for the baron, protecting him from himself, among others. When she packed her bags, he was left defenseless, an easy prey for the man who stalked him from another continent.

In early March, he was back. As professor de Mohrenschildt knocked about the library of Bishop College during spring break, perhaps wanting mostly not to be home alone in the empty apartment, he was greeted cheerfully by the old friend from Holland. This part of the story we have to take from Oltmans himself, unfortunately. He tells us that de Mohrenschildt was basically thrilled to see him and begged him to take him far away to Europe because he was receiving death threats. He was terrified, and also stricken with guilt, feeling "responsible for Oswald's role."[106] The latter obsession had already led de Mohrenschildt to act strangely in front of Russell back in July, when the baron was supposedly stronger and more put together. He "began pacing back and forth across the room," the unannounced visitor Russell recorded. "Suddenly he was shouting: 'It is defiling a corpse! Defiling a corpse! I don't want to talk about it, it makes me sick!'" The corpse the baron was talking about was Lee Harvey Oswald, not Kennedy.

"His wife," Russell had added, "motioned me toward the door."[107] Now she wasn't around for this purpose anymore, and Oltmans, possibly not believing his good fortune, plunked de Mohrenschildt on a plane and whisked him across the water back to the Old World.

En route, the beaming journalist explained that he had just the project for him, a tell-all book on the assassination. De Mohrenschildt listened on, without revealing whatever private reservations he may have had. Once in Europe, he panicked, however. This happened a day or so after the pair landed and drove together to Brussels, where Oltmans supposedly wanted to keep a luncheon date with an old friend who happened to be the Soviet chargé d'affaires. Again, this part of the story comes uniquely from Oltmans. He tells us in his magazine article a year after de Mohrenschildt's death that the baron told the two men he was going to take a little walk before lunch, but he never returned. He vanished, leaving behind at the Hotel Metropole (the FBI later discovered) his "luggage, raincoat, and pipe."[108]

The baron was in flight again. With a sudden jerk, he had pulled free from the Dutchman's grasp. At some time in the remaining three weeks of his life, he would write down why. "As I can see it now, the whole purpose of my meeting in Holland was to ruin me financially and completely," he said in a letter.[109] Then he was more explicit: Oltmans, who he thought may have been drugging him, "wanted to sully me into admitting things I did not do."[110]

During these dark epiphanies it may also have occurred to him that the Dutchman had invented the whole story of a psychic's revelation; that the man had been a fraud from the start.

What is known about de Mohrenschildt's March agony is that before reaching his final destination, the Tilton oceanfront mansion near Palm Beach, he stopped off at his apartment in Dallas to pick up some papers. He stuffed them in his briefcase and kept going. On March 16, a Wednesday, he showed up at the door of Nancy Tilton, the sister of one of his earlier wives, asking to be let in. Alexandra, who regarded this close aunt as her mother—and who had discarded Gary Taylor in Texas some years past—lived in the Tilton house. Her father, arriving with the clothes on his back and the briefcase, was invited to stay on as a houseguest by Mrs. Tilton. She, it would turn out, was a soap-opera fan and her favorite show was "The Doctors," both of which points would prove germane at the coroner's inquest.

About the Russian's final dash for freedom, Oltmans later wrote that he had been told de Mohrenschildt received word from Washington to "go to Florida where he would be less exposed."[111] That presumably explained why the baron showed up at the Manalapan estate. The Dutchman's source wasn't a psychic this time, but supposedly a Bulgarian man with the rank of general in the U.S. Army, Dimotor Dimitrov.[112]

Whatever the value of this unsupported assertion, the only thing the baron himself thought valuable enough to retrieve were the papers he made a special trip to Dallas for. Following de Mohrenschildt's death, the briefcase was found to contain his unpublished manuscript—his own version of the real tell-all story, which he had refused to revise for Oltmans' benefit or anyone else's. He was through revising.

Alexandra says that when she saw her father again on this occasion she was shocked and saddened to find him a "totally different" person. Whereas before he liked to argue and tease, tell jokes, and raise a bit of hell conversationally by talking about philosophical ideas instead of investments, he was now more dour and passive—"pathetic, really . . . I didn't even recognize his personality." Seemingly unhappy with the way he had lived, he did "very odd things," Alexandra recalled. "Like he would look at himself in the mirror, and he would look like he didn't know who he was looking at."

Or might he only have been seeing himself, and his life of self-invention, for the first time?

Maybe. Meanwhile, he desperately needed money, his daughter confirms. Sometime after his arrival at Manalapan he had an idea, perhaps inspired by Oltmans' decade-long attempt to cash in on de

Mohrenschildt's "involvement" in the assassination. He remembered the writer Edward Jay Epstein, who had long been trying to interview him for a book he was writing, a well-funded project, as de Mohrenschildt now recalled, financed by *Reader's Digest.* And Epstein was a Harvard man, the right sort of fellow. He could be expected to understand that a small honorarium was sometimes in order, for the inconvenience, that sort of thing.

The baron picked up the phone.

His proposal to the writer in New York was a four-day interview for a nominal courtesy fee, say four thousand dollars. Epstein agreed. They would meet in Palm Beach at a suitable gentleman's environment, the very GQ Breakers Hotel, with the initial interview set for Monday, March 28, 1977.

On the first two days Epstein doled out checks "totaling two thousand dollars," presumably a thousand per day, the balance payable upon completion of the interviews. As things turned out, of course, no balance was necessary.

On the fateful second day of interviews, the baron got up early and came down to breakfast already dressed. Lillian Romanic, the house cook who served him, remembered at the inquest that he left immediately for a short drive—in Alexandra's car, perhaps—and then returned. He had gone to a Palm Beach bank, it came out, to deposit the check he had already received from Epstein. Alexandra's father was home just a few minutes and left again, said the cook. She didn't see him until lunchtime, when he returned from The Breakers.

There, he continued talking to the New York interviewer, telling him a version of events that "if believed, would drastically change the picture of his relationship with Oswald and the CIA."[113] Ironically, Epstein *didn't* believe the hotel-room revelations and left them out of *Legend,* his Oswald-as-KGB-agent book, which came out the following year. It was only in July 1979, when the report of the House Select Committee on Assassinations disclosed a stash of CIA papers, that he found corroboration of the baron's distress-sale South Florida story:

> The documents found in de Mohrenschildt's CIA file showed that there was far "more contact between [CIA agent J. Walton] Moore and de Mohrenschildt than was stated" [previously by Moore]. In fact, they revealed that Moore had interviewed him numerous times over a course of years and prepared reports

based on this information. Moore himself testified that he had 'periodic' contact with de Mohrenschildt for 'debriefing purposes' and, although maintaining he could not recall any discussion about Oswald, acknowledged that these contacts may have extended to 1962.[114]

On Tuesday, the baron's last interview ended at 1:30 that afternoon, Epstein reports; "I may have been the last person to have seen de Mohrenschildt alive."[115] As the police reconstruction later noted, however, the writer erred on both counts. De Mohrenschildt left The Breakers around noon, arrived at the Tilton mansion on South Ocean Drive around 12:30, and talked both to his daughter in the kitchen (where he ate a lunch of three pieces of toast and appeared to her to be "happy" and "really quite normal") and, later, the maid, Anna Viisola, whom he would tease in a remarkable way. Strangely— perhaps unnerved by the whole experience—Epstein is also wildly off on the time of death, which he reports as 3:45 P.M. For once with irrefutable scientific precision on their side (as we shall see), the authorities set it nearly an hour and a half earlier, at 2:21:03. The Harvard interviewer agrees, however, that his subject gave no hints, by word or demeanor, of what he would soon do. Epstein was expecting de Mohrenschildt "to return at 4:00 P.M. as scheduled—especially since he had asked me to get a photograph for him that he said would prove important."[116]

What may have changed the baron's mind about returning—to anything—was a visit to the Tilton house that had taken place that morning while he was at the interview. De Mohrenschildt found out about it at lunch, talking to Alex in the kitchen. She greeted him in English—"Hi, how are you?"—then switched to Spanish as she gave him a card. She said a man had come by looking for him, and that she told the visitor he could call back at eight.

The card, which de Mohrenschildt looked at a moment and put in his pocket without comment, identified the caller as Gaeton Fonzi, a staff investigator for Sen. Richard Schweiker's office. Earlier, in front of Alexandra, Fonzi had crossed out Schweiker's name and penned in *House Select Committee on Assassinations.*

It's too bad de Mohrenschildt never met this investigator in person. The script would have been right out of "Columbo": the baron's sleek wiles versus the deceptively unassuming visitor from Miami, who "was excited about the opportunity to talk with de Mohrenschildt and thought it incredibly fortuitous that he should turn up in South Florida."[117] No doubt de Mohrenschildt would have liked him, as he liked Oswald and Epstein and all unusual smart guys who could put together a couple of sentences without lapsing into conventional inanities.[118] No doubt, indeed, he would have preferred him for a son-in-law to Gary Taylor, whom the baron considered an inept, spoiled, materialistic kid with shallow daydreams of becoming a billionaire like H. L. Hunt. Unfortunately, the manuscript had dryly noted about the ambitious son-in-law, "as most of his financial schemes failed, he had plenty of time on his hands."[119]

Fonzi, who had a similar wicked wit, later wrote *The Last Investigation,* a hilarious account of his days at the HSCA. The committee, "born in the septic tank of House politics," was initially hampered, according to Fonzi, by Texas congressman Henry Gonzalez. After House speaker Tip O'Neill passed him up for the HSCA chairmanship in favor of a mere lame duck colleague, Fonzi says, Gonzalez went on a scorched-earth rampage to destroy the committee. The congressman's take-no-prisoners tactics, writes Fonzi, included accusing the investigator—known to the congressman only as an Italian-sounding name on a list of new HSCA staffers—of having underworld connections. The night this news reached him, the enraged Fonzi wrote, "If Gonzalez had lived in Miami, I would have had his car blown up."[120] The baron would've roared.

It's possible that in some parallel universe, the young Columbo who drove up that Tuesday morning might have entered this other world of oceanfront mansions, become this preferred son-in-law even. Who knows about such things? Fourteen years after crossing the high hedges that hid the Tilton property from the common eye, Fonzi remembers the Alexandra who greeted him outside as "one of the most beautiful women I have ever seen in my life," he told Ray. The tall and striking daughter of the baron appeared from behind the garage as he got out of the car, which he had parked in the wide yard beside the main house. She had, he wrote,

> smooth olive skin, deep dark eyes and long black hair. Her statuesque body was clad in a clinging black leotard. She was carrying a small towel and glowed with a sheen of perspiration. She had obviously been exercising.[121]

But of course the investigator had come on business—serious

business. He was actually trying to get some work done, despite the disarray back in Washington with the committee. The next day, Wednesday, the House would vote whether to continue the investigation, and things didn't look too good right now. On Wednesday, however, after four hours of heated debate, the representatives finally voted affirmatively—due in large part to the unexpected action of George de Mohrenschildt that Tuesday afternoon. It was too flagrant to ignore.

During the previous weeks of legislative limbo, Fonzi was "isolated" in Miami, he tells us, lacking authorization or funds to go to Washington and find out what was going on. Not easily discouraged, he continued chipping away on his own while waiting for the committee's fate to be settled. On Monday, just the day before, he'd gotten a call from fellow HSCA staffer Bob Tannenbaum, who filled Fonzi in on the prospects of the upcoming Wednesday vote; he didn't sound optimistic.

"By the way," he told Fonzi, he'd just received a call from a tipster in California having to do with George de Mohrenschildt, Oswald's famous Russian friend. The caller told Tannenbaum he'd been "tracking" de Mohrenschildt, and had just found out he could be reached at a certain telephone number in Florida. Tannenbaum passed the number on to Fonzi, who, as we know, decided to drive, not call.

What was intriguing, and a bit chilling, was the name of the tipster, which Tannenbaum also passed on. It was "this Dutch journalist, Willem Oltmans."

Fonzi had heard of the Dutchman, it should be added. Oltmans had been on a publicity blitz of late, telling TV reporters and the HSCA itself that de Mohrenschildt had masterminded the assassination. The baron had "confessed" it to him, admitting he was part of a "Dallas conspiracy" and that Oswald had "acted at his guidance and instructions."[122]

All this was supposedly supported by some eighty crucial documents, but as the HSCA investigator would discover after returning to Miami,

> it was mostly just a bunch of crap. He [Oltmans] said he didn't have the other stuff, it was back in Holland. Then he told other people he wasn't going to give the committee everything, but keep it confidential. Then he's telling the press that he already did. It stank.[123]

Meanwhile, it wasn't exactly true that de Mohrenschildt had no response to the card Fonzi left with Alexandra.

He responded, but in another key. He asked if Mrs. Tilton, who was then away playing bridge with friends, would allow him "to stay at the house any longer, if [she] wanted him to leave," as Alex said at the inquest. Her aunt "did not want him to leave at all," she reassured her father. "She wanted him to stay."[124]

While Mrs. Tilton played bridge in Palm Beach, it wasn't necessary for her to miss another prized pastime, her afternoon soap operas. She had worked out a routine with her maid, Anna Viisola, to handle such unpleasant conflicts. At 1:30, Anna would go to Mrs. Tilton's bedroom on the second floor, turn on the portable nine-inch TV by the foot of the bed, and begin recording the first of her employer's two can't-miss programs, "Days of Our Lives" and "The Doctors" (which came on at 2:00). A small audiocassette machine was kept in the room for just that purpose, resting not far from a nightstand and a Chippendale chest.

Today was especially crucial, Mrs. Tilton had impressed on Anna before leaving; some really big event, an amnesia victim recovering her memory or something equally dramatic, was taking place on "The Doctors." She couldn't miss it. She'd been "waiting six months" to hear what would happen.

It might also be mentioned that against the corner of the bedroom, partly hemmed in by the chest and nightstand, leaned an elegant cane. Next to it was propped a similarly upright companion, a Utica 20-gauge shotgun just purchased the previous year by Mrs. Tilton. The weapon was for protection, not sport, and was petite as two-barrel shotguns went. "A relatively little gauge," a detective brought out at the inquest. "And we are talking about the skeet shot, which is much smaller than your BB that you use in your air gun."

Nancy Tilton had never fired the gun, but she kept it at the ready, just in case her expensive house-wide alarm system failed her or perhaps worked too well, informing her with a beep on some dark early morning that an intruder had crossed a forbidden barrier. A box of skeet loads was in the kneehole desk by the bed, and a single shell, the only one she had ever taken out, was in the drawer of the nightstand.

De Mohrenschildt's three pieces of toast that day represented a "light lunch" he had requested "because he anticipated going back out later that afternoon to another meeting."[125] The logic of this proposition is a bit elusive, but probably not worth pondering overmuch. The baron may have eaten three pieces of toast because he wasn't very hungry or because something Alexandra told him made him lose his appetite.

When the brief lunchtime conversation ended—they spoke for "a couple of minutes" only—the father and daughter went their separate ways for the last time. Alexandra prepared to go shopping in Boynton Beach with another Tilton houseguest, her friend Catherine Hudson Loomis, with whom she'd been exercising prior to HSCA investigator Gaeton Fonzi's arrival at the mansion. The two young women left together sometime after one. Among the items Alex would return with at 2:38 P.M. (seventeen minutes after the gun blast heard by no one, but recorded on Mrs. Tilton's cassette machine) was a can of shaving cream for her father, requested in their last conversation. He evidently had plans to shave again, or had simply been encouraging her to leave the house.

Anna Viisola arrived at the mansion to begin her chores at a quarter to one, in time to see de Mohrenschildt still eating his toast and speaking with "Donna," as Anna called Alex. Upon finishing his lunch, and prior to his daughter and Kate's departure for Boynton, the baron went upstairs to his bedroom across the hall from Mrs. Tilton's.

At that time, about one o'clock, Anna went to the laundry room and put two of de Mohrenschildt's shirts in the washing machine. He'd left his cuff links on one of them, however, and she went upstairs to his bedroom, where she found him "laying on the bed, reading." On a chair by one wall was the briefcase in which he'd brought his manuscript papers from Dallas. Whether it was this manuscript he'd chosen to review during his final calculations (and whether these calculations had indeed begun at this point), we don't know.

He had removed his shoes. He lay on top of the bed in a turtleneck sweater, tan slacks, and black socks.

"Here's your cuff links," she said to him.

"Oh, thank you very much, Anna," he replied.

She left.

At 1:30 Anna returned upstairs to turn on the cassette recorder in the bedroom opposite de Mohrenschildt's; "Days of Our Lives" was coming on. Either on this occasion or earlier, when she brought him the cuff links, she stayed on the second floor for a while to do some dusting in Mrs. Tilton's bedroom. One of the places where she cleaned, she'd later remember, was in the tight corner, beneath the stock of the 20-gauge shotgun propped against the wall.

De Mohrenschildt, just across the way, would have been well aware of her presence as she puttered in the other bedroom. From 1:30 on, he would also have heard the dramatic murmurings of the television voices, interspersed with bright jingles for Mop and Glo, Gala paper towels, and Playtex Living Gloves.

Perhaps only another White Russian, Vladimir Nabokov, could do justice to what ensued.

But—enough suspense!—it wouldn't be a murder novel he'd write, regardless of what Jeanne may have thought in her California refuge far from the deed, what Oltmans tried to impress upon the world to support his self-serving designs, or what Marrs and other conspiracy diehards may suspect to this day and go to their graves believing in their hearts. There were no "strangers" on the Tilton premises that Tuesday at the time of death. This was established beyond the reasonable doubt of jurors who unanimously returned a verdict of death by "self-inflicted wound," based on witness testimony and the fascinating taped record of Nancy Tilton's audiocassette machine. The reconstruction of Lt. Richard Sheets of the Palm Beach County Sheriff's Office was "exactly what happened," he summed up. "We know that. [De Mohrenschildt] wasn't accessible to anybody."[126]

That's the conclusion we're left with, unless, of course, we're prepared to consider seriously that "the butler did it"—that the baron was done in by the likes of Anna the maid, the gardener Coley Wimbley, the cook Lillian, de Mohrenschildt's own daughter Alexandra, her houseguest Kate Loomis, the Breakers interviewer Edward Jay Epstein, or the House investigator Gaeton Fonzi (the last two suspects having treacherously doubled back and entered the mansion without being seen by any of the wandering domestics or triggering the mad beeps of Mrs. Tilton's alarm).

Still, whereas Nabokov would hardly stoop to construct a sordidly commonplace whodunnit, he might well have been perversely interested in those final indignities of the Humbert Humbert-like baron, whose closing moments were laminated in Mrs. Tilton's tape machine together with soap-opera dialogue and cream-rinse jingles to "forget the greasies."

Relaxing on his bed, de Mohrenschildt came to a decision that early afternoon. It would be a repeat performance of sorts, except that this time he'd get it right and not swallow his dog's digitalis pills along with a flood of tranquilizers, the latter neutralized by the canine medication, as occurred the previous fall. Whether he reached his decision as Anna dusted in the bedroom across the hall, or an hour earlier, when Alex told him of the HSCA visitor, or in Brussels with Oltmans, or when Jeanne abandoned him, or just one day in front of his students at Bishop College, in despair over America's educational crisis, we're not likely to divine now. On balance it would appear that his daughter's lunchtime news was the deciding factor, perhaps with a slightly delayed effect as his situation sank in.

They've found out who you are at last, said one voice from the daytime serial across the way. *Everything's going to be all right now.*

We know that by 2:19 P.M., when Anna came back upstairs to turn the cassette over to side two, the baron had already tiptoed across the hall in his black socks, removed the shotgun from Mrs. Tilton's room, and tiptoed back with it into his own bedroom. He was once again quietly lying in bed as Anna walked past.

The time at which she turned over the cassette was determined by a Palm Beach detective who traveled to New York City for just that purpose. He checked the audio recording against the NBC computer log of programming. Side two of Anna's tape began in the midst of a Betty Crocker commercial, and was followed by another commercial for General Mills Golden Graham crackers. According to the NBC log, the latter began at 2:19:11 P.M.[127]

The shotgun noise from across the hall, though discreetly muffled by de Mohrenschildt's head and not heard by anyone in the house (or in the backyard, where the cook Lillian Romanic was sunning herself in her bathing suit), would be recorded on the machine about two minutes later—at 2:21:03, as previously noted. The bizarre preciseness of the record caused one conspiracy author to suggest that the police fabricated the entire tape in order to have a "documented" suicide scenario.[128]

When de Mohrenschildt saw the maid entering Nancy Tilton's bedroom, he didn't wait long to call or motion her into his room. He was afraid, police later reasoned, she'd discover the shotgun missing from its corner location next to the cane.

It's important that no one know about this. Especially my mother.

Anna, who appeared to harbor a slight resentment for Alexandra's old father at the inquest ("Never saw him before in my life until he came to the house," she glowered), finished her task with the cassette recorder and walked to his bedside. Whatever it was that later gave her the willies about the departed houseguest would be connected to this memorable (and unwanted) personal encounter in the last two minutes of his life.

She, at least, would never forget it.

"Did the girls leave?" he asked, looking up. His question referred to Alex and her friend Kate.

"Yes," said Anna.

One might as well have heard the wheels click in his head at this. He'd been waiting for his daughter to leave the house, apparently; she was the final restraint. Now the coast was clear—except for the maid, of course. And he needed her not just out of his room, but off the floor, away from the shotgunless bedroom of Mrs. Tilton.

True, he might've just swung out the naked double barrel from its present hiding place (under the covers? behind the bed?) and then told the terrified maid to move along smartly or he'd blow her head off too. But it wasn't the fashion just then to take a crowd with you, and anyhow brutality wasn't his way. So he launched instead, and for the last time in his life, into his socially playful manner, tossing off an effortless cameo as genteel lord harmlessly teasing a befuddled servant.

His head jerked, as if to note a strange noise out in the hallway.

"Did you hear *that?*" his expression asked.

She stared humorlessly. What *now?*

"I hear scratching," he said. "Don't you hear it?"

"No," she said.

"Of course, you do," he insisted, getting up and walking out in the hall ahead of her. "It's a cat. Don't you hear it?"

"Not really," she said.

So he went (she related at the inquest, when she'd finally figured it out and *still* didn't like it), "Pssst, pssst, pssst, pussycat," walking down the hall, leading her away from the room.

> So I followed him. I guess he wanted me out of the room or something. I don't know, but I followed him and he goes, "Pssst, pssst, pssst, pssst, pussycat."[129]

And that was how George de Mohrenschildt removed Anna both from his bedroom and the second floor, ultimately doing her a favor she wouldn't later appreciate.

I think never in my life have I seen a smoother operation . . . oh, I'm sorry! I just assumed that the gentleman was Dr. Aldrich. . . .

The cassette recorder marked his return into the room: a single pair of footsteps, incidentally. He wasn't shadowed.

He did not waste time. He scooped the shotgun from its hiding place and pulled a chair, sitting on the edge of it. He placed the stock of the gun firmly on the floor in front of him, trigger-side up. When he inserted the unpleasant double barrel into his mouth, flush against the upper palate, he leaned forward, extending his right arm. He rested his thumb against the trigger. It was a comfortable reach, with inches to spare.

I've made up my mind. I cannot see you again, not tonight, not ever. . . .

De Mohrenschildt met his end, one might say, in the Japanese manner. At an all-night bull session in his college days, Ray had heard a rumor, probably an urban legend, that in Japan, to show how sincerely annoyed you were with another party, you went to his front doorstep and killed yourself. It made quite a statement, at a price, of course. If the practice wasn't true, the larger idea behind it nevertheless had a fascinating ring: alien, uncompromising, pure. It had finesse. It was the way a continental gentleman with savoir faire and good breeding might take his exit, never mind the mess on the carpet and the shock to his daughter, who discovered him, or to his poor hostess, Mrs. Tilton, whose bridge party was interrupted when she was called to the scene. In time, they would understand.

Nancy Tilton had already taken steps in that direction by the following week's inquest. Asked by State Attorney David H. Bludworth if her late houseguest had ever discussed a previous suicide attempt with her, she'd said yes, "he was being harassed by different people."

"Did he mention any names?" the attorney asked.

"Just one man," she said. "His name is Oltmans." The baron had told her that in Holland Oltmans "was trying to force him to say things that weren't true"[130]—as we've seen.

The surprising appearance of the unlucky Fonzi that Tuesday had probably been the final destabilizer for de Mohrenschildt. Yet in his final madness, as he amiably led the deluded Anna Viisola from his room, it was Oltmans he may have seen, the obsessed shyster from Holland who represented all the lies of the world, his own included. If it took removing himself from the scene to make the lies stop, it was a bargain, a service to mankind, really.

He couldn't quite manage the doorstep part of the Japanese formula, but he had his briefcase with the unpublished manuscript in it; that would be left behind, on the chair by the north wall. Its pages would show Lee Harvey Oswald for what he was: a born patsy whom the baron unwittingly had led to slaughter. It would show what *he* was as well: a despicable wastrel who had tried to save himself by pitching in to revile Oswald's name.

But he was no Oltmans.

In the end, the truth mattered to the baron. There was just no other way to cleanse himself from the lies of the Dutchman, and from his own past, than to give his manuscript the official stamp that the fraudulent versions lacked, the imprimatur of death.

Let them read *that,* the bastards. And let the FBI try to explain it.

Sometimes the Japanese weren't all that weird after all.

Whatever the baron's final thoughts may have been, he needn't have worried that the world would take the consummate opportunist Oltmans seriously. His last scrambled thoughts on the assassination are remembered now only because of de Mohrenschildt, himself remembered only because of Oswald.

Sadly, the manuscript that the Russian took such pains to preserve (and to promote, as his final act) hasn't fared much better in the public mind than Oltmans' girlie magazine revelations. Though published in full by the HSCA in 1979—and supported by additional findings since that time—the baron's document languishes largely unread, an old but still new story. If it were a dog, it would have died by now. But it isn't.

De Mohrenschildt's pages bear close examination in the search for the real Lee Harvey Oswald.

CHAPTER FIVE
Summer of '63

On the evening of Easter Sunday, 1963, when George de Mohrenschildt was still very much alive and already packed to leave for Haiti, he and Jeanne paid a call on the Oswald family. They brought a toy rabbit for June, "a fluffy thing for the poor child" whose parents were living as social outcasts except for an occasional visit from Michael and Ruth Paine. Even Marina was now "abandoned by the conservative refugees as she had gone back to her 'Marxist' husband."[1]

A few days later, in a visit not recorded in his manuscript, the baron stopped at the home of Russian emigré friends Igor and Natasha Voshinin, who had never liked Oswald from the start. Natasha had "a sixth feeling" the Marine defector received KGB training while in Minsk, and wouldn't tolerate him in her house under any circumstances. "He stays out!" she'd long warned acquaintances—especially de Mohrenschildt, the eternal Oswald apologist.[2]

This time, though, George wasn't making the familiar old excuses for his irascible friend. On the contrary, Natasha reported,

> [De Mohrenschildt] said, "Listen, that fellow Oswald is absolutely suspicious, you are right." Thousands of times before, he would say we were wrong. "Imagine," George said, "that scoundrel took a potshot at General Walker. Of course Walker is a stinker, but stinkers have the right to live." Then he told us something about the rifle.[3]

The rifle de Mohrenschildt told the Voshinins about was one he and Jeanne claimed to have seen on their recent Easter-night visit

The house at 214 Neely Street, the last home of Lee and Marina Oswald in Oak Cliff. In the backyard of this duplex the "backyard photographs" of Oswald were taken. (Courtesy Dallas Municipal Archives and Records Center, City of Dallas, Texas)

to the Oswalds. Lee and Marina then lived in a rented house on Neely Street, their final Dallas address as a couple and the setting of the famous "backyard" photos.

As the baron described the Easter incident in his manuscript, the Oswalds now had a whole second floor, with a pleasant balcony and view—a great improvement over the dreary Elsbeth apartment the de Mohrenschildts had last seen them in. The improved surroundings seemed to have settled the couple's nerves. Marina was bubbly and Lee was smiling, "satisfied with his job and proud of being able to provide a better place for his family." For the "first time," he tells us, he and Jeanne "did not see any conflict between Lee and his wife."[4]

Of course, it was too good to last. While Oswald and the baron swapped some manly musings on the balcony, Marina led Jeanne through a guided tour of the apartment. Reaching the living room, she proudly opened the door to a large closet and began showing Jeanne her ample wardrobe, consisting largely of gifts from the affluent emigré community. That was when Jeanne couldn't help noticing:

> On the bottom of the closet was a rifle standing completely openly.
> "Look! Look!" called Jeanne excitedly. "There is a rifle there."
> We [de Mohrenschildt and Oswald] came in and I looked curiously.[5] Indeed there was a military rifle there of a type unknown to me, [a telescopic sight] dangling in front.[6]

"Lee bought it, devil knows why," Marina reportedly said of the weapon in the closet. "We need all the money we have for food and lodging, and he buys this damn rifle."

"But what does he do with a military rifle?" Jeanne asked, still marveling.

"He shoots at the leaves in the park, whenever we go there," Marina said.

All the time this initial interrogation was going on—there was more—Lee stood "curiously silent," de Mohrenschildt's manuscript tells us.

Suddenly, an irrepressible thought crossed the baron's mind. He was, it should be mentioned, a believer in ESP, which he thought he possessed (probably one good reason why he later fell easy prey to Willem Oltmans' introductory ploy, a Dutch psychic's "revelation"). Four days before the de Mohrenschildts' Easter visit, someone had taken a shot at the controversial right-wing general Edwin Walker. The general, who had been relieved of his command two years previously by President Kennedy, had become a leading player in the far-right John Birch Society and lived on Turtle Creek, close to the de Mohrenschildts. The recent attempt on Walker's life was still a topic of interest in the neighborhood, the town, and the nation. The baron also recalled, moreover, that at a gathering a few months back a man had described the general—in Oswald's presence—as "the most dangerous man in America, a potential neo-fascist leader."[7] Lee had kept on asking interested questions of the man, and "might have been influenced by this," de Mohrenschildt now realized.[8]

However it all worked, everything came together at that moment, as the baron blurted his famous "foolish joke":

"Did you take a pot shot at General Walker, Lee?" I popped a question spontaneously. And then [I] guffawed, "Ha! Ha!" [thinking] this a pretty good joke.

Lee's reaction was strange. I often tried to reconstruct it. He did not say anything. He just stood there motionless . . . became just a little paler. This was the last time I saw him and yet I cannot say with precision what his reaction was. I think he mumbled something unintelligibly and I did not ask. For sure he was embarrassed, possibly stunned, and Marina was definitely shocked.

Neither Jeanne nor I laughed much at my Walker joke. And certainly not Marina nor Lee. Only later we realized how stunning and unexpected this joke was to them. It hit the nail on the head.[9]

Marina would later testify to the Warren Commission and tell her biographer, Priscilla McMillan, that Lee had indeed taken a shot at General Walker, leaving her a mysterious note that contained instructions in the event of his capture (he didn't specify for what). Marina's revelations, however, did not come until *after* Walker himself had suggested to a German newspaper that Oswald had fired on him—a coincidence ignored by the Warren Commission.[10]

There are discrepancies in the Walker shooting story. A photograph of the rear of the Walker house found in Oswald's possessions showed a car in the driveway. Sometime after the photograph was found, the license number on the car was torn off. House Select Committee photo expert Cecil Kirk says committee investigators learned that it was cut out by Dallas police to protect a "prominent married female visitor." There isn't much evidence, however, that Walker was a ladies' man. Interestingly, though Oswald's possessions contained pictures of the exterior of Walker's house, the Dallas police, who investigated the case, have none in their files—a strange omission since the shots were fired from outside. The Dallas police photographs were taken by officer Bobby G. Brown of the Crime Scene Search division. As will be seen, Brown later played an important role in another photo mystery related to the case against Oswald.

In any event, there is little reason to doubt the outline of Marina's story (she stands by it today, now convinced of her husband's innocence in the assassination), or to doubt that the rifle was the

Mannlicher-Carcano ordered by mail from Klein's Sporting Goods in Chicago.

The Easter Sunday rifle-in-the-closet incident brought to a close the de Mohrenschildt chapter of Oswald's life, and vice versa. The two friends would not see one another again. On Friday, April 19, 1963 George and Jeanne de Mohrenschildt embarked on a journey related to their upcoming Haitian adventure; it would have, as we shall see, a significant layover in Washington, D.C.

Oswald, meanwhile, had his own new project waiting in the wings. Precisely at the time the Carcano was ordered, a new figure had entered his life. He was James Hosty, a Dallas FBI agent and investigator of right-wing groups, including the ultraconservative Walker and his followers. Consulting an informant in the city's postal inspector's office a month before the departure of the de Mohrenschildts, Hosty (whom we'll see again in later chapters) obtained the address of the Oswalds. The day after the agent made his first contact with Oswald, then still working at Jaggars, the order for the rifle was mailed to Klein's. By the end of that March, Oswald had lost his job.[11] Two weeks later, on the second day after Easter, the ex-Marine resurrected an old ideological flame, Castro's Cuba, as he began a new correspondence—another change accompanying his separation from the baron. He was moving in a new direction, and under new management, it would appear later. His letter, to the New York headquarters of the Fair Play for Cuba Committee, asked national chairman Vincent Lee for "40 or 50" of the FPCC's "fine, basic pamp[h]lets."[12]

The next week, on Wednesday, April 24, after arranging to leave Marina and baby June with Ruth Paine, he set out alone by bus for the Crescent City of New Orleans.

In spring of 1963 Lee Harvey Oswald was back in his hometown for the first time since passing through in September 1959, when he stayed long enough to board a freighter en route to France, the first leg of his journey to the Soviet Union. Before that, Oswald hadn't visited New Orleans since dropping out of Warren Easton High School within a month of starting the tenth grade. He had spent his free time then, it may be recalled, running messages to steamship lines, reading Marxist literature, memorizing his brother's USMC manual, and hanging out with school pal Edward Voebel, who'd been in the Civil Air Patrol with "Captain Dave Ferrie."[13] A recently discovered photo of Lee in his CAP days shows him standing wistfully at the edge of a group of boys gathered around Ferrie, who wears a military helmet.[14] (Why the owner of the photo, one of the CAP kids seen in it, hung on to the picture throughout the Garrison and HSCA probes is a question that hasn't been answered.)

Those early days on the Mississippi had been as carefree as Oswald's life got. If never exactly a version of Huck Finn even as a kid, the new arrival was still less so now as an adult with a wife and child (and another on the way), the baggage of a shady background as turncoat, no job, and no place to stay.

The last problem was solved by Oswald's Aunt Lillian, Marguerite's sister and wife of Charles ("Dutz") Murret, who put up her nephew while he looked for work.[15] Two weeks later, on Thursday, May 9, Oswald applied for, and was immediately offered, a job oiling machinery at the Reily Coffee Company. With this job in hand, he left the hospitality of the Murrets, found an apartment on Magazine Street, and sent for Marina and baby June. Ruth Paine, who had driven Lee to the downtown bus station when he left Dallas (and taken care of his family in the interim), now did the additional service of transporting the mother and daughter to New Orleans. They arrived on Friday, May 10, Oswald's first day on the job.

As in the case of his previous employment at Jaggars-Chiles-Stovall, Oswald's new company appeared to be an unlikely match for the ex-defector. The owner of the coffee firm, William Reily, was an ardent patriot and supporter of the Crusade to Free Cuba Committee, which in turn supported an anti-Castro CIA front, the Cuban Revolutionary Council of Antonio de Varona. On the practical level, to be sure, the job worked out no better than any of Oswald's other jobs, whether in Minsk, Fort Worth, or Dallas. For all his theoretical sympathies with the working class, Oswald disliked the actual grind of physical labor and had no patience for the niceties of socializing with common fellow workers—men who could not converse like the aristocrat George de Mohrenschildt. Thus his days at Reily Coffee ran a predictable course. He shunned other employees, shirked his maintenance duties in favor of reading magazines at a neighboring garage, and earned the considerable animosity of a supervisor, Charles Le Blanc. On Friday, July 19, exactly ten weeks after he reported for work, he was fired. The wonder may be that he lasted that long.[16]

But if Oswald had little stomach for the prosaic chores of an ordinary job, he exhibited both initiative and industry in the stuff he did on his own time, and which he surely perceived as his "real" work. In New Orleans, ironically consistent with the interests of coffee magnate Reily, he refocused his attention on Castro's Cuba. The revived interest in this area had shown up back in April, with his letter to the FPCC two days after he and de Mohrenschildt exchanged their awkward last goodbyes. Unlike the relatively quiet man of Dallas, the summer of '63 Crescent City Oswald metamorphosed into a flashy public pro-Castro butterfly. Somewhat incredibly, the new role was one for which he demonstrated genuine aptitude, indeed seemed to have been born to play: agitator, street-hustling ideologue, like American twenties commie star Jack Reed or the anonymous frumpy heroine in the Bronx who stood by the El handing out leaflets in support of the doomed Rosenbergs. In some ways it was she, not Marguerite, who was his real mother—the woman who imprinted on his imagination the romance of troublemaking, throwing monkey wrenches into the system. But which system was he sabotaging? With Oswald, that was always the question.

After thirty years of communal agonizing, two viable readings are left of the Oswald weirdness in New Orleans that summer. They can be called, after their most impressive proponents, the Posner and Summers-Scott theories. The first is a powerful upgrade of the version of events originally presented by the Warren Commission; the second builds on earlier contributions by Harold Weisberg and New Orleans district attorney Jim Garrison. Though radically different, both theories are entirely convincing, at least at first glance. The only consolation has been in knowing *one* of them *must* be true; there are no other explanations—or haven't been, until the next chapter.

In simplest terms, Gerald Posner's *Case Closed* (1993) argues that the New Orleans Oswald was a lonely Marxist wacko desperately staving off the reality of a failed life with escapist fantasy adventures. The adventures had no substance or connection to the outside world, but were later maliciously exploited by Garrison, himself mentally unstable, for his personal aggrandizement. By contrast, Anthony Summers' *Conspiracy* (1981) and Peter Dale Scott's *Deep Politics and the Death of JFK* (1993) present a competent Oswald collaborating in a dirty-tricks campaign orchestrated by U.S. intelligence to smear leftist groups by linking them with Soviet communism. The instrument for this linkage was Oswald himself, an agent or operative of some kind, though possibly without full knowledge of which organization was "running" him. Garrison, in this scenario, far from a malevolent degenerate as he is often depicted, was a courageous crusader ahead of his time.

The known facts can be marshaled to support both theories, but again, the two lines of thought are obviously mutually exclusive; only one can be right. Which is it?

On May 26, two weeks after hiring on at Reily, Oswald wrote another letter to Vincent Lee at the Castro-compatible FPCC in New York. He enclosed five dollars to join the committee, and noted: "Now that I live in New Orleans I have been thinking about renting a small office at my own expense for the purpose of forming a F.P.C.C. branch here in New Orleans. Could you give me a charter?"[17] Though the letter was deferential in tone and even requested a fan picture of Fidel ("suitable for framing would be a welcome touch"), Oswald was not put off by the stodgy response Lee sent back three days later. The FPCC chairman, discouraging the notion of trying to start a chapter "with as few members as seem to exist in the New Orleans area," suggested Oswald get in touch with the Tampa branch of the organization. He should not, at any rate, get involved in "unnecessary incidents that frighten away prospective supporters."[18]

Naturally, Oswald brushed aside all this bureaucratic timidity. Even before receiving Lee's reply, he had ordered a stash of handbills printed, reading in part: "HANDS OFF CUBA! Join the Fair Play for Cuba Committee, New Orleans Charter Member Branch."[19] Soon he'd be handing such flyers out on the streets, getting into an altercation in public, landing in jail, and appearing on television and radio, the latter including a prominent part in a bruising live debate. (The struggle was all, as he'd written to his brother.) On these documented facts, everyone agrees.

After receiving the FPCC's lukewarm answer in late May 1963, Oswald wrote right back. "Against your advice, I have decided to take an office from the very beginning," he told the committee chairman.[20] Two months later, on August 1, the same day the *Times-Picayune* announced a raid by the FBI of an anti-Castro paramilitary force operating in the New Orleans area, Oswald still had the office in mind. "In regard to my efforts to start a branch office," he reported to Lee in New York, "I rented an office as I planned and was promptly closed three days later for some obscure reasons by the renters, they said something about remodeling, etc."[21]

In general, Posner discounts the contents of Oswald's letters as part of his pathetic fantasy. His New Orleans FPCC chapter is "fictional," the claims in the letters "almost a complete fabrication," Oswald is "unable to write without embellishment," and so on.[22] In a number of instances, Posner is on firm ground with his sharp, sustained analysis. Oswald undeniably distorted, exaggerated, and sometimes simply invented things in his correspondence (sending out phony FPCC membership cards signed "A. J. Hidell," for example), though why he might have done so is another question. It didn't help matters that he chose to operate in a netherworld of radical polemics, where lies had status as honorary truth if they furthered some perceived historical purpose. (More significantly, there may have been other, conspiratorial, reasons for Oswald's "deceptions," according to the Summers-Scott line, as we'll see.)

Yet, even granting Oswald's lapses from literal fact, there was frequently some element of truth in his letters, as when he reported correctly to Lee that he printed up flyers but inflated the actual numbers, or said he received "considerable coverage in the press" though it was only a short article in the *Times-Picayune*. The central question in all of Oswald's New Orleans summer—more important even than the necessary conjectures on why he was doing the crazy things he appeared to be doing—is this: Was there an "element of truth" in his claim to Vincent Lee, repeated three times in two months, that he was involved in "renting a small office" for his FPCC chapter?

If Oswald can't be connected to such an office—whether as a room he really paid money for, was allowed to use for free, or just visited on occasion—and if that office can't be solidly placed in a specific Camp Street building that we'll see again in a moment—then the game's over. Posner wins. Only the Camp Street building can put Oswald in the company of other "conspirators." Without this connection firmly in hand, the proponents of a conspiratorial Oswald can save themselves the trouble of worrying about the different shades of tricks he might have been playing *against* the FPCC, and later, the American Civil Liberties Union. Such arguments, however ingenious and "scholarly," would all be built on sand.

Everything turns on the office, then. On this site, the battle of New Orleans will be decided.

The pamphlets that Oswald was seen handing out publicly in New Orleans were rubber-stamped with an address, often inside the back cover. The stamped information identified the "sponsor" distributing the literature (the FPCC), and where the recipient could go or write for more information. The *HANDS OFF CUBA!* handout, for example, promising "Free Literature, Lectures," followed up with the word "Location" and a colon. In the space after the colon Oswald stamped the pertinent address, the place to go for the free literature and lectures, and where presumably one could also join up, as the handout urged. That was the whole apparent point of the exercise, getting people to join this new local chapter.

As all buffs know, the most important stamped address on the Oswald FPCC literature—the address Summers called "an evidential time bomb"[23]—was that of a now-famous corner building with entrances on two different streets. By some dream logic mimicking the two faces of Oswald, the building had acquired two official addresses, one for each entrance. The front entrance constituted the building's "main" address—the one Oswald stamped on his handouts—544 Camp Street. The second address belonged to the more obscure side entrance, on Lafayette Street.

Interestingly, it was this lesser-known Lafayette address that the New Orleans FBI cited in briefly reporting an interview, three days after the assassination, with Guy Banister, a hard-boiled, fifty-eight-year-old ex-FBI agent whose private detective agency commanded the ground floor of the building. The two-sentence Bureau report noted simply that New Orleans Special Agent Ernest C. Wall, Jr., had "telephonically contacted" Banister at "Guy Banister Associates, Inc., 531 Lafayette Street."[24] Banister confirmed to the inquiring agent that the anti-Castro Cuban Revolutionary Council, headed locally by Sergio Arcacha Smith, had indeed officed "in the building located at 544 Camp Street." (This officing had occurred "some time ago"— a safe year and a half prior to Oswald's arrival.) Wall's report gave no hint that the two different addresses, Banister's and the CRC's, referred to the same location, or that Banister himself was the most prominent tenant of the Camp (and Lafayette) Street building.

The report also failed to mention, of course, that the real work of

Banister Associates ran to weightier matters than digging up dirt on errant marriage partners. Banister was a fire-breathing superpatriot, up to his ears in U.S. intelligence and anti-Castro associations. His files were organized under such classifications as *American Central Intelligence Agency, Anti-Soviet Underground,* and *Dismantling of Defenses, U.S.* Surprisingly, they also contained a more familiar classification: *Fair Play for Cuba Committee.* When Banister died of an apparent heart attack a few months after the 1963 FBI interview, his widow discovered, among his effects, numerous pamphlets of the FPCC—"odd propaganda to turn up in the possession of the man who had headed the Anti-Communist League of the Caribbean," as Summers observed.[25]

What was Oswald's literature doing in Banister's hands, and why was one of the files in his office labeled with the name of Oswald's "group"? Did the ex-FBI agent's interest in the FPCC mean he was monitoring the committee (which was little more than a fantasy, according to Posner) as a subversive pro-Castro organization? Or did his interest signify a more collaborative relationship, one that an embarrassed Bureau began trying to obfuscate as early as November 25, 1963? It's possible the Warren investigators would have been compelled to take a grudging look at these questions, had they been properly informed by the FBI. They were not.

Oswald and Banister shared the same "space," not in some sterile high rise, but a shabby three-story wooden building, the sort of unpretentious cozy quarters where other tenants were likely to know something about your business. A pro-Castro agitator had exactly a snowball-in-hell's chance of cohabiting peaceably with men like Banister and his passionately anti-Castro associates; three such firebrands would go into a reflex frenzy in August at the mere sight of Oswald passing out a few FPCC pamphlets on a public street. Yet, for all its apparent implausibility, the Oswald-Banister connection has been a matter of record for more than three decades. It is documented twice, as we've seen, and in both directions: Banister had Oswald's papers in his files, and Oswald had Banister's address on his pamphlets. The last is the killer, the Warren defenders' *Halloween* boogieman that refuses to die.

In 1978, Banister's former secretary, Delphine Roberts, dumped more discouraging news on proponents of a nonconspiratorial New Orleans scenario. She opened up to Anthony Summers, providing details of Oswald's alleged visitations to her boss's ground-floor office. Rather than taking up applications for the FPCC, Oswald himself appeared to be applying as one of Banister's "agents," she told Summers. That wasn't all. The ex-Marine allegedly returned to Banister's lair repeatedly, seeming to be on "familiar terms" with the old FBI man and his office. Delphine "understood," moreover, that Oswald was allowed the use of an office on the building's second floor, to which he would go "up and down"—understood so because, among other reasons, she herself visited the upper-floor office with Banister on several occasions and found it cluttered with FPCC leaflets.[26]

And when the secretary mentioned to Banister that she'd seen "that young man passing out his pro-Castro leaflets in the street," he reportedly told her: "Don't worry about him. He's a nervous fellow, he's confused. He's with us, he's associated with the office."[27]

As Posner recognizes in *Case Closed,* the Oswald office question must be dealt with, having "caused considerable debate." He concedes that "if Oswald had an office, even briefly, at 544 Camp, it could be significant."[28] This concession, to be sure, is only an hors d'oeuvre, served as Posner whets his machete. He knows full well that on this matter there can be no compromise or misguided, faint-hearted mercy. The Camp Street address rubber-stamped on the FPCC literature is a poisonous snake in the garden threatening the orderly creation of Posner's New Orleans Oswald. *That* Oswald, a lonely wacko who seldom strays from his apartment except for the occasional night in jail, can in no way coexist with his evil twin, the false and heretical Oswald who knocks around in a spook-filled building and has substantive associations with the likes of Banister, his Castro-hating Cuban exile gang, and their mob-tinged Anglo cohort from hell, David Ferrie.

Oddly, however, despite both the importance of this question and Posner's gleeful steamrollering of conspiracy arguments on other fronts of the assassinology wars, the feared neo-Warren avenger goes a bit limp on the must-win matter of the stamped address. Maybe he chokes, like Casey in Mudville. Maybe he just knows he has nothing to say here, and the sooner he goes on to something else the better for his side. Whatever the case, his response is uncharacteristically lame and speculative. Posner points out that "there is evidence" Oswald may have stopped by the Camp Street building one day and talked to the janitor about renting an office. This evidence is that the janitor told the FBI following the assassination that someone had once tried to rent an office, but that he had discouraged him. The janitor couldn't identify the man to the agents, and since the FBI interview took place after the Dallas tragedy, when Oswald's face was known the world over, it's evident the janitor didn't believe his would-be renter was Oswald. Even so, "there is a possibility" Oswald talked to the janitor, Posner insists, "and, if so, that was the extent of [Oswald's] contact to the building, though he still stamped it on some of his leaflets as the 'official' office address for Fair Play."[29]

It may be that such a single inquiry, to a janitor who later didn't remember him, accounted for Oswald's claims that he "rented" a Camp Street office. The question, however, is Oswald's association with the building, not whether he ever signed a rental agreement. It is this association, documented by Oswald's stamp, that Posner must dispose of in order to slay the terrible hydra of conspiratorial alternatives. Straining mightily, he tries to do so in a single, speculative swipe. "It is possible," he tells us, that Oswald "had decided when settling on a false address for his imaginary Fair Play chapter that it should embarrass his nemesis, the extreme right wing and the city's anti-Castro militants."[30]

That's it, the best Posner can do with 544 Camp Street, apparently. His explanation—his *only* explanation—is that the stamped address was another Oswald con, like the time he hired a couple of out-of-work guys at the state employment office to help pass out his FPCC materials, thereby creating the illusion that the organization had other members.[31]

But of course such an address con would make no sense—certainly not to Oswald, whose instincts were confrontational where ideology was concerned. By what strange logic was rubber-stamping the Camp Street address on flyers supposed to "embarrass his nemesis" if Oswald was desperately trying to build up his FPCC membership (as Posner also claims)?[32] If the ex-Marine had no functional address at Banister's building, how were recruits supposed to obtain their "Free Literature, Lectures" or be signed up for the local chapter? And would Oswald really have been sending valuable potential converts into the heart of the enemy camp, risking contamination of their tender minds with specious anti-Castro lies? As Posner himself reminds us, moreover, 544 Camp wasn't the only location the young New

Orleans native stamped on his literature. He also stamped his Magazine Street address and his post office box (the latter under the name
of FPCC "president" A. J. Hidell). These addresses were hardly
phonies. They were clearly intended to produce results, and could
only have done so by leading recruits directly back to Oswald. Was he
stamping his true addresses on some pamphlets and a nonexistent
"trick" address on others, and if so, how were passersby supposed to
know the difference?

Whatever its merits on other grounds, the Posner neo-Warren
explanation strikes out in the essential area of Oswald's connection
with the building at 544 Camp. To his credit Posner spunkily man-
ages to keep the game interesting with malicious zingers at witnesses
who place Oswald in the building: Banister aide Jack Martin is "an
admitted drunk," Delphine Roberts "a rabid anti-Communist and
racist," and her daughter "'a big fat lady.'"[33] Like Alexandra de
Mohrenschildt on the subject of her stepmother, Posner would
probably say more if he could find words damaging enough—but the
results would be equally futile. Nothing short of a proper accounting
for the stamped Camp Street address can save his position in New
Orleans. Failing this quest, he leaves the door open to other explanations of Oswald's behavior.

When the young Anglo walked into Casa Roca on downtown
Decatur Street, comanager Carlos Bringuier, then twenty-nine, was
mulling over a bit of bad news with a couple of young acquaintances
amidst an unclassifiable assortment of clothes, radios, Spanish
records, perfumes—everything necessary for body and soul, all in
one store. Bringuier, who had been a lawyer before fleeing Castro's
Cuba, was now more than a shopkeeper. He headed the New Orleans
chapter of DRE, the anti-Castro Student Revolutionary Directorate.
A few days earlier, Bringuier had received a package of one-dollar
DRE bonds from the organization's headquarters in Miami. He'd
recruited helpers to hawk the low-denomination bonds on the
streets, but one of the recruits, teenager Phil Geraci, had just been
explaining that he and the friend with him had been stopped from
selling the bonds by the New Orleans Police. You needed a city per-
mit to sell the bonds, they told him.

The niggling refusal to let the DRE raise funds by selling a few
scraps of paper was another hard knock to the legitimate aspirations

of the refugee community, they agreed. An even grosser insult had occurred just the week before, when the FBI found it necessary to raid an isolated vacation cottage north of nearby Lake Pontchartrain. The agents had confiscated a "cache of materials for bombs," according to the *Times-Picayune* headline of Thursday, August 1. The materials were intended for the CIA-supported Cuban-exile "Secret War" on Castro, which had included such reckless extremes as Alpha 66 attacks on Soviet ships in Cuban harbors, and a CIA-Mafia alliance churning out Rube Goldberg plots to murder Fidel Castro. Kennedy, whose brother Robert was secretly planning yet another invasion of Cuba, had nonetheless made an accommodation with Khrushchev after a heart-stopping missile crisis, and was determined to pull the plug on these operations, using the FBI, Coast Guard, and Navy to seize commando vessels, break up training camps, and confiscate matériel. Pontchartrain, where the raiders grabbed a ton of dynamite, napalm ingredients, and 100-pound aerial-bomb casings, along with DRE military section member John Koch (and Minutemen cofounder and mega gun-dealer Richard Lauchli), was one more skirmish in this campaign.

To the Cuban exile community, of course, such a policy was wildly misguided. The eleven men collared at Pontchartrain, arrested like common criminals, were preparing valiantly for a necessary purpose, a mission of honor and restoration. This was something Kennedy obviously didn't understand, as he showed when he martyred the Bay of Pigs invaders by denying them air cover. It took guts to be president; education and good looks weren't enough.

The Anglo newcomer who had entered Casa Roca—and who appeared to be lending a sympathetic ear to such deliberations—wasn't a sailor, Bringuier noted casually. The docks were close by, and merchant seamen just off the boat were frequent visitors in the Casa. They'd check their mail first at the post office across the street, and then, on the way to the bars on the same block, wander into the store for a quick look around. This visitor wasn't doing much looking, though. He seemed more interested in joining in on the shop talk. A small alarm went off in Bringuier's head. It grew louder as he saw the stranger actually reaching for his wallet, offering to buy a few of the DRE bonds which just that day the New Orleans PD had told Geraci and his pal they couldn't sell.

Bringuier politely refused, listening warily as Oswald (the

suspicious customer, of course) kept "hitting at the conversation," as the former DRE leader and recent novelist told the La Fontaines.[34] Oswald used the Mafia term *Cosa Nostra* (not then widely known) and in general impressed on the small group his Marine wiles and ardent belief in what the anti-Castro refugees were trying to accomplish.[35] He was ready to help them in the Secret War by training guerilla troops, he told them.

Rhetorically, Oswald's pitch probably wasn't that bad. He could talk impressively when the occasion required, and had wowed the dream girl of the evening at a Russian emigré party in Dallas with an intense three-hour monologue.[36] As we'll see, he would also (contrary to common opinion) give a decent accounting of himself in a radio debate shortly after visiting Casa Roca. But however slick Oswald's anti-Castro spiel may have been, the skeptical Old World mind of Bringuier (whose ancestors had arrived in Cuba from France in the nineteenth century) wasn't convinced. "I didn't trust Oswald from the beginning," he told Mary. "When he showed so much interest in our activities, it crossed my mind immediately that he could be an agent trying to infiltrate our organization. Pontchartrain had just happened, and I suspected the FBI might be checking to see if we were involved with that operation." It also occurred to Bringuier that "Oswald might be trying to entrap me with the bonds, which Geraci had just told me were illegal to sell."[37]

Oswald appeared to validate Bringuier's last suspicion a few weeks later, when he prepared a handwritten summary of his pro-Castro activities prior to seeking entry into Cuba via Mexico City. Indulging in a bit of résumé inflation, Oswald claimed that he shut down the DRE bond operation, having turned in proof of the organization's illegal activities to the New Orleans attorney general. The city did not have an "attorney general" and no records support Oswald's claim, but it shows he had some mischief in mind when he offered to buy Bringuier's bonds on the Monday afternoon of August 5. (There is now reason to suspect the date of Bringuier's alleged first meeting with Oswald. According to an April 1995 interview with a former New Orleans FBI employee, Oswald was the informant on the raid of the DRE arms cache. See chapter 10.)

The next day, supposedly August 6, Oswald made a follow-up visit to the Cuban store. This time he brought a copy of his Marine handbook as a document attesting to his military experience and guerilla know-how. Unfortunately, Bringuier was doing business in the docks that Tuesday, and Oswald ended up leaving the book with the comanager brother-in-law, Rolando Pelaez. (Bringuier shows the book to visitors to this day.)

Three days later, on Friday, August 9, Bringuier was behind the counter of Casa Roca when his friend Celso Macario Hernandez, forty-seven, rushed in breathlessly. Celso had seen some American on Canal Street wearing a pro-Castro sign and handing out pro-Castro leaflets, had gone insane, insulting him in Spanish, and then run all the way to Carlos's store to tell the news. Bringuier responded immediately, picking up nineteen-year-old Miguel Mariano Cruz and setting out at the head of the three-man posse to catch the perpetrator. Carlos, Celso, and Miguel cruised the streets on foot and by streetcar, with the DRE chief himself carrying their colors, a "Cuba Lies in Chains!" poster. But no luck—the quarry, commie or provocateur, couldn't be found.

But suddenly, like in the movies, after they'd almost given up, he was spotted again. It was back to the chase!

This time, arriving at the corner of St. Charles and Canal, the vigilant threesome caught the American in the act, still nonchalantly spreading the venomous doctrine. For Bringuier, whose jaw dropped at the sight, the story had a surprise ending. The guy handing out leaflets was the same Oswald character who'd been pestering him in the store earlier that week and professing such anti-Castro fervor. Now it turned out he was a *Fidelista,* and to add insult, a public one. Bringuier was amazed, but grateful. His instincts had been correct. He'd known from the *first* this character couldn't be trusted!

There was no physical violence in the ensuing scene, though it has come down to us as Oswald's New Orleans "street scuffle." The most flagrant act was by Celso Hernandez, who grabbed a bunch of the FPCC pamphlets, tore them up, and threw the pieces in the air. Otherwise, no one hit anyone, even when Oswald, passive-aggressive before it was cool, taunted, "Okay, Carlos, you want to hit me, hit me."[38]

When a policeman arrived and ordered the Cubans to move on and stop interfering with the leafleting, Bringuier refused to budge, telling the cop that Oswald had misrepresented himself and was a dangerous subversive. This apparently was enough for the NOPD. With two squad cars now at the site, Oswald was rounded up with the other three men and taken to the police station. A court hearing was set for Monday, three days away. Bringuier and his companions each paid a twenty-five-dollar bail and were released. Oswald, odd man out as usual, didn't have enough money and was jailed overnight. He was sprung the following day, Saturday, by a man named Emile Bruneau, a friend of his uncle Dutz with ties to the New Orleans underworld.[39]

Oswald's brief incarceration (examined more closely in the following chapter) did not derail his publicity blitz, which continued gathering momentum during the next two weeks. Interestingly, it was Bringuier himself who started this media ball rolling in earnest. On the Monday morning of August 12 he ran into local journalist William K. Stuckey at a bank and mentioned the upcoming hearing, as well as the existence of Oswald's pro-Castro organization, which in right-wing New Orleans was an oddity. Intrigued by the latter revelation, Stuckey sent a cameraman to cover the hearing for his station, WDSU, which had both television and radio facilities. At the courtroom Oswald was fined ten dollars for disturbing the peace. Charges against the Cubans—who had stalked Oswald, ripped up his pamphlets, and created a sidewalk disturbance—were dismissed. Present in the courtroom was Dr. Agustin Guitart, uncle of Silvia Odio, a Cuban woman living in Dallas who would herself later play a pivotal role in the legend of Lee Harvey Oswald.[40] The WDSU cameraman, who had not been allowed to shoot in court, cornered the young FPCC organizer after the hearing and interviewed him for the evening news in the midst of a shouting match with Bringuier's supporters.[41]

Encouraged by the attention he was arousing—an article on the scuffle had already appeared in the newspaper—and starting to get the hang of this PR flacking business, Oswald made a round of calls to the Crescent City TV stations. He let them know he was planning an FPCC demonstration in front of the International Trade Mart on Friday of that week, August 16, so that they'd be there with the cameras rolling.[42]

It was around this time that Oswald received a visitor—a Cuban named Carlos Quiroga—on the porch of his Magazine Street apartment. Quiroga, who had been directed to the right door by Oswald's landlady (and who came bearing FPCC leaflets that he would later claim had been gathered at the scuffle), represented himself as that rarest of breeds, a pro-Castro sympathizer swayed by Oswald's Fair Play promotions. In fact, Quiroga had been sent by Bringuier. Oswald wasn't fooled by Quiroga's professions of "interest"; he believed (as he later told Marina) that Quiroga had been sent either by Bringuier or the FBI.[43]

When the day arrived, the young self-professed Marxist had an inspiration worthy of the crassest capitalist on Wall Street. He showed up early in the morning at the state employment agency office and offered a deal that two out-of-work youngsters couldn't refuse: two dollars for thirty minutes' work and no heavy lifting, just distributing leaflets and incidentally lending their images for eternal misrepresentation. The plan worked perfectly. With his two-man crew, Oswald paraded in front of the summoned cameras, giving definitive "proof" that the organization had more than one member, himself. That evening, the deceptive display was aired on two New Orleans stations. Undeniably, life was good sometimes. But wouldn't you know, the young husband, no prophet in his own family, couldn't even get Marina to watch him on the tube. "I see you every day at home in all forms," she reportedly told him when he arrived from his Trade Mart triumph. "I don't want to see you on TV. Besides, how come you're not ashamed to telephone the stations yourself?"[44]

Marina obviously wasn't ready for prime time. Oswald was.

The next day, Saturday, August 17, the media pace quickened. At eight in the morning, journalist Stuckey showed up at Oswald's door to get a look at the American *Fidelista* with his own eyes. Not having caught Oswald's Friday appearance on TV, the newsman had come expecting to find some sort of beatnik in beard and sandals. Instead, he found this clean-cut shirtless kid in USMC fatigue pants, explaining how he'd like to invite him in for coffee, but his wife and daughter were still asleep. Impressed by the articulate homegrown leftist, Stuckey followed through with his original intent, which was to invite him to appear that same evening on his weekly radio show on WDSU, "Latin Listening Post."

Oswald agreed, and arrived at the station at 5:00 P.M. to tape an interview. The interview lasted thirty-seven minutes, of which only four and a half could be selected for use on the brief Stuckey program airing at 7:30. Oswald appeared pleased with the result, writing a letter to V. T. Lee that same night about the "considerable" TV coverage he'd been receiving.[45] The journalist continued to be impressed with Oswald's confident and "deliberate" manner, and suggested to the station's news director that the whole thirty-seven-minute interview be aired in a separate program. The director refused, noting that the FPCC organizer's appearance on the normally bland "Listening Post" had already caused an "angry public reaction."[46] He asked Stuckey to schedule a radio debate instead, in which Oswald's pro-Castro views could be balanced by those of local anti-Communists.[47]

On Monday morning, Stuckey proposed the debate to the ex-Marine by phone. Though the format would pit him against two opponents, Oswald immediately accepted, agreeing to appear Wednesday evening on a live twenty-five-minute program with a single intermission, "Conversation Carte Blanche." Finding a suitable opponent to debate Oswald wasn't brain surgery for Stuckey. His friend Bringuier had already called him on Saturday, the day after the Trade Mart demonstration, to complain that the TV coverage the station had given to Oswald's FPCC was only enhancing the group and providing a platform for commie lies. Instead of bloodless "equal time" on the next "Listening Post," as Stuckey offered, the passionate Cuban had wanted to confront Oswald *mano a mano*, in face-to-face combat. Now Stuckey was able to offer him this chance, and like Oswald, Bringuier jumped at it. The second opponent Stuckey selected for Oswald was Ed Butler, an expert in anti-Communist psychological warfare and executive director of the right-wing Information Council of the Americas.[48]

With the debate now set and only two days off, Stuckey thought it prudent to take a closer look at Oswald's background. Operating in an era less skeptical of government than our own, he gave a copy of the thirty-seven-minute interview tape to the New Orleans FBI office, which in turn provided him with information on Oswald from the Bureau's records. A top agent at the local office (unidentified by Stuckey in a 1976 letter to Priscilla McMillan) read portions of Oswald's file over the phone to the journalist, who thus learned for the first time of the former Marine's checkered past: how he'd defected to the Soviet Union and tried to renounce his citizenship, his marriage to a Russian wife, the undesirable discharge, everything.[49]

Meanwhile, the coalition against Oswald was zeroing in on the same damaging information. Bringuier had received Quiroga's report that Oswald spoke Russian at home and had been to the

Soviet Union. The two men visited Butler with this news on Tuesday, the day before the debate. The INCA director made a phone call to a Washington contact at the House Un-American Activies Committee, confirming the Cuban allegations and learning the full story. That same Tuesday he also called Stuckey, as the station journalist later reported in a 1976 letter to Priscilla McMillan, whose *Marina and Lee* remains the best read of the pro-Warren books. "Stuckey and Butler agreed over the telephone that they would bring Oswald's Russian past to light on the program, expose him as a Communist sympathizer, and destroy his organization," McMillan noted straightforwardly.[50]

And so it happened. From the program's opening drumroll, the young ex-Marine was hammered mercilessly for his secret Russian past by Stuckey, Bringuier, and Butler—three against one, if you counted the cohost starting the ambush with a chilling recital of the unpatriotic outrages discovered since the last interview. The unexpected revelation of his previous Soviet sympathies was more than a personal embarrassment; it knocked the props out from under the very organization Oswald had supposedly been trying to help, and "established" the FPCC by association as a Moscow-brand commie front. In a rare meeting of minds, Warren critics and defenders alike have generally agreed that the WDSU radio debate was a debacle for Oswald, though as usual they use this point to advance completely opposite arguments.

Conspiracy-siders such as Peter Dale Scott, Anthony Summers, and Philip Melanson explain the debate as an *intentional* disaster—an act of sabotage by Oswald, like the incriminating letters he was writing at the time, linking the FPCC on paper with American Communist and socialist groups. The debate fiasco wasn't an isolated misdeed, but part of a larger Oswald campaign of dirty tricks against the good name, such as it was, of the pro-Castro committee. The campaign implied cooperation with (or manipulation by) some controlling government intelligence organization, one still waging a Secret War on Castro, but on the propaganda front, manufacturing lies about the enemy. The CIA, to which ex-FBI agent Banister also had ties, was one of several likely candidates for this role.

Warren defenders Posner and McMillan found similar serviceable use for the debate-as-debacle scenario. In Posner's more recent account, the rout Oswald suffered that hellish Wednesday night at

WDSU was an unbearable reality check, sending the sadly delusional former Marine over the edge into depression, and eventually, the madness of the lone assassin . . . *Case Closed.*

An actual hearing of the debate tape, however, as opposed to simply searching the dead letters of the transcript, presents a somewhat different picture.[51] In a literal way, it's true that Bringuier and Butler achieved the technical objective of linking the FPCC with Soviet communism. But as a piece of on-air propaganda, the message of the debate was more mixed. The two-against-one format focused attention on Oswald and diminished the individual status of his opponents. It may also have aroused subversive subliminal questions (was he worth two of them?) and feelings of sympathy for the underdog, an emotion Oswald had craftily exploited a few days earlier, Bringuier reported, by sitting in the "colored section" at his court hearing.

It should also be noted that Bringuier wasn't an effective opponent that day. Though his English has much improved over the years, he spoke at the time with a thick Cuban accent and limited himself to quoting statistics on the comparative availability of consumer commodities in Russia and the pre-Castro Cuba of dictator Fulgencio Batista. It was the kind of wearying recitation you'd expect more from a party aparatchik than an impassioned freedom fighter. Butler was a more formidable foe, but at a price. His comments were both abrasive and unctuous, not exactly what one might prefer in the white knight defending capitalist democracy. As the debate wore on, moreover, it was Oswald who increasingly held the field, speaking in measured, reasonable-sounding sentences. He never came across to the radio audience as shaken, whatever his internal state may have been, and he was able to support his points with touches of detail without sounding merely pedantic, as Bringuier had done.

> BUTLER. Are you a Marxist?
>
> OSWALD. Ah, yes, I am a Marxist.
>
> BUTLER. What's the difference [between that and a Communist]?
>
> OSWALD. Well, the differences are primarily the difference between a country like Ghana, Yemen, Yugoslavia, China, or Russia. Very, very great differences. Differences which we appreciate by giving aid, let's say, to Yugoslavia in the sum of a hundred million or so dollars per year.

"That's extraneous," the INCA director complained, but another bit of damage was already done. In the crucible of live debate, the young challenger showed he could talk with the learned elders. What's more, he could backpedal and protect himself, take punishment. He'd been bushwacked by Stuckey and badgered by the stinging jabs of Butler, but they hadn't been able to put him away. What didn't kill you, the Spanish saying went, made you stronger. Oswald proved it as the program wore on. He took his lickin' and kept on tickin'.

The crisis point of the debate occurred earlier, however, in his first exchange with Stuckey. It was the sweaty moment just after the opening bombshell, when the cohost made the surprise announcement about Oswald's discovered past and went calmly down the line itemizing each misdeed. The rascal guest had obviously been caught redhanded. How would he respond? What could he possibly say in his own defense? Inquiring minds in Radioland probably wanted to know, and in the WDSU studio, every eye must have been on the ex-Marine.

> STUCKEY. [After itemizing.] Mr. Oswald, are these correct?
> OSWALD. That is correct, yeah.
> STUCKEY. You did live in Russia for three years?
> OSWALD. That is correct, and I think those—the fact that I did live for a time in the Soviet Union gives me excellent qualifications to repudiate charges that Cuba, and the Fair Play for Cuba Committee, is Communist controlled.

That had been the real test, the haymaker to the chin of a completely unprepared Oswald. He took it, wobbled . . . and stayed on his feet, turning the question around to his advantage.

The panel, almost as stunned by Oswald's reply as he himself had been by Stuckey's revelations, was momentarily disarmed. Stuckey's fellow cohost came to the rescue, asking Bringuier if he "would like to dispute that point." It turned out the Cuban did—but with his stultifying, heavily accented catalogue of commodity statistics. The pressure was off Oswald, temporarily. Surviving his first, and worst, moment, he established the pattern for the remainder of the debate.

Whatever was going on here, it didn't smack of a man intentionally sabotaging his own organization. On the contrary, he appeared to be fighting doggedly (and effectively, given the circumstances) to salvage leftist honor. Could it be that on the matter of Oswald's New Orleans summer, neither the Posner nor Summers-Scott line was on target? What other possibility *was* there?

For a starter, let's recall the Quiroga visit to Oswald.

What is initially noteworthy about the meeting isn't that Bringuier sent Quiroga to spy on Oswald (since Oswald was also supposedly spying on Bringuier), but the period of time in which it happened. That period was not, as Bringuier and Quiroga claimed in their Warren testimony, *after* the mid-August Trade Mart demonstration. The visit occurred almost a week earlier, Oswald's landlady told the Commission—"right after" his pamphlet scuffle on Canal Street, and thus *before* the Trade Mart event.

The reason the time of Quiroga's visit is important is that the landlady, Mrs. Jesse James Garner, had yet another revelation for the Commission. She told Warren attorney Wesley Liebeler that when Quiroga arrived at her door looking for Oswald, he brought with him a thick stack of FPCC pamphlets, "about 5 inches or 6 inches" high. Bringuier admitted to the Commission that yes, when Quiroga went looking for Oswald he did take a few pamphlets along (an admission forced by his knowledge that Mrs. Garner had seen Quiroga with them). Bringuier's explanation was that Quiroga had picked one or two of the pamphlets off the ground during the scuffle and had brought them with him on his spying expedition, presumably to show how he happened to have heard of Oswald. The account would have made some sense, except that as Mrs. Garner very explicitly noted, it wasn't one or two casual pamphlets Quiroga carried. It was a sheaf five or six inches thick—enough papers to fill a couple of ream boxes, at least.

The contradictions of the Quiroga visit begin to make sense only when we recognize the true likely purpose of his visit: not to "spy" on Oswald, but to *deliver the pamphlets* he would need for his upcoming exercise in political theater at the Trade Mart. This recognition also illuminates the real relationship of Oswald and the DRE in New Orleans. It was not merely spy v. spy, but (for a while, at least) a collaborative arrangement, the two sides appearing to work together for the common purpose of destroying the FPCC's reputation. In actuality, Oswald was playing the dangerous game of the classic double agent—cooperating with the DRE, but only for the higher purpose of penetrating Bringuier's anti-Castro organization. They thought he was one of them; he wasn't. (Later, Bringuier would claim he knew it all along.) What was perhaps more remarkable was that all the while Oswald was reporting to an organization both he and de Mohrenschildt were known to have loathed: the FBI.

CHAPTER SIX

I Was a Junior Crimestopper for the FBI

Three decades after testifying to the Warren Commission, Carlos Bringuier still refers new questioners to this testimony as his definitive statement, made when memory was fresh. But on one important point Bringuier has changed his mind concerning that summer in New Orleans—the result, he says, of years of research and reflection, during which he has written his own Kennedy assassination book (and more recently, in Spanish, a *Libra*-style fact-fiction novel focusing on CIA asset Rolando Cubela). It is mainly Bringuier's perception of Oswald that the years have altered. He no longer believes the ex-Marine was acting under FBI or CIA auspices in New Orleans (a conclusion he'd reached by the time of his Warren testimony), and, having read the Kennedy literature, he finds Oswald a more complex and sympathetic figure than he first supposed, a young man damaged by his relationship to a domineering mother. Not, however, a young man acting alone in a sad fantasy world a la Gerald Posner; on this matter the Cuban parts company with the author of *Case Closed*, a book he otherwise admires. Oswald killed Kennedy, Bringuier says, but he wasn't crazy, and he wasn't alone. He was operating under the control of Cuban intelligence.

"I can't prove this in my legal mind," says ex-lawyer Bringuier, "but in my *other* mind, as an ordinary person, I am certain Castro ordered Kennedy killed. He was a gangster and this was a matter of survival; the CIA was coming after him with all these murder plots. I can understand it." Bringuier's career-long absorption with the evils

163

of Fidel Castro (whose first murder victim, he claims, killed long before the Revolution, was Bringuier's own cousin by marriage, Manolo Castro),[1] though understandable, doesn't inspire great confidence in his objectivity on the subject of Cuban intelligence involvement in the Dallas assassination or with Oswald in New Orleans. As we'll see, Oswald did not murder President Kennedy on the orders of Castro, as Bringuier's "other" mind supposes. One needn't doubt, on the other hand, that Fidel (a name Marina claimed her husband wanted to pin on their second child, if male) was Oz's hero, especially after he'd seen with his own eyes how the Russians had "betrayed" their ideals. The bearded leader's annoying mug was on the wall of the Oswalds' Magazine Street apartment when Uncle Dutz stopped by following his nephew's night in jail, and four years earlier—before Castro had declared himself a Marxist—Oswald was talking late into the night with Marine buddies Nelson Delgado and Jim Botelho about how one day they'd join the Cuban revolution and become famous soldiers of fortune. Botelho believed that Oswald was recruiting for the U.S. government, which at the time backed Castro.

For all that, there is evidence that it was Bringuier's first intuition—that Oswald had some association with the FBI—that may have been closest to the mark. In many ways the postassassination role of Hoover's agents appears to have been more to interfere with, rather than conduct, serious investigation of the president's murder. In a book not otherwise preoccupied with FBI misconduct to this point, we have already seen a number of incidental examples of this behavior: how the Bureau lied about John Elrod's arrest record, its attempts to change Delgado's testimony, the lack of interest in (and destruction of) Oswald's Department of Defense ID, and the deceptive report on Banister's Camp Street office, among others.

It is clear, moreover, that the FBI pattern emerged from the first day of "investigation." Recently released audiotapes of conversations between new president Lyndon Johnson and Bureau director J. Edgar Hoover, held some twenty-four hours after the assassination, show that even then it was Hoover's contention that the case was already solved—that the man Dallas police were holding on the fifth floor of the downtown city jail, Lee Harvey Oswald, had shot Kennedy as a lone-nut assassin.[2] Johnson concurred, and a curtain was drawn shutting out all other investigative directions.[3] It remained only for the Commission, which LBJ would appoint, headed by U.S. Supreme Court Chief Justice Earl Warren, to formalize Hoover's foregone conclusion.

Why Hoover appeared so eager to reach this conclusion has remained puzzling over the years. Simple prudence alone, of which he had more than his share, seemingly should have restrained such a determination until the facts had been thoroughly sifted. "CBS Reports," hosted by veteran Warren apologist Dan Rather, suggested in its assassination anniversary program of November 1993 that the FBI's only cause of embarrassment was the Bureau's failure to notify the Secret Service of the potential danger posed by Lee Harvey Oswald. In actuality, Hoover had a far greater PR problem on his hands, and one from which he may have tried to divert attention by acting with the appearance of dispatch. The problem consisted of a suspicious string of preassassination events involving his federal agency. These events clearly suggested that Oswald served as an FBI informant or operative in both New Orleans and Dallas. With this perspective in mind, let's revisit a few scenes from the last chapter.

We know, first of all, that the day Bringuier claims Oswald first showed up at Casa Roca, August 5, 1963, the New Orleans FBI office had been paying calls around town trying to find the ex-Marine. This search had been undertaken by New Orleans agent Milton R. Kaack at the request of Dallas agent James P. Hosty, who advised the local office in a Teletype dated July 29 that he was "attempting to locate" the Oswalds, whose "last known place of residence was 214 Neely Street, Dallas, Texas, and [who] left giving no forwarding address."[4]

One of Kaack's calls that August 5 was to Reily Coffee. There, Mary Bertucci, a personal secretary, informed the agent that Oswald had worked at Reily as a maintenance man since May 15, and that his address, according to her records, was 757 French Street.[5] (The address was that of Uncle Dutz and Aunt Lillian, with whom Oswald had been staying when he applied at the coffee company.) Kaack's memo, prepared a week after the visit, didn't mention that Oswald hadn't worked at Reily since July 19. It noted, however, that the agent made another inquiry on Oswald on August 5, calling on his ex-landlady, Nina Gardner. Mrs. Gardner told Kaack that the Oswalds lived on her same block, at 4905 Magazine Street, and had been there for several months. The inquiries Agent Kaack made about Oswald on that day (and later) were not made known to the Warren investigators, despite Hoover's assertion to the Commission that he had obtained affidavits from all agents who had contacted Oswald. No affidavit from Milton Kaack was entered into the Warren record.[6]

As we have seen, Oswald tried to infiltrate an organization, Bringuier's DRE, with suspected ties to the Pontchartrain arms cache. The FBI had just shown a sudden interest in the whereabouts of the ex-Marine, tracking him down in New Orleans. Was there a connection between the Hoover agency's undisputed hand in these events and Oswald's attempt to sneak into the DRE nest of his supposed ideological opposite, Carlos Bringuier?

The paper evidence released by the FBI doesn't show such a link, and the Bureau has adamantly denied that any collaborative relationship with Oswald ever existed.[7] As we shall see in chapter 10, there is now persuasive reason to believe that such a relationship did exist, and that it was directly related to the FBI's raid on the DRE arms cache. Despite the years of denials, however, the Camp Street building (see chapter 5) glaringly tied Oswald to Guy Banister, the former Chicago special agent-in-charge—a tie that Warren investigators ignored and that Gerald Posner's *Case Closed* couldn't make disappear. In her account to Anthony Summers (and to the HSCA), Banister's secretary and mistress, Delphine Roberts, reported that her ex-FBI boss employed some strange characters. They included David Ferrie, an airline pilot and private investigator for both Banister and New Orleans mobster Carlos Marcello, and a young ex-Marine whom she believed had use of an office on the second floor. His name was Lee Harvey Oswald.

"He's a nervous fellow, he's confused," she said Banister told her of Oswald—a description eloquent in its cynical terseness and not far off the mark, given the one-time defector's zigzagging quest. Banister viewed this sometime visitor with a kind of amused contempt, gauging from his tone. For some unstated reason, however, Oswald was presently serviceable to Banister's organization—was, in fact, part of it. "He's with us," the private eye reportedly said when the secretary told him she'd seen the young FPCC organizer passing out pro-Castro leaflets in the street. "He's associated with the office."[8]

But the association with Banister wasn't the first such contact between Oswald and the FBI. The evidence that Oswald was an under-cover agent or informant for the federal agency both precedes and follows his New Orleans tenure in the spring and summer of 1963.

The curious story of the FBI's special interest in Oswald picks up back in March of that year. Oswald, then still in Dallas, was contacted by a Bureau counterintelligence agent of the same city, James P. ("Joe") Hosty. The relationship with the burly Dallas agent began on the day before Oswald filled out a money order in the name of A. Hidell and mailed it with an order coupon for a Mannlicher-Carcano rifle to Klein's Sporting Goods in Chicago. The pattern of FBI contact and apparent Oswald "response" would be repeated later, as some of Oswald's most intriguing (and incriminating) activities continued to followed hard on FBI visits. It happened in Dallas, in New Orleans, and again in Dallas a few weeks before the asssasination.

Hosty's documented entrance into Oswald's life, on March 11, 1963, marked a change in the way the Bureau had been handling the returned defector. Prior to that time Oswald had been interviewed twice by Fort Worth agent John Fain soon after the Oswalds arrived in America in the summer of 1962. According to a postassassination FBI summary of the Bureau's Oswald-related activities, Fain had closed his Oswald file.[9]

In March, however, Hosty reopened a file on Oswald, ostensibly because he was assigned the case after Fain retired and had information that Oswald had subscribed to a Communist publication. But the primary issue for Agent Hosty (as he described in his Warren testimony) was the concern for Oswald's employment in a security-sensitive industry. The agent expressed a similar concern in a report dated March 25, 1963, presumably prepared after preliminary investigations of Oswald's activities.[10] An FBI interest in examining this aspect of a former defector's employment wouldn't have been out of line, of course. In March 1963 Oswald was still working at the Dallas graphics firm of Jaggars-Chiles-Stovall, a company with government defense contracts that included the production of labeling for U-2 overflight maps of Cuba. (Indeed, he had started at Jaggars at a time when Russian missiles were first being photographed on the island.)

Despite their apparent legitimacy, however, the reasons Hosty provided for wanting to keep tabs on the ex-Marine appear today to be more of a pretext for making contact with Oswald than an expression of genuine concern with the national security threat he may have posed. The agent's reports of his March 1963 activities related to Oswald make no mention of any inquiries into his Jaggars job.

But on Tuesday, March 12, the day after Hosty reopened Oswald's file—and secured his Neely Street address through a confidential talk with an unknown employee of the postal inspector's office ("protect identity," the agent's report warned)—an event occurred that would figure directly in the assassination of the president of the United States. That day an order in the name of A. Hidell was placed for a rifle from Klein's Sporting Goods of Chicago. The gun was to be shipped to the post office box held by Oswald.

At the time of the order, mail-order gun sales were under investigation by the Senate's Dodd committee. For years, Oswald's alleged purchase of the rifle from Klein's under an assumed name has suggested to some Warren Commission critics that he was performing a task for the government in conjunction with its investigation of the mail-order house.[11] Why, these researchers ask, would Oswald order the Mannlicher-Carcano by mail, leaving a paper trail of the purchase, when he could have bought it (or one of numerous superior weapons) from any Dallas pawnshop for comparable money and with no trail at all—just as John Hinkley was to do almost twenty years later, prior to his attempt on the life of President Reagan?

But there was another important aspect to the order for the rifle from Oswald's post office box.

After the Dealey Plaza assassination, it was noted by the Warren Commission that the portion of the post office box application that authorized persons other than the boxholder to receive mail at the box was missing. Dallas postal inspector Harry Holmes made the false claim to the Commission that postal regulations provided for the destruction of that portion of the box application at the time the box was closed—in this case May 14, 1963.[12] In actuality, the regulations mandated keeping the whole application for two years after closing of the box.[13]

And this wasn't the only problem with the records provided by the Post Office. The receipt for delivery of the firearm to Oswald was never produced, despite the fact that postal regulations for 1963 also mandated the retention of *firearms* delivery records for *four years.*

846.5 RECORDS RETAINED
FOR PERIODS OTHER THAN 1 YEAR
(.53)

Postal Procedures	*Retention Period*
a. Delivery receipts for firearms, and statements by shippers of firearms (Forms 2162,1506).	4 years

What happened to the parcel post receipt for the gun, and more significantly, who signed it? This receipt, showing the signature of the person who received the rifle, should have been readily available to postal inspector Holmes and the Warren Commission—*by law*. More than a postal requirement, the receipt would also have served as the conclusive evidence that placed the assassination weapon in Oswald's hands. How could the government have passed up such a golden opportunity to make its case—indeed, have *gone out of its way* to miss such a chance by deviating from its own regulations—unless, perhaps, by some unstated logic, there was something to be gained by this deviation? What was it, though?

Consider, if it *had* been Oswald who signed the receipt, how eagerly the pro-single-assassin troupe would have rushed to wave it in front of the nation's face, like the Oswald backyard cover on the 1964 *Life*. The signed receipt would have been the perfect graphic representation of Oswald's guilt. In the last analysis there are only two possibilities to account for the failure to do this. One is that the receipt was "lost," a slim chance at best (especially if it bore Oswald's signature), but impossible to deny, given that the U.S. Post Office was involved. The P.O. is undoubtedly a great institution in a lot of ways, but every now and then you read how someone in the Midwest or California has just received a letter from a long-dead relative, mailed about thirty years ago. The other, far more plausible, possibility is that the receipt had been *signed by somebody else,* a person whose name appeared on the post office box application as authorized to receive mail at that box. The name had to appear there for the person who signed the receipt to have been allowed to do so. That was probably why that portion of the post office box application had never materialized either; it would identify this person—possibly an agent of the FBI.

The Post Office may have acted voluntarily, not needing to be reminded that the application would needlessly embarrass the Bureau. The Hoover organization had probably been acting in good faith, as we'll see. The agents couldn't very well have foreseen that the man they were employing for their own purposes—perhaps a mail-order firearms investigation—would wind up the accused killer of the president. It was like a terrible joke, something you wouldn't have imagined in your worst nightmare, if you were J. Edgar Hoover. The Bureau's nervous predicament called for sympathy and cooperation, a bit of the old team spirit. If the Post Office was a little short on this commodity, other steps might have had to be considered, but one way or the other, that portion of the application with the authorized recipients—and the receipt for the rifle—weren't going to see the light of day, and they didn't.

Yet, even if we assume that the Post Office was guilty of nothing more than incompetence, that it "lost" both documents, a problem remains.

The FBI files on the March 1963 investigation of Oswald opened by Hosty contained the information that Oswald had become a subscriber to the Communist party publication *The Worker.* Additional FBI reports reviewed by the Commission showed that in April 1963 Oswald was in contact with the Fair Play for Cuba Committee. We also know from the Bureau's own accounts that the Hoover agency consulted the postal inspector's office in Dallas in its March investigation of Oswald conducted by Hosty. Was the FBI running routine mail checks on the ex-Marine?[14] The presence of an unknown FBI informant in the postal inspector's office in Dallas, and the seemingly infallible collection of Oswald's mail by the Bureau, suggest that either the Bureau routinely accessed Oswald's mail, or that he himself provided copies to the FBI. If either case is true, why did the Bureau not take note of his order of a gun under an assumed name to be sent to his Dallas post office box? The probable answer is that the agents would have—had they themselves not instructed Oswald to initiate the rifle mail-order purchase for their own investigative purposes.

The strange circumstances surrounding the Carcano mail-order purchase add yet another layer of mystery to the ownership of the rifle, particularly in light of the fact that the Dallas police were unable to place the murder weapon in Oswald's hands on the day of the assassination.[15] On that day, former lieutenant Carl Day of the Dallas Police Department lifted Oswald's palm print from the Mannlicher-Carcano, though he didn't send it to Washington along with the rifle in the custody of the FBI on the Friday evening of the assassination. When the FBI couldn't find the print on the rifle, a controversy arose that lives to this day.[16] The pertinent point, however, as Day clarified in October 1993, is that the palm print was *not* made on the day he examined it—November 22, 1963. When Day saw the print that Friday it was already dry, "an old print, weeks if not months old," he told the La Fontaines—the same observation he probably made to Gerald Posner, who chose not to report it.[17]

What the FBI may have had in mind when Hosty arrived on the scene and Oswald immediately ordered a cheap Italian rifle through the mail isn't a question we can definitively answer here, beyond the guesses that have already been offered. Maybe someone will come forward some day and make a great confession, but don't hold your breath, and pray, if it happens, he (or she) isn't sponsored by one of the assassination impresario groups mentioned in chapter 11. The hidden real reason is probably benign, but rather inscrutable, dreamed up by one of the same cultural guardians who decided you shouldn't say "phoned," but "telephonically contacted," in FBI reports. Conjecturing what the thinking had been isn't as useful as simply noting that, for some reason, it seems to have led Agent Hosty to tap the services of a probably reluctant and resentful Oswald in March 1963. Later on, there are indications that the irritable ex-Marine may have grown to tolerate his servitude, to consider the brighter side of the picture, perhaps. He always did like spy stories, and of course adventure and ideology. He was fearless, though a puny fighter. In the end, it may not have been the idea of "working for the FBI" that rankled him so much as Hosty himself, whose "manner was very harsh," according to Robert Oswald, and who "harassed Lee in his interviews," as Marina told this brother-in-law.[18] The relationship with Hosty ended, according to the conventional stories, when Oswald left a threatening note at the agent's office a few weeks before the assassination (chapter 10). The note may not have been a threat at all, however, but a warning.

Two undeniable adolescent themes of Lee Oswald's were his

Marxist sympathies and a fascination with military adventuring. Both were "real," ingrained in his personality, not imposed by the exigencies of some later spy role. Though Oswald could scarcely stand any close association with his mother (like many radicals, his sympathies extended more to the type than the particular), Marguerite had been his object lesson on how capitalism exploited the poor. He'd seen in her struggle for survival, especially during their squalid tenure in the Bronx, the sorry underside of this system, the way it disregarded human misery and treated a sickness of the soul as a form of school truancy. The early poverty hadn't led him to dream of selfish riches, but of Marxist revolution, the great righter of wrongs for the oppressed peoples of the earth. Oswald's preinduction fantasies about the Marines may have resembled scenes from old Blackhawks comic books—stories about an international fraternity of leatherbooted commandos in slick uniforms who lived on an island with a Chinese chef, flew jet fighters, sported the latest assault weapons, and were ready to kick ass on any spot on the globe. The important thing, though, was that for all of their military pizazz, the Blackhawks were good guys at heart and the bane of Fascist-minded thugs and tinhorn dictators everywhere. They used their fab weapons on the side of the downtrodden masses, as Oswald himself no doubt would have done.

If Holden Caulfield wanted beyond all reason to save kids from their inevitable fall from innocence, Lee Harvey Oswald's aspirations were no less high-minded and quixotic. He wanted simply to take part in the Great Struggle for universal human betterment, and by so doing to reach the place with "no borderline between one's own personal world, and the world in general." His longing was a near perfect expression of the religious desire for the death of the self, the part that must be discarded if one is to attain a perfect union with God. Oswald of course replaced God with Marxism, but in all other ways he had the piety, if not the patience, of a saint. He lived his twentieth-century life following a script from an earlier age, as a devout Grail knight in search of the perfect political state. For this quest he was willing to die, as he'd shown in Russia. After the Soviet government's early refusal to let him stay, he attempted suicide twice, the first attempt accompanied by a poetic note (misspelled, as usual) rejecting an existence without meaning. The calamitous scene discovered by his female guide, of the pale Oswald in his blood-tinged bath water, could have been lifted from one of the great tear-jerkers of European romantic literature, *The Sorrows of Young Werther,* which set off an unfortunate continental fad of suicides (the suffering hero had finally shot himself) by sensitive young men foiled by life's cruelties and wearing Werther waistcoats. Oswald's willingness to follow this long-outmoded path appeared to strike a chord in the Russian soul, and the Moscow bureaucrats backed off. They let the volatile defector have his way, keeping close watch on him as a possible CIA plant during his remaining two and a half years in the U.S.S.R.

Whereas the Soviets only puzzled lengthily over Oswald's implications, the pragmatic operatives of America's intelligence agencies more likely saw in the returned scapegrace an available resource, about whom the only important question was not what he "meant," but how he could be put to use. Yet even this question wasn't so easy to answer. As knight and protector of the Marxist faith, ex-Marine Oswald had a knowledge of arms and guerilla tactics (you couldn't have a decent revolution without 'em) and an impressive record of high-stakes risk-taking. He was well steeped, moreover, in the lingo of political fanaticism, having read and argued leftist dogma from the day of his sudden conversion, at age fourteen, with the appearance of the Lady of the El offering her luminous Rosenberg leaflet.

All this was fine, no doubt, but how would you pop the question?

How would a U.S. government agency (and the FBI in particular) recruit, even temporarily, this weirdly intense and supposedly quick-to-sneer young idealist, who by the government's own reckoning was a born rebel and hater of authority? What could Hosty, Banister, or anyone else offer to induce him to collaborate docilely with a "brutal" Bureau that could only be an anathema to his revolutionary soul (the State Police of world capitalism!), and that he and de Mohrenschildt were known to despise? As noted earlier, there are no records yet released to give us this answer—though as we'll see, the trick may have been accomplished in the same way another federal agency possibly persuaded Oswald to undertake a grand Russian adventure—by appealing to his natural interests.

In March of 1963, Hosty may have had the leverage of blackmail, the threat of exposing Oswald's Soviet past to his employer if the defector did not cooperate. Though the story of "hometown boy" Lee Oswald's life in Russia had appeared in the Fort Worth paper shortly after his return from Minsk, no one at the security-sensitive

Dallas company of Jaggars-Chiles-Stovall knew anything about his previous defection to a Communist country. Oswald's bitter complaints to Marina that the FBI interfered with his employment have been commonly understood (by Warren-siders, especially) as typical Oswald excuse-making about losing another job. That may have been true at Reily Coffee, where the Bureau didn't check on him until after he was fired, but not at Jaggars. When Hosty made his sudden appearance, Oswald would have had plenty to worry about, especially if the agent wanted to play hardball.

Yet, five months later in New Orleans, the ex-Marine would be publicly exposed as a defector and Marxist at his WDSU radio debate. He continued his apparent association with the FBI even after this public exposure. Why? Was he simply a true chameleon with a pathological ambivalence, or was he what he usually said he was, a dedicated Marxist who shared with de Mohrenschildt a revulsion with right-wing extremists of the Gen. Edwin Walker—and Guy Banister—variety?

Assuming the latter, it must also be assumed that Oswald swallowed his revulsion for some sufficient reason. What this reason might have been, we'll see shortly. Meanwhile, one preliminary clue is the fact that guns were the apparent topic of every FBI-initiated contact with Oswald. In Dallas it had been a mail-order gun purchase the day after a visit from Hosty. In New Orleans, following the FBI's search for the ex-Marine, as well as contact with Guy Banister, he presented himself to Bringuier as a guerilla expert looking to provide arms training to anti-Castro combatants. Banister, it should also be noted, was a known gunrunner affiliated with the Minutemen, an agent working the heart of the clandestine underground railroad of arms trafficking extending from Texas to Florida. Still later, in November 1963 (and again in the wake of FBI contacts, as we'll note), Oswald would be snooping into the gunrunning underworld of Dallas.

The consistent motif suggests Lee Harvey Oswald may have believed he was participating in an investigation, under FBI auspices, of illegal gun-trafficking activities. It also suggests some of the buttons the Bureau may have pushed to win Oswald's cooperation. One selling point aimed at overcoming his left-wing scruples may have been a "concession" that he would only report on gun-hoarding right-wing subversives: anti-Castro Cubans, paramilitary Minutemen,

Birchers, perhaps American Nazis, Klansmen, and the like—all natural enemies of the genus Oswald. (Such a concession was one that
Hosty, as an investigator of right-wing subversives, would have been
in a position to make.) Whether the FBI, which only grudgingly
cooperated with Kennedy's curtailment of the Secret War on Cuba,
was all that sincere about going after far-right gun freaks is prob-
lematical, to say the least. It probably wasn't.[19] The actual facts of
the matter are secondary, however. It's the illusion we need to work
out first, what Oswald *believed* he was doing.

What he believed, evidently, is that he had been inducted as a kind
of Dick Tracy Junior Crimestopper for the FBI, an informal associate (like de Mohrenschildt with the CIA) "specializing" in illegal
firearms assignments. His letters showed a taste for irony, and Oswald
may have savored this one. He was helping to use the might of the
most dreaded anti-Communist agency in the world against commie-
hating primitives. He may also have been drawn by a boyish delight
in the undercover intrigue and phony ID possibilities of the thing,
sanctioned as part of the Crimestopper package. Scott has suggested
that Oswald and Banister may have been "working for what was in
effect a third force: an intelligence-mafia gray alliance, rooted in
the deep political economy of New Orleans."[20] A safer assumption
is simply that the real purpose of the FBI in recruiting the ex-Marine
was very likely something quite different from his perception.

The name A. J. Hidell was first used in January 1963 when Oswald
used it to order by mail a Smith & Wesson .38 revolver from Seaport
Traders in Los Angeles. As we've seen, the name (sans middle initial) was used again two months later when Oswald ordered, also by
mail, the notorious Mannlicher-Carcano rifle from Klein's Sporting
Goods in Chicago. Not coincidentally, perhaps, in light of Oswald's
apparent gun-trafficking Crimestopper "duties," both Seaport Traders
and Klein's Sporting Goods were being investigated in 1963 by the
ATF as well as by a congressional subcommittee chaired by Sen. (and
ex-FBI agent) Thomas Dodd. Both investigations were seeking to
establish the need for greater control of mail-order gun sales, and
Senator Dodd's subcommittee studied the matter by tracing firearms
through the mail in purchases involving the companies under investigation. Oswald's order of the .38 revolver was dated January 27, just
two days before the opening of the Dodd subcommittee hearings.[21]

The next known occurrence of *Hidell* (following his distribution of undated FPCC pamphlets) came during the ex-Marine's New Orleans incarceration. At this juncture Oswald was supposed to be under the influence of the Louisiana-based Banister, according to conventional conspiracy wisdom—an unjustified assumption, as we'll see. Regardless of this small detail, in a vintage Oswald move on the morning after his arrest (Saturday, August 10), the self-described FPCC organizer voluntarily summoned the FBI to his jail cell. He wanted to make a "report," he announced. To this day, no one has been sure why.

This Oswald shocker was, it should be added, his third of that week. We recall he had already appeared to outrage Carlos Bringuier by blithely handing out Marxist pro-Castro tracts in the street after having introduced himself to the Cuban as a far-right anti-Castro sympathizer. Yet even before Oswald's showdown with Bringuier and his two DRE compatriots, a letter from the ex-Marine to FPCC national director Vincent T. Lee, dated August 1, cast the Canal Street "scuffle" in a still different light. This letter (the same one in which Oswald claimed to have briefly "rented an office as I planned") complained—at least eight days prior to the public disturbance of Friday, August 9—that "through the efforts of some Cuban-exile 'gusanos' [worms] a street demonstration was attacked and we were officially cautioned by the police."[22] With just one slight imperfection (the "officially cautioned" part—Oswald would actually be thrown in jail), the letter predicted the future.

This annoying circumstance has bolstered the arguments of some Warren critics that the New Orleans Oswald was knowingly participating in a charade scripted by the FBI or another government intelligence agency—that he must have been, by extension, a hard-right Castro and Kennedy hater, like Banister and other Camp Street associates. But as we know, the latter assumption, that Oswald could have been anything like Banister, isn't supported by the historical record. Oswald was a leftist from the age of political reason, a Castro idolizer, and a man who according to George de Mohrenschildt frequently expressed admiration for President Kennedy. He was also, as we've seen, a dyslexic letter writer sometimes given to enthusiastic (and self-serving) exaggerations. His false anecdote about the attack by *gusanos* could well have been one of these exaggerations, a small bit of color emphasizing to Vincent Lee the romantic hazards that Oswald was enduring on behalf of their common goal. (The described attack also served as an excuse for his lack of progress, for, as he continued, "this incident robbed me of what support I had leaving me alone.")[23]

The precognitive letter and the later public quarrel with Bringuier on Canal Street were only warm-ups, however, for Oswald's Saturday morning statement, as recalled by New Orleans police lieutenant Francis Martello and translated by FBI agent John Quigley. Oswald, Quigley had written in his report, "was desirous of seeing an Agent and supplying to him information with regard to his activities with the 'Fair Play for Cuba Committee' in New Orleans."[24] This jailhouse call for an FBI agent in order to supply information on the pro-Castro organization was such an "unusual request" that even Oswald-did-it-alone author Priscilla McMillan couldn't help noticing its suspicious implications. She devoted some time to trying to decipher the enigma, musing that "perhaps,"

> as Lee's brother Robert has suggested, it [the request to talk to the FBI] was part of Lee's continuing effort to create mystery and drama around himself. Perhaps he wanted to impress the officers at the police station, encourage them to think that he had been acting as an FBI provocateur and thereby secure an early release. Or perhaps, finding himself in jail for the first time, Lee needed to feel singular and important, and summoning the FBI gave him that feeling. It is even possible that the FBI's lack of overt attention over the past year, relief though it was, had created a feeling of suspense in him and had strained his sense of self-importance.[25]

Priscilla McMillan's succession of guesses is a frank admission that the incident doesn't fit in well with her overall view of Oswald as a disconnected lone-nut assassin. Her candidly tentative tone is in refreshing contrast to the deceptive certainty of a later, less gifted Warren defender, Gerald Posner. For Posner, Oswald's request to talk to the FBI is only "seemingly unusual" and actually "strong evidence there was no association between him [Oswald] and the Bureau." Unable to explain the incident, he declares victory and argues that it supports his premise (as he does in the case of the Oswald

Department of Defense ID card, mentioned only in a footnote). It's probably not bad form as one-upmanship goes, but has nothing to do with the truth of the matter.

What *was* the truth of the matter, though? That hasn't been so easy for anyone, not just Posner, to explain. If, for example, Oswald made a voluntary attempt to report to the FBI, why did he "report" one lie after another? In an hour-and-a-half interview with the agent who came to his cell that Saturday, John Quigley, Oswald omitted from his background his defection to Russia (saying he met and married Marina in Fort Worth), and told an assortment of tales apparently cooked up in his spy-fan imagination. He provided FPCC membership cards to the agent and described five-man cell meetings for the virtually nonexistent New Orleans chapter, its members known to one another only by their first names.

And the true leader of the local group, he told Quigley, was "A. J. Hidell," a man he had never met in person, though he had spoken with him on the phone on several occasions.

The hard thing was rationalizing why Oswald would have lied just this way—that, and a related, equally relevant point: did he lie as the deceiver or the deceived? Had he been encouraged by Guy Banister, his New Orleans FBI contact, to "declare" himself to the FBI? Given all that Banister would have stood to gain from this, and the opportunities he would have had to do so (as attested by secretary Delphine Roberts, who placed Oswald and her boss together on several occasions), it would be almost inconceivable if Banister *hadn't* tried to put his young Camp Street associate up to calling in the FBI to tell them about the FPCC. Indeed, Oswald's direct report to the Bureau made sense only as someone's idea of what sort of action could be guaranteed to be immediately and devastatingly damaging to the FPCC and other pinko scumbags—the kind of thing Banister or Bringuier, but not Oswald, spent time creatively daydreaming about.

As a scheme of that sort, the talk with Agent Quigley appeared to constitute part of an incredibly successful one-man campaign to discredit leftists and the FPCC in particular. Consider the following results, all documented by researchers. First, with the Fair Play membership cards that Oswald showed to the agent, the former Marine discredited by association with himself both the FPCC and its national director, Vincent Lee. The "association" with Oswald would prove to be even more damaging later that month, with his exposure as a Marxist and Soviet defector in the WDSU radio debate, followed by his stunningly incriminating letter to the Central Committee of the American Communist Party (dated August 28, 1963), in which he blandly explained that "here in New Orleans, I am secretary of the local bra[n]ch of the 'Fair Play for Cuba Committee,' a position which, frankly, I have used to foster communist ideals."[26]

The copy of a Corliss Lamont pamphlet that Oswald turned over to Quigley—the kind of tract Lee sometimes passed out on street corners—had a similar negative effect. It generated an appendix in the Oswald New Orleans FBI file that linked the FPCC to the Communist party via the alleged remarks of former CP head Earl Browder, who (the appendix said) "had referred to Corliss Lamont as one of the 'four prides' of the CP because Corliss Lamont was ready to cooperate with any Communist front or any Communist cause."[27] And Oswald's lies to Martello about knowing Leonard Reissman—also incorporated into his FBI file—could not help but tarnish (again by association with the Marxist Oswald) the questionable peacenik-type causes with which the Tulane professor and other liberal colleagues were linked, e.g., integration and the Quaker New Orleans Council for Peaceful Alternatives.[28]

In surveying this awesome devastation, perhaps the result of a single mammoth Banister/Bringuier brainstorm, we shouldn't lose sight of the fact that of all the persons Oswald may have harmed with his jailhouse interview, he harmed no one more than himself. When he lied about "A. J. Hidell," proclaiming him the true head of the local Fair Play chapter and providing Martello and Quigley with an FPCC membership card in Oswald's name (and "authenticated" by Hidell's signature as the issuer of the card), he was continuing the false paper trail he had begun in Dallas earlier that year with his mail-order gun purchases.[29] The Hidell information learned by Martello was promptly passed on to the 112th Army Military Intelligence Group, which opened a file under the name Harvey Lee Oswald and A. J. Hidell.[30] On the day of the assassination, Col. Robert E. Jones at the 112th MIG immediately discovered the Martello-initiated file on Hidell as well as its link to Oswald, a fact that Jones communicated to the FBI by 3:15 that afternoon, less than three hours after the Dealey Plaza shooting.[31] Jones informed the FBI that Oswald was carrying a phony ID in the name of Hidell, though how the colonel knew this has never been determined; the phony Selective

Service Hidell card allegedly found in Oswald's possession following the assassination was not in evidence in New Orleans, and the card that *was* in evidence—the FPCC card "signed" by Hidell—was supposedly a legitimate issue. Even in sworn testimony to the HSCA in 1978, released in 1994, Jones never cleared up this matter. He claimed the army learned that "Oswald *was* using Hidell as an alias" from the New Orleans police; this is entirely false as confirmed by Lt. Francis Martello of the NOPD in 1993. In any event, the Hidell reference in Oswald's report to the New Orleans agent proved a fatal confession, "establishing" him later, via the forged Selective Service card, as the Hidell who purchased both the rifle reportedly used to kill President Kennedy and the revolver used to kill Officer Tippit.[32]

What did all these contradictions add up to? Given that none of the leading players were clinically deranged or even pathologically neurotic, there should exist some hidden line of reasoning, a consistent pattern of some sort, that tied the pieces together. Where was it?

The contradictions clustered around the unassimilable thought of Oswald and Banister (more so than Oswald and the less-primitive Bringuier) "working together." The two men clearly belonged to separate universes. If Oswald's alien quirkiness gave Banister a rosy sense of superiority, though, the private eye erred in this assessment, seriously underestimating his office visitor. The real question was how Oswald, so picky about ideological matters, could ever have consented to any alliance with this particularly noxious capitalist gargoyle—especially when he knew it would only help Banister achieve his corrupt ends and betray everything Oswald supposedly stood for. This was a nagging problem, not fully allayed by just considering the kinky ironic satisfactions of a short-term whirl with the commie-bashing FBI. Oswald was a "serious" young man, not someone looking for an entertaining life, like Marina in George de Mohrenschildt's unpublished manuscript. In Oswald's world, the most important things of all were ideological convictions, and you didn't mess around with these. You didn't sell them out, or shuffle them around at the behest of an uninspiring thug like Guy Banister. It would be profane, like trying to offer money to an angel, an insult of such baseness that Scripture celebrated it as the only unforgivable sin.

Finally, as if we didn't have enough already, there was yet another problem to consider and try to incorporate into the great enigma of

Lee Harvey Oswald. Was Oswald sufficiently distanced from his aspirations to see that the use of a Corliss Lamont pamphlet could be turned against him? Or that a letter in which he "frankly" (and who was to say it wasn't?) opened his heart to that sacred fount, the American Communist Party, could prove the ruination of the FPCC? While we're at it, was he really intent on tripping up a nice-guy liberal professor like Reissman, or was he just doing some more PR tap dancing, trying to impress by his elegant connections? In short, would all of this business, so "clear" to us now long after the fact, have been as clear in its real-time implications to an intelligent but self-absorbed dogmatist like Oswald . . . a Bobby Fischer-like idiot savant who may have had trouble seeing that if you wanted to fool Bringuier, it was probably a good idea not to wander around downtown a couple of days later, passing out pro-Castro pamphlets?

Enough; the envelope, please.

When Guy Banister reportedly reassured Delphine Roberts that she didn't have to worry about Lee Oswald because "he's associated with the office," the old ex-agent might have added, for accuracy's sake, that he hadn't developed the association; Oswald had sought *him* out.

Leaving for Louisiana in April 1963, the ex-Marine had passed into the hands of Agent Warren deBrueys, Hosty's counterpart in the New Orleans FBI office. A clerk in the office would note that deBrueys kept a confidential informant's file on Oswald (chapter 10), and indeed Oswald was almost certainly reporting to him during the final summer of his life. As surprising was the probable target of the former defector's covert scrutiny: the gunrunning New Orleans right wing, including ex-FBI agent Guy Banister himself (though no longer an official agent, Banister served as the FBI contact for such men as Sergio Arcacha Smith, whom we will meet in a later chapter).[33]

In the eyes of loyal company soldiers like deBrueys and Hosty, recent events and Bureau directives would have cast Banister's suspected activities in a new, unfavorable light. As we recall, Hosty probably "recruited" or otherwise dragooned Oswald into participating in a covert check of mail-order gun dealers. Looking into gun violations was a normal part of Hosty's FBI specialty, which, he told Mary, was "the investigation of mostly right-wing subversives, like Minutemen."[34]

Not exactly off the topic, Banister had been looking like nothing so much as a right-wing subversive for years at the time Oswald arrived in the Crescent City.[35]

Despite his affiliation to his old Bureau (maintained now with contract assignments), the private eye/ex-agent was the alleged organizer of the right-wing paramilitary Minutemen in the state of Louisiana.[36] More importantly, he was a probable gunrunner mixed up with anti-Castro exile groups just at a time when President Kennedy was calling on Hoover's Bureau to crack down on violators of a post-missile-crisis agreement with Nikita Khrushchev to lay off Castro. Banister topped off his dangerous-right-wing-nut profile with ties to Mafia leader Carlos Marcello (whom he tried, together with attorney Wray Gill, to keep from being deported to Guatemala) and virulent white-supremacist views, shared with secretary Delphine Roberts.[37] Behind the misleading doors of the Camp Street building, the private eye ground out a racist periodical, *Louisiana Intelligence Digest,* and supported young segregationists by letting them store their anti-integration picket signs in his office.[38]

If Kennedy's hands-off-Cuba credo was reviled by anti-Castro exiles and intriguers like Frank Sturgis (the CIA maintained a campaign of assassination attempts on Castro through the very day Kennedy himself was assassinated),[39] journeymen FBI agents like deBrueys and Hosty adhered to the official line. It was in enforcement of the administration's neutrality policy that the FBI would raid the anti-Castro arms camp near Lake Pontchartrain that summer, while Oswald was in New Orleans. In this operation, Banister and the journeyman loyalists almost surely found themselves on opposite sides. The New Orleans private eye, completely off the rails where Bureau policy was concerned, had probably himself been one of the major facilitators for the camp, a Mafia-CIA-Cuban-exile collaboration. He had a gunrunning history and ties to all of the participants, and his Camp Street location was the Grand Central Station of the arms-smuggling underground railroad reaching from Dallas to Miami.

If Oswald was in New Orleans to keep tabs on Banister and other right-wing subversives—and there is every indication he did just that, haunting the private eye's corridors and associating prominently with Bringuier—he still would have needed a cover activity. For that Oswald had the Fair Play for Cuba campaign. As everyone now agrees, the New Orleans Fair Play Committee existed only as a concept to be exploited, not as an actual entity. To Banister, the FPCC was no more than an entertaining front organization run by a kook whom the ex-agent encouraged by providing an upstairs office to store leaflets and other paraphernalia. To Bringuier, the mythical local chapter, complete with a pro-Marxist former defector at its head, provided the perfect anti-Castro propaganda campaign. To Oswald, the hollow organization was a way of adding to his legend as a pro-Castro activist (a "legend" that in his case reflected his true sympathies), and more immediately, his entry ticket to the Banister/DRE lair. The ticket came at a bargain price, ideologically speaking. Since the FPCC chapter didn't exist, if Oswald "betrayed" it he was betraying essentially nothing.

It was against this confusing background that Oswald would develop his seemingly collaborative relationship with the DRE. The relationship may have been planned by deBrueys from the beginning, or it may have been one of Oswald's unpredictable ad libs, like marrying Marina in Russia. In either case, the testimony of Mrs. Jesse James Garner about Carlos Quiroga's pamphlets (chapter 5) strongly suggests that the former Marine conspired with the DRE against the expendable FPCC (but not against Marxism, which he defended vigorously in his radio debate, he might have quibbled) in order to penetrate Bringuier's organization for the FBI. That the young informant succeeded in the latter effort is further suggested by the FBI's Pontchartrain raid—made possible, it would appear, by information Oswald gleaned from Banister and/or the gunrunning exiles of the DRE. As for the anecdote of Oswald's heavy-handed post-Pontchartrain "infiltration" attempt at Casa Roca, we should keep in mind that it comes down to us only from Carlos Bringuier, a man who like Silvia Odio (chapter 9) may have a lot to hide where Oswald is concerned. Bringuier's purpose in repeatedly trumpeting the alleged treachery at Casa Roca may indeed be much like that of Silvia's famous hallway tale, precisely to obfuscate the actual nature of a prior relationship with the ex-Marine.

As noted earlier, the double game was a dangerous one for Oswald. This would have been particularly true if, as one might expect, word gradually started to seep through via Banister's FBI grapevine about the identity of the Pontchartrain informant. Oswald's short-term gain would then convert to long-term losses, and in fact things would go downhill for him after his immersion

in the Camp Street milieu during the summer of 1963. By the end
of that summer he had apparently caught Banister's evil eye, or
worse, aroused the passionate animosity of the fanatically anti-Castro DRE. Later, as we'll see, even after he was back in Dallas with
Hosty, the long arms of his New Orleans antagonists would reach
out and enfold the fluttering ideological moth, Lee Harvey
Oswald.

It was after ten in the morning on a late summer day in 1963
when the glossy black Caddy—a limousine, some people said—
pulled up and parked near the voter registrar's office to take in the
unusual proceedings. The town of Clinton, Louisiana, some 1,500
strong, was undergoing a solemn and historical social transforma-
tion, part of the second Reconstruction then sweeping through the
South. A voter registration drive aimed at enrolling black citizens
was in progress. The event, one of the first efforts of its kind, was
spearheaded by a group of "outside agitators," the Congress of
Racial Equality, and had brought out virtually every adult in the
community. The all-white police, town marshal, and other local officials were conspicuously present, backed by an unsolicited posse of
angry white spectators. Together, they kept an intimidating eye on
the CORE organizers and the long line of rural blacks, extending
out into the dusty sidewalk, waiting to fill out forms in the registrar's
office.

The parked late-model Cadillac wasn't the kind of car you often
saw in Clinton. Neither were its two occupants, who continued sitting
in the plush comfort and staring impassively at the milling locals.
The man at the driver's wheel was a distinguished-looking silver-
haired gent with a ruddy complexion and fine manners, howdying
pleasantly to everyone who passed his window. The other occupant,
though quiet, was an unforgettable sight. He appeared to be wearing
a rumpled wig and had eyebrows that were painted on like two black
scrawls above his mouselike eyes.[40]

It wasn't long after the car's arrival that town marshal John Manchester noted the odd pair. Suspecting they were federal agents who
had come to Clinton to check up on the voter registration efforts,
Manchester decided to do a little checking himself. He called in the
limo's license-tag number to the state police and found out the auto
was registered to the International Trade Mart.[41]

Five and a half years later, Manchester would testify in a packed courtroom that the "easy-talking" man he saw behind the wheel—and not from a distance, but after he'd sauntered over to the car and chatted a while—was the defendant (and director of the same New Orleans trade mart), Clay Shaw.[42] A succession of other Clinton witnesses similarly picked out Shaw as the man sitting at the wheel of the limousine that day, and identified his shotgun-seat companion, from photos, as David Ferrie.[43] In the end Shaw was acquitted, of course—and the national reputation of prosecutor Jim Garrison ruined—but not because the jurors didn't believe the Clinton incident, which was well established in court. They couldn't find any motivation, however, for the respected trade mart director to have taken part in a conspiracy to assassinate the president.[44]

Before town marshal Manchester's attention was caught by the two men in the black Cadillac, there had been a third occupant in the car. Curiously, this man had left the deluxe vehicle and taken a humble place in the long line of persons waiting to be registered. He was one of only two whites in the line, and the tense onlookers took hard note of him. Two months later, following the assassination, they recognized his face on TV and learned that his name was Lee Harvey Oswald.

Whereas some writers have quibbled over whether the driver of the limo was really Clay Shaw (as Garrison believed, but not Anthony Summers, who argues for another hulking gray-haired suspect, Guy Banister),[45] there's little question that the others in the car were Oswald and Ferrie—except in the mind of Posner, as we'll see. Thus, former HSCA investigator Gaeton Fonzi notes in his recent book, *The Last Investigation*: "The House Assassinations Committee, for instance, found several very credible witnesses who saw Oswald during this period [August 21 to September 17] in Clinton, Louisiana [with] David Ferrie, an anti-Castro activist. . . . The Assassinations Committee could not determine what Oswald was doing in Clinton, but there was no doubt he was there."[46]

Another government employee with a similar certainty was Reeves Morgan, a Louisiana state legislator in September 1963. Morgan too had seen Oswald in Clinton during the voter registration drive—indeed, had received a visit from him—and dutifully reported this fact to the FBI immediately after the Dealey Plaza tragedy. The agent whom Morgan notified thanked him but said the Bureau already

knew of Oswald's visit to the Clinton area, the former legislator testified under oath.[47] Even the FBI, apparently, thought so public a
spectacle was hard to deny.

Oswald's visit to Morgan had occurred after the ex-Marine
stopped at the shop of yet another Clinton witness, town barber Ed
McGhehee. Here the story struck another Kafkaesque chord. As
McGhehee was cutting Oswald's hair, the young man struck up a conversation, telling the barber a bit about himself. He showed him, for
example, his Marine discharge card and mentioned he was trying to
land a job at a nearby hospital in the town of Jackson—presumably
the reason he was neating up his hair. McGhehee explained that
this institution was a mental hospital, a fact that seemed to astonish
(though not discourage) Oswald, and suggested he seek assistance
from the state representative for the parish, Reeves Morgan. The
Clinton barber further advised that Oswald might stand a better
chance of getting the job if he registered to vote in the parish. Later
the same day Oswald made the recommended visit to Morgan's
house, where the legislator also told him he could improve his
chances of finding employment at the Jackson hospital by registering
as a voter.[48]

Thus the widely witnessed registration attempt by Oswald apparently followed these contacts with McGhehee and Morgan, and
according to them was done for a reason no one could have possibly predicted—to pave the way for a job at a nearby mental hospital.
That Oswald did in fact apply at the Jackson hospital during this
period was later verified by Summers and Garrison investigator
Andrew Sciambra, based on interviews with hospital personnel.[49]

But again, what do we make of all this?

What Garrison made of it was that Oswald's "sponsors" were busily
adding to the incriminating legend they were inventing for the former Marine. He speculated that "a few weeks of menial work" at the
Jackson mental hospital

> would have been enough to complete the picture of Oswald wan-
> dering haplessly from one job to another, each more obscure
> than the last. With a bit of luck and a little orchestration, it might
> even have been possible—with a switch of cards from 'employee'
> to 'patient'—to have the right psychiatrist at Jackson describe
> the problems he had in treating this strange outpatient named
> Lee Oswald.[50]

Summers, though disputing some parts of Garrison's analysis, agrees that Oswald legend-building was probably involved in the Clinton episode. The visit by the threesome in the black Caddy, says the English conspiracy writer, may have been part of an FBI operation to intimidate blacks and thwart the civil rights movement (Clinton whites, by contrast, believed the feds were on the side of the CORE activists), in the process linking Oswald "with yet another left-wing cause [integration]" by placing him in line with the CORE members as a tacit supporter. The long-term impression, Summers adds, is of "an Oswald being manipulated by forces representing the precise opposite of his public posture," forces with "monstrous connections" to both the Mafia and government intelligence.[51]

But the significance of Clinton, Louisiana—an Oswald adventure never presented to the Warren Commission—isn't to be found in any one of the various conspiratorial spins it can sustain; these are legion, and historians can work out the details later. Its significance, rather, is in the hardwire connection the episode establishes between Oswald and David Ferrie—that underworld Renaissance man with multicultural talents as gay exotic, mad scientist, contemplative seminarian, fearless pilot, mega patriot, Kennedy hater par excellence, anti-Castro wild man, Mafia employee, and government intelligence operative. As in the case of the Camp Street building, this dangerous connection isn't one any self-respecting Warren defender can afford to admit into the canon of Oswaldiana; it must be extirpated root and branch, and Gerald Posner devotes six pages of *Case Closed* to the attempt.[52]

"The first problem arises over the time of the purported visit," Posner tells us—an announcement, incidentally, already tantamount to an admission of desperation. When the facts aren't on your side, the lawyers' maxim goes, you "argue the law," i.e., look for loopholes.

One such loophole that attorney Posner hopefully seizes on in trying to overcome the numerous credible witnesses who placed Oswald in Clinton is that the "time" was wrong; it couldn't have been in September. The visit to Clinton had to have occurred, for Posner's purposes, in October, a month when Oswald was no longer in Louisiana. Posner makes his claim for October on the basis of such matters as the fact that town barber McGhehee said he cut Oswald's hair on a day that "was kind of cool," and that state legislator Morgan "recalled lighting the fireplace."[53] In fact, however, the Clinton episode is calibrated to the CORE voter registration drive, which was known to have occurred in August or September.[54]

Ironically, while attempting to discredit Clinton voter registrar Henry Palmer (the man who "gave the most potentially damaging testimony identifying Oswald"), Posner ends by adding to the evidence that Oswald indeed was the man Palmer talked to that day.

We may recall that the former Marine was reported to have shown—somewhat curiously, since there was no apparent reason except perhaps to confirm his presence in the town—a discharge card (or Certificate of Service in the U.S. Marine Corps) with his name on it to barber Ed McGhehee. Later, Oswald would also show a card to Palmer when the registrar asked him for identification. As Palmer recalled in a 1978 interview with Anthony Summers, the applicant took out not a discharge card this time, but a "U.S. Navy ID card" bearing the name "Lee H. Oswald."[55]

Posner cites this Summers interview with Palmer as a prelude to switching into search and destroy mode. The Warren pit bull wants to show that whatever Palmer may have said to Summers in 1978, he said something devastatingly different eleven years earlier "in his 1967 statement to Garrison's office." Among the things Palmer said *then,* says Posner, was that "Oswald produced a 'cancelled Navy I.D. card' and that Oswald told him he had been living in Jackson for six months with a doctor from the hospital."[56]

The last part of Oswald's alleged statement has no more consequence than any of the other minor contradictions Posner dredges up in his six pages seeking to discredit the Clinton testimony. Oswald may or may not have said he lived with a doctor for six months in Jackson, and if he *did* say it he was lying. Nevertheless, Oswald's possible connection with the doctor at the mental hospital, identified in the notes of *Life* reporter Richard Billings as a Cuban exile, Dr. Francisco Silva, provides an interesting link to a group of Cuban doctors at a state mental hospital near Dallas, as we shall see in chapter 9.

Yes, Oswald had lied in other circumstances—to FBI agent Quigley about Hidell and the five-man FPCC cell meetings—but so what? The first part, however, about the *cancelled* Navy ID card, is an extremely interesting find, for which we owe Posner a debt of gratitude.

As we now know, none of the Oswald military cards included in the Warren exhibits bears a cancellation. There *is* one card, however—

not included in the exhibits or ever shown to the Warren investigators—that is "cancelled" not once, but twice. This is ID card No. N (for Navy) 4,271,617, the Department of Defense Form 1173 discussed in chapter 3. The apparent cancellations on the DoD ID are probably circular postmarks, one superimposed over the other. The clearer postmark is dated October 23, 1963. The previous postmark beneath it has only three legible letters: *JUL,* for July. Since October 23 would have been too late for a Clinton debut (Oswald was already back in Dallas by then), the cancellation that Palmer believed he saw on the "Navy ID" was probably the July postmark, though whether of 1963 or an earlier year remains unknown.[57]

In any case, the presence of Oswald in Clinton, Louisiana (and the connection this presence establishes between him and David Ferrie) remains today not just secure, but in better shape than when Posner set out to dismantle it. Not only has he contributed evidence by bringing the Department of Defense ID into the Clinton picture, but Ferrie, the man he said had never been in the Civil Air Patrol with Oswald, showed up together with fifteen-year-old Lee in a CAP photograph first seen publicly in a 1993 "Frontline" documentary. Despite the obvious differences between the ascetic Oswald and the lurid Ferrie, it may be that these two quirky men were also linked by a common fate. Both may have been, as Berkeley author and academic Peter Dale Scott has suggested, expendable "patsies" whose primary intelligence service was self-incrimination. "Ferrie," says Scott, "was most probably in the same position as Oswald: an employee of a private investigator, who at some point was hired, probably unwittingly, to create a record or 'legend' falsely linking himself to the assassination."[58]

CHAPTER SEVEN

You Don't Know Me

> You probably don't know me now, but you will.
>
> JACK RUBY, November 21, 1963
> (to Assistant D.A., Dallas County, Texas)

What would a discreet gentleman like George de Mohrenschildt, a high-strung Haitian banker named Clemard Charles, and Jack Ruby, a low trader in women's flesh, have in common? It was an avocation; all were involved, on the side, in gunrunning—an early sixties kind of rage, apparently, before dope and hippiedom kicked in following the Dealey Plaza tragedy. Running guns may have been a patriotic imperative for some members of the military, who facilitated the sourcing problem by cooperating covertly in the looting of armories. The Terrell break-in prior to the Thunderbird crash of Lawrence Miller and Donnell Whitter had all the earmarks of an inside job, and if so was only one of a string of similar armory thefts from Ohio to the Rio Grande.[1] The stolen weapons were seen as ending up, via an underground railroad of smugglers, where they'd do the country most good: in the hands of anti-Castro Cubans waging a Secret War, with U.S. intelligence support, against the Soviet-backed island dictatorship. There was also money to be made, of course; guns were the risky but profitable cocaine of the time. The mob was interested in any such venture, and Dallas hustler Jack Ruby scored his well-witnessed share. The witnessed accounts were ignored by the Warren Commission, however, since they could not be true: as far as they knew, Jack Ruby was not a gunrunner.

191

Ironically, George de Mohrenschildt, whose job in Dallas had been to keep a close eye on Oswald, became himself a subject of scrutiny shortly after his final separation from the former defector. On April 19, 1963, the week before Oswald set out alone on a bus to New Orleans, George and Jeanne left Dallas for a longer intelligence-related journey with stops at Washington, New York, and Philadelphia. Ten days after this departure, a CIA memo noted that an unidentified agency case worker (the name was blanked out) requested an "expedite check of George de Mohrenschildt."[2]

In mid-May, while the de Mohrenschildts were away, a private eye showed up in their Dallas neighborhood. For a couple of days he grilled neighbors and acquaintances of the couple, and trolled for dirt in police records, credit reports, and even old high-school files of de Mohrenschildt's daughter Alexandra. When the search was called off by one of two men named James Donovan, the unidentified gumshoe left behind a *National Enquirer*-worthy report titled simply "Re: George de Mohrenschildt." It was discovered by Mary thirty years later in the Dallas police files.

The detective's report provides a fascinating glimpse of the de Mohrenschildts' unconventional conduct, which had disturbed some residents in the conservative enclave of University Park. Though a friend of the rich and powerful, the baron shared Oswald's contempt for bourgeois values. He was considered a "Bohemian type individual," according to the report, even by the fellow Russian emigré who had sponsored his membership in the exclusive Petroleum Club, Paul Raigorodsky. The latter also told the snoop that George had "stopped playing around with women and the International set" and had been talking for several months about moving to Haiti, where he planned to "go into the hemp business and also do some oil development." De Mohrenschildt had shown Raigorodsky letters from oppressive dictator Papa Doc Duvalier "which were cordial in nature," and invited his friend to "put some money" in the Haitian ventures; Raigorodsky declined.

In the meantime, the de Mohrenschildts were three months behind in the rent on their Dickens Street apartment, which, the report claimed, was "generally ill kept," with the beds "practically on the floor, and maintained in keeping with their Oriental or beatnik type of life."[3] A woman neighbor who occupied the second-floor apartment directly across the hall told the detective that the couple liked "to entertain various types of people, both upper and lower social level, and that they appear to be highly educated—speaking several languages." The neighbor noted that Jeanne frequently let dishes pile up in the sink, but was "the type of person who can prepare a meal amid such disorder without concern or difficulty."[4]

George and Jeanne, early fitness nuts who spent plenty of time outdoors, scandalized at least some observers with their lack of inhibitions. "Mrs. de Mohrenschildt normally wears a bunny type bikini and seems to shower her affection on their two Chihuahua dogs,"[5] the investigator learned from landlord Josh Mayo. A captain in the University Park PD said he frequently saw the pair walking to and from the tennis court and that "they were always scantily clad, and in fact, Mrs. de Mohrenschildt had constituted somewhat of a traffic hazard by virtue of her abbreviated costume and physical characteristics."[6]

Mr. and Mrs. Mayo supposedly came in for a further shock when their liberated tenants returned from their Central American "walking trip" and showed them a movie of their exploits in the wilds. "The entire film was replete with scenes taken of both George and his present wife nude while they were bathing in various creeks and rivers." A more lurid version of de Mohrenschildts' south-of-the-border antics was related by a man officing at the Tower Petroleum Building. He reportedly told the investigator that George showed him a movie of a trip the baron made to Mexico with a Dallas geologist, Herbert Riley, and that the movie included scenes of Riley and de Mohrenschildt "dancing naked around a car in which a prostitute was seated naked in an extremely lewd position." George "also showed numerous photos of male nudes and bragged of wearing his wife's panties," the Tower Petroleum informant claimed.[7]

Happily for our peace of mind about the baron's character, it turned out that the unidentified private eye who made this report was identified in 1993 through FBI file releases obtained by Idaho academic and assassination researcher Larry Haapanen. The author of the unflattering de Mohrenschildt report was Bill Murphy, a "local [i.e., Dallas] detective" who carried out his investigation "in regard to a law suit in which George [de Mohrenschildt] was involved with a previous wife."[8] The ex-wife, who in 1963 resided in Philadelphia, was Wynne Sharples, represented by a City of Brotherly Love lawyer named R. Winfield Baile. George and Wynne were in legal combat at the time over custody of their preteen daughter Nadia, who suffered from cystic fibrosis. An FBI Teletype dated February 27, 1964 showed that Baile had a correspondent attorney in the exclusive Dallas enclave of Highland Park, James P. Donovan.[9] The local detective, Murphy, presumably on instructions from Donovan, had gone to known enemies of the de Mohrenschildts, asking informants whether they considered the free-spirited couple "the proper type people to take care of a sick child." The February Teletype contained another intriguing note about the Highland Park Donovan: he was recollected by Baile as "an ex-special agent of the FBI."[10] We'll return to the mystery of the Dallas lawyer in a moment. For now, it's sufficient to note that the Murphy report was not the result of a disinterested investigation, but plainly designed to advance the interests of Donovan's (and Baile's) client by demonstrating the unsuitability of de Mohrenschildt as custodian of Nadia.

After the assassination, the FBI had performed its own background check on George de Mohrenschildt, as a report dated March 6, 1964 showed.[11] Not surprisingly, the report painted a somewhat different picture from Murphy's anticustody tract. The couple's former landlords, the Mayos, indicated in this version that the "only complaint [Mrs. Mayo] had with regard to the de Mohrenschildts was that they had two obnoxious small dogs which ruined a carpet." If the couple hadn't left owing a month's rent, "they would have been considered very good tenants." And though the Mayos "attended a movie at the de Mohrenschildts' home" that showed a walking trip, nothing was made of it by the landlords except that George and Jeanne were "'out of the ordinary' tenants," people who "could not be condemned after you got to know them."[12]

The fact that the Murphy report was apparently designed to show the de Mohrenschildts in the worst possible light didn't end its interest, however. For all its aspersions on the baron's lifestyle, the report acknowledged that his credentials were verified by a "confidential source" at the Republic National Bank. The Russian had "maintained a satisfactory customer relationship" with Republic, which had extended him both secured and unsecured credit. He had the right contacts and degrees, and "was known to Dun and Bradstreet." In the previous month, April 16, 1963, the bank had written a letter of introduction, attesting to de Mohrenschildt's authenticity and worthiness as a client, to a bank in Port-au-Prince. As bottom line, Murphy "believed that [the bank's] letter may lend significance that [de Mohrenschildt] was, or still may be, planning to go to Haiti."[13]

The May 1963 background report of private eye Bill Murphy was dated two weeks after a CIA memo of April 29 had ordered an "expedite check" of George de Mohrenschildt.[14] The CIA memo had also made reference, though obliquely, to Haiti. The "interest in de Mohrenschildt," the memo noted, "coincided with the earlier portion of [de Mohrenschildt's] trip [east] and the info would suggest that possibly [name blanked out] and de Mohrenschildt were possibly in the same environment in Washington, D.C., circa April 26, 1963."[15] The agency's concern, in other words, was with whatever de Mohrenschildt was doing with some mystery man in Washington in late April 1963. As it happened, the man de Mohrenschildt was known to have done his main business with in Washington during that spring was Clemard Charles, a Haitian banker. It was on this relationship—and the baron's involvement in Haiti—that the CIA was focusing, as we'll see again in a moment.

Meanwhile, though, an "expedite" check wasn't something you waited almost a year for; it wouldn't have been the FBI background check of March 1964. Was it the check made by Murphy two weeks after the CIA memo, then? Was the vital part of his information the fact that de Mohrenschildt was following through on his plans to go to Haiti, and was this fact intentionally buried in the mundane slanders of a lawyer's brief, disguised as a dry banking detail?

Were these people *that* wily? Didn't they have anything better to do?

Maybe not; there were still more twists. Though private detective Murphy's investigation of de Mohrenschildt was "still in progress," his report complained, it was abruptly "terminated at 2:30 P.M. on May 17, 1963, upon the receipt of instruction from Mr. James Donovan, attorney."[16] The termination of Murphy's services occurred on the same day the U.S. suspended diplomatic relations with Haiti (an event accompanied by evacuation of embassy personnel and a threat by American ambassador Raymond Thurston to bring in the Marines).[17] Mary had learned more on this matter when she first sent the Murphy report to Larry Haapanen. Larry pointed out that the name of the man who had apparently ordered the investigation, James Donovan, was a familiar one to many students of the Kennedy era. Donovan was a prominent New York lawyer who represented

Russian spy Rudolph Abel in his trial for espionage. He had negotiated the exchange of Abel for American U-2 spy Gary Powers and the release of Americans held in Cuban prisons on espionage charges by the Castro government. The CIA once planned to use Donovan in a hare-brained scheme to infect Castro with tuberculosis using a contaminated diving suit. (The Cuban leader had foiled the schemers by surfacing unscathed in an uncontaminated suit Donovan had already given him.) Donovan, anyway, had manifest ties to the intelligence community, Larry emphasized.

And so he did—the New York Donovan.

As we've noted, though, there was a second James Donovan, also a lawyer, who practiced in Dallas in 1963. This James Donovan, who was also originally from New York, was listed in the city telephone directory and in the state bar, which showed him to hold a temporary Texas license. It was a slightly unusual note, since lawyers, unless practicing federal law, don't often leave the states where they are originally licensed and trained. The Texas Donovan wasn't practicing federal law, as we know. He was representing Wynne Sharples in a routine custody case, in pursuit of which he had ordered a routinely slanted background check by a private detective.

According to former *Houston Post* reporter Lonnie Hudkins, the New York high-powered Donovan made frequent visits to Dallas, and in fact "shared an office" with the Texas (Wynne Sharples) Donovan, precisely because they shared the same name.[18] "He was a very intelligent man," says Hudkins of the better-known Donovan, whom he claims to have met in the sixties aboard the private plane of Dallas millionaire John Dabney Murchison, brother of first Dallas Cowboys owner Clint Murchison, and himself president of the Allegheny Corporation. ("He'd come to Dallas and hide out," Hudkins adds.) The New York Donovan's files, now housed at the Hoover Institute at Stanford, show that *that* Donovan was indeed friendly with the older Murchison, with whom he maintained a cordial correspondence revealing shared intelligence confidences. As Donovan closed one letter: "This is my first opportunity to thank you for . . . your wonderful suggestion for exchanging Randolph Phillips. Many thanks for your note and I shall look forward to seeing you very soon."[19]

Still, the question remains. Did the high-profile Donovan, who had intelligence ties and a major role in ongoing negotiations with

Castro's Cuba, orchestrate the investigation of the Haitian-minded de Mohrenschildt? Or was it the Texas Donovan? Was it, perhaps, both?

Donovan confusion reigns, clearly. And is the confusion real or is it Memorex, an artificially generated illusion? Are we somehow *supposed* to be confused, like the victims of madcap twins who keep switching roles on alternate days?

The answer to this question came late. In April 1995, Larry Haapanen notified Mary that the confusion had been resolved by newly released CIA files. The Murphy report on de Mohrenschildt is a simple custody document prepared for the Texas Donovan. The CIA had conducted its own expedite check in late April, for the purpose of using de Mohrenschildt in Haiti, according to the retired agent who conducted it. The near conjunction in time of the two investigations was pure coincidence.

What *was* de Mohrenschildt doing in Washington, D.C. with Clemard Charles that spring of 1963 that the agency found so fascinating?

In one sense, nothing too exciting. The baron was doing what he did for a living, hammering out the final details of another in a long string of lucrative government-assisted "contracts" to do something or other in a foreign country. This time it was Haiti, and he was going as a geologist, his legitimate area of training, to conduct a survey for Papa Doc's government. That was the official story, and the one de Mohrenschildt presented in his unpublished manuscript. He expressed genuine enthusiasm for the coming days in Haiti, gushing about the island's tropical beauty and the snorkeling joys it promised. About the intrigue side of things that would accompany the days in the sun he said nothing, and he omitted the trip to Washington in the manuscript's version of his travel itinerary: "In April we were at last ready to leave to New York first and then to Haiti."[20]

Luckily, however, there was Dorthe Matlock.

In 1963, Matlock worked for the U.S. Army Chief of Staff as assistant director of army intelligence. She also served as Pentagon liaison to the CIA. Col. Samuel Kail, an army intelligence officer, suggested that she meet with the Haitian banker Clemard Charles that spring "because of Charles' relationship to President Duvalier of Haiti and Haiti's strategic position relative to Castro's Cuba," Kail told the

House Select Committee on Assassinations some fifteen years later.[21] The colonel had had an ongoing relationship with covert intrigue, serving as liaison for the CIA with Cuban exiles in some of the earliest plots to assassinate Castro from within Cuba.[22]

Dorthe Matlock, who also testified to the HSCA, arranged a luncheon meeting with Charles and invited CIA agent Tony Czaikowski to join them. The invitation to Czaikowski (who was introduced as a Georgetown professor) was more than a courtesy. As we'll see more closely in a moment with the case of Tom Davis, the agency was just then deep into a covert campaign to overthrow the unbearable Papa Doc—not from any humanitarian design, heaven forbid, but as a necessary step to convert Haiti into a beachhead for a Cuban invasion. Charles, a banker and sometime arms dealer who was as bitterly opposed to Duvalier as Bringuier was to Castro, represented an opportunity in that direction. At the Washington luncheon he nervously conspired against his own government, urging Matlock to have the Marines sent to Haiti and relieve the country of the brutal dictator.[23]

All this to the good, Dorthe Matlock had suffered a surprise when Charles first arrived—not alone as she expected, but in the company of a Dallas couple, George and Jeanne de Mohrenschildt. As the meeting wore on, she was further annoyed to observe that the baron "dominated" Charles; and she wasn't taken in by their claims to be in business together. "I knew," she said in a well-known remark, "the Texan wasn't there to sell hemp."[24]

Another army intelligence officer, Robert Pierce, later opined that de Mohrenschildt was playing the role of "introducer, interpreter, and general foot-rubber" for Charles that spring. The banker had become the protective baron's new Oswald, and like Oswald he would meet a violent end, dying in 1981 under "bizarre circumstances" that the Haitian government never explained.[25] By baby-sitting Charles (who had appeared "frantic and frightened" to Matlock), de Mohrenschildt contributed his modest part toward the CIA goal of converting Duvalier's country into a base for the invasion of Cuba. The evidence suggests that the pursuit of this end was the baron's true mission in Haiti, not his contracted mapping scheme (though it compensated him handsomely) or his side interests in sisal plantations.[26]

Meanwhile, the spreading Haitian fever was breaking out in Los

Angeles. An anti-Castro group, Alpha 66, had started up an L.A. branch on April 18, 1963,[27] and a month later (at the same time that Bill Murphy and the CIA were conducting twin background checks de Mohrenschildt and that the baron was meeting in Washington with Haitian banker Clemard Charles), the first unmistakable symptom erupted. It was a classified ad, addressed to "Ex-Rangers, Special Forces, and Paratroopers,"[28] in the *Los Angeles Times* of May 12: "If interested in military-type employment and are between 25-35 with honorable discharge, send resume to BOX-004."

The ad succeeded in corralling a group of unemployed men with soldier-of-fortune aspirations into an L.A.-area motel room a few days later. FBI reports prepared later that May captured the gist of the proceedings and confirmed their link to the Alpha 66 organization. One of the applicants told Bureau agents that five days after answering the classified he "received a Western Union Telegram which stated 'Need special forces men Alpha 66 operation Sat 3pm 13535 Lakewood Blvd.'"[29] When this ex-Marine arrived at the Lakewood address (the appropriately adventuresome-sounding Tahiti Village Motel), he found himself in a room with some twelve or thirteen other veterans who had responded to the ad. They were met by a man named Tom Davis, a six-foot-tall Texan with blue eyes, wavy hair, cowboy boots, and a large blond mustache. The flamboyant Davis, dispensing whisky, beer, and cigars, told the men he'd served in Korea, where he'd been captured twice, and had put in time in Africa with the "Belgian mercenaries." He explained matter-of-factly that the purpose of the present operation was to overthrow the government of Haiti. This feat, for which he had been given $25,000 by "a man in Mexico," was to be done with no more than twenty men, and without bloodshed: "if [bloodshed] was necessary the cause would be lost."[30]

The logistical details were straightforward enough. The twenty men would be picked up at LAX in a C-119 on or before Friday, May 24 and flown to Texas to be "equipped with automatic weapons, side arms, fatigue uniforms, berets, and jump boots."[31] Then it was on to Haiti, where they would land at an airstrip near Port-au-Prince, proceed directly to the palace, and seize Papa Doc Duvalier "without shots being fired."[32]

To dispel possible qualms over any of this, Davis reportedly assured the listeners that "the USS Boxer would be sitting offshore six miles with U.S. Marines aboard to back us up."[33] (He probably didn't add that the *Boxer* was the same aircraft carrier that had been stationed off Cuba during the disastrous Bay of Pigs invasion two years earlier.) The Alpha 66 coup "would be over in two days," Davis said, for once the Haitian dictator was captured they would have the support of five key men inside the Duvalier government as well as "the leader of the ton-ton [macoutes] and five thousand of their members."[34]

For their pains, the recruits would initially be paid $300 per month from Davis's funds. After Papa Doc's capture, however, they would have "between $200,000 and $2 million" to divide among themselves, courtesy of the new government; Duvalier "would post this amount as a bond to make his escape."[35] Thereafter, the twenty newly affluent members of the invasion team "would set up headquarters in Haiti to train Cubans as a striking force, which would conduct guerrilla warfare against Castro Cuba,"[36] the ultimate purpose of the Alpha 66 operation. In the unlikely event, however, that the operation was not successful, "we would be given $50, a map, and a compass and told to head for the Dominican Republic."[37] Another potential recruit later told the FBI that a majority of applicants surmised such an operation could only be run by the Central Intelligence Agency.

The FBI quickly obtained the names of the persons attending Davis's meeting, and interviewed most of them under the report heading of "Neutrality Issues." The Bureau also contacted the CIA to determine whether Davis's actions were part of an agency operation. When the answer came back negative, the Bureau interviewed Davis himself. Like de Mohrenschildt, who was ostensibly going to Haiti to conduct a geological study for the Haitian government, Davis told the FBI he did "field geology work," even though there is no evidence that he ever worked or had credentials in that occupation. (De Mohrenschildt, who did, was in a position to verify such employment should it have been required.) Davis also explained that what appeared to be an Alpha 66 recruitment with CIA backing was really only research for an article he planned to write on soldiers of fortune.[38] The agents accepted his deadpan story, and no charges were filed.

When the FBI questioned Davis's wife, Caroline, about her husband's activities she said she could not be compelled to testify against him—an unnecessarily defensive stance if Davis were conducting research for an article as claimed. Though she admitted being at the same Tahiti Village Motel room on May 18 while the soldier of fortune applicants met with her husband, she claimed she was bathing and washing her hair during the hours-long meeting and had no knowledge of what had occurred. She also asked the FBI to tell her what Davis had told them. They declined.[39]

Davis's May 1963 claims to his potential mercenaries at the Tahiti Village were accurate. The U.S. Ready Amphibious Squadron of the Atlantic fleet with the Fourth Marine Expeditionary Brigade aboard the USS *Boxer* was indeed off the shore of Haiti between May 15 and June 4, 1963 (the latter date was a day or two before Davis was interviewed by the FBI), and there were expectations by some of the imminent invasion of Haiti, as the U.S. ambassador to the island had already threatened.

After the assassination, tough talker Jack Ruby confided to his first lawyer, Tom Howard, that there was one man on earth he feared— the blue-eyed mustachioed Texan, Thomas E. Davis III. The discovery of his ties to Davis could hurt his defense, Ruby told Howard. The bar owner explained that he had been involved with the Texan, who was a gunrunner, and that he planned to continue this partnership after his release.[40] Warren Commission counsels Hubert and Griffin wanted Ruby questioned about his relationship with Davis, but noted in a memo (dated March 19, 1964): "The FBI has been unable to identify anyone engaged in the sale of arms to Cuba who might be identical with the person named Davis." Davis appeared to be a secret only to the Bureau, however. His activities, and indeed the man himself, were known to newsmen in Dallas, who had compiled bulky files on the adventurer with the assistance of Ruby lawyer Howard.[41]

But the Bureau's blindness to Davis (and therefore to any connection between Davis and Ruby, which would violate the Warren Commission credo that the portly Oswald murderer had no ties to illegal mob activities such as gunrunning) was official, set at the top. The director himself, J. Edgar Hoover, adhered to it strictly, as he showed in a telegram to the State Department regarding Davis, dated less than a month after the assassination, December 20, 1963.

What had happened was that the globe-trotting Davis got himself in a jam in Tangier, where he happened to be selling guns when the news came that Kennedy had been shot by a man named Oswald.

The same cosmic jokester who dreamed up the two lawyers from New York named James Donovan may have had a hand in deciding that the Kennedy saga would also have two Oswalds, and that the name of one of them, not Lee Harvey, would be in Davis's possession when the assassination occurred. The Texan was immediately clapped in a Tangier jail when the name was found on him, though it was that of *Victor* Oswald, an international arms dealer in Madrid and the Adnan Koshoggi of his day. On the first leg of the journey that would take him to Tangier, Davis, carrying a letter of introduction, stopped in Madrid to pay his respects to the esteemed gun trader Oswald; they had serious business to discuss, no doubt, but it had nothing to do with a planned assassination.[42] (Ironically, when Davis's innocence on this question later became evident, his release from jail may have been arranged by CIA asset Q J/WIN, a foreign agent in charge of the agency's top secret ZR/RIFLE assassination program.)[43]

Meanwhile, though, in mid-December 1963, Davis was still rotting in a Moroccan cell, and FBI director Hoover had just been informed of it by the State Department—which like the arresting authorities had confused the Oswald reference found in the Texan's possession. As far as State and Hoover still knew, Davis had been caught in Tangier bearing the name of Lee Harvey Oswald. The director had to make an official reply on this matter, and did so in his telegram of December 20. The telegram adopted the line Davis told agents in Los Angeles back in May, that he was a noncriminal fellow, a researcher, whether or not he may have had Oswald's name on him. As Hoover explained:

> In May, June, and July, 1963 you were furnished several memoranda concerning Thomas Eli Davis, III, possibly identical with the individual arrested in Tangier. He reportedly had been recruiting men for an invasion of Haiti; however, it was developed that his scheme was actually to become acquainted with the "soldier of fortune" type of individual so that he might acquire background information for an article he planned to write.[44]

With this, a potentially tricky situation was defused. Hoover acquitted Davis, and did so before Warren mavericks Hubert and Griffin got to wondering, a few months later, about his possible associations with Ruby, and why Ruby was afraid (as he'd told his lawyer) that the Texan could damage his case.

In any event, the big picture once again tied Oswald and Ruby together. Not only were they connected through the supported revelations of John Elrod, but now, more tangentially, through close associates of each man. Oswald's "best friend" in Dallas, de Mohrenschildt, was working in Washington and Haiti to bring about the invasion of that country, while (at just the same time) Ruby's gunrunning partner, Davis, was busily recruiting a mercenary invasion force for Alpha 66 to carry the invasion forward to Castro's Cuba.

It was the spring of '61 or '62—she had a hard time with dates. History has proven her right, though, on a lot of other details. Nancy Perrin, who lived in Belmont, Massachusetts, commuted to a public relations job in the New Hampshire state legislature. Her gritty account of what happened next survives from her interview with Warren Commission attorney Leon Hubert in 1964. Though the attorney was intrigued by what he heard, the Commission eventually discarded Nancy's story on the grounds that it couldn't be true, since Ruby was never known to have been involved in gunrunning or other illegal activities. Today none of the researchers know where Nancy Perrin is, or even whether she is still alive (living, perhaps, under a new married name).

What Nancy told Hubert when she was still available was that one day (which turned out to be in May 1962) she finally finagled a job for her husband, Robert Perrin, at the same place where she worked. Her elation over this coup quickly turned to distress, however, as she informed Hubert:

> I telephoned to Massachusetts to tell him [Robert] to come on down, and there was no answer. And I had a feeling something was wrong. So I hightailed it back to Massachusetts, and there was a note. And the note said that he was going to Dallas. I called halfway over the United States, thinking of places he told me he had been, and I couldn't find him.[45]

Nancy, who was no slouch as an investigator, having previously worked undercover for several police departments in Massachusetts and California, included the Dallas PD in her long-distance calls. The boys in blue were affable on the phone, but no help in finding Robert. She then called a man who her husband had claimed "was some sort of a Government agent, which was in all probability true," though she was certain he'd never admit it. His name, the only part of it she could recall, was Youngblood. Anyway, he hadn't seen Robert either.

Within a week the determined Nancy caught a bus and set off on her own adventure to Dallas, still looking for her man. She went directly to the Dallas police station, where she ran into one of the same persons she had talked to on the phone from Belmont, Massachusetts. His name was J. D. Tippit, and he and several other officers pitched in to help out the new arrival. "They get the Black Maria," she told Hubert,

> go down to the bus depot and get my bags. And I had called Associated Press. I have many friends around the press world. Being in public relations, I would. And this Brice someone or other said, "You can go and stay with my wife for a couple of days until you get settled." Three o'clock in the morning we start punching doorbells, with the suitcases in the Black Maria, trying to find Ann, and I couldn't remember the last name. So the next day they send up to pick me up and help me find a place and job.[46]

The "they" who arrived from DPD were two:

> One Mr. Paul Rayburn, detective, juvenile, came to pick me up, along with his partner, Detective House. Well, we managed to find a place to live. And Paul suggested he had a friend. And did I know anything about bartending; well, I did.[47]

The police friend who hired Nancy as a bartender turned out to be the owner of a downtown nightclub called the Carousel, Jack Ruby. Given the players involved, it wasn't surprising. A federal convict in Alabama, Jack Hardee, Jr., told FBI agents four days after the murders of President Kennedy and Officer Tippit that Tippit was "a frequent visitor to Ruby's night club," together with another officer who was a motorcycle patrolman in Oak Lawn; that "there appeared to be a very close relationship between these three individuals."[48] The other two lawmen mentioned by Nancy, Rayburn and House, are confirmed by records as 1963 partners in Juvenile, the division that ultimately would come under the greatest suspicion by conspiracy researchers for supposedly tipping Jack Ruby to the imminent transfer of Lee Harvey Oswald.[49]

An interesting sidebar to Nancy's Carousel days was her uncomfortable discovery that even though Texas law barred the nightclub from serving hard liquor (restricting sales to beer, wine, and setups), Ruby had a "standing order" for a "particular group of people." Whenever, she elaborated,

> he would come in and say, "This is private stock stuff," that would mean for me to go where I knew the hard liquor was and get it out, and get it ready for the people in his private office.
>
> HUBERT. What was the particular group—who did it consist of?
>
> MRS. [PERRIN] RICH. The police department.
>
> HUBERT. Are you saying that Jack Ruby told you that when any member of the police department came in, that there was a standing order that you could serve them hard liquor?
>
> MRS. [PERRIN] RICH. That is correct.[50]

But Nancy didn't stay at the Carousel long—not after Ruby tried slapping her around a few months after she hired on. He became incensed one night because "the bar glasses were not clean enough to suit him" and "I wasn't pushing drinks to the customers fast enough," she told Hubert. "Ruby threw me up against the bar and put a bruise on my arm, and only because Bud King and one of the dancers there pulled me off, I was going to kill him."[51] The incident was hardly unusual at the Carousel; bullying women was what its owner, the man who was supposedly maddened by sympathy for the widowed Jackie Kennedy, did best. (The 1992 film *Ruby,* starring a protective and loveable Danny Aiello in the title role, must have seemed a bitter farce to the real-life Ruby's former "girls.")

Nancy quit her job on the spot after the fracas, but when she threatened to sue Ruby for assault and battery, she suddenly found her former Samaritans at the police less helpful than before. "I was told [by a Dallas detective] if I did that I would never win it, and get myself in more trouble than I bargain for," she said, adding: "I was also advised—I was not told to leave the city or anything like that, but that it was nice in Chicago, for instance, that time of year."[52]

Meanwhile, the long lost Robert Perrin showed up, and though his progress to Dallas had been delayed by a romantic detour to South Bend, Indiana with Nancy's own former secretary, she took him back with open arms. She loved the kinky lug; what can you say? Robert (whose death not long afterwards was caused by "arsenic voluntarily consumed," as Hubert delicately phrased it) reciprocated the love by "turning me out," she stated. Her phrase, equally delicate to Hubert's in its way, caused a bit of consternation in the sheltered mind of the Warren attorney. "Don't ask me why I didn't leave him," Nancy went on before Hubert could interpose a question. "Everyone else asked me that. It is not easy being something that is against everything that you believe in or stand for . . . when I worked, he worked. When I quit, he quit."[53] Then:

> HUBERT. What was the significance of your remark that when you worked he worked, and when you did not work—
> MRS. [PERRIN] RICH. As long as I was hustling he would work, and as long as I wasn't hustling he would not work.
> HUBERT. Does that mean he was—
> MRS. [PERRIN] RICH. My husband turned me out. That is what it means.
> HUBERT. Turned you out of the house?
> MRS. [PERRIN] RICH. This is an expression used in that particular trade.
> HUBERT. What you mean is—
> MRS. [PERRIN] RICH. He taught me how to be a prostitute, obtained dates for me, et cetera, et cetera, et cetera.[54]

Then another proposition came Nancy's way. Sometime in the summer of 1962, she and her husband were asked by a man named Dave Cherry—a bartender at another Dallas bar, the University Club—about performing a service. The job was to get some refugees out of Castro's Cuba, he told them. The Perrins sounded interested, and Cherry arranged to take them to a sparsely furnished apartment in Oak Lawn. There he and the couple, who cautiously introduced themselves as Jack and Nancy Starr, met a fourth party, a U.S. Army colonel in summer uniform. The colonel, balding, fortyish, and slightly built, as Nancy recalled him, offered the "Starrs" $10,000 for their part. He wanted someone

> to pilot a boat—someone that knew Cuba, and my husband claimed he did. Whether he did, I don't know. I know he did know boats. So they were going to bring Cuban refugees out into Miami. All this was fine, because by that time everyone knew Castro for what he appears to be, shall we say. So I said sure, why not—$10,000.[55]

At the same time, the offered amount struck Nancy as "awfully exorbitant for something like this; I smelled a fish, to quote a maxim." The couple asked to think the proposition over. They were told that "there were more people involved" and that "we were to attend a meeting at some later date, of which we would be advised."

Five or six days later, they were. At the second meeting, again at the same Oak Lawn apartment with its few pieces of cheap Danish Modern, the colonel once more was present in uniform, joined now by a "rather mannish" middle-aged woman with a "granite face," and several other men in addition to the University Club bartender Dave Cherry. Among them was one who looked "pugnacious," like an ex-prizefighter, and another with a dark complexion who "might have been Cuban or Latin American." The colonel seemed to be the head of the group and did most of the talking, but it was the Latin who first confirmed the fish Nancy had smelled at the first meeting. There were *two* parts to the $10,000 assignment, should the Perrins decide to take it. The second part, as they'd been previously told, was to bring refugees back. The first, however, was to deliver a shipment of weapons to Cuba. These were Enfield rifles, the colonel clarified. He added that the guns had been methodically stolen from his military base "for the last three months getting prepared for this," and that at present they were stashed in Mexico. Two of the men at the meeting were to pick up the weapons and transport them back to Dallas, where they would be pooled with other weapons that the colonel, Nancy discovered, had already stored "in a little storeroom outside of the apartment building." The Perrins saw the latter cache of military armaments during this meeting, as she told another investigator:

> There were guns, there was one B.A.R. [Browning automatic rifle] which I thought was left over from World War II, used, and there were hand grenades. There was some kind of a land torpedo, there were mines, I'd say half a dozen land mines, and, why, there must have been 20 or 30 packing cases of hand grenades. And I assume—in fact I more than assume, because I got the general impression from what was said that these were pilfered from the United States Army or Air Force bases.[56]

The growing complexity and danger of the plan made Nancy nervous. And she sensed yet another problem. Despite the colonel's grandiose scheming, there was now an air of evasiveness and delay, as if some kind of money hitch had materialized since the first meeting, and the financing wasn't quite in place.

Suddenly, however, the answer to the money snag arrived. It came in a form that gave Nancy "the shock of my life," she told the Warren attorney. "I am sitting there. A knock comes on the door and who walks in but my little friend Jack Ruby."[57] With the entrance of the bar owner (whom Nancy hadn't seen since quitting her too-much-crap-for-a-nickle job at the Carousel several months earlier), everyone in the apartment broke into a big smile,

> like here comes the Saviour, or something. And he took one look at me, I took one look at him, and we glared, we never spoke a word. I don't know if you have ever met the man. But he has this nervous air about him. And he seemed overly nervous that night. He bustled on in. The colonel rushed out in the kitchen or bedroom, I am not sure which. Ruby had—and he always did carry a gun—and I noticed a rather extensive bulge in his—about where his breast pocket would be. But at that time I thought it was a shoulder holster, which he was in the habit of carrying.[58]

Well, the bulge turned out to be far less menacing than a filled holster, apparently. When, ten or fifteen minutes later, the two men returned from the back room, Nancy noticed that Ruby's pocket was noticeably flat. The Carousel owner walked out of the apartment immediately after emerging from his conference, but left joy and fulfillment in his wake. Whereas before there was only the gloom of some obvious hitch in the procurement of the Enfields, that hitch now had vanished; the air was positively electric. The "pugnacious-looking fellow and one of the Latins" were ready to go "down to Mexico to make arrangements and pay for the guns," Nancy recounted. "All of a sudden just before Ruby come in they couldn't go, and right after Ruby left they were on the plane the next morning, so to speak."[59]

It was time, Nancy saw, to render her decision. "All right, we will go," she reportedly said. "But you can take the $10,000 and keep it. I want $25,000 or we don't move." This, at least, was what she announced to the group. In reality, she "was stalling when [she] asked for the $25,000," and intended to "notify the Federal authorities," she claimed to Hubert. "As I say, bringing the refugees out is one thing. Running in guns is another thing, for a Communist country which at that time [Cuba] was."[60]

In any case, the colonel replied that Nancy's $25,000 counter offer had to be discussed "with some other people that were higher up."

> HUBERT. They told you they were higher up?
> MRS. [PERRIN] RICH. Yes; the colonel said that they were higher up. I do not know the exact words.
> HUBERT. What happened then?
> MRS. [PERRIN] RICH. I think his exact words were something like "I will discuss it with my bosses."[61]

Three or four days later, notified as usual by Dave Cherry, the Perrins attended their third and final Oak Lawn meeting. When they arrived, the ubiquitous colonel was once again present, as was the granite-faced woman, the pugnacious-looking guy (who supposedly had already "gone to Mexico and been back"), and the dark-complexioned Cuban or South American—all the regulars of the Conspiracy Cafe. This time, however, there was a new face in the crowd, and it chilled Nancy's heart. "I smelled an element [at the meeting]," she told Hubert, "that I did not want to have any part of."

> HUBERT. And what element was that?
> MRS. [PERRIN] RICH. Police characters, let's say.
> HUBERT. Well, specifically it was, as I understood your testimony, that you suddenly identified the man who was at the third meeting, but not at any other, as possibly being the son of Vito Genovese.[62]

Nancy indeed came to this conclusion, she confirmed. She suddenly realized that the mob "element" of Genovese was "involved in this matter," and that he was "perhaps the higher-up the colonel spoke of," as well as the figure who "was running the guns in, and God knows what else."[63] Paralyzed by this discovery, she and Robert managed to slip from the third meeting without agreeing to the gun shipment (which in any event was postponed by the colonel), and without, as she supposedly planned to do later, notifying federal authorities. "Quite frankly, I am not stupid enough, shall we say," she testified, "to believe if I ever went to the authorities and that element was involved that I would ever live to tell a second story."[64]

Shortly thereafter, Nancy was arrested on multiple charges—vagrancy and prostitution were the ones she'd remember. As soon as she was released, she demanded of Robert that they leave town. Within a couple of hours the Perrins had packed a U-Haul and put Dallas in their side-view mirror, bound for New Orleans. A few months later, in the fall of 1962, Robert would die in the Crescent City, an apparent suicide. (In one of his fabled weird moves, New Orleans D.A. Jim Garrison allegedly sought to charge Robert Perrin—who had left this world a year before the assassination—with the murder of President Kennedy.)[65]

Nancy would live to tell her story, as we know, and it must have crossed the minds of her Warren interrogator and his memo-swapping friend Griffin to wonder what, if she were lying, her motivation might be. The matters she described weren't grand enough to win her great attention, if that was what she wanted; they were obscure, back-room Ruby-without-Oswald dealings, guaranteed to go nowhere on the conspiracy hit parade, but which nonetheless cast her in a degrading light, as a onetime careerist "from a respectable family" who fell to prostitution. Gratuitously confessing such things wasn't widely considered therapeutic just yet. On the other hand, if her story were the truth, it wouldn't require a "motivation," only a conscience. Mary believed Nancy Perrin had a conscience. She told what she knew about a gunrunning jerk, Jack Ruby, and of the mob and military associations with whom he trafficked.

We recall that the National Guard armory of Terrell, Texas was burglarized a week before the assassination. The reported theft occurred in the early hours of a Thursday morning, November 14, 1963. Eleven weapons, locked in a vault "awaiting repairs," were taken. The FBI was notified, bringing Dallas agent Joe Abernathy on the scene. The fact that the stolen guns were stored in a location other than their usual storage place, and that all but one of the weapons had been declared "defective" and placed in the vault within a day or so of the burglary, must have raised some questions in the agent's mind. It seems likely, knowing what we now know of ATF agent Frank Ellsworth's activities on the night of November 18, that the weapons were handpicked for their intended recipients, forming part of a prespecified list "requested" by Ellsworth in his attempted sting on gun dealer John Thomas Masen. There is no evidence, however, of any investigation into the personnel at the armory, even after the guns were recovered, and no one was ever charged with the Terrell burglary. Miller's conviction was only for possession (and unlawful receipt, etc.) of stolen weapons, not for theft.[66]

Four days after the armory break-in, on the same Monday,

November 18 that Dallas hoodlums Miller and Whitter did in their Thunderbird and any immediate plans for a gun delivery, Jack Ruby entertained a female visitor at the Carousel for several hours.[67] Described in an FBI report later as blonde and "modish," she was the years-younger sister of Lee Harvey Oswald's last housekeeper, Earlene Roberts. Ruby's attractive fortyish visitor was also the land-lady of Dallas policeman Harry Olsen (her next-door neighbor, who himself would spend several hours with Ruby later that week, on the troubled night of November 22) and of some of the Carousel strippers. She was Bertha Cheek, a successful businesswoman who would become even more successful within the next year. Ruby car-ried Bertha's phone numbers on a slip of paper the day he mur-dered Oswald.

Bertha Cheek's sister Earlene was the last person Oswald admit-ted seeing prior to his arrest at the Texas Theater. He encountered Earlene briefly when he went to his room a half-hour after the assas-sination and picked up his pistol. Oddly, even after his picture was shown on television (Earlene acknowledged seeing it), she never called the police. Her employers, Mr. and Mrs. A. C. Johnson, owners of the boardinghouse, were the ones who finally made the call.[68]

Bertha had a younger boyfriend, Wilburn Waldon Litchfield, who had been at her house when the FBI knocked on the door five days after the assassination, on Wednesday, November 27. Litchfield wit-nessed her interview with the agents, and five days later, on Decem-ber 2, contacted the FBI on his own. He told the Bureau then that sometime during the first two weeks of November he had seen a man closely resembling Oswald at the Carousel Club. Jack Ruby would acknowledge that Litchfield had been in his club at the time in ques-tion, but insisted the man Litchfield had seen was someone else, not Oswald. Litchfield was not supported by a lie detector test.[69]

The day after Bertha's boyfriend made his FBI statement, another man who knew her, Jess Willard Lynch of Page, Arizona, told the FBI that he recalled Bertha had rented to two Cuban men during 1959, and that Earlene Roberts was friendly with these tenants. The two reports, one following so closely on the other, led Warren attor-neys Hubert and Griffin to speculate that Litchfield and Lynch sus-pected Ruby, Bertha Cheek, or her sister Earlene Roberts of some involvement with the assassination.

Earlene Roberts' employers, the Johnsons, said Earlene suddenly disappeared immediately prior to the issuance of a Warren Commission subpoena to her. They said they had tried to contact her through her sister Bertha, but that Bertha put them off, saying vaguely that Earlene might not talk to anyone for some time, if she were pouting. Contacted by Mary in 1993, Bertha's daughter said that her mother was still living, and that she had a hard time after the assassination because "she had to take care of my aunt." (Earlene died in January 1966.) Protective, as many persons might be with an ageing parent who should be spared harassment, whatever may have happened many years ago, she wouldn't give her mother's present name or whereabouts.

Bertha Cheek was of interest to Warren attorneys Hubert and Griffin for several reasons. The most obvious was that she provided a link between Ruby and Oswald through her sister Earlene Roberts. The attorneys speculated she might have been involved in gunrunning deals with Ruby, and noted that through her sister Earlene she could have had access to Oswald's room at the boardinghouse. These were serious possibilities weighed by two members of the Warren investigation team, not later scenarios of assassination buffs. Hubert and Griffin also pondered the fact that one of Bertha's former husbands (she had three) was a convicted counterfeiter; his skills would have come in handy, they saw, in producing the phony "Hidell" ID cards allegedly found on Oswald after the assassination.

Bertha explained to Griffin in an April 1964 interview that her interest in meeting with Ruby on November 18 was to discuss a possible investment in one of his nightclubs. She passed on that chance but not many others, apparently. County records showed that Bertha Cheek acquired more than a dozen additional apartment buildings in 1963. Her new prosperity moved her from a seedy Gaston Avenue neighborhood to an address in the toney Park cities, Dallas's version of Beverly Hills. In her 1964 interview with Griffin, Bertha listed her current holdings. These were modestly fewer than county records showed, but included an apartment building at 5917 Gaston Avenue. Ten years later, Lawrence Reginald Miller would die at 5917 Gaston, at age forty-three. Records showed the cause of death as a heart attack brought on by acute alcohol intoxication. It isn't clear whether Bertha still owned the apartment building when Miller died.[70]

Griffin made a valiant effort to extract more information from

Bertha Cheek in the form of tenant records on her apartments and boardinghouses, but got no help either from Bertha or the FBI. "We went as far as we could go with some of these questions at the time," the former Warren attorney told Mary, "but we weren't conducting the investigation. That was being done by the FBI." Griffin lost another opportunity when he uncharacteristically overlooked one bit of information himself—Bertha's acquaintance with Officer Olsen, who admitted spending time with Ruby on the troubled night of November 22, 1963, and who later married one of the bar owner's strippers. It was Olsen, Bertha suggested to the Warren attorney, who recommended Ruby to her as a good nightclub manager.

Jack Ruby—the gunrunning paymaster who in the summer of 1962 greased the skids for an armory-pilfering U.S. Army colonel by showing up with a pocketful of cash; who was tagged as the western kingpin of an arms-smuggling "corridor" extending eastward through Louisiana to Santos Traficante in Miami;[71] and who, some five days before the assassination, reportedly advanced money under "some type contract" to four men in a Dallas motel room, one of whom was probably Lee Harvey Oswald—hung another greasy bauble on his low-rent legacy November 19, 1963.

On that Tuesday (the day after FBI agent Joe Abernathy and four anonymous Dallas detectives chased Miller and Whitter into a utility pole), Ruby met at the Carousel with a member of the U.S. Army in Terrell, Samuel Baker. According to an FBI report,[72] Baker paid Ruby on that occasion a sum of money in travelers' checks, three of which the bar owner would have in his possession when he was arrested for the murder of Oswald the following Sunday, November 24.

The explanation Baker provided to Bureau agents in December 1963 for the travelers' checks and how they came to be in Ruby's possession stretched FBI credulity regarding the bar owner's innocence to new lengths. As Baker told it, he was in the Carousel on the night of November 19 to celebrate his reenlistment in the army, for which he had received a thousand-dollar bonus. Rather than having the bonus sent to his installation at Terrell, Baker told agents, he traveled more than a hundred miles to pick it up at Fort Wolters in Mineral Wells, Texas. The reason for this inconvenient maneuver, he said, was to prevent the bonus from "being lost or stolen in the mail." (The implication of this rationale was that the army planned to send the bonus to Baker in cash, hardly a conventional procedure, but not a troublesome point for the FBI, apparently.)

After collecting the bonus in Mineral Wells earlier that same Tuesday, Baker reported, he backtracked twenty-five miles or so to Weatherford, Texas, where he purchased $600 in travelers' checks. He did not explain why his concern with protecting his money did not cause him to convert the bonus to travelers' checks immediately in Mineral Wells, why he did not convert the full amount, or why he chose Weatherford for the purchase of the checks. After taking care of these financial details, Baker said, he met other army buddies at Ruby's Dallas club for his "celebration." The buddies were "not identified," according to the report. No connections were attempted by the intrepid agents between the curiously explained Baker-Ruby money transaction of November 19 and some rather glaring attendant circumstances. Among these were the fact that Baker was stationed at Terrell, that a theft of weapons from Terrell's armory had occurred five days earlier, on November 14, and that two Dallas hoods had been spectacularly captured on the previous day, November 18, with a car full of Terrell weapons.

If Ruby's connection to Baker remains one unsolved mystery, his tie to a lawyer, Pete White, is another. We may remember that ATF agent Frank Ellsworth, thwarted in his quest to nail gun dealer John Thomas Masen by the capture of Miller and Whitter, arrested Masen two days later on minor charges. On the following day, November 21, 1963, Masen's lawyer Pete White visited the courthouse and met Jack Ruby—who, as we've seen, was also circumstantially connected with the Terrell armory theft. Later, after Ruby's arrest for the murder of Oswald, White's name, address, and phone number were found in the address book of Ruby's clerical employee Larry Crafard. Crafard was unable or unwilling to explain why he was maintaining this information when interviewed by the Warren Commission. (Similarly, though Ruby's roommate George Senator was questioned about all other Ruby phone notations, this one was skipped in Senator's interrogation.)[73]

On the same eve of the assassination that the Carousel owner talked to lawyer Pete White in the Dallas courthouse, he also visited a bail bondsman. Ruby himself was under no charges at the time, nor, as far as is known, were any of his employees. Later that day, he stopped at the office of a Dallas County assistant district attorney, Ben Ellis. It isn't known what Ruby went in to talk about, but upon leaving—as he handed out cards advertising one of his strippers, Jada—he introduced himself to Ellis and told him: "You probably don't know me now, but you will."[74] Ruby would become a prophet and a murderer within seventy-two hours.

The actions of Jack Ruby on the weekend of November 22-24 have been exhaustively studied by many reputable researchers, notably the late Seth Kantor, a journalist who knew the bar owner well, and the authors of a chronology compiled by the House Select Committee on Assassinations. (It was Kantor who witnessed Ruby's presence at Parkland Hospital as the president lay dying in trauma room one while Ruby's mechanic, Donnell Whitter, remained in a coma on another floor.)[75]

Although Ruby was later said by his family to idolize Jack Kennedy, the bar owner seems to have made no effort to catch a live glimpse of the president on his single postelection visit to the city. While the motorcade cut through the confetti of downtown Dallas, Ruby indifferently whiled away the time at a newspaper, the *Dallas Morning News*, preparing bar ads. In this low task he was both at home and in character. Following the assassination, however, he appears to have gone into a state of frenzy. He rushed to Parkland Hospital, closed his bars, placed ads announcing the closings, visited the Carousel, made numerous long-distance phone calls, went to a deli for pounds of cold cuts, visited his sister, attended a prayer service at his synagogue, stopped at the police station (and entered the room where Oswald was being interrogated), attended the suspect's midnight press conference, talked to a disk jockey at radio station KLIF, visited with policeman Harry Olsen and stripper Kathy Kay in a parking garage until two or three in the morning, went home, awakened his roommate George Senator and employee Larry Crafard, photographed a billboard reading "Impeach Earl Warren," and finally returned to his apartment, only to arise on the morning of the 23rd to start his frenzied activity all over again.

While there is no doubt an element of true chaos here (a chaos in some ways reminiscent of Bloom's odyssey through the back streets of Dublin), the underlying pattern is this: Ruby stalked Oswald after the assassination until he killed him, simultaneously leaving "clues" that his actions were randomly driven. Beginning with his intrusion into the interrogation room where Oswald was being questioned on Friday evening,[76] through his presence at the midnight press conference where Oswald was displayed to reporters (and where Ruby corrected D.A. Henry Wade on Oswald's affiliation with Fair Play for Cuba), to his shady entry into the basement of the Dallas police station on the Sunday of Oswald's murder, Ruby was never far from the accused presidential assassin.

On Saturday the bar owner was spotted numerous times by policemen and journalists as he haunted the police station and Dealey Plaza, where the county jail (the next stop for Oswald, should he be transferred that day) was located.

The next morning, Sunday, November 24, Ruby awaited a call at his apartment from a hoodlum/cop that Oswald was being transferred,[77] as well as a call from a stripper, Little Lynn, supposedly related to some money she desperately needed to buy groceries. In reality, as Kantor demonstrates, Ruby was less interested in Little Lynn's plight (which was authentic enough) than in setting up a later argument that his behavior of that morning was spontaneous, not premeditated.

> Ruby's chief concern now would be in making the [Oswald] shooting look a spur-of-the-moment matter so he could be back out in the street as soon as possible to reap the rewards of being a popular hero. He already had the perfect reason for being in the same block as the police station by going on a legitimate errand to the Western Union office there [to wire the money to Little Lynn]. Next he would need a reason for the gun. He stuffed nine $100 bills, 30 $10 bills, 40 $20 bills and a number of smaller bills into a pocket. It was supposed to be the federal excise tax money Ruby owed. By carrying it with him, he created an understandable reason under Texas law to pack the gun, too, even though he had no license to carry any hidden weapon. But the excise tax payment story was a phony. Only five days earlier he had signed the power-of-attorney in the office of his tax lawyer, Graham Koch, granting Koch the right to negotiate with the IRS for an extended time period to make those federal tax payments. There was no logical reason for Ruby to be carrying all that money, except to establish an alibi.[78]

As important as the much-bruited matter of Jack Ruby's premeditation in the murder of Lee Harvey Oswald may be (and as obvious, except to the likes of Gerald Posner and Dan Rather), the less settled

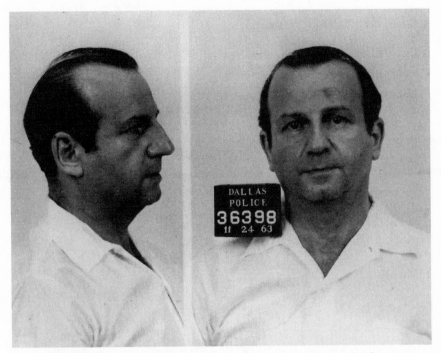

Jack Ruby after his arrest for the murder of Lee Harvey Oswald. (Courtesy Dallas Municipal Archives and Records Center, City of Dallas, Texas)

question of Ruby's motivation for killing Oswald remains. Did he, as some conspiracy scenarios have suggested, receive mob "orders" to do in a patsy who properly should have been killed on the spot (as was done with the "assassin" of Philippine patriot Benigno Aquino), perhaps by a policeman rushing into the school book depository— but a patsy who, in this case, smelling a rat, reflexively took wing to his Oak Cliff boardinghouse in preparation for a more permanent escape to Mexico or some other distant point? Was it then necessary for Ruby, whether he received orders from higher-ups or not, to silence Oswald in order to sever his own recent ties to him as part of an anti-Castro gunrunning ring (and possibly more, an anti-Castro ring tasked with assassination)? Was it the realization of Ruby's own impending exposure, as Oswald inevitably started talking, that changed the Carousel owner's demeanor from indifference to frenzy during his nightmarish assassination weekend?

In the area of Ruby's motivation (as distinct from his premeditation) we are clearly on more speculative grounds. Yet even here the
mists have cleared somewhat, with the recent discovery of a long-overlooked document suggesting that Ruby was not a mere gunrunning
profiteer but a man privy to a much deeper level of insider knowledge.

One spring Saturday afternoon in 1993, idly rolling through a
microfilm of FBI documents in the Dallas Public Library as she
waited for her daughter Eugenia to complete work on a research
project (a noxious way for a school mom to spend her time, Eugenia thought), Mary slowed down and backed up when she noticed an
item she'd never heard of before.

In an FBI report filed under the category "Jack Ruby," a fascinating, perhaps crucial, detail emerged. The report, buried in the hundred thousand or so pages mostly available on non-indexed
microfilm, wasn't released until 1977 and to Mary's knowledge had
never been cited in any of the books written about the assassination,
or about Ruby in particular. (She'd read almost all of them by now.)
Dated February 2, 1964, the document had been dictated January
31 of that year by Special Agent Estes G. Coleman at Lake City,
Arkansas, and supplemented with information gathered by another
agent, Alfred E. Neeley of the Dallas office.[79]

"Mr. John Basinger, minister, First Baptist Church, Lake City,
Arkansas, furnished the following information concerning his
brother, Rex Harding Basinger," the report began. It would go on
to provide an account strikingly similar, on superficial points at least,
to the Elrod story. Once again, there would be two brothers, one of
whom would end up in a Dallas jail, and who following his release
would relate a strange tale to the stay-at-home brother concerning a
run-in with a famous assassination principal. And again, the FBI
would deny the jailed brother's story.

According to the document, Rex Basinger, forty-five, who claimed
to have worked in Denver as a cab driver and police informant prior
to showing up in Texas, "was arrested at Parkland Hospital, Dallas,
December 14, 1963, on a charge of vagrancy." (Rex Basinger's arrest
report, still available in the records division of the DPD, confirms the
date and circumstances.) He was then "released by the Police Department to the same hospital on December 17."[80]

A little over a month later, on January 21, 1964, Rex showed up at the doorstep of his older brother John in Arkansas, and brought the Baptist preacher up to date on his whereabouts for the last several years. He told him of his days in Denver driving a taxi and being an amateur narc, and how he'd decided to leave town in December 1963, after someone had taken a couple of shots at him. Rex went on to describe a still more curious event that had happened after he arrived in Dallas and got himself arrested. He was put in the same jail block with Jack Ruby, the notorious killer of Lee Harvey Oswald, he told John. And that wasn't all. He actually got into a conversation with Ruby, and Ruby told him about "an invasion of Cuba which would take place on May 1, 1964," the report said. "The invasion groups were to meet at Key West, Florida, and others were to meet in Mexico, place unknown. Rex said he was going to join the group at Key West, Florida, but could not furnish any information as to the leaders of this group, but claimed the invasion was being sponsored by the United States Government."[81]

As would be the case with John Elrod in Memphis a few months later, the author of the FBI report showed little mercy for the tall-tale artist—for really, what else could he be? The report explained (in the addendum by Dallas field-office agent Neeley) that "since Jack. L. Ruby had been removed from the Dallas City Jail to the Dallas County Jail prior to [Rex] Basinger's confinement at Dallas City Jail, Ruby and Basinger could not have been in the same jail block." It added that Rex was released by the Dallas police "with [the] notation 'lunacy,'" and that a doctor at Parkland "subsequently reported to the Police Department his diagnosis as 'probable psychosis, possible brain syndrome.'"[82]

Finally, the report noted that upon hearing the brother's account, "[John] Basinger stated that he could not believe the story told to him by Rex and feels sure that he was not in the same jail block with Jack Ruby in Dallas, Texas."[83]

Well, would a nice backwoods Baptist preacher lie?

He probably wouldn't, to be sure. But the same couldn't be said for the federal agency reporting these words, of course—as Mary discovered when she picked up the phone and called the Reverend Mr. Basinger at Lake City, Arkansas. Now in his mideighties, but hale and alert, the brother of Rex told her he'd never heard of the report till the moment she quoted it to him—that, moreover, "to my knowledge, I have never talked with the FBI in my life."

John Basinger told Mary that contrary to the Bureau report, he *did* believe what his brother had told him. One reason for this was that right after Rex visited him in January 1964—he stayed in Lake City for four days—Rex set out for Florida with the intention of acting on what Ruby allegedly told him. He wanted to get "involved with the invasion" that was supposed to happen in May of that year. Shortly after Rex left, the Baptist minister said, he received a letter with a South Florida postmark saying his brother was in the Sunshine State.

John Basinger also told Mary that the day after Rex set out for Florida with machismo on his mind, the preacher was visited by a man identifying himself as "a local policeman," though he didn't recognize him. The man told John he was there to "check on Rex" because "the police in Denver were worried about him." The "policeman" didn't explain how he knew Rex had been by to see him, John said. He emphasized that in any event he never told this visitor (or anyone) that he didn't believe his brother's story.

What about, though, the Parkland Hospital doctor who (the FBI report tells us) "subsequently" diagnosed Rex Basinger as a possible nut case? Subsequent to *what*? Rereading the report, Mary realized that the good doctor, not necessarily a quack or dullard, probably offered his tentative remarks after having been told, as helpful contextual information, that Ruby, the man his patient claimed to have seen in the ample flesh, had been removed from the Dallas cell "prior to Basinger's confinement." Given that supposed circumstance, even a layman could have easily delivered the same diagnosis . . . particularly if he or she weren't familiar with the FBI record on such matters as John Elrod.

We are left, then, with the information Rex Basinger—now no longer an obvious teller of tall tales—passed on about Ruby. Might Ruby actually have made the jailhouse remarks Rex attributed to him, and if so, is there any basis for believing them to be true?

Once again, as in the remarks Elrod reportedly heard from a cellmate, there is. In January 1963, twenty-one months after the Bay of Pigs fiasco, U.S. Attorney General Bobby Kennedy had decided to have another fling at storming the island citadel of Fidel Castro.[84] Inviting former Bay of Pigs leader Manuel Artime up from Miami for a skiing weekend on the slopes of New Hampshire, Bobby put the Cuban military hero on a $1,500 monthly retainer from the CIA to revive his Movement for the Recovery of the Revolution. The MRR itself was soon receiving $250,000 a month to launch an operation with the code name Second Naval Guerilla. Though the objectives of the operation were formally limited to attacks on Cuban shipping and shore installations, its spirit was one of joyous preparation for all-out war.

> It was like old times in [Miami's] Little Havana. The MRR battle flag, a gold trident on blue, hung outside a newly opened headquarters. General Edward Lansdale flew down for a personal inspection. Recruits banged on the door, and Bay of Pigs veterans were sought out as war fever again spread through the exile colony. A group holding maneuvers in a field proudly told quizzical Miami police that they were "training for the next invasion of Cuba."[85]

By the summer of 1963 Artime easily persuaded dictator Luis Somoza to allow the Second Naval Guerilla operation to establish a military base in Nicaragua, and Somoza in turn prevailed on President Francisco J. Orlich of neighboring Costa Rica to allow two additional camps in that country. With the help of the CIA, money flowed in to the MRR's Miami home office for the purchase of modern military equipment, from torpedo boats to the latest German rebreathers for frogmen.

While Manuel Artime's Bobby-sanctioned project went swimmingly forward, the Kennedy administration continued to maintain a public posture of honoring its agreement with Nikita Khrushchev, reached after the Cuban missile crisis of October 1962, to lay off Fidel's regime. Other anti-Castro free-lancers, however, were creating havoc with JFK's attempt to maintain even a hypocritical semblance of restraint and neutrality. With the covert assistance of CIA handler Maurice Bishop, Alpha 66 and other renegade exile groups deliberately whacked Russian ships off Cuba, looking to bring about another U.S.-Soviet confrontation. One such instance occurred on March 27, 1963, when Tony Cuesta led a commando naval attack on the Russian merchantman *Baku,* mailing it to Davy Jones' locker (Caribbean division) along with 10,000 bags of sugar. This and other similar provocations would only backfire, though, as the president responded by sending conciliatory statements to the outraged Soviets, confiscating the boats of the commandos, and restricting their leaders to the dull confines of Dade County.

The anti-Kennedy mood of the more militant exiles may have

reached a critical mass in late July 1963, when, as we've seen, an FBI raid near Louisiana's Lake Pontchartrain netted a large DRE cache of armaments, together with the cofounder of the Minutemen, Richard Lauchli. (As we shall see, it was Lauchli's fellow Minuteman, John Thomas Masen, who apparently served as a middleman for military weapons moving from Fort Hood through Dallas to the DRE, an operation in which Jack Ruby served as paymaster.) As a recent Cuban TV documentary not yet shown publicly in the U.S. has suggested,[86] Pontchartrain was a "turning point" in the eyes of extremist CIA, Mafia, and Cuban exile elements—the incident that finally convinced this alliance of convenience that John Fitzgerald Kennedy was hopelessly ambivalent, a condition for which a permanent solution was required. With Kennedy out of the picture, the second invasion of Cuba could proceed.

May 1, 1964, the day allegedly blabbed by Jack Ruby to Rex Basinger, was a plausible postassassination target date for the more fervid invasion plotters (if not for Artime's Second Naval Guerilla contingent, which reportedly planned to hold off until May 1965), allowing a decent interval of mourning before getting on with important business. In reality, the mood of the U.S. government changed radically after the assassination, when Lyndon Johnson, revulsed by the Cuban madness (as well as by any project having to do with Bobby Kennedy), moved to shut down the training camps. He was focusing on Vietnam, as it turned out.[87] Ruby, by then in prison and out of the loony loop of anti-Castro scheming, wouldn't have known of this latest change in plans; but that he knew enough to hit on May 1 at all would argue an insider's knowledge of the arcane mechanics of advanced Castrophobia. That knowledge, though obsolete by the time he supposedly talked to Basinger, was apparently sufficient to send the former Denver taxi driver looking for his final address—and dream of adventure—at the southernmost tip of America.

CHAPTER EIGHT

Running Man

Running man. Please call me. Please. Please.

—Lee

Personal Ad, *Dallas Morning News, Oct. 15, 1963*

One early evening in April 1963 Michael Paine had an unusual errand. His wife, Ruth, had sent him to pick up a young couple and bring them to dinner. The couple, whom Ruth had met at a Dallas party a few weeks earlier, lived across town in Oak Cliff and had little money and no car. They did, however, know Russian—Marina was a pretty native of the Soviet Union, Paine had been told—and Ruth, a Quaker with peaceful coexistence on her mind, wanted to practice the language.

As Paine, a Bell Helicopter engineer from Pennsylvania, climbed the stairs leading to the second-floor apartment of the small two-story house, he idly noticed that the clapboards were closer together than those on houses in his part of the country. The door was answered by Marina's husband, Lee Oswald. While waiting for his wife to get ready, the young man showed Paine an 8x10 print of himself in which he was dressed in black and held up a rifle and some newspapers. Paine noticed that the house behind Lee in the picture had the same clapboards he had just noted. The photograph had been taken here, he gathered. But he didn't know what to make of the picture, or what reason Oswald had for showing it to him. Paine's attention was distracted from the matter as Oswald yelled at Marina to speed up her departure. "I wasn't in any particular hurry," Michael Paine says today, "so any rush was of Lee's own making."

The dinner with the Oswalds that night was otherwise uneventful, except, as Paine recalls, for a "sharpness in Lee's tone" with Marina, even though he couldn't comprehend the Russian words. Marina and Ruth Paine did strike up a friendship, however. Less than two weeks later, Ruth took Lee to the bus station for his relocation to New Orleans that summer. Marina and baby June moved in with Ruth, as we've seen, until Oswald was able to send for them in May. Four months later, in September 1963, Ruth stopped by New Orleans en route from Philadelphia to pick up Marina and June for their return to Dallas.

By the fall of that year the Paines were separated. One Friday afternoon, Michael, stopping by their house in Irving to drop off a check as was his usual custom, met another visitor at the house—widebody FBI agent James Hosty. Hosty, Paine remembers, was "very polite" and "detailed to Oswald," investigating his whereabouts.

In fact, this visit—which Hosty entered in a report as occurring on November 1—wasn't the agent's first visit to the Paine neighborhood. Learning that the New Orleans post office had a card forwarding Oswald's mail to the Paine address on Fifth Street in Irving, Texas, Hosty had made a preliminary foray in October, asking neighbors if a Russian-speaking woman, Marina, lived at the Paine residence. On this occasion, as on his next visit to the area on the first of November, the agent discreetly parked his car "down the street," because the Bureau didn't "like to draw attention" to such interviews—a detail that would have some bearing on later testimony to the Warren investigators.[1] Told by neighbors that such a woman did indeed stay at the Paine house, Hosty made his first formal appearance at Ruth Paine's door, and it was she who fielded his questions for the then-non-English-speaking Marina.

Ruth told the agent on that Friday that only Lee's wife lived with her. Oswald himself currently lived at a boardinghouse in Oak Cliff, she explained, and had recently found employment at the Texas Book Depository Building. Marina's benefactor withheld Oswald's address and phone number, however, believing (as she later told the Warren Commission) that an organization with the investigative capacity of the FBI should be able to discover such details for itself.

Ruth Paine also did not elaborate on several additional points that have since become common knowledge—that, for example, she herself had been instrumental in securing the book depository job for Oswald, who had returned to Dallas from Mexico on Thursday, October 3, once again unemployed. After spending that night at the YMCA, he had shown up at the Paine house to visit Marina the next day, explaining (whether truthfully or not isn't known) that he had been to Houston to look for a job. As luck had it, some ten days after Oswald's early October visit, Ruth and Marina were chatting at the house of a Fifth Street neighbor, Linnie Mae Randle. Allegedly hearing of Oswald's plight, Linnie Mae volunteered that her brother, Buell Wesley Frazier, who lived in the house with her, had just landed a job as a warehouseman at the downtown book depository, and that the same folks might possibly be looking for additional help. That same day, Ruth Paine had phoned Roy Truly, manager of the TSBD. Truly sounded receptive, and Ruth called Oswald at his boardinghouse at 1026 North Beckley. Oswald followed up on the tip and visited Truly on October 14. The ex-Marine was offered a job on the spot—as a warehouseman, like Frazier—and had begun his new job on the following day.

Hosty left his name and phone number (and perhaps his address) with Ruth Paine, so that she might call him when she "found out" where Oswald was living.

With the exception of a few details—the presence of Michael Paine at his house during the first Hosty visit, and his witnessing of the famous Oswald backyard photo in April 1963 (which, if true, would make it a certainty that the backyard photos are real, not forged)—every fact cited above has been well known for thirty years. The official Warren-sanctioned story is that Agent Hosty, once again on the trail of Lee Harvey Oswald, missed his quarry on that Friday, November 1, and did not talk with him until exactly three weeks later, on November 22—after Oswald, now the accused assassin, was in custody.

The new evidence indicates that this official story is dead wrong.

On Tuesday, October 15, the same day Oswald started his new job at the book depository, an evocative personal classified ran in the *Dallas Morning News*. Addressed to "Running Man," the ad begged this special reader: "Please call me. Please. Please." It was signed, "Lee." Understandably, such an urgent plea appearing five weeks before the assassination had piqued the interest of at least two Warren staffers, Ruby specialists Leon Hubert and Burt Griffin.[2] Though nothing would come of their curiosity (the ad was later determined to be a teaser for a movie), Warren investigators eventually examined the same central question suggested by the newspaper message: Was it possible Oswald was reporting in some way to a "running" man, perhaps an agent of a federal agency like the FBI?

This question wasn't grounded in the flimsy vapors of an anonymous classified, but in a notation Oswald had entered by hand in a personal notebook later found in his belongings. This notation contained the name, phone, address, and even car license-tag number of a Dallas FBI agent with a now-familiar handle: James P. Hosty. But what in the world was an FBI agent doing in Oswald's notebook, and why was this information deleted (as the Warren investigators would be none too happy to learn) from the transcript of the notebook provided by the FBI to the Commission? These matters needed explaining, and were later exhaustively analyzed in a 1974 manuscript by Paul Hoch, as well as reconsidered by the House Select Committee on Assassinations.[3] They have still not gone away.

The facts were as follows. At some unknown point, Oswald entered these lines in his notebook:

Oct Nov 1, 1963 [*Oct* scratched through]
FBI agent (RI-11211)
James P. Hosty
MU 8605
1114 Commerce St
Dallas

According to a Dallas police memo, three days after Oswald's death, on November 27, 1963 and at the odd hour of one in the morning, FBI agent James Hosty picked up a "notebook recovered from room of Lee Harvey Oswald at 1026 No. Beckley on 11-22 [November 22] from Capt. Will Fritz, along with Oswald's billfold and 16 cards and pictures, and a 6.5 rifle hull recovered at [the] Texas School Book Depository."[4]

The FBI made a transcript of the contents of the notebook, and the Warren Commission was provided with a copy of the transcript. Two of its pages, however, the cover and the page that should have contained the Hosty notation, were retyped. The notation was deleted from the retyped page, and was the only deletion from the transcript.

The explanation given to the Commission by the Bureau (after Warren investigators got wind of the existence of the Hosty notation from newspaper stories) was that the Hosty entry in Oswald's notebook had no value as a "lead."[5] The Commission noted, however, that other material that had no lead value was included in the transcript first provided to the investigators. The House Select Committee considered the issue, initially raising questions, but finally letting the FBI off the hook by allowing corrected testimony from agents involved.[6]

A second piece of the notation puzzle revolved around the question of the license-plate number, MU 8605, which had been included in the Hosty entry. If Hosty missed Oswald on November 1 (and on a subsequent follow-up visit on November 5), as claimed, how did Oswald obtain this number and what did it mean that he had it?

The explanation provided to Warren investigators for this question was that Marina jotted down the license tag of Agent Hosty and passed it on to Oswald. The Warren *Report,* eyeing contradictions in the testimony, was intentionally vague on the matter of the date on which Marina passed this information to her husband;[7] but let that slide for a moment. According to Marina's sworn statement, "Lee had asked me that if an FBI agent were to call, that I note down his automobile license number, and I did that."[8]

The problem was (and remains) that to arrive at the truth of the matter we must navigate, as the Commission tried thirty years ago, a morass of contradictions caused by Marina's conflicting reports. She said one thing under oath to her Warren listeners (testimony contradicted by that of Ruth Paine and James Hosty), and another entirely different thing years later to her authorized biographer, Priscilla McMillan. Both versions of how she might have learned the Hosty license-tag number in order to pass it on to Lee were physically impossible.

Marina testified to the Commission that she saw the tag on Hosty's car during his first visit of November 1. During this visit she stayed mostly in a back room, a point on which both Ruth and Hosty's testimony concurred. Therefore, if Marina saw the tag then, she would have to have seen it from some window of the Paine house. However, since Hosty's car was parked "down the street," this would have been impossible. The Warren investigators studied the views available from windows of the house and confirmed that the tag could not have been seen even if the car were parked in front of the house or as the vehicle was turning around and pulling away.[9]

Marina also testified that when she told Oswald of Hosty's visit, he became quite angry, telling her, as we've already heard in part, that if he showed up again she should get his license-tag number (a weird enough request, but again, let's let it pass temporarily). Of course, this constituted yet another contradiction in her testimony, for she couldn't have both elicited this response and also have succeeded, as she claimed, in seeing the tag on the "first" Hosty visit.

More than a decade later, Marina "clarified" her story for Priscilla McMillan. She had really seen the tag, she told the writer, on the *second* Hosty visit—on Tuesday, November 5. However, as we learn from Warren and HSCA testimony, on this visit Hosty and a fellow agent only chatted with Ruth at the doorstep for a few minutes. Hosty, ever interested in postassassination days in distancing himself from the Oswalds, claims Marina did not so much as come to the door; he did not see her on this visit. Ruth Paine says that she did, that Marina "appeared toward the end of the visit," so that (as McMillan recorded) "both Ruth and Hosty were surprised to see her."[10] Marina then weighs in with her own recollection that on this occasion she talked to Hosty even longer than on his first visit, and that she was impressed by his "nice personality." In the end, however, she had "appeal[ed] to him not to come again because news of his first visit had upset Lee very badly."[11]

But regardless of whether Marina talked to Hosty for a long or short time, or whether, as Hosty says, she did not see him at all, the important fact is that the brief visit was conducted on the doorstep, during which time the agent would have had the car in sight, at least peripherally. We know this from his HSCA testimony. He explained to the investigators that on this return to the Paine house, on Tuesday, November 5, he had skipped the ceremony of parking down the block somewhere and instead pulled the car into the driveway. Like any polite guest with a "nice personality," he wouldn't have jammed the car all the way into the back of the driveway, out of sight from the front yard. He would have kept it respectfully in the vicinity of the entrance, even if it hadn't been a fact that Ruth Paine's own car was already parked in the driveway when Hosty arrived.

All this makes a shambles of Marina's second, and belated, version of how it was that she acquired the agent's license-tag number. What happened, she reported to McMillan, was that "at some point,"

> she slipped out of the bedroom, into the kitchen and dining area, out of the kitchen door, and around the house. She had no trouble finding Hosty's car [particularly since it was in the driveway, McMillan refrained from adding] and, without the smallest feeling of being in a hurry—"I am a sneaky girl," she laughs— she walked around and around it, trying to figure out what make it was. This she was unable to do because she could not read English. But she studied the color and memorized the license number. Then she came back inside the house. Once Hosty had gone, she wrote the number on a slip of paper and left it for Lee on their bureau.[12]

If Marina did as she told Priscilla McMillan, she would have been immediately spotted regardless of whether she tried to come through the front door, where the others were standing, or sneak out the kitchen door. This would have been especially so in light of her dopey antics of walking "around and around" the car "without the smallest feeling of being in a hurry." Her car-locating adventure sounds as if it was plotted with a car parked down the street in mind, where Hosty usually left his, but which despite this caution she is cleverly able to find. The car she describes is at a distance, which is why once she gets to it she can take her time without feeling any rush; Hosty wouldn't be able to see her. Marina's amended story may have been more lively than the first, but as the FBI agent's HSCA testimony about his parking location showed, it was no more truthful.

We may believe, however, one last point of Marina's testimony in this affair, supported by the testimony of Ruth Paine. The two women told Warren investigators that they withheld the information about Hosty's second visit from Lee until the following Friday or Saturday, November 8 or 9. They knew he'd be disturbed by the news, and waited until his weekend visit to tell him.[13] They knew this because Hosty's visits had in all likelihood happened before, as we will see.

But there was a yet more perplexing difficulty, unrelated to such relatively gross matters as the FBI's possible chicanery in withholding the Hosty entry from the Commission, or the physical obstacles purportedly preventing Marina from seeing the car tag. This more sublime dilemma resides in the inherent illogicality of Oswald's Hosty notation. Consider that this entry begins with a thoroughly scratched-out, barely legible *Oct*. The blotch is "corrected" alongside it to read *Nov 1, 1963*. Accordingly, whether we rely on the official FBI-Warren-HSCA explanation or on that of any other previous commentators on the matter, we must accept one of the two following scenarios.

1. Oswald began a notation on Hosty on November 1, made the common mistake of starting to write the previous month—*Oct*—and then, realizing his mistake, changed it to the new month. He then wrote the agent's name and phone number from a card Hosty had left with Ruth on his first visit, but not the address. A week later, when Marina brought him the news about the second Hosty visit and the license-tag number, he entered the tag number and followed it with the address he had failed to enter the previous week.

2. Oswald began his notation on Hosty on November 8 or 9, the date on which he received the data on the license tag. (But why then would he have entered *Nov 1, 1963*? Was it to mark the date of Hosty's first appearance at the Paine house, per the Warren testimony? If so, why didn't he mark the later and presumably more grievous appearance of November 5 as well? And what about the scratched-out *Oct*? Was he still making first-of-the-month mistakes on November 8 or 9?) After entering the date, Oswald proceeded as in the first alternative, by mixing the information from Hosty's card and Marina's license-tag note.

Unfortunately, neither of these scenarios makes much sense, even for Oswald at his quirkiest. And anyway, why would he have wanted Hosty's license-tag number in the first place? What use could he conceivably have made of it?

Such contradictions had long nagged at Mary. One day, stewing in a hot bath, where she did her best thinking (usually fogging the mirrors for forty-five minutes after a majestic, turban-swathed departure), she had the solution.

It required a bit of patience, she told Ray smugly; he'd need to pay attention.

The Friday, November 1 of Hosty's first visit to the Paine house was a busy day for a man who put in a full day of work at the Texas School Book Depository. By 2:30 in the afternoon, Oswald had opened a post office box—his last, after the earlier boxes in Dallas and New Orleans.

We learn from the application for this final postal box that he listed his home address as 3610 North Beckley Street. Again, a contradiction surfaces. The procedure for opening a box at any U.S. Post Office involves a preliminary check on the home residence address written on the application. The postal-route carrier must confirm this address before the box is issued—a precaution, among other things, against postal fraud. But in Oswald's case, for two entirely sufficient reasons, this confirmation could not have been made. First, the home address Oswald listed on the box application was nonexistent; there *is* no 3600 block of North Beckley. Second, Oswald was supposedly living under the name O. H. Lee at his actual residence, 1026 North Beckley. With neither a name nor an address that worked, the carrier could hardly have confirmed the validity of the application.[14]

Another facet of the November 1 postal-box application is noteworthy. Under the heading of "name of firm or corporation" to be using the box, Oswald listed two organizations: the familiar FPCC, and a new group, which he would join that same day, the American Civil Liberties Union. The double listing served the apparent purpose of linking two entities that otherwise, apart from Oswald's membership in each, had no connection. Less than a week after the assassination FBI director Hoover would have occasion to use this fortuitous association, claiming it as evidence that the supposed assassin was a Communist—for "he was a member of the ACLU in New York, and the Fair Play for Cuba Committee."[15]

But whereas the implications of this double listing have been previously noted, Warren critics have hitherto failed to mark a more subtle and significant problem with the November 1 P.O. box application. As had been the case with the earlier Dallas box that was used as a return address for the mail-order gun purchases, *the portion of the application authorizing other persons to receive mail would also turn up missing for this, Oswald's last postal box.* Dallas postal authorities appear to have been quite thorough in losing all paper trails that might have led to other persons involved in either the receipt of the rifle or in receiving mail at Oswald's post office boxes. In the case of the November application, however, the authorities couldn't use the fraudulent excuse used for an earlier box in Dallas: that postal regulations called for destruction of this portion of the application upon closing of the box.[16] (They didn't.) The last box was still open when Oswald died. Unfortunately, none of the Warren investigators noticed this discrepancy, which appears to implicate the postal authorities in the willful destruction of evidence.[17]

After opening his P.O. box of November 1, Oswald was still not done for that Friday. He sent a letter (postmarked 2:30 P.M.) to the American Communist Party, giving his new box number, 6225, as his return address. The letter informed the party officials that he had joined the American Civil Liberties Union and asked about the advisability of "attempt[ing] to heighten its progressive tendencies"[18]—about as helpful to the ACLU as his earlier letter, in which he claimed to be using his position "to foster communist ideals," was to the Fair Play for Cuba Committee.[19] Finally, on the same date, Oswald posted his application for membership in the ACLU.[20]

In some ways, Oswald's busy day was reminiscent of another day in March of that year, when he also conducted business with the post office, purchasing a postal money order and sending his mail order for a Mannlicher-Carcano rifle in the name of A. Hidell. On that earlier occasion he appeared to have been prompted by a visit by FBI agent Hosty. On this occasion as well, Hosty was part of the picture. That was precisely what the Hosty notation in the Oswald notebook showed.

"Hold it," balked Ray when Mary had rounded this unmapped curve. "What was that last part again?"

"You have to look at the notation," she said. She fished it out of a foot-high stack of papers and held it up to her slow student.

"Don't you see? It's obvious."

Maddeningly, when she explained it, it was.

Oswald met Hosty in the agent's car on November 1, the same day the agent stopped by, supposedly looking for him at Ruth Paine's house. The ex-Marine needed the license-tag number to help identify the car. It was not an unusual FBI practice to "meet in cars," as Oswald had done with agent John Fain in Fort Worth in the summer of 1962 after arriving from Minsk. The brilliant Sylvia Meagher, universally respected by nonfrauds on either side of the conspiracy question, made a strong case close to thirty years ago that Oswald almost certainly had been meeting with Hosty in Dallas. She pointed out the Warren testimony in February 1964 of Lee's brother Robert Oswald, who noted that Marina "had an aversion to speaking to him [Hosty] because she was of the opinion that he had harassed Lee *in his interviews*" [emphasis added].[21] Robert's testimony about prior meetings between Hosty and Oswald flatly contradicted Marina's; she told the Commission that Hosty had never seen or met Oswald. Despite misleading the investigators, Marina had quite obviously discussed the meetings in some depth with Robert. Her denial of the earlier contacts with Hosty was but one of a number of lies the frightened immigrant from a nightmarishly repressive country docilely fed to the intimidating American authorities. Today, though far more settled and secure (and though saying she now believes Oswald did not kill Kennedy alone, if he did at all), she has continued to cling to some of the old stories, but to no great harm. We need keep in mind only that in 1964 Robert said Marina told him of preassassination meetings (both in Irving and Dallas) between Lee and Hosty, and that on this score, Robert, with no apparent reason to lie, had the greater credibility.[22]

But granted that Mary's analysis was on firm ground on the matter of a prior Oswald-Hosty relationship, what about the rest of it— the date on the notation, for example?

Not surprisingly, she had an answer for that, too. She had an answer for *everything*, as she did as the smartest little girl in the second grade, the kind you'd like to throttle when nobody was looking.

Oswald was first contacted by Hosty sometime in October, probably in the latter part of the month. The contact was likely no more than a brief phone call, the point of which may have been simply to set up a later meeting. Oswald wrote down *Oct* initially not because he made a silly mistake eight or nine days into November (thinking it was still the previous month), but either because he first started to write the date on which the call occurred, or because he assumed the proposed meeting would take place that same month. In any case, he scratched out the *Oct* he had begun to write and substituted *Nov 1, 1963*, the Friday for which the meeting was actually set (and on which, in fact, Hosty showed up at the Paine house supposedly looking for him). Oswald then entered Hosty's phone number (probably because it was given to him next) and followed it with the license number of the car in which the meeting would take place.

On November 1, we find Oswald once again carrying out a slew of postal "duties," following the instructions, seemingly, of a "running" man.

Meeting with Hosty that day, and perhaps agreeing then to resume his role as an informant for the agent, Oswald obtained a post office box with Hosty's assistance, using a nonexistent address (as, in earlier mail orders, the nonexistent name *Hidell* had been used), and listing on the P.O. box application either Hosty or another government contact (or alias for the contact) as persons also authorized to receive mail at the box. At this November 1 meeting Oswald could have reported on the ACLU meeting he had attended with Michael Paine the previous Friday, October 25, and Hosty may have instructed Oswald to go ahead and join the organization, as well as to continue his contacts with the American Communist Party.

The drill was becoming an established procedure for Oswald, however resentfully he may have performed his chores or hated to see Hosty coming, as Marina had complained to Robert. And more than postal duties were involved, apparently.

By strange coincidence, November 1 was also the date of an FBI airtel that Hosty had received from San Antonio, to which he responded fourteen days later.[23] The subject of the exchange of airtels was "John Thomas Masen, IS [Internal Security]—Cuba." As we'll see in a later chapter, the Bureau was involved at this time in snooping on rumored anti-Castro plans, reportedly with CIA backing, for a second major invasion of Cuba—the same one Ruby may have popped off about to Rex Basinger in his jail cell. The airtel from San Antonio had called on Hosty to do some checking on a man named George Perrel,[24] believed a Cuban exile in the Dallas area. (Though not known at the time, the name "Perrel" would prove to be an alias for an important figure.)

In Hosty's mind, the ex-Marine would have been an asset experienced in mixing with Cuban exiles, and quite possibly the best one to involve in a street-level search for Perrel. The search was triggered on the same day Hosty appears to have met with Oswald and sent him rattling through the P.O., restyling once again his postal identity. That was one coincidence; there was another. Looking for Perrel may have been only a variation of another regular assignment for Oswald as Ruby watcher. Both tasks involved high-volume gunrunning and a new story Hosty had been starting to hear in recent days about a second major invasion of Cuba. He had first heard of it, an FBI document would suggest,[25] on or about Friday, October 25. If so, that time would nicely coincide with the probable date on which Hosty first called Oswald to set up their meeting of November 1.

The coincidences were starting to pile up. Either that, or they weren't coincidences.

Meanwhile, there was yet another round of strange Dallas doings around this period for the professed leftist and Castrophile Oswald. He was being sighted at meetings of anti-Castro militants.

CHAPTER NINE

It Takes a Woman to Know

How do we know that Oswald attended anti-Castro Cuban meetings in Dallas during the fall of 1963?

Well, a female witness—termed "credible" even by J. Lee Rankin, general counsel of the Warren Commission—let the matter out more than three decades ago. Remarkably, no one has appeared to notice as yet, possibly blinded by the klieg lights of her *other,* more sensational, assertions. To this day, the latter have comprised an important structural prop for conspiracy arguments, and continue to generate enthusiastic assessments of the witness's reliability. Anthony Summers has called her claims "the strongest human evidence" [of a conspiracy], HSCA investigator Gaeton Fonzi remains "absolutely convinced" she was telling the truth, and—no!—the angelic Sylvia Meagher, mistress of reason and noblest spirit ever to examine the Kennedy conundrum, titled the exposition of her tale "the proof of the plot." But with both new and overlooked information at hand, the flashy old tale suddenly looks very much like an invention, proving only that even the Divine may (though very seldom) err, like mere human scribblers.

The mysterious witness in question was beautiful Silvia Odio, perhaps the most exotic Cuban creature to hit Dallas in 1963. Her charms turned the head of a priest (probably not an easy thing to do back then), a department-store tycoon, and an important Warren investigator, only among others. But despite the unfair punch that Silvia's looks may have added to her persuasiveness, where men were concerned, at least, not all of the faith placed in her account has been unwarranted. On one significant Oswald matter, missed to date by Warren critics and apologists alike, we can probably believe her. Ironically, the matter is not connected to Silvia's famous story of the "loco" ex-Marine standing shabbily in the hallway of her Dallas apartment one early evening in the last week of September 1963, except by way of undermining the story's trumpeted credibility. Rather, it has to do with Oswald's attendance at meetings of anti-Castro exiles during the same period—as, after many a twist and turn, we shall see.

Meanwhile, we should resist the temptation to race ahead, for as Fonzi reminds us in his recently published book, *The Last Investigation,* "Silvia Odio's background is important." So it is.

The first part of Silvia's life, if not quite as privileged as Princess Di's, had something of the same storybook air. She was the second of ten children born (on May 4, 1937) to Sara del Toro and Amador Odio-Padron, a Havana trucking magnate who was to become one of the richest men in pre-Castro Cuba. After spending her early years of schooling at Mercy Academy in Havana, Silvia was sent to the U.S. for high school at Eden Hall Convent of the Sacred Heart in Philadelphia, where she graduated in 1954. She then returned home, enrolling at the University of Villanova with a concentration in law. Intellectually accomplished as well as comely, she wrote stories that were published in Latin-American journals. The charmed life continued through a grand wedding in 1957 to Guillermo Herrera, whose family was reportedly characterized by knowledgeable exiles in Dallas as even higher than the Odios in the Havana pecking order: "cultured, old, extremely wealthy and socially well known." By contrast, the Odios were considered nouveau riche, and "it was whispered that Silvia had married above her social status."[1] Possibly so, but who cared? Life was good. A nine-month sojourn to New Orleans accompanied the wedding festivities.

But the first rumblings of trouble were on the horizon. The year before Silvia's marriage, Fidel Castro, a former student leader at the University of Havana, had put together a rebel force; the year after, his men were moving virtually unchecked. By the first day of 1959, the corrupt dictator Fulgencio Batista fled the country, and six weeks later Fidel Castro was premier of Cuba.

At first, Silvia's family welcomed the change. Despite their wealth,

Amador and Sara were gifted with a crusading spirit that made them the natural enemies of all tyrants. Amador, exiled twice by the Batista regime, had given his active support to the pro-Castro underground. After the revolution, however, he quickly realized that his hopes had been misplaced; Castro was an avowed Marxist. Again, Amador joined the underground, this time fighting against his former ally and hiding other secret dissidents. Among Amador's closest compatriots in such efforts was a democratic socialist named Manolo Ray, founder of the anti-Castro *Movimiento Revolucionario del Pueblo* (MRP), forerunner of the *Junta Revolucionaria* (JURE)—a group we'll shortly meet again.

With the unmasking of Castro, the many children of Amador and Sara were dispersed to the safety of the U.S. Silvia's younger sisters Annie and Sarita, and two of her brothers, ended up in the Dallas area. Silvia, Guillermo, and their own children reached Miami on Christmas Day of 1960 for processing by immigration authorities, and quickly took up residence in Ponce, Puerto Rico.

Meanwhile, Amador Odio's luck was running out.

After a planned bazooka attack on Castro went amiss in October 1961—one of numerous CIA-sponsored attempts on the life of the Cuban leader—the senior Odios were discovered harboring a man implicated in the aborted assassination plot, Reynol Gonzalez. Arrested at the Odio country estate outside Havana, Sara was imprisoned on the same grounds (which Castro, with grim delight no doubt, converted into a national women's prison) for eight years. Amador's fate was worse: a cell on the notorious Isle of Pines.[2]

If, as Aristotle said, tragedy required a precipitous fall from high to low estate, Silvia qualified in spades. The girl who once had everything was soon to have nothing. The final blow was struck when her husband—the one from the culturally superior family—departed on a company trip to Europe and never returned.[3] She had been abandoned with four young children. Penniless, her parents in jail, separated from her brothers and sisters—who themselves were scattered to the four winds—and living in a foreign land, Silvia began to experience emotional difficulties. They manifested primarily as fainting spells.

While Silvia languished in Ponce, her sister Sarita, now a student at the University of Dallas, had made the acquaintance of a Dallas society matron, Lucille Connell. It was a fortuitous connection. Mrs.

Connell, a Protestant contributor to the local Cuban Relief Committee (part of a national Catholic effort to help resettle the waves of
Cuban refugees washing up on U.S. shores at a rate of 2,000 a week)
and vice-president of the Dallas Mental Health Association, was sympathetic to the tales Sarita told her of her beautiful sister in Puerto
Rico. Moving quickly to help, Lucille Connell sent Silvia the air fare to
reunite her with Sarita in Dallas. "I came from Ponce because I was
mentally sick at the time," Silvia would later tell the Warren Commission. "I was very emotionally disturbed, and they [Mrs. Connell and
Sarita] thought that a change from Puerto Rico to Dallas where my
sister was would improve me, which it did, of course."[4]

Leaving her children behind temporarily, Silvia reached Dallas in
March 1963 and soon made fast friends with her benefactor Lucille
Connell, who became her closest confidante. After several false
starts, Mrs. Connell helped Silvia locate a psychiatrist, Dr. Burton C.
Einspruch, who began treating the pretty Cuban arrival in April. As
her symptoms diminished and she regained her confidence, Silvia
found a small apartment on Oram Street, located employment, and
eventually went back to Puerto Rico—on June 29—to retrieve her
four children. On her return to Dallas, she moved to a somewhat
larger (but still cramped) unit in the Crestwood Apartments on
Magellan Circle. Her long-term dream remained to reunite her scattered siblings. In the meantime, however, she had already succeeded
quite remarkably, despite her destitution, in establishing herself in
the highest circles of the Dallas community.

Though Silvia attended meetings of anti-Castro exiles, "she was
never really part of the Cuban community [in Dallas]," psychiatrist
Einspruch explained to Warren attorney Burt W. Griffin in 1964. Her
"real place was at the very top of the social ladder among American
Dallas socialites"—the same kind of people Baron George de
Mohrenschildt might have felt at home with as he guided Oswald's
fortunes in Dallas in the months immediately prior to Silvia's arrival.
Among her "closest friends" were the John Rogers family (owners of
Texas Industries), with whom she stayed following her postassassination hospitalization. She was also reported to have dated Lawrence
Marcus, one of the owners of Neiman-Marcus, where she worked
for a while. Such was Silvia's success, the psychiatrist said, that she
"unquestionably passed Mrs. Connell on the Dallas social ladder"
and may have aroused "a certain amount of jealousy," causing Lucille

Connell to cool on her protégée "because Miss Odio was more of a social success than Mrs. Connell."[5]

But as in the case of George de Mohrenschildt, not everything about Silvia was quite as it seemed. It wasn't exactly true, for example, that she was disengaged from exile politics except for the nominal attendance of a few meetings. Indeed, the "beautiful brilliant, well-spoken, charming woman," as a Griffin memo described her (via Einspruch), had much of the baron's inner guile beneath the pleasant froth. Despite her faints and the encumbrance of four children, she was at some real level a Cuban patriot, busily dabbling in arms deals like any of the guys. (With imprisoned parents and a lost society to avenge, it would have been contemptible for a person of spirit not to try to do *something*.) Her trip to Puerto Rico to pick up the kids was also a trip to report on a gunrunning meeting to Manolo Ray, her father's friend and founder of JURE, to which she too belonged. The meeting had taken place in her own apartment on Oram Street.

All this was told by Silvia to interrogator Wesley J. Liebeler of the Warren Commission ("I don't know if this is legal or illegal; I have no idea," she sort of put in). The day she arrived in Puerto Rico to collect her children, June 29, 1963,

> was exactly the day that I saw [Manolo] Ray again. We had been trying to establish a contact in Dallas with Mr. Johnny Martin . . . [who] had heard I was involved in this movement. And he [Martin] said that he had a lot of contacts in Latin America to buy arms . . . and that if he were in contact with one of our chief leaders of the underground, he would be able to sell him second-hand arms that we could use in our revolution. . . . So I called Eugenio ["war name" of Rogelio Cisneros] long distance from Dallas. . . . This was before I left for Puerto Rico. June 28, Eugenio arrived from Miami to see Johnny Martin. . . . So they went to my house. Now, I was living at the time at 6140 Oram Street, the day they arrived. But when I went back to Puerto Rico, the same day, June 29, I saw Ray, and I explained to him what Johnny Martin here in Dallas was up to, and then [Ray] said that he was planning a trip also to see if something could be worked out. Mr. Ray himself was planning a trip in connection with that. He was going to Washington to be interviewed by some high official.[6]

That JURE leader Manolo Ray was probably looking to bankroll

Silvia's arms deal by visiting a "high official" in Washington is less pertinent to our story than the simple confirmation that she was actively
engaged in arranging such deals. In this case she set up the June
meeting with Rogelio Cisneros (alias Eugenio), a trusted man who
had known her father, at her place of residence—on Oram, not yet
the Crestwood Apartments.

It is also worth noting that though Silvia sought to mislead the
Warren Commission on a number of points (as we'll see), this
wasn't one of them. Here she was telling the truth, as we know
from the verification provided by Cisneros himself to the Secret
Service on May 4, 1964, approximately two months before Silvia's
testimony to the Commission:

> Mr. Cisneros said he went to Dallas, Texas, from Miami, Florida,
> in June, 1963 . . . specifically for the purpose of contacting Sylvia
> Odio who was to introduce him to a person in Dallas who was
> interested in selling them small arms. Cisneros said he contacted
> Sylvia Odio only once, and at that time he was accompanied only
> by Jorge Rodriguez Alvareda, their [JURE's] Dallas delegate, and
> no one else.[7]

Rodriguez, Cisneros' companion at the late June meeting in Silvia Odio's apartment, confirmed the same information in an FBI
interview conducted September 8, 1964. So did Antonio Alentado
Leon, who had succeeded Rodriguez as president of the Dallas unit
of JURE,[8] and had learned secondhand of the visit to Silvia's by Cisneros and Rodriguez.[9] In the same FBI interview, Alentado observed
that Silvia, who of course knew both English and Spanish, "had done
some translation work" [for JURE] and "could be useful in the translation of propaganda material to be used in the organization of the
group at Dallas."[10] Silvia supposedly wanted to become secretary of
propaganda for the JURE group in Dallas, but Rodriguez "would
not allow this," as he reportedly told Dallas agent Wallace R. Heitman, because "Odio was too emotional and would, therefore, not
make a good officer of the organization."[11] She talked too much and
tended to be "unstable," he believed. Alentado put in that her
divorce was another mark against her, notwithstanding her alleged
abandonment, because it carried "a social stigma among Cubans."[12]

Silvia's meeting with Cisneros, Rodriguez, and the Uruguayan gun
trader who owned a washateria down the street, Johnny Martin,
proved unsuccessful. Cisneros did not like Martin's way of doing

things, and no deal was made. The meeting was, however, productive in a different way. It appeared to serve as precursor and model for a later meeting that Silvia claimed to have had at her apartment house with three *other* men in "late September" 1963, three months after the Cisneros-Martin meeting. It was this second meeting that constituted Silvia's most celebrated claim, described by her to FBI and Warren interrogators, as well as to two reputable investigators to whom she granted interviews, Anthony Summers and Gaeton Fonzi.

As Silvia told the story, all of the men who came to her door on that second occasion—which she pinned down to September 26 or 27—had been strangers, and consequently never allowed inside the apartment; instead, she had put on a housecoat and talked to them in the outside hallway for the fifteen to twenty minutes that they stayed. Two of the unknown men were anti-Castro Cubans who claimed to be members of JURE and to have known her father in Cuba, she said. They explained that they had just driven in from New Orleans. In fact, they looked grubby and "very greasy," presumably from the road, but also in that way suggesting "low Cubans, not educated at all," not the sort of persons with whom her father would have associated, Silvia suspected. The purpose of the visit, the Cubans told her, was to ask her to translate a Spanish letter, which one of them showed her. The letter's content, she explained, was "something like we represent the revolutionary counsel [JURE], and we are making a big movement to buy arms for Cuba and to help overthrow the dictator Castro." They asked her "to translate this letter and write it in English and send a whole lot of them to different industries to see if we can get some results."[13]

As she supposedly replied when the request was made, this was the "same petition [that] had been asked of me by Alentado," and with four children to look after, she had no more time for this latest request than for the previous one, which she had also turned down.

The third man in the party, meanwhile, was an American. And this was the punch line, the cause of all the fuss in connection with Silvia's story: he was Lee Harvey Oswald, introduced to her as "Leon Oswald."

In September 1963 the name meant nothing to Silvia, as she explained, since she didn't know Oswald or that he would end up accused of killing the president. It was only two months later, when the brutal assassination actually happened, that she would fully realize the horror of once having encountered the man who would do such a thing. Her shock on the Friday afternoon of November 22, 1963, when she collapsed at work upon hearing that the president had been shot downtown, was compounded when she learned, upon waking up in a hospital bed, that a suspect had been apprehended in the assassination, and that he was the same "Leon Oswald" she had seen in the hallway with the two JURE Cubans in September, even to the same name. What was most eerie and disturbing, she had even been *told* what Oswald was capable of by one of the Cubans who accompanied him. This Cuban, who identified himself only by his JURE "war name," Leopoldo (and who remains unknown to this day), had called Silvia the day following the visit. As she recalled for the Commission, she thought at first that Leopoldo might be "trying to get fresh" with her on the phone, being "too nice" as he'd been the night before, telling her how pretty she was and so on.

Leopoldo had started the call in the same spirit, but then moved on. He asked her what she thought of the American he'd introduced her to the previous evening. "I didn't think anything," Silvia told him. Leopoldo's question seemed unusual, inasmuch as she'd barely noticed the American companion, she testified. The conversation had been conducted almost entirely in Spanish, and the ex-Marine hadn't said more than a few words. Once, though, "trying to be nice," she'd tossed a question his way. She asked him, "Have you ever been to Cuba?"

> And he said, "No, I have never been to Cuba."
> And I said, "Are you interested in our movement?" And he said, "Yes."[14]

That was pretty much it, as far as "Leon" was concerned. But Leopoldo told her more in the phone conversation—volunteered it—and following the assassination, she would never forget the words. Oswald was an ex-Marine who was "kind of nuts," Leopoldo said. Oswald had told the Cubans, Leopoldo claimed, that they didn't "have any guts," because "President Kennedy should have been assassinated after the Bay of Pigs, and some Cubans should have done that, because he was the one that was holding the freedom of Cuba actually."[15]

Silvia's claim of a hallway meeting with Oswald in the company of two anti-Castro Cubans was rife with conspiratorial possibilities. One could envision almost any scenario, from Oswald's being set up as a patsy two months prior to the assassination, to his willing collaboration with Cubans who were not really members of JURE but pro-Castro agents looking to implicate the anti-Castro group in the coming disaster. (The Oswald quantum jinx continued, apparently; he could be "observed," but not pinned down.) Like certain vintage UFO tales—the famous sighting by Deputy Marshal Lonnie Zamorra in Socorro, New Mexico, the bizarre seduction of Brazilian farmer Antonio Villas-Boas by a beautiful slant-eyed alien with red pubic hair, or the dual abduction, retrieved under hypnosis, of Betty and Barney Hill one night in New Hampshire—Silvia's close encounter with Oswald has been repeated and anthologized over the years to the delight and wonder of Kennedy assassination buffs, as well as the consternation of several investigative bodies.

The story's dramatic power was felt even by the Warren Commission, hardly a friend of conspiracy scenarios. On Sunday, August 23, 1964, with the publication date of the *Report* looming barely five weeks away, Warren chief attorney J. Lee Rankin remained troubled by the unresolved aspects of Silvia's claims. He sent a letter on that Sunday to J. Edgar Hoover calling on the Bureau to check her story out further; it was "a matter of some importance to the commission that Mrs. Odio's allegations either be proved or disproved."[16]

The FBI responded exactly three weeks later by locating a man named Loran Eugene Hall in California. Hall, a soldier of fortune, claimed that he too had been in Dallas in September 1963 trying to raise funds for "anti-Castro activities" and accompanied by two men, one of whom resembled Lee Harvey Oswald. Then, in a follow-up interview with the Bureau, he backed off the story (which had not been supported by his two named "companions," Lawrence Howard and William Seymour).

Though the Loran Hall story may have been bogus, it served the necessary purpose of allowing the Commission to write off Silvia's story (though not her credibility; she was still believed to have seen three men in September—Oswald just wasn't one of them). In the end, of course, the story would have had to have been turned down by one means or another; *all* conspiracy angles were automatically excluded from serious consideration by the Commission, except for the consideration of how best to exclude them. Justice Warren's dedication to the nonconspiratorial lone-nut theory regardless of all

possible indicators to the contrary, it should be added, was not simply a perversity but in all probability a perceived obligation to a
higher end than the discovery of truth, namely the preservation of
the country. On this level, at least, it is difficult to fault the Commission's action. Who knew what might have resulted in that tense post-
missile-crisis era from an imprudent discovery that the president of
the United States had been murdered as a result of an international
conspiracy involving, say, agents of Fidel Castro with the suspected
assistance of the KGB? And would a different kind of conspiracy,
implicating only American intelligence operatives and anti-Castro
Cubans, have been much better in its toll on public trust? Understandably, the Commission wasn't eager to run into any such complications. There were some things it was better not to know, as
Oedipus's wife tried to warn him.

What was surprising, at any rate, was that Silvia's conspiratorial
allegations weighed on the Commission's mind for as long as they
did. They didn't succumb in a fifteen-second TKO, as did most other
such allegations, but were still hanging around in the fifteenth
round. Fonzi notes that even one month after Rankin sent his letter
to Hoover, when the *Report* was already in galleys and practically out
the door, Warren staff counsel Wesley J. Liebeler, the man who had
interviewed her, was still agonizing over the potential importance of
the Silvia Odio case. "There are problems," Liebeler writes to his boss
in a memo in the last days prior to publication. "Odio may well be
right. The commission will look bad if it turns out that she is."[17]

Naturally, the Commission ignored this sort of shilly-shallying and
put out its report on schedule. Though cagily admitting that "the FBI
had not yet completed its investigation into this matter" at press time,
the report's authors nevertheless concluded that "Lee Harvey
Oswald was not at Mrs. Odio's apartment in September 1963."[18] The
implication was that the Silvia Odio mystery had been laid to rest
with the discovery of Loran Hall and the supposedly Oswald-like
William Seymour (who therefore had to be the "Leon Oswald" Silvia saw).

The Warren Commission did not feel the need to consider, apparently, that the use of the name "Leon Oswald" alone, two months
prior to November 22, 1963 and in connection with the assassination
of President Kennedy, was a problem of seismic proportions regardless of who might have been standing in Silvia's doorway. "Identifying"

him as Seymour (whom he obviously wasn't), or anyone else, proved nothing. Hoover was finally reduced to suggesting that, "phonetically," Loran Hall sounded something like Leon Oswald.

But if Silvia's story was the scandalous "unfinished business" of the Warren Commission, as Sylvia Meagher said (or as Fonzi called it, "the most flagrant of all the commission's distortions"), fans of the Odio Oswald scenario would be gratified to see it finally attain the offical respect it seemingly deserved fifteen years later, when the House Select Committee conducted the second major investigation of the Kennedy assassination. Silvia's testimony, the HSCA report concluded, was "essentially credible," and there was "a strong probability that one of the men [in the hallway] was or appeared to be Lee Harvey Oswald."[19] Partly on the basis of this circumstance, the committee found in favor of a probable conspiracy.

Silvia's story, though attacked by Posner as the work of an emotionally disturbed person (a frequent charge with Posner), and though conflicting with Oswald's official itinerary (he was in, or en route to, Mexico City at the time of his alleged visit to the Crestwood Apartments), has made it through the gauntlet of time essentially intact, with its most vital questions still unresolved. (So, too, the great UFO stories appear to defy the passing years, growing stronger precisely because they have survived so long without explanation.) Silvia's story remains today, as in the beginning, a source of solace for conspiracy-siders, and for Warren defenders an unsettling possible skeleton in the closet.

But the defenders can finally relax, at least as far as the story itself is concerned. There's nothing to it. Silvia made it up. She did it with finesse, and for the noble reason of wanting to liberate her country from the tyrannical rule of Fidel Castro, who was holding her parents captive. More immediately, she probably also wanted to help save the skin of some acquaintances—fellow patriots—who she appeared to have good reason to believe had pushed their luck beyond all reason by involving themselves in the assassination of the American president; but more on the whys later. Silvia's narrative skill, which she had previously employed in writing published stories ("Do not abandon literature," her father implored in a letter from his jail cell—"write a good book even though it takes you years"), allowed her to weave together persuasive details from several actual events.

One of the real events Silvia used in her fabrication was the period

of confusion during the days preceding the move from her Crestwood apartment. This apartment, though larger than the one she
had on Oram Street, where the Cisneros meeting had taken place
late in June, was still inadequate for Silvia's needs. She had her children with her now, and they were probably getting into everything,
including the enticing cardboard moving boxes scattered throughout the apartment. Silvia had already put down a deposit on a larger
place (and closer to her work at an Irving chemical company) and
would be taking possession on October 1, only a few days away. That
was how she and her sister Annie had pieced together that the knock
on the door had been on a Thursday or Friday, September 26 or 27.
Annie, a student at an upscale Catholic girls' prep school in north
Dallas, Ursuline Academy, had been called in to help with the packing and baby-sitting, and was staying at Silvia's until the move was
finished. On the night in question, Silvia had been dressing in the
bedroom—she was going out that evening—when Annie heard a
knock at the door. The invention begins with that knock.[20]

It is quite possible that a group much like that in Silvia's story came
to the door on that or some other night when Annie was present to
answer. It isn't difficult to imagine (and no one can refute) that at
some time Silvia and her sister—two young women alone in an apartment with four small children—may have been visited by some fresh-
talking strangers making dubious claims and wanting to continue the
conversation inside the apartment. (Silvia herself cited some other
such instances in her Warren testimony: "I never open a door unless I
know who they are, because I have had occasions where Cubans have
introduced themselves as having arrived from Cuba and known my
family, and I never know" [WC II 370].) As protectress of the brood,
Silvia may well have handled herself with her usual social aplomb by
hearing them out, but in the hall, as she later described. The probability that some such incident actually happened is vastly increased by
Annie's "corroboration"—which, however, remains a gray area.

"I'm the one who opened the door when Oswald and the two
men came," Annie told Mary in 1995. In 1964, however, Annie was
unwilling or unable to make such a positive identification of the
American; she merely agreed with her sister that he had to be
Oswald based on Silvia's recollection. Silvia herself made the same
crucial distinction in her Warren testimony regarding the extent of
her sister's corroboration.

MR. LIEBELER. Did your sister hear this man introduced as Leon Oswald?

MRS. ODIO. She says she doesn't recall. She could not say that it is true. I mean, even though she said she thought I had mentioned the name very clearly, and I had mentioned the names of the three men.

MR. LIEBELER. But she didn't remember it?

MRS. ODIO. No; she says I mentioned it, because I made a comment.[21]

Silvia's carefulness was no doubt increased by the knowledge that her sister Annie, though not called before the Commission, would likely be interviewed by the FBI. Just so, the week following Silvia's session with Liebeler, Bureau agents questioned Annie at the southwest Miami home of Cesar Odio, one of Silvia's nine siblings (and today Miami city manager). Annie told the agents that she had indeed been present at Silvia's Crestwood apartment under the circumstances described above, had heard the knock, and opened the door. She reportedly saw "three men in the hallway outside the apartment, two having the appearance of Cubans and one who appeared to be an American." One of the Cubans asked for Silvia, and Annie left the door secured by the chain latch, called for her sister, and returned to her business. That was the extent of Annie's actual participation in the claimed incident of late September, as she told the Bureau interviewers. But in fact there was another important incident in which Annie and Silvia participated jointly. It was the *re-creation*, two months later, of the September visit—a postassassination period of intensive conversations with Silvia in which the "American" was transformed to "Oswald" in Annie's mind. As Annie told the FBI in her Miami interview of July 1964,

> when she returned to her home [on November 22, 1963] and heard of the assassination, she turned on the television set. Subsequently, Lee Harvey Oswald appeared on television as the leading suspect. Miss Odio [Annie] said that as soon as she saw Oswald on television she had *a distinct impression that she knew she had seen him before.*
>
> A short time thereafter, while visiting her sister Silvia, *Miss Odio mentioned to Silvia that she had had the feeling that she had either met or seen Oswald previously.* Silvia *then remarked* that Oswald was the American who had accompanied the two Cubans to Silvia's

apartment in late September 1963. Miss Odio [Annie] said that
she *then recalled* that incident and realized that this was in fact the
person of whom she had been thinking when she saw Oswald
on television.[22] [Emphasis added.]

Despite the amply described influence of her older sister in the
formulation of her knowledge, Annie concluded by telling the
agents she "was almost certain that the American who came to Silvia's
apartment with the two Cubans was Oswald."[23]

Annie's statement to the FBI was strangely reminiscent of the poor
Hills of New Hampshire, who were rounding a turn one night in
1961 and ended up being sperm- and egg-counted (or some such) by
aliens—who then rewarded the interracial couple for their good
behavior at the Doctor's by showing them a "star map" of their true
home. The Hill incident was followed by a gradually increasing number of reported abductions, all of which were characterized by supposedly forgotten alien abductions that were later "retrieved" under
hypnosis. The Hill case was interesting, however, in that it was not
only the first of the pattern, but uniquely a dual abduction—as, in a
sense, the Silvia-Annie collaboration (unwitting on Annie's part)
appeared to be.

As skeptics explained the dynamics of the Hill phenomenon,
Betty, the dominant personality, "imprinted" a dreamed or otherwise
mistaken perception on her younger and more passive husband. As
their "memory" of the event was refined through repeated discus-
sions, neither was aware that it was Betty who was really telling the
story, while Barney was only rephrasing it. (He remained convinced
till his death in 1969 that he had undergone an alien experience.)
Whether, like Barney, the helpful Ursuline student Annie was consciously or unconsciously led in her postassassination memory
retrieval by the dominant personality of her dazzling twenty-six-year-
old sister, Silvia (as Annie essentially admitted to the FBI), it is evident that this partial presence of a second malleable witness does not
provide the corroboration that Silvia's hallway claim requires. The
claim remains today essentially a one-person account.

The rest of Silvia's story was elaborated by bonding details onto the
late-September Crestwood apartment setting from another real event
she drew on for her fabrication, the June visit at Oram Street by Cisneros. The two hallway Cubans of Silvia's invented story "knew" her
father, as did Cisneros, and they wanted her to translate materials for

JURE fund-raising purposes—the same thing that Rodriguez, her other visitor with Cisneros and Juan Martin, thought she could do well; the latter had been the small talk of the previous, real meeting. In Silvia's fabricated version, Leopoldo offered her the publicity tasks that she had told Rodriguez, in the June meeting, she wanted to do as "secretary of propaganda." Rodriguez turned her down for the job, we recall, but in the improved imaginary scenario it was she who turned Leopoldo down—a small creative touch that did no harm to the overall Oswald-at-the-Crestwood picture, since that itself was an invention.

That the Silvia Odio story is a deliberate invention and not a confusion in her mind is apparent from a later lie she told to the priest who had been her lover, Fr. Walter M. Machann—as a precise old pamphlet of his north Texas diocese spells it, or *McKann* as the Warren Commission prefers, or *McChann* as he is usually known in the literature. (There were still other variations.) No one seems to have been too certain about the name except the father himself, and he wasn't around to help. A few weeks before the assassination, he had mysteriously dropped out of sight, perhaps from a breakdown, in the city where he had been a lifelong resident. Some weeks later, after the assassination, he quietly left town and has not lived in Dallas since, though returning occasionally to visit his mother. He was last seen (in 1993) in Bangkok. (Machann's mother told Mary in a recent interview that he was visited by the Secret Service or other government investigators as recently as 1992 or 1990.)

But in the spring of 1964, Father Machann hadn't yet made it to Bangkok. That April, apparently at the behest of Warren general counsel J. Lee Rankin, the Secret Service had launched an all-out search for the unusual padre, who was rumored to have bedded a number of women parishioners during his tenure as assistant pastor at a Catholic church in east Dallas. After agents failed even to identify the father in Miami (where he had received his training as a Cuban refugee adviser), Secret Service inspector Thomas Kelley managed to locate Machann in New Orleans, interviewing him on Thursday, April 30. The former Dallas priest (he was now on indefinite leave) had been attending classes at Loyola University, and was, as he told Kelley, a frequent visitor of Silvia's uncle, Dr. Agustin Guitart, a physics professor at the university. Guitart, it may be recalled, happened also to be a friend of Carlos Bringuier's, and had attended

the New Orleans court hearing of Lee Harvey Oswald following his
"street scuffle" with Bringuier and two other members of the local
chapter of the Student Revolutionary Directorate (DRE) the previous summer.

It wasn't, of course, Machann's vow-breaking proclivities that interested assassination investigators like Kelley, but the role he was said
to have played from 1961 through most of 1963 as chaplain of a Dallas group assisting Cuban refugees; for if rumors were flying concerning the priest's sexual liaisons, they were even more rampant
on a more relevant matter, the possible participation of Cubans—
whether pro- or anti-Castro one couldn't say—in the assassination
of the president. On the latter matter, Machann had been in a position to be an invaluable informant.

Organized in 1961, the Cuban Catholic Committee of Dallas had
sought to help Cuban refugees by finding them jobs and planning
social and religious functions for their families. In March 1963 the
committee had gone a step farther, setting up a resettlement office
funded through the Catholic Relief Service. Responsibility for conduct of the new office, which offered food and other living assistance
for arriving exiles (who were frequently met by committee members
as they stepped off a plane at Love Field), had been given to the committee's capable director, Father Machann. In his capacity as benefactor and spiritual liaison with the Church, the clean-cut father had
been a popular figure with refugees. He knew virtually everyone in
the Dallas exile community, and everyone knew him—this despite
the fact that (as Machann told Inspector Kelley in April 1964) he had
made it a policy never to attend "any of the political meetings of the
Cuban groups that were represented by the Cubans in Dallas,
although he was often cajoled and entreated to attend them."[24]

That the father had often been cajoled as well by ladies of the flock
wasn't hard to believe. He was twenty-nine—three years older than
Silvia—tall, and movie-star handsome. (However, the Secret Service
mistakenly reported Machann's age at this time as twenty-six.) He
had dimples; he was intelligent; he was polite; he was perfect.
"Caught in the embrace of love's glance, I floated anticipating just
the very sight of my beloved," one woman would later write about the
man who gave her Communion. She wasn't alone, nor the only one
to despair when he suddenly dropped from sight. Of all his female
admirers, however, the most spectacularly beautiful was Silvia Odio,

the 1963 arrival who was said not only to have been one of his mistresses, but (as the story is told today by those who remember) his true love, the only one he really cared for.

For all its good works, the Cuban Relief Committee of Dallas had been abruptly disbanded immediately after the president's murder, by which time the handsome and seemingly competent father, though still in town, was nowhere to be found. He had reportedly taken shelter at his mother's house, and was there on the Friday of the assassination—when he, like Silvia that day, was said to have suffered a collapse.[25] But whatever the priest's personal problems may have been at this time—the ones that had driven him underground—the Secret Service and other federal agencies knew nothing of them, except for the whispers of his sexual entanglements. That Silvia had been a conquest of Machann's (or vice versa, perhaps) had already been reported to authorities by her old socialite confidante, Lucille Connell, and tacitly acknowledged by Silvia's psychiatrist, Dr. Burton Einspruch. The psychiatrist told Warren interviewer Burt W. Griffin that he "did not believe the affair with Father Mac Chann was as serious as [the Commission] had been led to believe," a rather ambiguous assessment. Griffin closed the delicate topic in his memo (dated April 16, 1964) on the interview by noting, "We did not press him [Einspruch] on this matter, however."

In April 1964, having located the missing priest, and armed with the knowledge of his suspected past with Silvia Odio, the Secret Service concocted a devious plan that in efficacy, at least, was miles ahead of the "straightforward" approaches of the FBI and Warren Commission. Instead of grilling Silvia directly on her hallway-Oswald story, Inspector Kelley wanted Father Machann to call Silvia long-distance in Dallas (he would be "furnished the necessary funds") and see if he could get her to tell him "the name of the JURE representative who had accompanied Oswald."[26] As Kelley may have calculated, she might well confide things to the former lover—her "father confessor," she called him in a 1993 documentary—that she wouldn't say under oath or the glare of a federal inquiry. In this the inspector was probably right, but would Machann be snake enough to go along?

It turned out he would. He was, in fact, remarkably docile and cooperative, reportedly stating that "it was the duty of every citizen to cooperate to the fullest extent in the President's Commission's investigation and that he felt he was bound in conscience to give whatever assistance he could."[27] It is possible that Machann's docility was caused (as Secret Service head James J. Rowley, Kelley's superior, wrote on the father's behalf) by the fact that he "did not realize at the time that she [Silvia] had not made a full and frank disclosure of the names of the people who brought Oswald to her."[28] Toward the end of December 1963, while the priest was still lying low in Dallas, Silvia had spoken to him about the Cubans who had supposedly shown up with "Leon Oswald" in September, but she also told Machann she had already "discussed this matter fully" with FBI agents. Later, after Father Machann moved to New Orleans, she had written him a letter saying she had again "discussed her meeting of Oswald with Government officials." Consequently, Machann told Kelley, he didn't feel that he would be "violating a confidence in giving any information previously given [by Silvia to] the proper authorities."[29] Even so, the eagerness of Machann to participate in this game—"stating that if he could not induce her to tell him who the people were, he could induce her to tell it to the proper authorities"—sounds a bit edgy somehow, as if fear or nervousness is driving it, if not the passivity that sometimes accompanies convalescence from a mental breakdown.

The deal was struck, and it was agreed Machann would call Silvia that same Thursday evening around 6:30. He requested, and received, privacy for his call. Then,

> upon his return to Inspector Kelley's room about 7:30 pm, he said he had made the call to Mrs. Odio in Dallas and she was very anxious to discuss the entire matter. She advised him [Father Machann] the only information she could provide on the people who visited her was that one of them said he was using the code name Leopoldo, that the second man she could identify as Eugenio Cisneros, and the third man was introduced to her as Leon.[30]

This was amazing. Where did the *Cisneros* come from? Silvia hadn't said a word to the FBI or any other investigative body prior to this phone call about one of the two Cubans being Cisneros. Indeed, the second Cuban—the one who wasn't "Leopoldo"—was so vaguely discussed in Silvia's FBI interview of December 18 that the report made no individual reference to him at all. Obviously she didn't volunteer then who she thought he could be (nor did the agents apparently think to ask). The second Cuban was similarly inconsequential in all of Silvia's later official tellings (he was "on the heavier side and had black hair" was all she could recall for the Warren Commission)—so much so that he was the only one in her story not to have a name. Now, suddenly, he was Rogelio Cisneros (alias Eugenio), the man who had traveled from Miami to Dallas to trade arms in her Oram apartment three months prior to her alleged hallway sighting.

Silvia provided an explanation of sorts that could conceivably account for the discrepancy. The explanation can be dismissed, however. She told Father Machann there were some things she did not tell the FBI "because they did not ask her these questions" and that anyway the agents had "interviewed her improperly"; they had embarrassed her by barging into her place of employment with questions about the story she'd told Lucille Connell concerning Oswald and the two Cubans, and caused her to lose her job. (One of the two agents involved was the familiar James Hosty, whom Oswald so resented and for approximately the same reasons.) But that Silvia withheld some matters from the FBI is irrelevant—or rather, would only be relevant if the matters withheld had been true. The part about Cisneros wasn't.

What was Silvia thinking of, to tell her old lover such a thing? One day she may decide to tell us, but until then the only thing we can know for certain is that the statement was yet another intentional lie (hers, of course, not the ingratiating Father Machann's, who would appear to have no reason to mislead the Secret Service on this score). It wasn't a mistake on her part. She couldn't possibly have confused a man she knew (and whose visit, which far from being a surprise she had helped to plan, had occurred at an entirely different time and place) with the "greasy" nameless blob, Cuban No. 2.

Besides, wasn't she supposed to have asked the men in the hallway, "Were you sent by Eugenio?"[31]—meaning that one of them couldn't have been Cisneros? Well, yes, she had, but that was in another variation of her hallway tale—what might be called the definitive Warren version. This was just the point. Silvia, the creative artist, tinkered with her story lines as any good writer will, and that she did so demonstrated once again that the claimed September visit was a fiction. The Cisneros variation enters the literature only by a kind of happy fluke, as the result of the Secret Service's admirably sneaky maneuver. Silvia didn't realize she was practicing her lines into an open mike, or she undoubtedly would have been more careful, as she was when she spoke to the Commission three months later, on July 22. She wouldn't, and didn't, make the "identification" of Cisneros to any official authority, since she knew it would only fracture the credibility of the hallway story she had been telling since her first FBI interview of December 1963; Cisneros himself would immediately jump up and deny the assertion with corroboration of his whereabouts elsewhere in late September of that year. (As it was, none of the JURE Cubans believed her story of an Oswald visit at that time.)

Thus Silvia had to cover her April lie to Father Machann with another lie to her Warren interrogator, Wesley Liebeler, in July.[32] She steadfastly refused to admit the obvious, that she had told the priest that one of the men in the hallway had been Rogelio Cisneros. After repeated questioning, the exasperated Liebeler brought out his trump card, the report on the Secret Service-sponsored New Orleans phone call that Kelley's superior had sent the Commission.

> MR. LIEBELER. Now, I have a report before me of an interview with Father McKann by a representative of the U.S. Secret Service in which it states that Father McKann told this Sercet Service agent that you had told him that one of the men was Eugenio. But you indicated now that that is not so?
>
> MRS. ODIO. No. Perhaps he could have misunderstood me, because he has the same problems with names. Probably I did tell him that the man was not Eugenio.[33]

Silvia wouldn't budge from her position even in the face of documentation. Nor could Liebeler shake her from an even greater— indeed, her greatest—Warren lie: that she hadn't known Oswald before the assassination, except for the alleged one-time September encounter.[34]

Dr. Burton Einspruch had treated Silvia once a week from April 1963 "until the President was assassinated."[35] He was still seeing his patient five months after the assassination (though presumably on a less frequent basis), and had an appointment scheduled with her the morning after Warren counsel Burt W. Griffin's interview with the psychiatrist on Monday afternoon, April 13, 1964. Griffin's memo on that little-known interview (supplied by researcher Paul Hoch with

the marginal notation "Probably released by accident") was overlooked by Posner and sadly twisted by one conspiracy adherent.[36] It
stands, nonetheless, as one of the most important documents of the
assassination. Griffin noted to fellow Warren counsel W. David Slawson:

> Dr. Einspruch stated that he had great faith in Miss Odio's story
> of having met Lee Harvey Oswald. He stated that, in the course
> of psychotherapy, Miss Odio told him that she had seen Oswald
> at more than one anti-Castro meeting. One of these meetings
> was apparently at her house, he believed, and Miss Odio's sis-
> ter also saw Oswald at the house. Dr. Einspruch says that Miss
> Odio reported to him that Oswald made inflammatory com-
> ments about Cuba. The term "inflammatory" is Dr. Einspruch's
> and he could not clearly indicate what it was that Oswald had
> said. In fact, I got the impression these comments were pro-Cas-
> tro.[37]

This astonishing statement, coming from a man who talked of
his attractive patient in the most glowing terms and whose last intention would have been to injure her reputation, provides the key to
understanding Silvia's hallway hoax, as we'll see. Let us note immediately, however, that Einspruch's revelation that Silvia had known
Oswald prior to the assassination was not unique. It was supported
by a similar revelation from Silvia's *other* confidant, Lucille Connell.
The two friends were no longer as close as they'd once been, but in
Silvia's turmoil following the president's murder she had reflexively turned to Mrs. Connell to unburden herself. If she thought the
former benefactor would keep the information quiet, however, Silvia would be sadly disappointed. Lucille Connell called the FBI on
the heels of her conversation with Silvia. When Bureau agents interviewed Mrs. Connell on the following day, November 29, 1963, she
told them Silvia had revealed to her that "she knew Lee Harvey
Oswald, and that he had made some talks to small groups of Cuban
refugees in Dallas in the past."[38] There was no mention of a hallway, the Crestwood Apartments, late September, or two JURE
Cubans, one named Leopoldo. There was, however, the same kind
of supplemental assessment of Oswald—persuasively indicating a
knowledge of his peculiarities—that Silvia had provided to her psychiatrist, Einspruch. Silvia (Lucille Connell reported) had stated
that she

personally considered Oswald brilliant and clever, and that he had captivated the groups to whom he spoke. Odio further reported to Connell during this conversation that a call had been made in recent months by a Cuban associate of hers to an unknown source in New Orleans, Louisiana, requesting information on Lee Harvey Oswald. Odio volunteered that information was in turn received from the New Orleans source to the effect that Oswald was considered by that source in New Orleans to be a "double agent." The source stated Oswald was probably trying to infiltrate the Dallas Cuban refugee group, and that he should not be trusted.[39]

Silvia denied everything, of course. She gave Wesley Liebeler a blank-eyed "I don't think so" when the Warren interrogator asked if she'd ever told Einspruch she "had seen Oswald in more than one anti-Castro meeting."[40] And in a second FBI interview (on September 9, 1964), Silvia could only conjecture that Mrs. Connell must have made up those terrible things about her out of catty malice:

> In reply to a question as to why Mrs. Connell would attribute such a statement to her, Miss Odio stated that, "You would have to be a woman to understand." She stated that Mrs. Connell and she had been friends, but due to personal reasons, they had had a falling out. She believes that Mrs. Connell in attributing the aforementioned information to her was using a "double-edge knife," that is, she was trying to help in the investigation of the assassination and at the same time was trying to embarrass or get her, Miss Odio, in trouble.[41]

But Dr. Einspruch, who was the authority on these matters, did not subscribe to the old double-edge-knife-trick theory. While granting to Griffin that there may have been "a certain amount of jealousy" between the two women, he had no doubt that Silvia had said the things to Mrs. Connell that the confidante had passed on to the FBI. Silvia had said essentially the same things to him and, as Griffin closed off the doctor's analysis of the matter, "it should be emphasized that *at all times Dr. Einspruch felt that the story about Lee Oswald was completely true*" (emphasis added). (Again, of course, the story the psychiatrist felt was "completely true" was that Silvia had prior knowledge of Oswald through his attendance at anti-Castro meetings, not the September hallway meeting that she had yet to fabricate at the time of her November 28 conversation with Lucille Connell.)

What the doctor felt needed explaining wasn't the behavior of Mrs. Connell (she had only told the truth), but why Silvia had confided her postassassination jitters to the friend in the first place at a time when the friendship had cooled. For this, however, he had an answer. He told Griffin

> that Mrs. Connell, at the time of the President's assassination, was Miss Odio's closest friend in Dallas. He [Dr. Einspruch] stated, however, that their relationship had begun to cool at that time. He stated that Sylvia Odio had slept at the Connell house on more than one occasion. I [Griffin] drew the inference that it may have been possible that Miss Odio wished to confide in Mrs. Connell as a means of cementing their deteriorating relationship. Dr. Einspruch observed that he thought the anxiety which Miss Odio felt after the assassination may have caused her to tell Mrs. Connell about Oswald and that that episode was one of lack of self-control.[42]

What Dr. Einspruch tells us, though in more restrained tones, is that Silvia was out of control with panic in the days immediately following the assassination. She had to talk to someone besides her psychiatrist and chose Mrs. Connell, who was older by some twenty-five years and perhaps represented the closest thing she had to a mother in her new country, no matter that they'd had their differences. It is in this stressful climate, made even stormier when her friend relayed her confidences to the FBI (ever reluctant to pursue a possible conspiracy angle, the Bureau took three weeks to show up at Silvia's job), that we can clearly see the evolution of the hallway hoax—how and why Silvia dreamed it up.

Silvia's story of the late-September hallway visitation (the only one she has ever told officially to assassination investigators) is a cover story to mask a real story, which, in great stress, she partly confided to a few trusted persons. The tale of Leopoldo, Oswald, and a quiet guy without a name (he would become "Angelo" in Silvia's later renderings) saw the light of day in her first interview with officialdom, when the FBI belatedly rushed in wanting to know what she had been telling her friend, Mrs. C. L. Connell. Whether Silvia invented the hoax then in one inspired flash, or had received some forewarning and pondered it a while, she came through magnificently. She whipped up a plausible-sounding scenario, told in her intelligent melodious voice, that provided an innocent explanation (you weren't responsible for the people who came to the door, especially if they were perfect strangers and you didn't even let them in) for the potentially ruinous things Lucille Connell had let out, the noxious busybody. As Silvia explained to the FBI (and forever more thereafter), she'd had contact with Oz, yes, but only once—a safely meaningless encounter in a hallway—and it was this single meeting that she had mentioned to Mrs. Connell, but the poor excitable woman had misunderstood everything, indeed had gone off the rails completely, inventing wild things—that business, for example, about checking up on Oswald in New Orleans and finding out he might be trying to infiltrate anti-Castro groups in the Dallas area. Where did *that* come from? You had to be a woman yourself to understand how such things could happen, and so forth.[43]

The story got the job done, we already know. It was bought, even becoming an assassination classic in the process, like the three tramps. More importantly, it has exculpated Silvia and her associates for more than thirty years.

But from what? What was the cover story covering up?

To explore this question, we should first revisit a couple of details from Dr. Einspruch's statement to Griffin. The psychiatrist, we recall, told his interviewer that "one of these meetings" (retaining the plural) at which Silvia claimed to have seen Oswald had occurred at her house; and that her sister had been present. At first blush these details have a familiar hallway ring—as if Silvia might have also told Einspruch the cover story, in which little Annie figured, but had intermingled it with descriptions of *other* times she had seen the "inflammatory" Oswald. The two "greasy" Cubans, the hallway setting, and the next day's phone call by Leopoldo had been omitted from the psychiatrist's conversation with Griffin, or else Griffin had failed to note them in his memo. Of course, such a loss of details was the kind of thing that could happen when a story was transmitted through several parties—but wasn't there a limit? Wouldn't Einspruch at least have reported, if Silvia had told it to him, the punch line of her hallway story—that Oswald had supposedly said Kennedy should be murdered? And wouldn't that have been the first thing the reliable Griffin, or any other competent witness, wrote down? More likely, Silvia simply hadn't delivered her punch line to Einspruch. But why, if she told the story at all?

There is an even greater problem to the supposition that the psychiatrist's reference to an Oswald visit during the presence of Silvia's sister (who wasn't identified by name in Einspruch's telling) stemmed from her usual hallway story. This usual story, we have seen, was a cover presumably designed to hide what Silvia had confided privately, that she and her anti-Castro acquaintances had consorted with Oswald prior to the assassination. But if cover was the apparent purpose of her famous claim, why would she have defeated this purpose by also telling the doctor about *additional* encounters with Oswald, where he had been his recognizable horse's-ass self with "inflammatory" pro-Castro comments at anti-Castro meetings?

The probable answer is that Silvia did not not tell Dr. Einspruch her patented hallway cover story at all. What she described to him, as she did to Lucille Connell, were events that actually happened, including a meeting "at her house" (as Einspruch said simply)—not in the hallway, or with strangers, but under her roof and with people she knew—including, apparently, one of her sisters. But if so, was this sister necessarily Annie? Annie, who had been present at the irrelevant Crestwood Apartments—where nothing of note happened—was a thirteen-year-old prep-school student, not likely to have been involved in political meetings. At the time of the assassination, however, Silvia had been living on Davis Street in Oak Cliff (where she had moved on October 1) with another sister, Sarita. Sarita was older than Annie and a senior at the Catholic (and ultraconservative) University of Dallas, where she had made numerous anti-Castro Cuban acquaintances. Though Oswald wasn't in Dallas on September 26 or 27 (the fly in the ointment of Silvia's cover story), he had arrived back in town from Mexico City on or around October 3. During the time Oswald was actually available to visit Silvia's apartment, in other words, she was living with Sarita (about a mile and a half from Oswald's boarding house on North Beckley) at 1826 West Davis, Apt. A. That, in all probability, is where the Oswald meetings she spoke of to Einspruch had taken place.

It's possible to envision one such meeting at Silvia's Davis apartment in which Oswald—brilliant, clever, and perverse, as she described him—may have been holding forth in the company of a youthful anti-Castro group, male friends and acquaintances of Silvia and Sarita. Let's suppose further that at this gathering Silvia found herself listening with concern as the conversation took a slightly crazy turn. President Kennedy was coming to town shortly, and the guys had started dwelling on how he needed to be killed, not only for his string of "betrayals" beginning with the Bay of Pigs, but to precipitate a U.S. invasion of Cuba (the assassination would be pinned on Castro's agents). As we'll see in the next chapter, this extremist turn of mind could only have been exacerbated by the CIA's rejection of the DRE's lofty military plans in the Caribbean—a rejection officially announced to the exile student group three days before the assassination.

If Silvia indeed heard some talk along these lines—with a Kennedy visit to Dallas looming—it would help explain why the man she saw weekly during that time, Dr. Einspruch, told Burt Griffin that it was "the period *just before* the assassination" (emphasis added) that was "of great anxiety for Miss Odio." As the psychiatrist also noted to Griffin, he "thought that Miss Odio and all of the local Cubans were afraid that they would be blamed for the Kennedy assassination"; that was the "fear [that] precipitated Miss Odio's blackout on November 22." What, if not some troubling knowledge, would have caused this great fear on Silvia's part? Not many people outside the Catholic circle were talking much about anti-Castro Cubans as possible suspects in the days immediately following the assassination (when the work of the refugee committee was abruptly discontinued by Msgr. Thomas Tschoepe)—the same days when Silvia was so "lack[ing] self-control" that she couldn't stop talking of her prior associations with Oswald, and finally had to invent an official story declaring herself, and by extension, her exile associates, innocent. Her massive dread of somehow being "blamed for the Kennedy assassination" suggested either a well-advanced case of paranoia (not what the doctor was treating her for, however) or the guilty conscience that protesting too much usually reflected.

Who or what was Silvia hiding?

> Sylvia [Odio] stands tall next to Father [Machann], my love, as we descend the great stone steps of the Sacred Heart Cathedral after the monthly Cuban mass. Marcella [Insua] introduces me to the attractive young woman. The acknowledgement on her part is as though she has not even heard my name, as if I do not exist. She ignores the introduction entirely! Vivacious, captivating, she addresses the padre instead, isolating him from us all, seeming to own him. The young, beautiful woman is incredibly asking Father to dinner, saying, "Father, I'd love to have you for

supper. Why don't you come home with me right now?" Formally, he responds, "I am sorry, Sylvia, I really cannot make it. I
have another engagement this evening." Michael [Father
Machann] is deliberately brushing Sylvia off as he breaks away
quickly from our little group.

Jealous? No reason. So far however, strange unfamiliar stir-
rings within, gnaw at the senses. Instinctively, I dislike Sylvia.[44]

Reading a few lines of Marianne Sullivan's *Kennedy Ripples: A True
Love Story,* you know you've entered a new zone. The book, though
published (in 1994) by a small San Clemente press, could glibly be
called the Harlequin Romance version of the assassination. In reality,
and despite some naïve factual confusions,[45] it is a refreshing contribution to the Kennedy literature that allows us a firsthand look at
the preassassination world of Silvia Odio, Father Machann, and their
Catholic circle of affluent Anglos and rabidly anti-Castro Cuban
refugees. After a while, even Marianne's style may grow on you. It has
attitude. Marianne *hated* Silvia Odio. Silvia stole the father from her.
There was nothing in all of heaven or earth you could do that was
worse than that.

Kennedy Ripples is a memoir despite its title. Its true topic, as the
subtitle suggests, is the author's undying love for Father Machann;
the assassination is largely a backdrop for the days of her remembered love, which sadly was not requited by the fleeing priest. The
fact that the assassination occurred during this intense emotional
period in Marianne Sullivan's life, and that it appears to have some
real but inscrutable connections to the tortured love story she is
telling, causes Marianne to do a bit of conspiratorial speculating
about this and that, but without the proper Kennedy-nut background
to distinguish consistently between what is plausible and what has
long ago been hopelessly discredited. No matter; it's what Marianne
Sullivan remembers that is important, not always what she thinks it
may mean. She was an insider in Father Machann's Catholic helping circle for Cuban refugees, and her insider's recollections make
her work a valuable source book of preassassination information by a
first-person observer of events.

As Marianne Sullivan tells us, she and her closest friend, "Hope
Larsen" (so called in the book), were drawn into the Cuban relief
group on an October day in 1961. Hope had just received "a hurried call from Father Walter [Machann]," she rang to tell Marianne.

"He would like us, you and I, to assist with the Cuban Resettlement Program, as volunteers, since he has been appointed the Director. Do you think you can find the time?"[46]

Marianne found the time, of course, since the request involved the man she loved. (As her heart jumped "leap frog," she immediately thought to herself: "Father has engineered this maneuver to involve me . . . for Hope is my inseparable companion.") In the Cuban assistance program, Marianne and Hope would join such other members as once-prosperous Havana executive Jose ("Papa") Insua and his family, including his buxom daughter Marcella, a Col. Robert Castorr and his wife, Trudy, both close friends of Gen. Edwin Walker, and (in spring of 1963) two strikingly blond latecomers, Lucille Connell and her luscious Cuban protégée, Silvia Odio.

The "Hope" in Marianne Sullivan's memoir is Faith Leicht, today a grandmother of twenty-six who recently celebrated her golden wedding anniversary with Robert, a retired pilot for American Airlines; like Faith, he looks far younger than his years. In 1963 Faith was in her thirties and the mother of seven young children. Family and church obligations didn't leave much spare time, but she and Robert enjoyed socializing with Marianne (then Rahmes) and her husband, Ralph, a former baseball player. Marianne, a striking dresser who favored shocking pinks and purples (with jet-black hair and white lipstick), frequently created a small wake of murmurs and raised eyebrows as she boldly made her way down the aisle to receive Communion, but she had a good heart and kept the Leichts in stitches with her stories. "She was adventuresome and very funny—we felt dull and conventional by comparison," says Faith.

Marianne's most unconventional turn was her madcap pursuit of the young parish priest some twelve years her junior, Fr. Walter Michael Machann, to whom she once had planned to declare herself in confession. "I have desired a man other than my husband," she'd tell him—"YOU."[47] Whether she ever did or not she doesn't say, but the relationship began, and it clearly wasn't at his instigation; his failure was in not withstanding the onslaught.

But if Marianne was impressive in her determination to win the reluctant father, she was even more so in her no-holds-barred campaign to track him down after his disappearance. The last time Machann was seen in his public role as shepherd of the city's Catholic exile community was the Tuesday night of October 1, 1963.

On that evening, he and other prominent members of the resettlement committee had shared the stage of Highland Park Town Hall with a guest speaker, John Martino, a fifty-two-year-old American and Mafia associate who was on a Bircher-paid tour to talk about his recently published book, *I Was Castro's Prisoner*. Martino had been imprisoned in Cuba for some thirty-nine months (during which time he had befriended Silvia Odio's father, Amador), and his three-hour book talk dwelled on the barbarism of his confinement by the revolutionary regime—balm to the ears of the gathered refugees and their circle of benefactors on the Town Hall stage. Marianne, who was in the audience, had of course been oblivious to the finer ideological points of the speech. Her main concern was in positioning herself so that "the beautiful priest [wasn't] blocked from my view [by] the speaker's podium." As Martino droned on with his list of Castro's cruelties, she found herself wondering, "Is he [Father Machann] trying to signal me, crossing and uncrossing his legs . . . the frequent motions radiating uncontrollable desires within me?"[48]

Trudy Castorr, meanwhile, who also sat on the stage with Father Machann that last evening, gathered a different impression, as she told an assassination investigator several years later. Though no one doubted (and she least of all) that the young priest performed his duties sincerely and with total dedication, Mrs. Castorr had noticed that he seemed to have started wearing down in the days prior to the Martino talk; he was distracted, "terribly worried, terribly pressed."[49]

In the ensuing days the father's absence was noticed not only by Marianne (though she was no doubt the first) but by everyone in the circle, Cubans and Anglos alike. All were mystified by the sudden and seemingly permanent departure of a young man who had given his all to the Catholic Cuban assistance program since its inception, who had believed in it and loved the people involved, as virtually everyone agreed.[50] Now he had vanished and no one knew why. Trudy Castorr still said years later:

> I have no idea why he [Father Machann] left. . . . After a week or two went by, of course, the Cubans were all talking about, well, "Where is Father McCann?" After all, this was their spiritual leader and no one seemed to know where he was or what had happened.[51]

The last one to take this mysterious business lying down was Marianne, naturally. Seven weeks after Father Machann dropped from sight, she showed up unannounced, and with her "Hope," Faith Leicht, in tow, at the apartment of Silvia Odio. Faith corroborates the visit, as well as the date: Thursday, November 21, 1963, the night before the assassination.

The reason for stopping by, Marianne told Silvia at the door, was to bring her a box of children's clothes from the "Cuban closets" of spare clothing that the benefactors maintained in their homes for the refugees. Though Marianne may have savored its implicit insult, the charity box was only a pretext "to gain a smooth entry" into the apartment; her real reason for the visit was to discover if her love rival—as she had pegged Silvia since their first meeting on the steps of Sacred Heart Cathedral—had some knowledge of the whereabouts of Father Machann, or if she might possibly even be hiding him in her house (against his wishes, presumably). Marianne also admitted to a more morbid, but fascinating, reason for showing up unannounced: she wanted "to catch Sylvia unprepared[;] to observe her in her natural habitat." What she got to observe wasn't pretty, Marianne complains for several pages—the apartment was untidy, the kids and TV were too loud, and Silvia was ungracious (which did not, however, prevent Marianne and Faith from staying three hours). Yet for all of her catty intentions in dropping in unannounced, and despite her many complaints about Silvia's housekeeping (and more), Marianne did Silvia a service: she demonstrated for the historical record that for at least three hours on the night prior to the assassination, nothing suspicious or untoward could be detected at the Davis Street apartment of Silvia and Sarita . . . no uptight meeting of anti-Castro gunrunners... no presence of a weird American ex-Marine would-be infiltrator answering to "Lee," "Leon," or "Oz," receiving (or providing) last-minute instructions. The place was clean in that respect; it passed Marianne's malicious little pop quiz.

As for any signs of Father Machann, there were none of those either. He wasn't hiding in a closet and his name wasn't visible on any of the envelopes and things Marianne snooped through (per Faith's recollection) while Silvia took a long phone call in another room. Finally, the frustrated Marianne dropped all pretense (Silvia hadn't been fooled about the purpose of the visit) and attempted one more question, off the wall, what can I lose? "Sylvia, have you by any chance seen Father Michael since his departure?" The furious woman flinches, her eyes blasting, she speaks coldly, directly at me, "You care too much . . . you are too interested . . . too involved!" . . .

Ending our conversation she walks toward the door, saying, "Father is not in hiding. He is simply trying to make up his mind. He was not meant to be a priest . . . you know that, Marianne."

For once, Sylvia and I are in total agreement. We [Marianne and Faith] do not kiss her good-bye.[52]

With the shock of the assassination on the following day, compounded by the suspicious collapse of Silvia at her job, Marianne went into an even greater investigative frenzy. On the day after the president's murder, she visited Silvia at the Irving hospital where she had been confined. She found the patient alone in a darkened room, her attention riveted on the TV, where the assassination coverage continued.

I venture delicately, "Hi, Sylvia . . . are you all right? What in the world happened to you, you were fine the other night." Frozen. Sylvia responds, "News sure travels fast. How did you find me?"

"Well, Marcella told me you were ill and asked me to visit you as she is working today." I lie. Tearfully, the golden woman replies, "If you found me, *they* will find me." What does that mean?

Who are *THEY*? I am afraid to go further . . . "I am sorry, Sylvia, I hope it is not serious . . . you seemed so well Thursday. I do hope our little visit was not upsetting for you. . . . Uh, is there anything you need, anything that I can do for you?" She does not answer, she does not hear me. Tears slide down her pale drawn face as she murmurs, "Everything is lost now."[53]

Silvia, who would try to ease this despair by opening up in a few days to Lucille Connell and her psychiatrist, persons she trusted, clearly had no intention to do so with the old enemy Marianne Rahmes.

In coming weeks, the stymied Marianne would hire a private detective (who informed her that Silvia had betrayed her parents to the Cuban authorities and was in reality the mistress of Fidel Castro), consult her "trained astrologer" for hints, and discuss the recent bewildering events ad nauseam with her dear friends Faith and Marcella. Father Machann's disappearance was somehow connected to the assassination of the president, Marianne believed; he had heard, perhaps in confession from one of the refugees, perhaps from his mistress Silvia, something about the impending event.[54] This wasn't an absurd or uncommon opinion, it should be noted. Even Colonel Castorr (who, as Father Machann believed, had some sort of intelligence interest in the Cubans) speculated that the priest had learned something he shouldn't have. Machann was at his mother's Dallas home on the day of the assassination, the mother would later reveal, and Colonel Castorr had heard, probably from Mother Machann, that the father "went to pieces in hearing the telecast."[55] This reaction, the colonel agreed, showed "some special extra shock" to the news of the assassination because "of his [Father Machann's] association with the Cubans who were tied in with some affair or other [of the assassination]," and that "it had to be something that he knew prior to the assassination for him to react [in that manner] to the assassination."[56]

As the girls continued their marathon brainstorming sessions, Faith pitched in with her own ideas about Silvia's possible links to the disappearance-assassination equation.

> We dig, discussing the disappearance and the immediate reaction of Father's friends . . . his family, the church officials, the parishioners, the Cubans, the Insuas, Lucille, Patty [Link] and finally Sylvia. Hope [Faith] asks some reasonable questions, "Do you suppose Sylvia fainted out of fear for her own welfare?" "Now what could she have done that would generate such awesome fright? And what connection did she maintain with Father causing her to search frantically for his whereabouts?" "And how about this idea, was she afraid Father might reveal a plot that had been told to him prior to the assassination?"[57]

After the assassination, when Father Machann supposedly "went to pieces," Marianne heard from his mother that he had been admitted to "the psychiatric division of Parkland Hospital for several months."[58] Similarly, the investigator Harold Weisberg had also heard that Father Machann entered "a home to rest" following the assassination.[59] The news did not sit well with Marianne (who suspected the mother of committing the son herself), but she admitted

that "Michael" might have "unwittingly become a part of the assassination plot through Sylvia," in which case "his sensitive mind might
have cracked, resulting in a breakdown."[60]

Three years passed. Finally, Marianne—now divorced—got a
break. She learned that Father Machann was in West Palm Beach—
learned this deviously, being the prize snoop that she was, after having tracked him to New Orleans and written a heart-rending letter.
His reply had arrived a few days later:

> Marianne,
>
> You are to leave me alone. You must not come here [New
> Orleans]. I am going to move and change my address. I am get-
> ting a different phone number. Do not write again, do not look
> back.
>
> Michael[61]

Father's letter betrayed a certain ambiguity, Marianne believed. To
the untrained eye it might have suggested that "Michael does not
love me," as she conceded. But look closer: "Michael's handwriting
appears strange, fragile, almost unfamiliar." Had an impostor written
the letter? ("I have been *deceived* many times," she reflected.) She had
to find out, to "be certain for peace of mind." By the time she picked
up the phone, however, it was too late; he'd already left the Crescent City without a forwarding address. This might have discouraged a lesser mortal—not Marianne. After lying to a former
employer of Machann's in New Orleans about a family emergency
(the priest was her brother and their mother was dying, she told the
operator), she finally received her blessed reward: not only his new
city, West Palm, but the new phone number.

This time, receiving her call, the father sounded resigned. He
knew when he was beat.

> "Michael . . . Michael, are you there?" The sound . . . his sound
> . . . only one man in the world emanates his voice, "Yes, hello
> Marianne, yes it is me. I've been expecting your call."[62]

On a Tuesday, November 22, 1966, exactly three years after the
darkest day in Dallas, Marianne was stepping off a plane in West Palm
Beach, "body faint with excitement." He was waiting. She would find

him strangely detatched, "thinner, more solemn," but with his sexual appetite intact. Between their elaborately described bouts of lovemaking (mystical unions, really), they went shopping and Marianne discovered he didn't know his shoe size. He was "like lobotomized," she told Mary recently. But the book itself, between the lines, shows a more competent Father Machann, though perhaps like many lapsed priests still bookish and unworldly despite his occasional lusts. He had obviously given some thought beforehand to the question of Marianne's insult-proof ardor, and reached a Solomon-like decision. He would grant her her paradise in South Florida, but only for six days (all the time God needed to create the world, after all), making her promise the moment she landed in West Palm to be back "on the plane by Sunday noon." Marianne accepted the conditions, for "I do not question Mr. Walter Michael Machann, private citizen USA . . . and possibly undercover agent or protected citizen."[63]

But even three years after the terrible days in Dallas, Marianne's love life was haunted by the specter of Silvia (who had moved to nearby Miami shortly after the issuance of the Warren *Report*). One morning, while the father was away playing his ritual morning tennis game, Marianne compulsively began going through his things at the apartment. Inside a kitchen drawer, she came upon a leather wallet she had given him years before. She hoped to find her picture inside it, or perhaps one of her many effusive notes, sentimentally saved. "Instead I find inside the frayed, stained glossy photo flaps, a picture of Sylvia! A younger Sylvia, around twenty, in blue jeans, a casual shirt, a casual look, hair longer, the blonde tossing in the wind. If only I could bleed openly!"[64]

Later, having recovered from the cruel blow and seeing another opportunity to snoop, Marianne made a yet more ghastly discovery— the final confirmation of love that she feared.

> While he showers I have a few moments to quickly gaze around again. He has so few belongings, mostly books. I can find nothing that I have sent him. Slide a drawer open quickly, a card from Sylvia, deliberately set there, over a pair of cuff links. Seemingly deliberate. It says, "I've got you by the neck and I won't let you go. I love you." The pain goes deeper as I catch my breath.[65]

Meanwhile, in the same old wallet with Silvia's picture, Marianne had found a mysterious photo—of Father Machann himself. It showed

> Michael, his head shaved, Michael thin, emaciated, in a strange shirt, a shirt or jacket. Michael with a black card bearing white numbers marching across his wide chest! No, dear God, he couldn't have been a prisoner. Michael in prison? Never. Synapses flash to higher energies, an "Agent" . . . an agent would be identified by a code number. I suspect Michael is a government agent . . . or an inmate? No, banish the thought.[66]

Yet a shaved head isn't exactly the signature of a "government agent," and whether Father Machann was ever an inmate somewhere isn't really our business. The photo, for all we know from Marianne's fevered search, may have been a prank ID of some kind.

The pursuit of the elusive Father Machann ends unhappily for Marianne, who was faithful to the end, and deserved better. Happily for us, her fixation on the priest leads past two important pieces of information that are worth our serious attention. One she reveals in her book; the second she gave to Mary in an interview.

(Ironically, neither has much to do with Father Machann himself, who after many years remains largely a mystery, as does the role of the Catholic church in his disappearance. Was he fleeing from some assassination-related matter, as the timing of his departure and his rumored Silvia-like "collapse" on the day of the president's murder suggest, or, as Faith and Robert Leicht now think, from Marianne? Whatever his reason for going underground, the still-devoutly Catholic Leichts believe that the Church helped to hide him, and that its haste to dissolve the Cuban assistance circle immediately after the assassination stemmed from the Dallas hierarchy's suspicion that local Cubans had been somehow involved. ["The Church won't admit it, of course."])

The first important piece of information, reported in *Kennedy Ripples,* is an incident that allegedly happened to Marcella Insua late one Tuesday—October 1, 1963—a date Marianne's astrologer may have found propitious for strange conjunctions, for it certainly had them. It was on that first October Tuesday that Silvia moved into her Davis Street apartment, that Martino gave his book talk at the Town Hall in Highland Park, and of course that Father Machann, who had been on the Town Hall stage with Martino, was seen publicly in Dallas for the last time. That ordinarily should be enough conjunctions for one night, but on this one there apparently was room for one more, at least for Marianne's friend Marcella, who never forgot it.

(Yet another curious event was alleged to have occurred on the night of October 1, 1963, though the source is suspect. At a study group in [Dallas suburb] Farmer's Branch, a man was reported to have said something in a taped conversation about the Cubans "taking care" of Kennedy when he came into town. The story was told to Weisberg by the Castorrs and, as they explained, was being promoted by Nelson Bunker Hunt, Dallas police lieutenant George Butler, and Gen. Edwin Walker, all ultra-right-wingers who themselves had questions to answer about the assassination. The alleged taped statement has the appearance of a red herring.)

That night, Marianne Sullivan writes,

> Marcella receives visitors after her return home [from the Town Hall talk by Martino]. Already in bed, she answers the door bell with trepidation, due to the late hour. Two men state they are in a hurry as their "American Friend" "Lee" is waiting in the car and will she please tell them the whereabouts of Sylvia Odio as they had found her apartment empty. Innocently, Marcella explains Sylvia's move that very day to an apartment in the Oak Cliff area of Dallas.[67]

Our options in dealing with this story attributed to Marcella (who died in 1985) are limited. Either Marianne made up the incident from later published accounts of the hallway fable, or the incident is true and therefore—when the visitors reached Silvia—the probable prototype of her famous story. This is what actually happened that she had to hide (or one of the things, at least).

Unlike Silvia's cover version of an Oswald visit set in late September, Marcella's version (which also featured two Cubans, one of whom she recognized as a man "she had assisted in resettling") did not conflict with Oswald's known travel itinerary. The men at Marcella's door had arrived at a "late hour," Marianne tells us twice, when Marcella was already in bed after a long social evening dominated by Martino's lengthy talk. The night had undoubtedly stretched into the early hours of Wednesday, October 2 when the visitors rang the bell. It was on October 3 that Oswald was thought to have arrived back in Dallas after his journey to Mexico City. (The men in Silvia's hallway cover story had supposedly just arrived in town, we recall.) The time frame of the Marianne-Marcella story, far from conflicting with Oswald's itinerary (as the hallway story did), actually coincided with the approximate time of his return to town. This arcane non-Father Machann fact wasn't the sort of detail that Marianne Sullivan was inclined to know.

If Marcella's alleged claim of a late-night October 1-2 visit is true (as appears, but *¿quién sabe?*), it would be just the kind of preassassination Oswald story that Silvia told about herself to Lucille Connell and Dr. Einspruch in her hysteria following the Dealey Plaza shooting. The main difference was that the October story wasn't self-inflicted; it leaked out on its own, via the stop at Marcella's house to ask directions—as Silvia would quickly learn when the three men arrived. She couldn't have been too happy with this knowledge, since, as she also knew, Marcella was an intimate friend of her worst nightmare, the obsessed love rival Marianne. After the assassination, she would also know that the ladies of the Catholic circle would be talking up a storm about her, putting a lot of twos and twos together ("Do you suppose Sylvia fainted out of fear for her own welfare?"), as indeed Marianne's book tells us they did. These circumstances would again explain why Silvia would find it necessary to tamp down the rumors (her own to Lucille and those Marcella might add to the fire) by means of the long-lived Crestwood Apartments cover story first told to the FBI on December 18, 1963.

It appears quite possible that in backdating an early-October Oswald visit by one week, to late September, Silvia would have been craftily aware that she was creating an "impossible" Oswald (the real one having been out of town at the time). But why would she also choose to implicate JURE—her father's group—as the sponsors of Oswald in the cover story? That is a harder question to answer, and it is here that Marianne Sullivan's second piece of information—the one that she told to Mary—comes in. The information wasn't a particular secret in the community, Marianne says, though understandably she omitted it from her book as a superfluous detail. It didn't have much to do with her theme, Father Machann, but with Silvia's sister at the University of Dallas, Sarita.

Sarita, Marianne Sullivan alleged to Mary, was a member of the *Directorio Revolucionario Estudiantil,* or DRE. Characteristically,

Marianne did not know the organization as the "DRE," nor was she familiar with other anti-Castro Cuban organizations such as Alpha 66, the Second National Front of Escambray, or even JURE, the group Silvia claimed as her own. JURE was the party of her father and of Manolo Ray, the man she had reported to in Puerto Rico about the Dallas gunrunning meeting between two other JURE members, Cisneros and his sidekick Rodriguez, and the unsatisfactory Johnny Martin.

But if Marianne was unfamiliar with the term "DRE," she was well acquainted with the "student directorate"—the anglicized version of the same organization. Silvia's sister, the one attending the University of Dallas, was in the "directorate," Marianne insisted. Everyone knew it; it wasn't a secret. True or not, this information wouldn't have been something Marianne Sullivan cribbed from Silvia Odio's statements to the Warren Commission or to any of her interviewers. Silvia has consistently denied any connection to the DRE, much as she consistently denied talking about Oswald meetings to Lucille Connell and Dr. Einspruch, or telling Father Machann that one of the two men in the hallway was Cisneros.

There was, however, an illuminating exception in Silvia's Warren testimony to her many disavowals of DRE knowledge. Though she hadn't had anything to do with the DRE in Dallas ("not at all"), she told counsel Wesley Liebeler, she *had* heard "about the directorate in New Orleans, because I have family there and they told me about all the incidents about him [Oswald] in New Orleans, about Oswald giving propaganda in the street and how he was down in front of a judge and caused a fight with Carlos Bringuier, and that, of course, this man [Oswald] had been working pro-Castro in this Fair Play for Cuba."[68]

This admitted knowledge of the DRE head in New Orleans, Bringuier, was something Silvia couldn't easily deny because of her known family connection to Bringuier's friend, her uncle Agustin Guitart. It was, in fact, through Guitart ("my family") that she'd learned of the street scuffle and subsequent court hearing, she emphasized to Liebeler; she hadn't read about the affair in the papers.

> MR. LIEBELER. Who in New Orleans told you about this incident between Bringuier and Oswald?
> MRS. ODIO. My family discussed it in New Orleans how he

had been handed the propaganda. The other member of the directorate came along, and they had a problem with him [Oswald], because they were taken in front of a judge. This was true.

MR. LIEBELER. Have you read about that in the newspapers?

MRS. ODIO. No; I haven't. This I know from my family, the information we heard from New Orleans.[69]

All this was clearly true, since Guitart, as we know, had accompanied Bringuier to the court and witnessed the proceedings with his own eyes. That was the basis of his information—and of Silvia's, who hadn't been in New Orleans during the summer of 1963, but who had a firsthand informant in her uncle; and he could hardly have failed to have added, in telling her his Bringuier-Oswald story, that the reason he knew it was that he'd "been there."

Twelve years later, however, Silvia chose to change this account, as a recently released House Select Committee document reveals.[70] The document shows that on January 16, 1976, Silvia claimed to her sympathetic HSCA investigator Gaeton Fonzi that she had no knowledge that her uncle ever had associated with Bringuier at all. When the investigator showed her a photograph of some persons leaving the New Orleans courtroom following the Oswald-DRE hearing, Silvia identified one of the men "as her uncle and said she didn't know her uncle was involved with Bringuier." Fonzi told her that "according to an FBI report, her uncle, Dr. Agustin Guitart, admitted to being at that court hearing." She replied that "her uncle never mentioned his involvement with Bringuier [except] that she knew he was a 'fierce' anti-Communist."[71]

Apparently, having forgotten what she had told Liebeler, Silvia wanted to distance herself from Bringuier and his DRE as much as possible. Fonzi did not ask about the contradiction with her Warren testimony or mention it in his *Last Investigation*. He did add parenthetically, "She herself, she earlier said, was associated with the more liberal element of Manolo Ray's party [JURE] and had always been a Kennedy fan."[72]

But were Silvia's true affiliations with JURE?

JURE was probably the party of Amador Odio-Padron, a friend of Manolo Ray, but we should also keep in mind Silvia's volatility during the early sixties, as well as the fact that she was a woman scorned by JURE, according to Rodriguez Alvareda's statement to the FBI of

September 1964. Silvia had "assisted in the organization of JURE,"
but because of her perceived instability "had never been an official of
the Dallas unit," specifically "secretary of propaganda," as she desired
to be, Rodriguez alleged to the Bureau. Moreover, there was nothing
to suggest that Silvia or her siblings were in harmony with such socialist ideals as JURE's "Fidelism without Fidel," whereas explicit associations did exist between the Odios and known Dallas-area DRE
members. Thus Felix Guillermo Othon Pacho, an exile who in October 1963 was appointed Dallas delegate to the DRE by the group's
military head, Juan Manuel Salvat, told the FBI he knew "of" Silvia
Odio and was "acquainted with her sister Sarita," as of course would
have been the case if Sarita were in the directorate.[73]

For Silvia and Sarita, the DRE was quite likely a slicker, more mil-
itantly with-it version of their father's party. The students of the
directorate were the Red Guard of anti-Castroism, as exemplified by
Bringuier's bizarre streetcar crossing of New Orleans with bannered
slogans in search of the leafleting Oswald. The DRE, the enfant terrible of Cuban exile groups, as its own CIA sponsors lamented,[74]
wasn't for the faint of heart, or for wooly-minded old-line pinkos
merely offended by a cult of personality. Its adherents were cultured
counterrevolutionaries dispossessed of their previous status (nothing like the "greasy" lower-class Cubans whom Silvia, perhaps a bit
maliciously, put into JURE clothing in her hallway fiction).

It was precisely this class of elite, dispossessed emigrés that the
children of Amador and Sara represented, as was the case with
another young man from a wealthy Cuban family who too would
have been acquainted with Sarita. He was Fermin de Goicochea
Sanchez, her fellow student in the fall of 1963 at tiny and ultraconservative U. of D. (one president of which, Robert Morris, was a high-
ranking official in the John Birch Society). Young de Goicochea, a
veteran of the Bay of Pigs invasion, was also in the DRE, and like
Othon had met with Salvat when the military "secretary general" traveled to Dallas from Miami in October 1963, some five weeks prior
to the assassination. As we learn from documents released in 1994,
de Goicochea admitted to the FBI that Salvat recruited him on that
occasion to serve as DRE "secretary for military affairs" in Dallas.[75] In
practice, this meant that Sarita's fellow student and directorate member was to locate arms for guerilla strikes against Castro.

As noted in the previous chapter, FBI agent Hosty received an airtel on November 1, 1963 requesting the search for an exile named George Perrel, believed to be in the Dallas area. By the spring of 1964 the Secret Service, conducting its own earnest investigation of the assassination over J. Edgar Hoover's protests, had also joined the search for "George F. Parrel"—one of the names agent Thomas Kelley asked Father Machann if he recognized. (He didn't, he said.) Despite the FBI's November 1 call for Perrel, the FBI would not conduct an interview with the mystery figure until September 1964, after the Warren Commission had safely folded its tent. In fact, however, the Bureau had known both his identity and whereabouts since the day of the assassination, when ATF agent Frank Ellsworth relayed the information from a man he had arrested in Dallas on November 20, gun-shop owner John Thomas Masen. On the ride to jail, Masen had pointed out a man on a black Honda motorcyle; that, he'd told Ellsworth, was George Perrel. The motorcycle rider had turned out to be Sarita's DRE classmate, Fermin de Goicochea Sanchez.

How the FBI knew that Perrel-de Goicochea was too conspiratorial a package to take to the Warren Commission (with which the Bureau worked in perfect harmony of spirit, having its own reasons for not wanting to unveil an Oswald-related conspiracy) is part of the story related in the next chapter. The one-sentence version is that de Goicochea, alias George Perrel, was found to have been a key participant (together with other DRE bigwigs) during the weeks prior to the assassination in planning a second major Cuban invasion armed by weapons stolen from a large U.S. Army post at Killeen, Texas, Fort Hood. (The weapons were stolen with the collusion of Fort Hood ordnance officer George Nonte, as well as the knowledge of the FBI—one likely reason the Bureau wasn't eager to publicize what it knew about de Goicochea prior to the dissolution of the Warren Commission in September 1964.) De Goicochea, the DRE military rep entrusted with the chore of acquiring weapons to fuel the anti-Castro effort, may well have been one of the persons involved in meetings with Oswald at Sarita and Silvia's apartment, and consequently one of the persons Silvia may have sought to shield with her cover story of two anonymous and never-to-be-found Cubans.[76]

And there may have been one *other* young Cuban, closer to the family circle, whom Silvia's story protected.

A dozen years after mob (and CIA) associate John Martino gave

the exiles of Dallas a three-hour anti-Castro pep talk as part of a
"book tour" funded by the John Birch Society, he became talkative in
a different way—as mob figures sometimes do near the end of their
days. In June 1975, some two months before his death, Martino
allegedly admitted to a then-NewsDay reporter, John Cummings, that
he himself had "played a role" in the Kennedy assassination—an
admission first reported twenty years later by Anthony and Robbyn
Summers in *Vanity Fair.* "Two guns, two people [were] involved,"
said Martino reportedly: anti-Castro Cubans.[77]

When Mary called Cummings in Long Island, the former reporter
confirmed the admission by Martino—whose claimed role was as
"facilitator," not triggerman—but added something not mentioned
in the Summers article. Martino had also told him, Cummings said,
of "a woman he knew in Dallas who knew a lot of things" about the
assassination. At first, said Cummings, he had no idea whom Martino
meant. Later he discovered, however, that it was Silvia Odio. (Cummings thought of "going somewhere with what Martino told me,"
he explained, "but where would I take it? The government doesn't
care.") Perhaps as intriguing as the mention of Silvia was the fact that
the association between the Odios and the assassination was made by
the guarded Cummings himself, volunteered independently *prior* to
any mention of the Cuban family.

> M.L. Did you have the feeling that he [Martino] was a major
> player in the assassination?
> CUMMINGS. Not at the time . . . not until later when he told
> me [about his involvement] just before he died. *Although I won-
> dered, I remember reading about the Odios, him telling me about them.*
> M.L. What did he have to say about them?
> CUMMINGS. He never referred to them by name. Just by, a
> woman he knew in Dallas who knew a lot of things. [Emphasis
> added.]

Asked if Martino had mentioned any other persons involved in the
assassination, Cummings maintained that he had, but cautiously
refused to go farther.

> CUMMINGS. He did mention names—a couple of names to
> me.
> M.L. Can you say who they were?
> CUMMINGS. Well, I can tell you that he mentioned a name
> to me of . . . well, I don't think I'd better. There was one name he

Author, mobster crony, CIA asset, and Odio family friend John Martino, who confessed a role in the Kennedy assassination shortly before his death in 1975. (Courtesy John Woods II)

mentioned to me in particular that I didn't know at the time and who has become quite well known.

M.L. Is he still in Miami?

CUMMINGS. Oh, yeah, you'd know him right away if you heard.

M.L. Did he [Martino] ever talk about her [Silvia's] story that she had been visited by Oswald and two others?

CUMMINGS. No.

End of conversation. The last could hardly be called a surprise, of course. Whatever John Martino (a prison friend of Silvia Odio's father who met with her sisters in Dallas) had to say about Silvia, who "knew a lot of things," it wouldn't have had anything to do with a well-rehearsed cover story about Oswald and two Cubans in a hallway. It would have been a *real* story . . . the one we are still waiting to hear from Silvia, when and if she decides to come forward.[78]

CHAPTER TEN

Meaningful Glances

As FBI agent Joe Abernathy would testify in the February 1964 trial of car-crash victim Lawrence Miller, the agent was alerted to the Trunk Street transfer of guns—from a white Dodge to the blue Thunderbird—by the Burglary and Theft Division of the Dallas Police Department. How the B&T detectives who invited Abernathy to accompany them to the stakeout at Trunk and Main knew that something would occur at just that location in the early evening hours of November 18, 1963 has never been determined. There was a tip, obviously, but whether from their own intelligence sources or an anonymous informant remains unknown. For that matter, so do the detectives themselves (as we saw in chapter 1). Abernathy was not required to reveal their identity at the Miller trial, and claims today he can no longer remember their names. The peculiarity of this lapse of memory, as well as of the general proceedings of Abernathy and the unknown B&T detectives on November 18, was remarked by retired ATF agent Frank Ellsworth in October 1993.[1] Had he been at the Trunk Street stakeout, Ellsworth noted, he wouldn't have had to call in a patrolcar to make the arrest, nor would the white Dodge have been allowed to slip from the scene. Under the laws enforced by the ATF, he explained, the mere observation of the transfer of weapons would have permitted him to arrest the occupants of both vehicles on the spot.

Was there a reason for the tenacious withholding of the identities of the B&T detectives, and was it in some way connected to the sting

Ellsworth had in store that same night for gun dealer (and reputed Oswald lookalike) John Thomas Masen? Ellsworth's ATF, together with two other government agencies, had been investigating a string of inside thefts at a major Texas army post, Fort Hood. Millions of dollars' worth of stolen weapons were leaving the base and passing through Masen en route to Cuban groups like the Dallas chapter of Alpha 66, according to admissions made by the gun dealer to the ATF agent, Ellsworth claimed. Ellsworth himself had talked on the phone at Masen's shop with an army officer at Fort Hood, and later informed Warren counsel Burt Griffin that the gun dealer was selling stolen arms to Dallas Alpha 66 leader Manuel Rodriguez Orcaberro.[2] The arrest of Whitter and Miller as they were on the way to deliver similar goods to two other "customers"—Ellsworth and his partner— was a fortuitous event for Masen, sabotaging the planned bust and protecting the gun dealer and intended ATF target. Was the sabotage by design or coincidence? Where did the tip come from, and why hadn't Abernathy and his quartet of unknown detectives arrested the suspects on the spot during the stakeout? The event raised questions that wouldn't be answered until a fresh wave of FBI releases and other documents arrived from San Jose in March 1994, shortly before the manuscript was due at the publisher. The releases had the effect of mangling yet another deadline, but otherwise couldn't have been a more welcome sight. The Bill Adams cavalry had arrived just in time.

An interesting (and little-known) meeting occurred in a downtown Dallas office four days after the curiously roundabout apprehension of Whitter and Miller. It was held on the Friday morning of November 22, 1963, while the rest of the city buzzed in anticipation of the president's arrival from Fort Worth.

Three men, all federal agents, were present at this session, which finally broke up around 11:45, approximately forty-five minutes before the Dealey Plaza shooting. The agents were Frank Ellsworth of the ATF (at whose Commerce Street office the meeting took place), the FBI's James Hosty, and a figure we haven't met to this point, Agent Ed J. Coyle of army counterintelligence, who was identified (in sworn HSCA executive-session testimony) by his superior, Col. Robert Jones of the 112th Military Intelligence Group of San Antonio, as the army's liaison for presidential protection that day.[3] To spare needless suspense, it should be said straightaway that the three feds hadn't gathered that morning to put finishing touches on a plot to assassinate the president. Ellsworth had called the meeting to discuss the continuing theft of weapons from Fort Hood, Texas, and the possible involvement in this affair of members of the Minutemen and supporters of Gen. Edwin Walker. The agent's credibility as illegal arms purchaser had been blown by the ambush of Whitter and Miller, and he had already arrested John Thomas Masen two days before, though on a minor charge, lacking the evidence that would have been delivered by the hapless Ruby henchmen in the doomed Thunderbird. (Masen shrugged off the arrest and was sprung the next day, Thursday the 21st.)

Right-wing subversives were Hosty's FBI specialty as we recall, and the reason why Ellsworth had invited him to the Friday meeting; the ATF agent wanted to share the findings he had uncovered as part of his investigation of the slippery gun dealer. Coyle, stationed in Dallas but with the 112th MIG of San Antonio, represented the army's interest in solving the pilfering at Fort Hood.

Hosty later reported that after the assassination the army counterintelligence officer Coyle was sent back to Korea "so reporters couldn't get at him—since Korea was a combat zone.[4] It wasn't clear, however, why reporters would want to quiz Coyle about anything. There was no apparent connection between the topic of the Friday morning gathering in Ellsworth's office and the cataclysmic event that followed it by less than an hour—would *be* none for thirty years, until details of the John Elrod Memphis FBI report began to surface in 1992.

When Mary pressed Agent Hosty, he changed his story somewhat about the date he learned of the topic of the meeting (the Masen-Nonte arms deal, as we'll see shortly). He had learned of it on the previous day, he said, explaining that he and Coyle had also met on Thursday, November 21, because the two agents "had already started to work on the [Fort Hood arms thefts] case." There was a third party present on this earlier occasion as well—not Ellsworth, but a Dallas police intelligence officer, Jack Revill. What happened, said Hosty, was that Revill "made a comment about not wanting to guard that son of a bitch Kennedy tomorrow." The remark made Hosty see red, he claimed, and the two men had heated words. The FBI agent "wanted to pop 'im one," he told Mary.

Coyle, being present at the Thursday meeting, overheard the angry exchange; and "it was because he overheard what Revill said," Hosty explained, "that Coyle was sent back to Korea."[5]

Revill today refuses to discuss the incident and Coyle can't be found.

That the army would ship one of its own officers halfway around the world simply to keep a lid on the fact that a Dallas intelligence cop made an indiscreet remark the day before the assassination was hardly a credible concept, of course. But then, the army was known to do strange things. One had to grant that it was barely possible (though only in a world where *anything* is possible) that something like that may have happened—that a higher-up, reacting with ultra-paranoid sensitivity to the alleged Revill remark in Coyle's presence, may have decided Coyle would best be sacrificed for the good of the U.S. Army, i.e., sent to some inaccessible point on the globe. If so, the "reasoning" may have been that *if* the story came out, the November 21 session could be maliciously construed as preassassination plotting, based on Revill's comment; and though Coyle was entirely innocent on this score (as, presumably, were the two other men), better to err on the side of prudence than to have to explain what an army intelligence officer was doing in a room, one day before the assassination, when a Dallas cop groused that he didn't want to protect "that son of a bitch Kennedy."

That, as we say, is the anything-is-possible scenario.

But there's a more reasonable possibility, not quite so premised on either army strangeness or the quaint assumption that Agent Hosty told the truth. He didn't. How much he revised on this matter only became evident with the newest wave of file releases, including FBI materials dating back to October 1963. In addition to shedding light on the relatively minor detail of Agent Coyle's Korean reassignment (and the weightier question of Whitter and Miller's arrest), documents on John Thomas Masen and the military operation of Capt. George Nonte lay bare a tale of high intrigue and interagency dirty tricks. It was, the documents tell us, a plan for a second invasion of Cuba—and the FBI's interest in uncovering it—that served as the hidden driver of murky Dallas doings in the month of President Kennedy's assassination.

The story begins in the early fall of 1963 when, as we've seen, ATF agent Frank Ellsworth was on the trail of gun dealer John Thomas Masen. As the agent would testify to HSCA staff counsel Lee Matthews in 1978, he represented himself to Masen as an Irving policeman who was "not terribly honest" and "hungry for a little extra money," which he hoped to make in the gunrunning game. He himself lacked the means to buy anything significant, he told the dealer, but he did know a wealthy New Mexico veterinarian who was "very much in the market for military ordnance"—machine guns, mortars, antitank guns, and the like, all of which had to be "in good operative condition."[6]

In time, Ellsworth introduced Masen to the "vet"—fellow ATF undercover agent William Fuller. As the relationship became chummier, Masen offered to put Ellsworth in touch with a bigwig in Fort Hood who was "in a position to give us unlimited supply of almost anything the military had in the way of ordnance."[7] This sounded more promising than anything in the original case the agent had been building against Masen; naturally, he told him he was interested. Not long thereafter, while Ellsworth and his friend were once again visiting Masen's gun shop, the dealer picked up the phone and had the agents talk long-distance to a man named Nonte at Fort Hood. Masen, meanwhile, didn't stray far from the conversation, making it clear he was "interested in staying in this thing," Ellsworth would testify. "In other words, he [Masen] did not want to get cut out, he wanted a cut of any business we did with Nonte. He wanted to be a middleman."[8]

Having verified that a man claiming to be a U.S. Army ordnance officer at Fort Hood was offering his government-owned wares to buyers, Ellsworth set out for the army post. (His recollection as to the date of this visit is "a little hazy," but an FBI Teletype suggests his visit occurred shortly before October 24, 1963, as we'll see again.) At Fort Hood the ATF agent stopped by two agencies housed in the same building, the FBI and the army's Criminal Investigation Division (CID). He talked to agents from both offices, asking "if they had been missing any ordnance down there." The question drew blood immediately:

> They told me that somebody was stealing them blind. They said the stuff was going out in truck load lots. They lost I don't know how much stuff. They enumerated large quantities of all sorts of ordnance, including a medium tank that disappeared off the

post. They knew exactly what the serial number and everything else was. But they did not know who got it and how it got off the base.[9]

Ellsworth then reportedly told the Fort Hood feds the good news. He thought he knew where the stolen arms were going, and asked "if they knew anybody by the name of George Nonte." They "certainly did," they said; "he was the ordnance officer there at Fort Hood . . . in other words, all of the stuff that was stockpiled and warehoused and all of that sort of thing was under his control."[10]

Not yet a major (the rank at which he'd be retired six months later), Nonte turned out to be a U.S. Army captain with a top-secret clearance, George Charles Nonte, Jr., commanding officer of D Company, 123rd Maintenance Battalion, Fort Hood. Nonte was thirty-seven years old, a less than staggering five feet, seven inches tall (a deficit partly overcome with a handsome walrus mustache), and quite likely the same gunrunning "colonel" described by Nancy Perrin (chapter 7).

"The CID and the FBI were naturally pleased to get a break in the case," Ellsworth explained in his HSCA testimony. The Fort Hood-based feds asked him to return to Dallas and "continue the line of investigation that Mr. Fuller and I were pursuing, and attempt to make a deal with this George Nonte and take some delivery on this stuff."[11]

Ellsworth headed back for Dallas, eager to start building his case against Nonte as requested. That the ATF agent never got a chance to land his big Fort Hood fish he still ascribes to an unfortunate and puzzling mishap a few weeks after his return to Dallas, the ill-timed interception, on November 18, 1963, of Whitter and Miller by an FBI agent and four purported B&T detectives. The incident so rattled Masen that the gun dealer nervously backed off from any further scheming with Ellsworth and Fuller, thereby scuttling the ambitious plans to bring down the big-time Fort Hood arms supplier. Reluctantly, after "a good deal of conversation," the two agents concluded that "our ability to proceed with the investigation of George Nonte was at an end."[12]

It is worth emphasizing (as Ellsworth did in his testimony to HSCA counsel Matthews) that he and Agent Fuller were as shocked as Masen himself by the unexpected arrests of Whitter and Miller. The morning following the car wreck, after Masen's initial panic had subsided, Ellsworth was able to infer partially from "the things he [Masen] told us and partially [from] reading between the lines, that evidently what had happened was that he had hired these fellows [Whitter and Miller] or he had made a deal with these fellows, and in some manner, shape or form they were supplying the ordnance he was getting from them and they were delivering to him."[13] That Ellsworth could extract even this much information from the shaken gun-shop owner was due to his ability to convince him that he and fellow gun-buyer Fuller hadn't themselves set up Whitter and Miller. This part wasn't playacting, Ellsworth explained to Matthews. Masen

> was able to see that we [Ellsworth and Fuller] really were mystified as to what was going on because we genuinely were mystified. . . . I think partially the reason that we were able to convince him that we were what we said we were, is that we were genuinely mystified . . . we obviously were very bewildered and I think he could sense truthfully our bewildered state. And of course, if we had set him up we would not be bewildered.[14]

But the sabotaging of Ellsworth's investigation wasn't an inexplicable accident. It was the result of government intervention. This much is made clear by a remarkable five-page FBI Teletype dated October 25, 1963, shortly after Ellsworth's visit to Fort Hood.[15] Instead of placing the ordnance officer under close surveillance following the ATF agent's revelations, the FBI, the Teletype tells us, interviewed army captain George Nonte on Thursday, October 24 and "briefed [him] as to scope of discreet inquiry to be made of Masen on contact."[16]

In a word, the proposed "investigation" of Nonte and Masen was a polite scam designed to send the ATF agent home happy. Nonte himself was reporting to the FBI, and his involvement with stolen weapons the ones that were supposedly leaving the post in "truck load lots" was apparently neither news to the agents nor of great consequence. Indeed, the "discreet inquiry" that he was to make of Masen didn't address the matter of stolen arms at all. The Bureau, with weightier matters in mind, wanted only "information pertaining to the military operation in the Caribbean."[17]

In October 1963 the Kennedy administration was continuing the struggle to honor its post-missile-crisis neutrality agreement with Nikita Khrushchev to lay off the Castro regime, even as eager-beaver presidential brother Bobby dabbled with invasion schemes, the CIA bungled its umpteenth plan to slay Fidel, and Alpha 66 and other renegade exile groups deliberately whacked Russian ships off Cuba attempting to provoke another U.S.-Soviet confrontation. In the chaos of this Secret War, J. Edgar Hoover had been impressed as the reluctant ally of the harried president. The Bureau was tasked with enforcing neutrality by such avenues as raiding armed anti-Castro camps (as had occurred in July near Lake Pontchartrain) and, most importantly, staying abreast of the dangerous adventures concocted by the mad swashbucklers of the Langley agency.

It was precisely the latest such information on CIA antics that the ordnance officer with the walrus mustache could provide to the FBI. In his capacity as crooked supplier of arms, he had contacts with shady Dallas middlemen like Masen and Ruby, who in turn were plugged into the activities of CIA-supported buyers in the Dallas exile community. As arms flowed from Nonte to the exiles, information flowed back to him and the Bureau to which he was reporting via the middlemen. (In this game, the Texas entrepreneur Masen, described by the pilfering army captain in an FBI document as an "opportunist" willing to do anything for money short of involving himself in "white slavery or narcotics," sought to capitalize twice: by selling the Nonte-supplied arms to buyers, and then selling the buyer-supplied information back to Nonte or the highest bidder.)

What Nonte reported to the Bureau after talking with Masen was that the upcoming Caribbean operation "centered upon Cuba" and involved a huge rebel force "staging at unknown Caribbean bases." The action would be big—would send the stock market plunging, Masen implied—and appeared to be a second major invasion of the island, not another hit and run on Havana harbor. The information reached Masen, he reportedly told Nonte, from a man "by name of Martinez," a Miami-based "weapons buyer" who had come "through Dallas on [a] recent buying trip."[18]

In one respect the importance attributed to Masen's information by the FBI was justified and in restrospect appears even more so, thanks to yet another newly released Bureau airtel dated November 1, 1963. The planned second invasion of Cuba was to "begin with the *last week of November* against the Cuba mainland" (emphasis added), initially with an "extended series of small size commando type raids," followed by "a large scale amphibious operation."[19] This invasion, structured by anti-Castro Cuban exiles on the payroll of the

CIA, appears today to be the probable key to understanding the motivation behind the assassination of President Kennedy.

But who were the players, and what did they have in mind?

Decades ago, Warren Commission member Gerald Ford called the murder of Officer J. D. Tippit the "Rosetta Stone" to the solution of President Kennedy's murder. It wasn't. (Whether Oswald killed Officer Tippit or not, the identification of the ex-Marine as the killer of Tippit is seriously flawed. See Appendix B, "The Case Against Oswald.") Today a more likely candidate for the status of Rosetta stone may be a document released by the National Archives in 1993 and first obtained by Bill Adams under the Freedom of Information Act (FOIA). The document, a 1964 FBI interview of Cuban exile Fermin de Goicochea Sanchez (the fellow University of Dallas student of Silvia Odio's sister Sarita), is perhaps second only to the long-buried FBI report on John Elrod in its ultimate importance to the case.[20]

The FBI meeting with Fermin de Goicochea revealed the identity of his anti-Castro associates, Cuban and Anglo, ca. October 1963— among them, the "Martinez" mentioned by Masen. He was Joaquin Martinez de Pinillos, who, like de Goicochea, was a member of the DRE, the Cuban "student directorate" that had been linked to Lee Harvey Oswald since August. Originally students of the University of Havana, the group had fought as a second front against Batista during the revolution, hoping to reach the capital before Castro. Though failing in this effort, the DRE survived as a fiercely vigilant anti-Communist organization, and had made a genuine contribution to U.S. security. Its members, through persistent and valiant efforts— not initially heeded—were the first to alert the nation about the existence of offensive Soviet missile installations in Cuba.

Meanwhile, the group's ties to the CIA extended to the days before the Bay of Pigs, when DRE infiltration teams were trained by the agency and then left stranded in the disastrous invasion, resulting in the capture of seventy-four men.[21] Paradoxically, despite its displeasure with the agency, the directorate appeared to grow increasingly dependent on CIA funds.[22] Recent CIA releases indicate that at one time virtually the entire leadership of the group was on the agency's payroll—to the consternation of many older and more seasoned exiles.

As de Goicochea explained to the FBI, Martinez traveled from

Miami to Dallas in mid-October 1963 with DRE military chief Juan Manuel Salvat.[23] The ostensible purpose of this October trip was fund-raising for medical relief to Cuban exiles, and in fact several public meetings designed to generate money were organized in the Dallas area. One, at a bank, was attended by Gen. Edwin Walker and local conservatives sympathetic to the anti-Castro cause. Other gatherings took place on the Southern Methodist University campus and the residence of Sarita Castillo (where Trudy Castorr dropped in), an acquaintance of Silvia Odio and the Dallas rep of the DRE prior to Felix Guillermo Othon. (It was at such anti-Castro Cuban meetings, we may recall, that Silvia claimed to Lucille Connell and Dr. Burton Einspruch she had seen Oswald during this same period—probably in his usual role of "infiltrator" under FBI instigation.) The various sessions reportedly raised some five thousand dollars, an amount the visiting DRE organizers were "very disappointed in," de Goicochea told his Bureau interviewer, Wallace R. Heitman, in September 1964.

But though the total take may well have been disheartening, money wasn't the sole point of the October 1963 excursion to Dallas. As in the June trip of JURE's Rogelio Cisneros, the true interest of Salvat and Martinez was in acquiring arms. In this case, the arms were specifically intended for the upcoming "military operation in the Caribbean" that Captain Nonte (and the FBI) had caught wind of by way of the industrious Masen, who stood to gain as the weapons broker.

To this end, young de Goicochea, who had proven himself at the Bay of Pigs, was appointed by Salvat on his October trip as the DRE's "secretary for military affairs" in Dallas—functionally, the local buyer of arms for the group. As part of the appointment, de Goicochea was introduced to Martinez's old contact, John Thomas Masen. He presented the gun-shop owner with a shopping list of supplies that included machine guns, anti-aircraft weapons, bazookas, and plastic explosives, de Goicochea would tell the FBI. Later in the same month, he also got to meet Masen's supplier "George," described by de Goicochea as a military man with an inordinate knowledge of arms and "an extremely large handlebar mustache" who "indicated to him that [he] knew what Goicoechea was doing."[24] (Like Nancy Perrin, de Goicochea believed that the military man was a "colonel," though perhaps retired.)

The meeting between Fort Hood ordnance officer Nonte and

young gun buyer de Goicochea (introduced only as George Perrel) took place at Masen's "Dallas home and gunshop" on Thursday, October 31.[25] The next day, November 1, Nonte reported the event to the FBI, describing the motorcycle-riding "Perrel" as twenty-one or twenty-two years old, five feet seven, and with dark hair worn in a crewcut.[26] It was undoubtedly this report by Nonte that generated an FBI Teletype that same Friday, November 1, asking Dallas agents to be on the lookout for Perrel, as we've seen.

For our account, however, the larger significance of the October 31 gathering at Masen's digs is that it allows us to identify the planned invasion not as a generic anti-Castro campaign, but as a specific DRE initiative. As Nonte stated in his FBI interview of November 1, he "further determined *from inquiry of Perrel* that the small commando type raids would be water borne rather than airborne"[27] (emphasis added). "Perrel" knew this, of course, because the exiles who would be conducting this operation were his own DRE compatriots. As we'll see shortly, they had already made their rep as William Pawley's "water borne" version of Flying Tigers; the small-craft "commando type raids" that would form the first stage of the Cuban invasion were only a new application of established DRE expertise. It was for that first stage, planned for the last week of November, that de Goicochea's shopping list of weapons was intended.

Fermin de Goicochea's Rosetta-stone interview with the FBI, in which he revealed the DRE's activities in Dallas one month prior to the assassination, was not conducted until September 1964. Why the FBI waited so long to contact the DRE is "explained" with a lengthy excuse in the de Goicochea report by Agent Wallace Heitman. The fact that someone felt such an unusual step was even necessary suggests the Bureau was aware appearances were none too good on this matter. (The FBI had known of de Goicochea's whereabouts since before the assassination, when the ATF's Frank Ellsworth had informed the Bureau of his whereabouts after arresting Masen.) The FBI waited until it was too late to include the de Goicochea interview in the Warren investigation, and did not question Martinez or Salvat on their associations with the weapons sources Masen and Nonte, with whom the anti-Castro Cubans were known to have been in contact. Martinez was asked instead whether he'd seen Oswald in the public meetings the DRE held in Dallas in October, and Salvat, about a propaganda story he and others had put out linking Ruby to Castro. Martinez didn't recollect seeing Oswald; Salvat wasn't asked.[28]

In addition to the picture provided by DRE insider de Goicochea (and Nonte via his FBI reports), a scathing secret dispatch by the chief of the CIA's JM/WAVE station in Miami, Theodore Shackley, offers a fascinating perspective on the directorate during the same period—as well as further details of the proposed military operation that the DRE had its heart set on beginning the final week of November 1963. The dispatch, dated November 8, 1963, suggests not only the scope and intent of the "Caribbean operation" for which Salvat and other members of the DRE leadership were gearing up on their October arms-buying foray to Dallas, but the internal dissension that was wrenching the Langley agency on the subject of the exile group's proper role.

As background to Shackley's dispatch, we should note that the DRE (once called "the most unruly stepchildren of the CIA")[29] had friends in high places. Among these were two of the richest and most accomplished Americans of their day, Clare Boothe Luce and William Pawley. Luce, a Broadway playwright, former ambassador to Italy, member of the U.S. House of Representatives, and international socialite—all in addition to being the wife of *Time-Life* publisher Henry Luce—served as patron of a three-man DRE raiding-boat crew whom she fondly called "my boys."[30] She got the idea of sponsoring a DRE boat from her South Florida friend Pawley—oil baron, Eisenhower-era ambassador to two South American countries, dispossessed investor in assorted pre-Castro Cuban enterprises, and longtime influential personage in CIA circles (particularly close to the agency's director, Allen Dulles), though never himself an agent. Above all, perhaps, Pawley was a born swashbuckler. He had achieved his greatest fame, and probably his most satisfying moments, as organizer of the Flying Tigers (with Claire Chennault) during World War II.

The DRE had caught Pawley's eye following a JM/WAVE-planned strike on a Cuban beachfront hotel, the Icar of Miramar, where Castro was thought to dine frequently with Russian, Chinese, and East European advisers. After spraying the hotel with machine-gun bullets for five minutes, missing everyone but leaving the lobby in shambles, two DRE motorboats scampered back to the safety of Marathon.[31] When Manuel Salvat called a press conference with the two boat skippers (the story landed in the *New York Times*), the flamboyant Pawley probably recognized a kindred spirit in the bold Cuban group, and it was apparently then that the inspiration struck him to organize an aquatic version of his famous Flying Tigers, asking wealthy friends to sponsor one armed boat apiece; Mrs. Luce had promptly complied.

The following year, in the summer of 1963, Pawley himself had participated in a CIA-backed boating adventure he had cooked up that would raise the hackles of JM/WAVE chief Ted Shackley. The elaborate scheme involved Pawley's own yacht, dubbed *Flying Tiger II*, and an amphibious airplane provided by the agency. The purpose of the raid was to land eleven CIA-trained exiles in Cuba, kidnap a couple of Soviet missile technicians, and bring them back to American shores, after which Mrs. Luce's *Life Magazine* would publicize their presence as proof that the Russians still had missiles in Cuba, despite the post-missile-crisis Kennedy-Khrushchev accord. The mission was a disaster, however; the raiders were all lost, including their leader, Alpha 66's Eddie Bayo (Eduardo Perez). Pawley returned to Florida with the other dejected noncombatants, including *Life* staffer Richard Billings and another figure who (as we saw in the previous chapter) would travel to Dallas a few months later to talk about his imprisonment in Cuba: the American mob associate John Martino.

It was the presence of Martino on this CIA-aided mission that JM/WAVE's Shackley had cited in a letter complaining of Pawley's irresponsible influence within the agency. Martino, Shackley noted, was not the kind of person with whom the CIA should be doing business. Shackley's later dispatch to his Langley superior, dated November 8, 1963 (and elegantly turned, in contrast to the FBI's brutish reports), did not mention Martino or Pawley, but it, too, appeared to be a criticism of the "Flying Tiger"'s influence—though this time, more veiled and indirect. As implied evidence of Pawley's flawed judgment, the dispatch launched into a detailed description of the DRE's "military plan" in the Caribbean—the proposed operation described secondhand by Masen to Nonte—and of the undisciplined and money-grubbing ways of Pawley's (and Clare Boothe Luce's) pets, the student directorate. They were arrogant and impractical, insisted on doing things only in their own ways, and had proposed

"600 deodorants and 500 bottles of after shave lotion" for their guerilla training encampment.

That wasn't to mention the DRE military plan itself, which, Shackley observed dryly, was "somewhat romantic." The costs were bound to go up far beyond the initially requested amount, and the scheme was marred by logistical blunders, like too conspicuously long a supply line for a secret operation.

> Supplying it [the proposed DRE base, "Martha"] in a clandestine manner . . . would not be possible for any extended period of time. We cannot say how long this base could function without coming to the attention of the local authorities but probably no longer than six months. Discovery is a matter of eventual certainty. And when this occurs, [KUBARK, i.e., CIA] involvement is certain too. For it is a matter of general knowledge that [AMSPELL, i.e., DRE] is dependent on KUBARK funds.[32]

The DRE plan called for buying a farm (with CIA funds) outside the U.S. and relocating from the JM/WAVE base on the "south campus" of the University of Miami to the new foreign base, which would be named "Martha." (As Capt. George Nonte reported to the FBI on October 24, 1963, the impending invasion of Cuba "involved rebel forces allegedly staging at unknown Caribbean bases"— "unknown" because, like "Martha," the DRE base[s] had not yet been designated [and ultimately would not be approved]). This grandiose relocation was another matter Shackley frowned on, since for one thing it would create the conspicuous supply line he objected to. "Meanwhile," the JM/WAVE director noted, "[AMSPELL] is "also anxious to infiltrate (within three weeks) a force of 14 guerrillas, as well as selected individuals to support 'underground forces.' After eight months of apparently casual searching, [AMSPELL] suddenly is seized with a sense of urgency."[33]

This sudden urgency appeared to puzzle Shackley, who speculated it may have stemmed from a desire to beat a rival anti-Castro exile group (perhaps the Bobby Kennedy-backed Manuel Artime encampment in Central America) "to the punch." Whatever its reason, the new DRE urgency had developed during, or shortly after, the mid-October Salvat-Martinez trip to Dallas, where the upcoming visit by President Kennedy was already an old story.

Finally, there was the matter of the DRE members themselves. They had a "known penchant for insecure behavior" and constituted only an "amorphous" mass, concerned primarily with "economic survival" and thereby willing to coalesce temporarily around any activity "KUBARK is willing to finance."

> If we supply the money, [AMSPELL] will do the job but in its own way. Today, [AMSPELL's] own capabilities are indeed limited. Outside of the fifteen or twenty-man "military section" which [AMSPELL] has succeeded in maintaining as a unit, it really has no qualified or trained personnel to undertake any of the intricate and complex tasks which their operational plan requires.[34]

"Rather than encourage them further," the best Shackley was willing to do for the group was urge the "more militant and activist [AMSPELL] elements" to merge with the forces of another anti-Castro camp, and to "maintain" fifteen or twenty of the remaining student directorate members—but only "provided they were fully matriculated at a junior college or college in the JM/WAVE area." Shackley continued, "In two words, we would support only students who were willing to be and act like students. We have no further need of [AMSPELL] members who act the equals of generals or ambassadors or teachers or lawyers or doctors merely because KUBARK funds have given them the power to do so."[35]

Shackley concluded his dispatch to the headquarters office not only recommending against the DRE's proposed military operation, but requesting approval to rein the exile group in "along the lines indicated above."

The request was apparently approved, and the bad news about the CIA's decision was officially broken to the DRE on November 19, three days before the assassination, as we learn from another secret CIA Teletype released in 1994. Strangely for a terse government document, a lot of body language is described, as if someone is straining to tell us something not visible on the surface text. Just what, though, or why the CIA writer would want to imply this, isn't too clear. The suggestion seems to be that the man receiving the news (perhaps DRE secretary general Luis Fernandez Rocha) had already heard what was coming, or had had reason to guess it ahead of time, possibly with the help of Pawley's network within the agency.

> When [CIA man] had just about reached half way mark of above
> statement [the announcement of the rejection and cutting back
> of CIA support], [DRE man] smiled and eventually broke into
> laughter. When [CIA man] finished talking and [DRE man]
> stopped chuckling, [DRE man] declared, "I just knew you were
> going to say something like that." Meaningful glances were
> exchanged and the subject was dropped. The parting was ami-
> cable. [End of message.][36]

Whatever the "meaningful glances" are supposed to mean (it's
anyone's guess), the more tangible point is that the CIA's rejection of
the DRE military plan in the Caribbean, intended ultimately to goad
the U.S. into an invasion of Cuba, had leaked out to Pawley's favorite
exile group in the ten-day interval between the negative dispatch to
Langley of November 8 and the day of its official announcement,
November 19.[37] It was during this same interval that the first whispers were heard by the Bureau of a plot to assassinate the president
in Dallas. One report came from an FBI clerk in New Orleans (later
a bank executive and owner of an insurance company) who claimed
his office received an early-morning Teletype warning of a coming
assassination attempt on the president in Dallas by a "Cuban faction"
(part of, or synonymous with, a "militant revolutionary group"). A
second warning may have occurred just a few hours earlier, during
Oswald's little-known last interview with the FBI prior to the assassination. This interview had taken place on November 16 (a Saturday,
as in Oswald's jailhouse report to Agent Quigley in New Orleans).
The few hours separating the two possible warnings implied a connection between them, or else another incredible coincidence.

If at this mid-November meeting Oswald passed on to the FBI
something he'd heard about a coming assassination attept (obtained
either by infiltrating Ruby's circle of gunrunners or Oswald's more
customary infiltration target, the DRE), the agents would have put
out the word at once. That would explain an internal Teletype to
"ALL SACS" that allegedly reached the New Orleans Bureau at close
to two in the morning following Oswald's report.

A still earlier warning attempt may have been made by Oswald,
who was known to have walked into the Dallas FBI building looking
for Hosty and then left him a note when told the agent wasn't in.[38]
The date of this established Oswald visit was probably November 12,
after the unhappy news of JM/WAVE's devastating dispatch of

November 8 had a chance to filter unofficially to the DRE. The note Oswald left for Hosty, which was later intentionally destroyed by the FBI, may have been intended, like Hosty's phone call to Oswald prior to November 1, to set up another meeting between the Bureau and its informant. That would have been the November 16 interview. Might Oswald have reported on that Saturday something he'd recently learned bigger than anything having to do with gunrunning or military operations in the Caribbean a plot to assassinate the president at the end of the next week? If so, that would have explained why that same night the FBI director's office in Washington teletyped an assassination warning to New Orleans and at least two other field offices.

All the pieces seem to fit together nicely on our impetuous preliminary run. But of course such things would only matter if the Oswald warnings (the "so-called" Oswald warnings to the gravel-hearted) are real possibilities, not disguised urban legends of some kind. Are they? We'll need to take a closer look later, just to be sure.

John Thomas Masen, eager to fill the shopping list of orders from his DRE clients, continued to barrage Capt. George Nonte into November with chummy letters and phone calls about gun deals, which the captain, under the watchful gaze of the FBI following ATF agent Frank Ellsworth's trip to Fort Hood, felt compelled to report.

"Dear George," Masen wrote to the ordnance officer in an undated letter received some two weeks before the assassination,

> Need prices on 75-millimeter recordless rifle and tripod; 20-millimeter automatic with base assembly for fix and placement; 50-caliber machine gun with base assembly for fix and placement. This is some stuff for our friends. Have you talked to Scot about the amo?[39]

Later, Nonte had to explain to the FBI that he "was perplexed as to why Masen would contact him" about such weapons, and Masen would deny, in testimony to the HSCA, having any "recollection of [the letter] at all," though he also refused to swear that he hadn't written it.[40] But of course Masen wrote it, all right. The list corresponds directly to an official shopping list the DRE compiled for the operation it had proposed to the CIA in late September 1963.[41]

In his dealings with Nonte, it is possible the communicative Masen may have told the ordnance officer of a deal he was working on the side with the two men who had talked to Nonte on the phone earlier in the fall from Masen's gun shop. They were picking up a shipment from Nonte by way of Terrell (trial records showed that the weapons stolen on November 14, though kept at a National Guard armory, came from Fort Hood)—the same two men who, as Nonte now knew, thanks to Ellsworth's visit to the base, were trying to bore into his operation. This would have concentrated the ordnance officer's attention about as powerfully as accidentally catching his walrus mustache on fire. Though Nonte obviously didn't warn Masen directly (to do so would have tipped the dealer to Nonte's role as informant), he undoubtedly would pass the alarming information to the Hoover agents, as he'd been routinely doing. In this case the Bureau would have known that a valuable asset, Masen, a man not highly disciplined as Nonte had reported, was about to be busted with unpredictable results. (A second possible source of this information was Ellsworth himself, though no FBI reports of Ellsworth interviews have been released. We know of Ellsworth's first report to the FBI in the fall of 1963 from his HSCA testimony only, as noted earlier.)

The FBI, which easily had the investigative capacity to ferret out such details as when and where a planned transfer of stolen weapons was to happen (and had planted Oswald in Ruby's midst, as evidenced by the information the ex-Marine knew about Miller), moved in to sabotage Ellsworth's sincere efforts. So it would appear, at least, from the needless secrecy and deviousness surrounding the apprehension of Whitter and Miller. As Ellsworth would point out, the whole charade of the car chase was unnecessary. The suspects could have been lawfully collared on the spot, on Trunk Street, and then both cars would have been nabbed, not just one.[42]

The simplest explanation that answers the questions haunting the arrest is that the Bureau itself initiated the Trunk Street stakeout (not anonymous "B&T detectives," as Agent Abernathy reported), possibly for the purpose of protecting the line of communication between Nonte and Masen, not to say keeping them out of jail. The ruse of the stoplight infraction for the apprehension may have been intended to keep the staight-arrow ATF agent Frank Ellsworth from realizing the elaborately contrived machinations behind the arrest. The whole thing had to be seen as a lucky accident, the story angle in the morning paper, or as Ellsworth more likely saw it, a disheartening cosmic thunderbolt ruining his best-laid plans. Whom could he blame, though? There wasn't a complaint department for cosmic thunderbolts.

But if the intervention of the FBI in the mysterious arrest of Whitter and Miller is evident enough, its purpose remains ambiguous. The protection of Masen and Nonte was only one possible (and perhaps secondary) consideration. Another may have been still more pressing.

On Saturday, November 16, 1963, two days before the expendable Ruby henchmen were sacrificed on a tip from an unknown informant, Lee Harvey Oswald provided the Bureau with his last known preassassination report. The story of this report was told in a long-forgotten *Dallas Morning News* article headlined "Oswald Interviewed by FBI on Nov. 16." This account, by *DMN* staff writer James Ewell, appeared on Sunday, November 24 remarkably, the same day that Ruby shot Oswald in the basement of the Dallas police station.[43]

As the opening paragraphs of Ewell's story noted, the meeting with Oswald had all the earmarks of FBI secrecy wherever its apparent informant was concerned.

> Lee Harvey Oswald, charged with murdering President Kennedy, was interviewed by the FBI here [Dallas] six days before the Friday assassination.
>
> But word of the interview with the former defector to Russia was not conveyed to the U.S. Secret Service and Dallas police, reliable sources told The Dallas News Saturday.
>
> An FBI agent referred all inquiries to Agent-in-Charge Gordon Shanklin, who could not be immediately reached for comment.

The "reliable sources" of the story, Ewell explains today, were DPD chief Jesse E. Curry and his police intelligence unit. Publicly—for attribution in the article—Curry refused to blame the Bureau for failing to cooperate, telling the reporter: "I do not want to accuse the FBI of withholding information. They [the FBI] have no obligation to help us [the Dallas police]." As the anonymous "sources," however, the chief and his intelligence personnel (Ewell wrote) "maintained the Nov. 16 interview [with Oswald] by the FBI *did take place* with no mention of it to the Secret Service and police" (emphasis added).

Many years later, of course, the issue is no longer whether J. Edgar

Hoover's Bureau was remiss in sharing information with local authorities, but rather, was the interview with Oswald yet another instance
of a special relationship with the ex-Marine as informant, what did
the Bureau learn from him on that occasion, and what were the consequences of this knowledge? With FBI silence on such rude questions as pervasive today as in the days following the assassination, we
needn't think of turning to the Bureau for help. But the circumstantial evidence is perhaps as eloquent as any direct testimony we
might obtain. Consider the following.

Oswald's final preassassination meeting with the FBI occurred on
a Saturday, November 16. Late that same night—at approximately
1:45 on the morning of Sunday, the 17th—a Teletype was said to have
been received in the New Orleans office of the FBI by William S. Walter, a Bureau security patrol clerk who (as he would later testify to the
HSCA) was "the only employee on duty at the New Orleans office
between 12:00 midnight and 8:00 in the morning."[44] As Walter
reconstructed the early-morning message from notes that he stated
were based on a copy of the original Teletype (the original and all
copies would disappear shortly after the assassination, he noted), the
text went like this:

> URGENT: 1:45 AM EST 11-17-63 HLF 1 PAGE
>
> TO: ALL SACS
> FROM: DIRECTOR
>
> THREAT TO ASSASSINATE PRESIDENT KENNEDY IN DAL-
> LAS TEXAS NOVEMBER TWENTY TWO DASH TWENTY
> THREE NINETEEN SIXTY THREE. MISC INFORMATION
> CONCERNING. INFO HAS BEEN RECEIVED BY THE
> BUREA[U]S BUREAU HAS DETERMINED THAT A [Walter
> handwritten insertion: *CUBAN FACTION QOU*] MILITANT REV-
> OLUTIONARY GROUP MAY ATTEMPT TO ASSASSINATE
> PRESIDENT KENNEDY ON HIS PROPOSED TRIP TO DALLAS
> TEXAS NOVEMBER TWENTY TWO DASH TWENTY THREE
> NINETEEN SIXTY THREE. ALL RECEIVING OFFICES
> SHOULD IMMEDIATELY CONTACT ALL CI'S; PCIS LOGICAL
> RACE AND HATE GROUP INFORMANTS AND DETERMINE
> IF ANY BASIS FOR THREAT. BUREAU SHOULD BE KEPT
> ADVISED OF ALL DEVELOPMENTS BY TELETYPE. OTHER
> OFFICES HAVE BEEN ADVISED. END AND ACK PLS.

Upon receiving the Teletype (Walter said under oath),

> I immediately contacted the special agent-in-charge who had the
> category of threats against the president and read him the tele-
> type. He instructed me to call the agents that had responsibility
> and informants, and as I called them, I noted the time and the
> names of the agents that I called. That all took place in the early
> morning hours of the 17th of November.[45]

When Walter's claims came to light, however, none of the agents
whose names he had jotted on the face of the reconstructed Teletype
would officially corroborate that they had been informed by the
clerk of a preassassination threat against Kennedy in Dallas, nor
would any of his fellow lower-level FBI employees.

In addition to having been on the midnight shift when the alleged
Teletype warning of an impending assassination attempt arrived, it
was Walter's further occupational misfortune to have been the clerk
on duty some three months earlier, on the Saturday morning in
August when Oswald voluntarily summoned the FBI to his jail cell
to make a "report" (chapter 6). As we recall, it was Agent John
Quigley who met with Oswald for the requested interview. On that
occasion, as Walter testified to the HSCA in 1978,

> Agent Quigley handed me a memorandum with Lee Harvey
> Oswald's name on it and asked me to check the indexes and
> determine whether or not there was any file or files on that
> named individual in the New Orleans office.
>
> I recall searching the indexes and finding a card that showed
> more than one file number, which would indicate we had more
> than one case . . . that sometime during the New Orleans office
> inquiry into Oswald there were cases that his name appeared in
> other than one file.
>
> When I searched for these [Oswald] files in the normal fil-
> ing area of the Bureau, which was in an open bay filing, the files
> were not there. From looking at the numbers . . . they *fell in the
> category of security-type, informant-type files, 105 classification, 134
> classifications* [emphasis added].[46]

That was the last notice Walter took of the Oswald files until after
the assassination, he told the HSCA. When the president was murdered, Walter would learn, of course, that the accused assassin was
none other than the man who had reported to Quigley. At that time,

> I was curious and went back to look to see what the files would
> indicate that had been done by the New Orleans [FBI] office to
> Oswald, curious as to whether or not our office had an ongoing
> investigation before the assassination.
>
> What I found was a file in the Special Agent in Charge's safe,
> or his locked file cabinet, and I don't recall the file number but
> I recall on the jacket of the file a Special Agent [Warren]
> DeBrueys' name.

(If so, this is appropriate, for Agent deBrueys' specialty—unlike
Quigley's—was monitoring the Fair Play for Cuba Committee and
anti-Castro Cubans such as Orest Pena of the Cuban Revolutionary
Council.)[47]

Well, what are we to make of the incidents reported by the former FBI clerk William Walter?

His claims about an incoming Teletype at the New Orleans office
of the FBI in the early hours of Sunday, November 17, 1963 (he gave
seventy pages of sworn testimony on March 23, 1978 for the HSCA's
subcommittee on the assassination of the president) were predictably discredited by the Bureau and the HSCA itself. The latter
(which concluded in its *Report* that a probable conspiracy did
occur—but only if the probable conspiracy involved the mob) found
it hard to believe, and perhaps understandably so, that such a teletyped message could have been sent to "ALL SACS" without some
special agent-in-charge or other FBI employee "coming forward in
support of Walter's claim." The FBI (in a memo of October 6, 1975
from Director Clarence M. Kelley to the office of then U.S. Attorney
General Edward H. Levi) focused on the procedural sins of the
reconstructed Teletype. "The terminology, 'ONE PAGE,' should be
on the same line as and follow 'FROM: DIRECTOR,'" for example.
"It should read '1 P' instead of 'ONE PAGE.'" Similarly, the Teletype operator initials *HLF* were wrong, Kelley wrote, because the
name of the operator on duty in the originating Washington office at
the time of the alleged transmission was Harry F. Louderback—ini-
tialed HFL instead of HLF.

However, "the most significant variance is that the alleged teletype
says that a 'militant revolutionary group' may attempt to assassinate
President Kennedy," claimed the FBI director. "The instructions
issued to the field in the alleged teletype are to contact several
different types of informants [CI's, PCI's, etc.], but security

informants, SI's, and potential security informants, PSI's, are not included."

To all these objections, Walter could only wearily repeat to his HSCA interrogators that his version of the Teletype was never represented by him as anything but a roughly typed copy from handwritten notes based on the vanished message; that "what is important about that teletype is whether it was sent or it was not and not whether or not the Bureau can pick it apart as to typographical errors and age of paper and terminology used."[48]

As Walter also noted,

> the point is, if I wanted to make a teletype look like a teletype, I had the knowledge and the ability to do just that. I made teletypes myself that were approved by supervisors and sent to other field offices. If I wanted to use the correct terminology because I thought that at a later date I was going to use this particular document to make myself look good or for publicity, I certainly would have done a better job than I did with it.[49]

As for the important question of why no FBI employee corroborated his claims, Walter had no answer, but perhaps some belated realizations—among them, that "the primary goal, I should say, at that time [from the assassination to his FBI resignation in September 1966] was to try to protect the Bureau's image, don't allow the Secret Service or the CIA, or whoever else . . . to throw blame at the Bureau."[50] For all that, Walter remembered "a lot of conversations about that teletype with the people I came in contact with, and we discussed it openly and freely among ourselves as to how it was going to be handled."[51] The conversations delved not only into the "phantom teletype" (as his Bureau inquisitors dubbed it) but into "informant contacts" and "Oswald's relationships with agents in the New Orleans office."

Today William Walter has a better insight on the lack of corroboration from other FBI employees. When his story of a warning Teletype began to leak out some five years after the assassination, Bureau personnel were pressed to sign affidavits—not to the effect that the Teletype did not exist, but that they would not disclose "confidential information" (with appropriate reminders of stiff penalties for noncompliance). Among Walter's former co-workers who signed such a statement was a once good friend, Tom McCurley, one of the

persons with whom Walter recalls discussing the warning Teletype
in the days immediately following the assassination. (The FBI
attempted to show that Walter never talked about the Teletype until
1967.) Alas, when Walter testified about these conversations to the
HSCA in 1978 by which time both of the friends were bankers
McCurley allegedly could only complain to Walter that the testimony
put him on the spot. He had children at home now, he told the former colleague, and "the FBI was all over my house."[52]

Seventeen years later, in April 1995, McCurley was still maintaining his distance from his old pal, Mary discovered.[53] He barely
appeared to remember Walter, much less the Teletype. The brief
conversation was in this vein:

> M.L. Did you know him [Walter] well?
> McCURLEY. Well, I knew him while we both worked at the
> FBI at that time, you know.
> M.L. Did you believe this was false testimony that he made?
> McCURLEY. (Pause) I couldn't say yes or no.
> M.L. Did he ever discuss it with you at the time [of the assas-
> sination]?
> McCURLEY. I cannot recall that.
> M.L. Do you have any idea why he might make it up?
> McCURLEY. I really don't, you know.
> M.L. Did you ever know him to fabricate stories?
> McCURLEY. No, not really.
> M.L. Did the FBI ever talk to you about it, after it came out
> that he had seen the Teletype?
> McCURLEY. (Long pause) I can't recall. I really don't remem-
> ber. It seems like I might have. I might have signed a statement.
> M.L. Was he best man at your wedding?
> McCURLEY. Yes.
> M.L. Thank you.

There was, however, one ex-FBI employee who did support Walter's story, though he never got a chance to tell the House Select
Committee. He was onetime Bureau deputy director William C. Sullivan, whose duties included overseeing *all* informant files for the
Hoover organization.

In October 1977, as Sullivan was preparing for his testimony to the
HSCA, the former number-three man in the FBI hierarchy placed a
surprising call to a man who had previously served the same Bureau

as a lowly file clerk. Bill Walter still prizes the chair he sat in when he picked up the phone. Sullivan wanted to discuss the Kennedy assassination, and the men found that they agreed on two major points. First, they both knew that Oswald was an informant for the FBI. Second, they believed, nonetheless, that he was probably a lone-nut assassin.

That Sullivan would call Walter at just this period, and to talk about Oswald as an FBI informant, was not, from another view, all that surprising. He had told a previous government committee (and essentially said the same thing to author Curt Gentry),[54] "I think there may be something on that [Oswald as FBI informant]. I don't recall having seen anything like that but I think there is something on that point." Clearly, Sullivan had reason to touch base with the one man who had actually seen Oswald's informant file and was willing to talk about it.

As noted, however, Sullivan never told his story to the HSCA. Two weeks after his call to Walter, and one week before his scheduled interview, William Sullivan was shot to death in a hunting accident near his secluded cabin. A young neighbor, the son of a state trooper, explained that he mistook Sullivan for a deer. Once again Walter was left high and dry.

Even so, Walter stuck to his guns. "I had the Bureau tell me in Memphis, Tennessee," he told House Select Committee counsels Robert W. Genzman, Michael Goldsmith, and Gary Cornwall,

> that Mr. Hoover sent them down, two agents down, to set me straight and they wanted me to admit that I had had—was going through an emotional trauma, change of jobs, and I had all these problems. . . .[55]
>
> My answer to all that is, I have had every opportunity to back out. I could have said, "Okay, Mr. Hoover and Mr. Bureau, what I did is confuse the teletype of the 17th with the teletype of the 22nd."[56] In good conscience, I am not going to do that, because one day it is going to come out that the teletype did exist and it is there and I just don't want to in any way try to make that job any harder than it is going to be already.[57]

One day it is going to come out. Unlike Nancy Perrin, an admitted sometime prostitute, and John Elrod, an admitted alcoholic, William S. Walter went on to become senior vice-president of Patterson State Bank in Morgan City, Louisiana. It has made no difference to the FBI

and its allies; his testimony was discredited just the same as Nancy
Perrin's and John Elrod's, and with almost as little justification.

Meanwhile, we are left with perhaps the most tantalizing and mysterious of all the pieces of information on Walter's claimed Teletype
of November 17: "Cuban faction QOU"—the phrase he had written
in by hand, as an afterthought, modifying "militant revolutionary
group" on his typed reconstruction of the message. This group—
the one that the message warned would try to assassinate the president in Dallas on November 22 or 23—was therefore a Cuban faction
of some sort, according to the sense of the revised Teletype.

"I have no idea of the meaning of that" (the notation *Cuban faction
QOU*), Walter told the HSCA interviewers when asked; and no doubt
he didn't. It was simply something he remembered from the "phantom teletype" after he'd finished typing the reconstruction, and he
had added it by hand, as he had added a semicolon in one location
and an apostrophe to *CI'S* (confidential informants). Like Marianne
Sullivan, William Walter's knowledge of the pieces of the puzzle was
stronger than his knowledge of the whole—the picture the individual puzzle pieces were inextricably forming.

Before proceeding to this picture, however, we should examine
one more piece. Like Walter's Teletype, it, too, is a "phantom" of
sorts, and relates to Oswald's role as FBI informant. It is the famous
missing note that the ex-Marine left for his runner and hated tor-
mentor, Special Agent James Hosty.

The story goes this way. One day, sometime after Hosty's second
November 1963 visit to the Paine household, Oswald, depressed by
the agent's visits, scribbled a short note, stuffed it in an unsealed
envelope (scrawled with the endearing misspelling *Hasty*), and
rushed it to the FBI office on Commerce Street. When he found
Hosty out to lunch, Oswald left the envelope with a receptionist,
Nancy Fenner. As Gerald Posner admits, "No one at the FBI office
can remember the exact day Oswald visited," though he theorizes it
may have been Tuesday, November 12.[58]

The incident, in any event, took a grotesque turn for the FBI when
it was discovered, twelve years later, that the Bureau had once again
shredded evidence that would tie it to Oswald. In this case it turned
out that Hosty's superior, Dallas special agent-in-charge Gordon
Shanklin, ordered Hosty, immediately after the police basement

shooting of Oswald, to destroy the note. In Hosty's words, the "agitated and upset" Shanklin told him: "Oswald's dead now. There can be no trial. Here—get rid of this." Hosty complied by carrying the note (already in pieces) to the bathroom and flushing the remnants "down the drain."[59]

What was it about the note that caused such despair at 1114 Commerce that Sunday, November 24? According to Hosty, the long-vanished message from Oswald was to this effect: "If you have anything you want to learn about me, come talk to me directly. If you don't cease bothering my wife, I will take appropriate action and report this to the proper authorities."[60]

This uncharacteristically mealymouthed rendition of Oswald-speech rings false, stylistically. What about its substance? Was that equally false? Did Oswald, in other words, leave behind not a whining note about visits to his wife (hardly the kind of thing that should have so agitated Agent Shanklin), but something more monumental, perhaps? Two days later, on November 14, an armory was going to be burglarized in nearby Terrell. But since Oswald was willing to wait four days, until November 16, to give his report, the impending burglary wasn't likely what he wanted to talk about. The assassination attempt was a different matter, however. It was still far enough away that Oswald could afford to wait a few days to report it, if he needed. He did.

The suggestion that Oswald tried to warn Hosty with this note isn't new, and Posner addresses it in his breakthrough update of the Warren arguments, *Case Closed*. If the note left for Hosty was indeed some great "warning," Posner asks, why wouldn't Oswald have followed it up with a phone call? And

> when finally arrested and charged with the crime, instead of telling the Dallas police and the FBI that he had actually tried to warn them ten days before the assassination, Oswald quietly sat in the station and denied his guilt. Even when Hosty came into the interrogation room, Oswald did not say, "What happened to the warning I gave you?" but rather attacked Hosty for having bothered Marina.[61]

The problem with this seemingly plausible point is that because no tape recordings of Oswald's interrogation were made, Posner must rely on the word of the very people who are known liars (Shanklin told the HSCA he had never seen or known about the Oswald note until 1975)[62] and destroyers of evidence. As the Assassinations Committee would note in 1979, it "regarded the incident of the note as a serious impeachment of Shanklin's and Hosty's credibility," adding that "it was not possible to establish with confidence what [the note's] contents were."[63] Or put a different way, how does Posner know, on the word of these same agents so clearly terrified of the contents of a note, that Oswald did *not* make a follow-up phone call, or that he quietly sat in the police station (he wasn't quiet in the presence of Elrod) and didn't in fact say to Hosty, "What happened to the warning I gave you?" Would Hosty, who may have destroyed the note precisely because it *was* a warning that the FBI didn't heed, then have turned around and announced to the world that Oswald asked him what happened to his warning?

On balance, however (and despite the temptation to find fault with Posner on every occasion), it would be wise not to push the Oswald note to Hosty too far. The incident happened, to be sure, but it remains inconclusive, primarily because the "unreliable" Nancy Fenner did not keep the note to herself. She reportedly showed it to an assistant special agent-in-charge, Kyle Clark, and to a "girl from the steno pool," Helen May.[64] None of them remember it as a warning of an assassination attempt (it was more a threat to "blow up" the office, according to Mrs. Fenner). Pent-up frustration with Hosty's demands may account for a threat to blow up the office, or it may have been more: William Sullivan allegedly told Walter in his phone call that Hosty had some unwritten-up visits to Marina and may, in fact, have been carrying on an affair with the pretty Soviet immigrant. On the other hand, if Oswald was in a jealous or irascible snit with Hosty during this time, would he be willing to give a helpful report to the FBI a few days later (relayed by Teletype to Walter's New Orleans office, among others) concerning an assassination attempt? Given that paradox was the soul of Oswald, the answer is yes; anything was possible, particularly where a higher cause was involved. (There should be "no borderline between one's own personal world, and the world in general," recall.)

But if the note itself remains inconclusive, what it demonstrates is not. The FBI was clearly and unquestionably in the business of both destroying and lying about evidence related to Oswald. And the business went all the way to the top. "Hoover ordered the destruction of the note," William Sullivan told Gentry; "I can't prove this, but I have no doubts about it."[65]

But the original question remains. What did all this have to do with the mysterious arrest of Whitter and Miller?

The HSCA testimony of William Walter, who could not have known that Oswald had been interviewed in Dallas just before the alleged internal Teletype started clacking in, suggests that the FBI did not ignore Oswald's warning. Immediately after receiving his report, the Bureau acted to start protecting the life of the president by putting out the word to its field offices.

But that in itself, though impeccable, was not a protective action. There had to be more. Consider that if we accept at all the possibility that Oswald may have warned the FBI of an attempt on the life of the president in his November 16 report, it doesn't damage reason to suppose further that the protective response the FBI might take would be related to the very people—gunrunning associates of a "Cuban faction"—who Oswald may have claimed were talking about the rumored assassination attempt: Ruby, Miller, and the others in the motel room, as described secondhand by John Elrod. As Hosty's probable infiltrator on gun-related/right-wing subversive matters, Oswald would have been looking for just such information as when a shipment of military rifles was arriving or being transferred to some other point—on Trunk Street November 18, for example. That information, too, may well have been passed on in Oswald's report. It isn't hard to imagine that agents, not liking the sound of this combination of assassination talk and a car stashed with rifles, cracked down two days after the report and impounded the weapons as well as their transporters, Whitter and Miller, as a preemptive precaution. It was the Bureau's response to Oswald's warning.

While hundreds of books have been written on the Kennedy assassination, one burning question, always answered vaguely, has remained. If not Oswald (or not *exclusively* Oswald), who? Who finally killed JFK?

The culprits *had* to be persons or groups intimately associated with the Castrophile ex-Marine. For many, the guilty parties necessarily included a monolithic CIA, or military, or both. For many others, it was the Dallas right wing, the mob, or Castro's agents. Less popularly, the guesses have run to the KGB, a tricky rifle accident by a member of the Secret Service, or the occasional extraterrestrial in a supermarket tabloid. It may have have been a revulsion with the swarm of contradictory suppositions that smoothed the way for Gerald Posner's *Case Closed,* by contrast a rigorous presentation of a refreshingly different idea: Oswald did it alone.

But if Oswald did it, it wasn't alone. Again, who were his associates?

For years, Lee Harvey Oswald has been linked through misinformation (frequently of his own making as he built his legend as an intelligence asset) with the radical left: Communists, Marxists, the Fair Play for Cuba Committee, or Fidel Castro. There is no evidence that the ex-Marine, despite his Marxist sympathies, ever associated with any of these groups. Oswald never attended a known Communist, Marxist, or FPCC meeting. And he never made contact with Castro or any of Cuba's intelligence community. His history as a defector to Russia (probably as a U.S. intelligence operative) had spawned the theories. He did make contact in the final months of his life with the Cuban and Russian embassies in Mexico City (and perhaps earlier, as his barracksmate Delgado suspected, the Cuban consulate in Los Angeles). Both embassies seem to be as puzzled by the contacts as anyone outside of U.S. intelligence would be.

The only groups intimately associated with Oswald were the right-wing Dallas Russian community, and the militant, CIA-funded DRE. The new evidence strongly suggests that Oswald first attempted to infiltrate the DRE in New Orleans as an FBI informant on neutrality and weapons issues. As we may recall, the leftist former defector was likely sent to the Crescent City to inform on gunrunning by right-wing subversives. Guy Banister and the equally gun-happy student directorate, which, though supposedly a propaganda group, had stockpiled the Pontchartrain arms cache raided by the Bureau in late July, were obvious targets. Indeed, Oswald's informant file, seen by former FBI employee William S. Walter, identified Oswald as a Bureau informant on the DRE's Pontchartrain arms cache.[66]

It was, however, as an FPCC organizer that Oswald was most visibly (and ambiguously) identified during his New Orleans summer. Various cases can be made accounting for his confusing behavior in this area, as we've seen. One conspiratorial favorite is that Oswald and Bringuier were basically on the same anti-Castro side, a proposition rejected in this book. It is possible, however, that some degree of cooperation may have occurred between the two ideological antagonists. At some point during the summer of 1963 the DRE unquestionably identified Oswald, as did Banister, as just the kind of "nut" who could be a useful tool in the war against Castro and Fair Play for Cuba subversives. (Undermining the Committee was one of the student group's CIA assignments.) For his part, Oswald may have agreed to serve the DRE's ends—participating in a media blitz "unmasking" the FPCC as a Communist-controlled organization for propagandist Bringuier—in order to gain the confidence of the exile group and obtain information on such matters as the Pontchartrain operation. In this, Oswald, a lifelong fan of *I Led Three Lives*, would have been acting as a classic double agent.[67]

Obviously, however, if such cooperation existed, it was as doomed from its inception as the momentary alliance between Hitler and Stalin. It couldn't possibly last, and didn't.

Returning to Dallas from Mexico City in October 1963, most likely by private transport and in the company of DRE members, Oswald entered the gunrunning world of Silvia Odio, Juan Manuel Salvat, John Masen, George Nonte, Silvia's family friend John Martino, and Martino's CIA contact (and DRE sponsor) William Pawley. It was a murky milieu, which the ex-Marine himself could hardly have understood fully; empathy for the masses was his strength, not self-awareness. The unsuspecting "double agent" could well have believed he was fooling some people in Dallas he wasn't.

There is no telling what Oswald was thinking when—if he actually did so, as Silvia claimed—he bragged to anti-Castro Cubans in Dallas that he was a crack shot and that the Cubans should take out Kennedy. (Her story of the hallway visit is fictitious, of course, but perhaps a selectively—and incriminatingly—pruned version of an actual occurrence in the company of DRE comrades.) Was he playing the anti-American game to de Goicochea's group, as he played the anti-Castro game at Bringuier's Casa Roca? If so, we can be certain the game didn't work. Silvia would say so to Lucille Connell, we may recall—that "in recent months" (i.e., October or November 1963) a "Cuban associate" of Silvia's had learned in a phone call with "an unknown source in New Orleans" (Bringuier or his friend, Agustin Guitart, Silvia's uncle) that Oswald was considered a "'double agent'" who was "probably trying to infiltrate the Dallas Cuban refugee group" and "should not be trusted."

John Martino, the man who late in life admitted having "played a role," together with "anti-Castro Cubans," in the murder of the president, and who revealed to a reporter that Silvia Odio "knew a lot of things" about the assassination (chapter 9), also allegedly told a Texas businessman, Fred Claasen, that it was "the anti-Castro people" who "put Oswald together." Martino continued:

> Oswald didn't know who he was working for—he was just ignorant of who was really putting him together. Oswald was to meet his contact at the Texas Theater. There was no way they could get to him. They had Ruby kill him.[68]

Whether ending up at the Texas Theater and so on was part of the plan or not, we can't be certain—only that the *rest* of Martino's alleged description sounds right on target. It was "the anti-Castro people," specifically the DRE, who "put Oswald together." Oswald, infiltrating the group for the FBI, "didn't know who he was working for," was "just ignorant of who was really putting him together." Oswald thought he was "working" for the FBI; he didn't realize he had been exposed—that the Cubans in Dallas knew all about him, as Bringuier did. They appeared to tolerate (and underestimate) him at their meetings as a goofy but potentially useful figure, much as Guy Banister had done, who had also worked with Oswald in New Orleans.

In short, the DRE re-created Oswald, altering his role from informant to patsy. Silvia, the beautiful young woman who "knew a lot of things," may have witnessed, or in some way aided, this process of re-creation. If so, that was one of the "things" she knew—the most important one of all, in fact—and which she has yet to share with us.

As the plans were laid by CIA operatives Salvat, Martinez, and de Goicochea in Dallas for the planned invasion of Cuba to commence the *last week in November,* according to the previously cited FBI airtel of November 1, 1963, Oswald blithely reported on the activities of the DRE, Masen, Nonte, and Ruby. The underestimated ex-Marine caught wind of the plot to kill the president, and reported it to the Bureau on November 16. The FBI took action with the arrest of Whitter and Miller, and perhaps believed the plot had been foiled. But history played a cruel trick—not only on the hapless investigative agency, but most of all on Lee Harvey Oswald.

The "Cuban faction" itself, the DRE, had been pondering the leaked rejection of its invasion plans, a rejection made official three days before Kennedy was to arrive in Dallas. Things did not look too hopeful. But there was more than one way to skin a cat, which may account for the DRE's jovial acceptance of the CIA's bad news, if not the "meaningful glances" of November 19. If the agency was not willing to help goad the timid Kennedy administration into attacking Cuba, the assassination of the president by a Marxist Castrophile (preferably acting in collusion with Castro agents, as Bringuier still "theorizes") would surely bring about the desired effect—an all-out retaliatory invasion by the American colossus. In the person of George Nonte, later an editor of *Soldier of Fortune* magazine who authored stacks of books on guns, the enfants terribles of the exile community had a consultant of world-class expertise in target shooting with an arcane specialty in cartridge conversions; in John Masen and Fort Hood, endless supplies of weapons; in the FBI, bumbling miscalculation; in Oswald, the perfect patsy. The jagged kid from New Orleans may have borne the DRE's guilt for more than thirty years.[69]

Following the assassination—and more specifically, the murder of Oswald by Ruby—there would have been a chilling recognition by the intelligence agents involved in the Friday morning meeting of November 22 (as well as by the superiors to whom they reported) that the dreadful events of that weekend were very likely tied to the same case the three men had met to discuss. There was no public knowledge of the Fort Hood arms thefts, and therefore no public association to be made between the murders of Kennedy and Oswald on the one hand, and on the other, the Fort Hood gunrunning mill providing arms to anti-Castro exiles for a planned second invasion of Cuba. With the exception of Ellsworth (who, knowing only part of the story, was the only one to speak up to Warren and HSCA investigators, revealing his suspicions of Minuteman involvement in the assassination, his dealings with Masen, and Masen's gun sales to Cuban exiles), only the federal intelligence operatives and their associates knew enough to have made the necessary connections.[70] Their information was never revealed—was apparently covered up, in fact, by such extreme measures as sending one of the three intelligence investigators to a new "mission" in Korea.

Agent Hosty, whose big mouth on a single high-stress occasion supposedly caused "irreparable harm" to the Bureau, was nonetheless
the soul of discretion on many matters that he knew, once the dust
settled. He was obviously aware, for example, that the men arrested
in the Thunderbird could be tied by association to another Nonte
middleman, Jack Ruby, that Ruby indeed had *other* ties to gunrunning, and that gunrunning was the core activity of anti-Castro, anti-
Kennedy Cubans. Hosty later also had to learn the testimony of
Nancy Perrin, who talked to the FBI before she talked to the Warren Commission, and who presented to both the most important
(and graphic) testimony given on the subject of Jack Ruby. The bar
owner had appeared with pockets bulging, she said, in the guise of
an operational paymaster, at a meeting of gunrunners that included
a U.S. Army "colonel" and a hoard of stolen military weapons. The
agent did nothing, though he knew, as Nancy did not, of the large-
scale theft of arms at Fort Hood involving army officers, paramilitary right-wing groups, and militant anti-Castro Cubans.

Why, knowing what he knew, did Hosty remain silent?

More to the point, what might have accounted for the refusal of
J. Edgar Hoover, the ultracompetent director of the greatest investigative agency in the world, to conduct a true investigation of the
assassination?

Hoover insisted that the murder of the president had been solved
with the capture of a "silly little Communist" (as Jackie Kennedy
despaired) and member of the ACLU who acted alone—a conclusion reached in the first twenty-four hours after the Dealey Plaza
shooting, and from which the director would never waver, regardless of any and all evidence to the contrary. The conclusion was
accompanied by Hoover's demand, also made on the heels of the
assassination, for the immediate release of an FBI report that would
be definitive, preventing a "rash of [independent] investigations."
The latter, he told President Johnson, would be "very bad."[71] As Curt
Gentry notes, however, "Hoover's plan to wrap up the case with a
single report, thus avoiding the risk of exposing the FBI's deficien-
cies and cover-ups in the case, ran into a major obstacle."[72] The
obstacle was LBJ himself, who insisted on establishing the Warren
Commission. Temporarily stymied, the pugnacious bachelor director
retreated to a fallback position: sabotage. He

publicly offered it [the Commission] his full cooperation—after all, it was a creation of the president—but instructed his agents to volunteer nothing beyond what was requested, and then only after prior approval of FBIHQ. He delayed responding to its requests, until the committee was under tremendous pressure to issue its report, then inundated it with materials he knew its staff wouldn't have time to examine carefully.[73]

The tactics of Hoover's FBI aroused the astonishment, distrust, and fear of Earl Warren's men, even though they, like the president, and Hoover himself presumably, otherwise agreed that a finding of conspiracy in the assassination ran a terrible national risk. But not to investigate at all? To want to shut things down, in essence, in the *first week*? It made no sense to persons of integrity (Gerald Ford, Hoover's spy on the Commission, excepted).

Some plausible-sounding reasons for the senselessness offered themselves. Conducting a true investigation would have made public the note Oswald left for Hosty (successfully suppressed by the Bureau for twelve years), as well as such additional embarrassments as the FBI's preassassination knowledge of Nonte, Masen, Ruby, and the flood of contraband weapons gushing from Fort Hood. But would these matters alone account for Hoover's irrational behavior? One would think there had to be something more, even for a small-minded man like the Bureau director. There was. An investigation—a *real* investigation—ultimately risked exposing the nightmarish joke that fate had played on his empire: its Dallas informant had turned up an accused presidential assassin. It was quite likely this grim surprise—cruel and unfair as Hoover himself—that changed all the rules, and made denying its Oswald past a higher priority for the FBI than investigating the assassination of an American president.

And the Bureau wasn't unique in its horror over such a thing coming to light. In secret session on January 22, 1964, the Warren Commission itself reacted with utter panic to the suggestion that Oswald may have been an FBI informant.[74] Similarly, it may have been the possibility of this ghastly revelation that precipitated the civic-minded cooperation of other right-thinking organizations like the U.S. Army, the Post Office, and the Dallas Police Department. In effect, "losing" Coyle in Korea was the military personnel equivalent of other, usually paper, losses in the national interest: the disappearance of records on Oswald's P.O. transactions, of the identities of the "B&T detectives," of the tramp and John Elrod reports, and, as seen most recently, of the Bureau's own New Orleans Oswald informant file, Teletype of November 17, 1963, and report on the Oswald interview of November 16 (supposedly never made).

One final example of the FBI's "investigation" of the assassination is illuminating. After the president was shot, Bureau agents looked into the sources of the ammunition used. They contacted all gun shops in the Dallas-Irving area, and found that only two dealers had carried Mannlicher-Carcano 6.5-mm ammunition prior to Kennedy's murder. These two were John Thomas Masen and his sometime partner Johnny Brinegar, who had purchased the entire lot of ammo with Masen. In his testimony to the HSCA, Masen described the ammunition as "unusual."[75] The FBI purchased bullets Masen had reloaded for examination. They were soft-nosed "hunting load" bullets. There has always been controversy as to whether the ammunition used in the assassination was "military" (full metal jacket), as the Warren Commission claimed, or hunting load. The FBI's purchase from Masen would appear to confirm the latter. Though the Hoover agency took a sample of Masen's ammunition for analysis, there is no indication that the Bureau ever acknowledged to the Warren Commission the connection between the massive illegal gun-trafficking involving Masen that the FBI was aware of, and the tracing of possible assassination ammunition to the gun shop of the same man. Similarly, there is no evidence that Masen was ever questioned about another Dallas gunrunner, Jack Ruby.[76]

Approaching the twenty-first century, the FBI's investigation of President Kennedy's assassination has yet to begin.

On Monday, December 9, 1963, the *Dallas Morning News* carried a small AP wire article datelined Mexico City. It was a DRE announcement that "126 Cuban militiamen were killed in one of the bloodiest and longest clashes between Prime Minister Fidel Castro's forces and guerrillas in the Escambray Mountains of Las Villas Province."

The fighting had taken place three months earlier, "in mid-September," according to Angel Gonzalez, identified as head of the DRE in Mexico City. The anti-Castro guerillas reportedly lost eighteen men in the action, of whom "a Negro peasant guerrilla leader,"

Andre Tartabull, and three "captains" were singled out for mention: Carlos Roca, Julio Garcia, and Sergio Perez.

In December 1994, Eric Hamburg, a former congressional staffer instrumental in the passage of the JFK Records Act and now a film producer for Oliver Stone's Ixtlan Productions, interviewed Gen. Fabian Escalante, head of Cuban intelligence. General Escalante told Hamburg that of the four mentioned names, he could confirm only the death of Tartabull in the Escambray, and that the report of the deaths of the other three men was false. He had it from a "human intelligence source," the general said, that Carlos Roca had been seen in Miami a couple of days after the assassination in the company of a DRE member. Roca then traveled to Monkey Point, Nicaragua (near the Costa Rican border) with the same DRE member and did not return, Escalante alleges. The wire story was a misinformation plant, according to his theory. He speculates that Roca was involved in the assassination plot, and that he died in Nicaragua (where a Cuban exile encampment was preparing for an invasion of Cuba) between November 24 and December 8, after which his death was "backdated" via the newspaper article to disassociate him and the DRE from the assassination. DRE military leader Manuel Salvat and the source of the wire story, Angel Gonzalez, were "very close," Escalante added. Recently obtained CIA information indicates that Salvat traveled to Central America in the first week of December 1963.[77]

The Cuban intelligence general, though not a disinterested party, paints a provocative picture.

Were Carlos Roca, Julio Garcia, and Sergio Perez, the captains whose bodies could not be found in Cuba, sacrificed participants in the assassination of President Kennedy?

Justice of the Peace Jim Botelho believes that his old Marine buddy Oz may indeed have tried to warn authorities of the assassination, we may recall—though Botelho speaks from afar to be sure and must base his assessment on character rather than factual knowledge. He only knew the real Oswald, not the postassassination media cartoon influenced by Clare Boothe Luce's *Life Magazine* or the bewildering thirty-year-plus compendium of "evidence" beloved by buffs and Warrenologists alike. Still, his words, from the heart and innocent of empirical certainty, are haunting: "If he [Oswald] was involved, it was as an informant of some kind, someone who was probably trying to stop the assassination, not participate in it. He was a hero of our time, not a killer."

Regrettably, such pure sentiments will not likely impress the flinty soul of the hard-minded reader. (Don't even serial killers have friends or neighbors who remember them as nice, quiet guys?) An appendix, "Countdown to the Assassination," offers something more by way of objective analysis, as well as relief from the muddle of words that can sometimes obscure the big picture. The appendix summarizes in chronological order significant events related to the deaths of President Kennedy and Lee Harvey Oswald, many of them either newly learned from recent releases of evidence or newly rediscovered. The new evidence may not do much for hard-core Warren defenders or conspiracy fans addicted to a favorite hobbyhorse. They will no doubt regroup and find new excuses for continuing to believe as they do (one possible reason CompuServe once classified the Kennedy assassination under Paranormal Events).

That, however, is *their* problem.

They say longtime prisoners, who have heard all the stories there are to know (and categorized them for the sake of convenience), no longer have to go through the trouble of telling a joke; they just call out a number. The listeners respond with a belly laugh, polite chuckle, or killer stare—depending, of course, on just how funny they think it all is.

It was in this spirit, more or less, that one revered old hand in the Kennedy Correctional Institute, Peter Dale Scott, got together with a relative newcomer, Mary the Knife, at a Dallas conference not so long ago.

"Nancy Perrin Rich," said Peter.

"Yes."

Then Mary had one of her own.

"Elrod."

His kind eyes twinkled.

"In four months," he assured her, "it will all be over."

CHAPTER ELEVEN

White Lies

In the classroom
the past is only vivid
when it smells like yesterday's garbage
and old men with fragile teeth
write it up as history.

PATRICK BARBER
Poems, 1972

By the end of January 1992 America was mired in the War of *JFK.* The *Washington Post*'s George Lardner had launched a preemptive strike by savagely criticizing director Oliver Stone and his film before the movie had even been completed. Stone had retaliated by producing an epic masterpiece, released in December 1991, that Norman Mailer would call "one of the worst great movies ever made." To accusations that the film mixed fact with fiction, the director replied that he was creating a "countermyth" to the Warren Commission's lone-assassin fable. Whatever the fine points of the matter, his film succeeded in boosting the numbers of the already considerable majority of the American public that believed President Kennedy died as a result of a conspiracy, as well as in generating irresistible pressure for the release of classified files on the assassination. The government, Stone told a "Nightline" audience on the occasion of *JFK*'s premiere, should "trust the American people with their history." The Dallas City Council became the first political body in the nation to respond to the call, voting unanimously that

January to release all of the city's Kennedy files. News of the tramp arrest records and other finds by Mary broke in February 1992, as we've seen, on the front page of the *Houston Post* as "A First Look at Dallas' JFK Files."

When the paper hit the streets, the La Fontaines waited curiously (and a bit naïvely, it turned out) to see how the Associated Press would play the story. The couple had their usual nonnegotiable differences on this point, but one possibility neither considered turned out to be the AP's top pick: it would ignore the *Post* story. The "reason" for this, Ray discovered when he called the AP office in Dallas, was that the story needed to be "checked out." That the story had already *been* checked out, was documented, and had run as a bannered Sunday lead in a major mainstream newspaper didn't seem to fit the bill, nor for that matter, that the news was of national, not just regional, importance. Nor did it appear to be relevant, suddenly, that the AP was a wire service, and not in the business of "checking out" the stories of its reputable subscriber newspapers—that even if a paper somehow were to go temporarily haywire and publish a complete hoax, the sad deed would redound, when uncovered, to the discredit of the paper, not the wire service.

The AP obstruction did not stop there, however. The *Post* management registered a complaint to the wire service about the refusal to distribute the trumpeted Dallas file discoveries to other papers. In time—a week later—the AP did grudgingly move its own version of the story. This version reduced the story from a documented investigative news account to a small whimsical feature akin in spirit to a claimed UFO sighting. It also matter-of-factly identified the original authors of the *Post* article as "conspiracy theorists"—code for nuts. When the La Fontaines read this, they did in fact go a bit nuts. They called the AP back in a rage, and Mary's rage, having Irish redhead breeding, was far superior to Ray's. She threatened to sue, citing La Fontaines' previous news stories and documentaries (including PBS prize-winner *Murray and Arlene*) on a variety of topics, and noting that this was in fact their *first* Kennedy story. The writers were obviously not "conspiracy theorists," moreover, since the disclosure of the tramps' identity showed them to be real tramps, not the disguised CIA hitmen of conspiracy lore.

Finally, the AP issued a correction to its story, this time identifying the fearless (but slightly shaken) duo as "documentary makers." Either way, arguing over what they were going to be called was the last thing they expected to result from the story. They had evidently strayed into some strange new realm, and Eugenia, as usual the bemused spectator of her parents' misadventures, was happy to chime in with a few bars of appropriate theme music . . . from "The Twilight Zone," of course.

On Wednesday, February 19, David Lee Miller, a reporter for the TV tabloid "A Current Affair," called. He had read the *Houston Post* story and wanted an interview for his program, which at the time neither Ray nor Mary had seen. Eugenia had, however, and promptly pronounced it "the sleaziest show on television." She also pointed out that the 20th, the day Miller wanted to do his interview, just happened to be her birthday. She was turning seventeen, and how many times does *that* happen in a lifetime? Despite this clear warning and the risk to their daughter's psyche (the candle-blowing was delayed an hour), the La Fontaines met with Miller in Dallas and eventually agreed to produce, under their name, a segment of the tabloid program. It would focus on the tracking of tramp Harold Doyle, on whom Mary had ferreted out a lead, as we'll see. Another segment, to be produced by "ACA"'s own people, was to air on the first day, and would focus on the Dallas document discoveries.

Ray's qualms about the tabloid world weren't helped much by watching Miller stare deeply into the camera at the beginning of the first taping. "I have very dark eyes," he was cautioning the local Texas camera guy. "Make sure they come out." Later, trapped in a motel room in Klamath Falls, Oregon, the town to which they'd finally tracked Doyle, the intrepid travelers were astonished to learn (why, Eugenia wouldn't know) that in the segment not produced by them, running that night, "A Current Affair" was taking credit for discovering the tramp files in the Dallas city archives. To underline this "discovery," the program showed Miller cruising through the stacks and conferring with city archivist Cindy Smolovik. The lawyers wrote letters back and forth, and the tabloid, without admitting culpability, paid up. The days wore on in the mazy Kennedy waters, with Ray only now and then bothered by brief involuntary flashbacks to a poem he'd never much cared for at school, *The Rime of the Ancient*

Mariner. The mariner, he recalled none too comfortably, was hallu-
cinating with sunstroke, lost at sea, and felt compelled to tell his story
to strangers.

For Mary, the whole experience was only bracing and invigorating,
of course, the kind of thing that made it possible to face the day.
She had a weak heart according to the cardiology charts, but her
courage had exposed the shady doings at one major university and
helped send the president of another Texas school packing for his
damnable deeds. She did these things on the phone mostly, from her
bedside, alongside her calculator and the latest issues of *Vanity Fair,*
Elle, Vogue, and *Mirabella,* for when things slacked off a bit. She took
some pride in this feat, and pointed out that a certain Russian character, Oblomov, never got out of bed at all because there was nothing
important enough for him to get up for. One should only get up for
important things; otherwise, why bother? Ray wasn't always sure
whether he was in the presence of moral genius or clinical depression, but it came with a cyclotron brain and the irritability, when
crossed, of the princess who could feel a pea under a hundred mat-
tresses. Wrongdoers messed with her only at their peril.

In tiny Canyon on the Texas Panhandle the bad guy had been
Mesa Limited Partners oil tycoon Boone Pickens, then of nearby
Amarillo and of eighties corporate-raider fame, which may be how
he got the idea for the hostile takeover of a state university. Pickens
was chairman of the board of Canyon's West Texas State, a school
he had designated as "Mesa's university." He wanted to set an example to America of how a college should be run, which was like a corporation, conforming to business principles and with "wellness"
programs to get everybody exercising. To this visionary end, Pickens
had inflicted on the school and town an unfortunate dictatorial buf-
foon (and Adolf Hitler buff, interestingly) as president, Ed Roach,
who the terrified faculty swore practically clicked metal balls in his
hand, like Captain Queeg in *Caine Mutiny.* If he hadn't been so
vicious in firing competent faculty, violating every shade of academic freedom, and censoring the school paper, he might have been
tolerated as a merely eccentric wild man; you don't expect much
from a college president, God knows. But Roach, who had built himself a new presidential mansion with a zillion rooms and, by actual
count, fourteen telephones (the architectural splendor didn't stop
the house from becoming immediately known as the Roach Motel, of

course), went beyond all limits. And Pickens, with his ego involved long after he must have realized he'd made a mistake, refused to remove him.

That was the scenario, a modern replay of a B western. Pickens was the Black Bart who owned the whole town, and Roach was his evil stooge, the guy who'd show up in Bart's back-room office to take his wicked instructions. Decent citizens couldn't speak out for fear they'd lose their jobs, and the local Amarillo paper was almost helpless, bullied by Boone, who had pressured all his Mesa employees to give up their subscriptions as a kind of holiday pledge of goodwill, which they were to sign before they left the happy company Christmas party.

Mary, hearing about this case from a friend whose husband taught on the West Texas faculty, started calling. She gathered information for weeks from the small community 350 miles to the west, becoming better known there on the phone, Ray didn't doubt, than some actual lifelong residents. In the end, it had all been worth it. Stories by the La Fontaines in the *Dallas Times Herald* and elsewhere helped get the little known Roach-Pickens situation out of the secluded Panhandle and into the media stream, and Ed Roach was finally clapped away in a special attic for dysfunctional presidents within the administrative bureaucracy of Texas A&M.[1] He was last heard of still on the public payroll in another state, but the little town of Canyon and its school are once again free. Pickens, who hasn't talked much about Mesa's university lately, has moved to Dallas and is said to have thought of running for governor, no doubt with a strong educational platform.

The search for Doyle—the subject of the La Fontaines' "Current Affair" segment—would lead through Amarillo, Mary had been told by a high-level source in the Texas state bureaucracy. The publication of the tramp arrest records story had launched a mad search for tramps across the country, and everyone with a PC modem and a Kennedy compulsion, as well as the FBI, jumped into the act. The gold rush of 1848 was only a little less desperate. Only Mary, however, had a genuine clue. This was supplied by her nervous Austin pal, who informed her, if she wouldn't reveal the source, that the name Harold Doyle had turned up on a Texas ID card.

Texas ID cards are issued for identification purposes to residents who for some reason do not want or qualify for driver's licenses. It turned out that Doyle's ID had expired December 9, 1989 and showed an Amarillo address that Mary's source described as "skid row." The data on such IDs is purged from state Department of Public Safety computers two years and sixty days after expiration, which in Doyle's case would have fallen on February 8, 1992—one day before the date of the *Houston Post* story. The source had searched the DPS computer in the week prior to publication, while the La Fontaines were still working up the story. If she'd waited a few days more, the information would have been lost forever.

In Amarillo, the La Fontaines met their camera crew—another husband-and-wife team, Ron and Nellie Zimmerman, who had flown in from San Antonio—as well as Al Dooley, a deputy sheriff from a nearby county. Ray and Mary had met Al four years earlier, when they'd finally traveled to Canyon to interview President Roach and other members of his West Texas administration. Al had then been a student reporter for the school newspaper, and had earned Roach's enmity by writing articles critical of his presidential mansion. Mary had recognized a kindred spirit in the budding troublemaker, in addition to a fine investigative mind, and had asked him to join the search.

Al had already turned up a bit of bad news—the Doyle "skid row" address on the Texas ID was a hotel. With a two-year-old hotel address as their only lead, Ray was composed to hear the worst: that the anonymous drifter they technically knew as Harold Doyle had come and gone without a trace, not only not remembered, but never even noticed.

True to his word, Al Dooley had already rounded up several people who had worked at the hotel in the eighties. Shown pictures of Doyle-as-tramp from thirty years before (and without identification by name), none of them seemed to recognize him, not even Kay Ingram, who had worked at the hotel at the time Doyle used it as his address.[2] One woman, however, sat quietly, working cross-stitch embroidery at a coffee-shop table. Finally, exasperated, Mary announced: "Well, has anyone here ever heard the name Harold Doyle?"

"Harold Doyle?" "Harold Doyle?" The name echoed through the room, suspended in the air for a moment. People chuckled softly in recognition; some even assumed a slightly wounded air, as if asked an insultingly easy question.

"Why, we *all* know Harold Doyle," said Kay, at whom Mary had aimed the question. "But I don't think that's him."

"Sure it is." The woman with the cross-stitch finally looked up. "I recognized him right away. Look at that chin. That's Harold all right. I think I have a picture of him at home."

"You do?"

"You bet I do. And you know, the people who knew him best were the Taylors."

Doyle, the La Fontaines were told, had worked at the hotel as a dishwasher. And almost everyone gathered in the restaurant (after news spread word-of-mouth of Al's calls that morning) had known him. There was soon a cacophony of conversation about Doyle, mostly centering on his quaint ways. He didn't drive, and no one quite knew why he had settled in Amarillo. Everyone remembered that a few years back he had been run down in front of the hotel by a police car in hot pursuit of a Cadillac. Doyle had spent quite some time— months, maybe—in a nearby VA hospital, and collected a substantial settlement from the city. He also regularly collected a government check both before and after the accident, but nobody knew what it was for. He wasn't old enough for social security, or retirement.

Fifteen minutes later the cross-stitch lady, who had quietly slipped out of the cozy hotel coffee shop, returned with her pictures.

When she held one up, the La Fontaines and Zimmermans looked at each other and laughed. It was him! Jowly, thirty years older, but with the same scar on his forehead, the same glowering eyes. A late middle-aged version of the "Frenchy" tramp had stared benignly into some camera, no longer sullen and frightened, as he'd been that earlier day in Dallas. One of the tramps had finally been identified. Mary handed the picture to Kay.

"There is no doubt in my mind," Kay said as Ron's Betacam purred, glancing again at the old photos of the tramps for comparison. "This is Harold Doyle."

Having spoken her piece, Kay piled into the cramped rental car with the La Fontaines and Zimmermans to lead the way to the house of the Taylors, the people who had known Doyle best.

The Taylors, a kindly elderly couple, were just preparing to leave when the entourage arrived. Ray talked his way into the house and was able to persuade them to postpone their departure in order to contribute a few on-camera recollections of America's most famous tramp. They warmed to the task, obviously having only the fondest memories of the gentle man who had passed through town some years before, who had been treated with kindness, and who had returned it, leaving the rails and settling into Amarillo—for a while, at least. As it turned out, Doyle had worked for the couple in their furniture repair business, and had confided to Mrs. Taylor that he indeed had been one of the men arrested behind Dealey Plaza on November 22, 1963. He had shown her a story in a magazine—*Playboy*, she thought—that contained his picture and those of two other men. He told her about being fingerprinted and taken before a judge, and about spending several days in jail.

Sometime four or five years before, the kindness had stopped. Doyle had been run down by a police car in front of the very hotel where he had worked as a dishwasher. When he recovered, he had left for a "vacation." He had never returned—leaving all his belongings in his small apartment in Amarillo. He was back on the rails.

Out of the blue, Mrs. Taylor added a seemingly incidental point. "I have his address somewhere—on a Christmas card, I think. He lives out of state and sent us a card a little while back. What state was that, dear?"

"Mmm . . . Indiana, I think," said Mr. Taylor. "Or was it Arkansas?"

Two hours later, after the Taylors left on their errand and returned, Mary called back from the hotel. Mrs. Taylor had turned up the Christmas card. Harold had found a new place that he liked, and taken the time to describe it in a few lines for his old friends the Taylors. It was called Klamath Falls, and wasn't in Indiana or Arkansas, but Oregon. He thought it was beautiful.

Five minutes later, Ron Zimmerman was on the phone with "A Current Affair." He was talking to Barry Levine, managing editor of the program, and had already mentioned the Klamath Falls information. Levine asked to talk to Ray; Ron handed him the phone. Levine was wired. "You got to get out of there and on a plane to Oregon," he shouted from New York. "The future of the country *depends* on it."

Klamath Falls, into which Ray and Mary descended in a two-engine prop puddle jumper, reminded Ray from the air of the little lumber town in *Blue Velvet,* and turned out to be as full of nasty surprises. Harold Doyle was no longer in town. He'd been whisked away by "A Current Affair" to Dallas, which the La Fontaines had just left eight hours earlier. "ACA" tried to take credit for the discovery of the arrest documents, and, almost as shocking to Ray, misspelled his name on the producer's credit as "Roy."

Despite the woes with the tabloid, there was no longer a question, after Doyle's later appearance on camera, that he had been the man long known to conspiracy adepts as "Frenchy," the shorter and stockier of the two younger tramps. The La Fontaines took some satisfaction in knowing that the truth the AP had refused to tell was now out with a vengeance (the Doyle discovery segment received a 14 share, they were told, the highest rating in "ACA" history). Shortly after the program aired, the FBI confirmed the tramp identities with follow-up interviews. Doyle was interrogated by the Bureau aboard an Amtrak train in Portland, which agents, tipped off by "ACA," had halted for this purpose. Doyle was subsequently released and the FBI announced he had nothing to do with the assassination, having spent the morning of November 22, 1963 in a shelter in Dallas, where he got clean clothes, a haircut, and a meal. No explanation was forthcoming as to why his arrest record had disappeared for almost thirty years.

For all that, the news wasn't well received among the fringier elements of the conspiracy community. Alan J. Weberman and Michael Canfield, who collaborated in one of the true nut books of assassinology, *Coup D'etat in America,* were displeased by the implications that their book was entirely baseless, since it was devoted to the exposition of the hidden agenda behind the three tramps, who in their world are supposed to be Watergate burglars E. Howard Hunt and Frank Sturgis, and a CIA operative named Dan Carswell. In a recently released printing of *Coup D'etat,* the two authors have added an "Aftermath," chapter 19. Chapter 19 is their retort to a ridiculous idea, recently promulgated by "the couple who had written the [*Houston Post*] story" and who "sold the story to the tabloid-style TV Show, 'A Current Affair.'" This suspicious-sounding pair, say Weberman and Canfield, failed to notice a long list of significant details, such as the fact that Doyle had only "learned to make his mouth look a little like that of Carswell." It isn't explained why the sweet-natured Doyle, who found happiness in Klamath Falls after leaving it in

Amarillo, started practicing in the bathroom mirror to look like a CIA guy named Carswell, but perhaps Chauncey Holt would have some insight on the matter.

Holt, who claims to have also been in the Mafia, is a self-confessed "tramp." He admits it; he was part of a special CIA tramp contingent flown in to knock off the president. The claim has earned him TV appearances and serious consideration in a *Newsweek* article published in December 1991, two months before the *Houston Post* story. Like Weberman and Canfield, Holt's assertions haven't been affected by the appearance of mere pieces of paper, like arrest records. He still claims to have been the "old man" in the pictures, who we now know was Gus Abrams, who died in 1987. Holt looks younger today than old Abrams did thirty years ago, but listen, a lot of things are possible.

One you probably wouldn't have thought of, if it hadn't been pointed out in yet another spirited tramp defense, is the argument in the "Chameleon" section of Bill Sloan's *JFK: Breaking the Silence*.[3] Doyle wasn't impersonating a disguised hitman, Sloan's source ("the Chameleon") says; the hitman was impersonating Doyle. You see, there were three killer tramps and three *real* tramps, and the killer tramps knew about the real tramps and adopted their identities. . . .

Reading this stuff had a soothing effect on Ray's rattled nerves. He sometimes wondered if in the solitary cocoon of pounding out pages he wasn't growing imperceptibly weirder every day. His darkest fear was that one day he would wake up and realize he'd been typing, "All work and no play makes Ray a dull boy," like Jack Nicholson in *The Shining*. Reading guys like Weberman and Canfield, though, you had to figure you were possibly still OK after all. He liked them for that.

It was a year and a half before locating Doyle that the La Fontaines became interested not only in the Kennedy assassination, which till then they assumed was the work of a single deranged gunman, but in the curious ways of conspiracy promoters, the PR wing of assassinology.

It all began with listening to the car radio on the way back to Dallas after a brief trip to Wichita Falls. It was early August 1990, and the big news was the invasion of Kuwait by Saddam Hussein, but another, more local, story had also caught Ray's attention as he stared hypnotically over the wheel. Astonishingly, it appeared that a young man named Ricky White was announcing that very day, at a press conference in Dallas, that his late father, a Dallas policeman, had been the true assassin of President Kennedy. The seeming straightforwardness of the approach intrigued Ray; who would declare to the world that his own father killed JFK if it weren't true?

By the time the La Fontaines reached home, Ricky White was appearing hourly on CNN. Later that week, they watched him on "Larry King Live." In his own inimitable Bubba style, Ricky seemed convincing. Ray, meanwhile, had been telling Mary that *this* was a story they could have, and should have, done; it was happening in Dallas, after all. Mary for once actually considered his advice—did so, in fact, long after he started wondering what in the world he could have been thinking of. By then, of course, there was no turning back. She'd already locked on.

And not just on Ricky White. Ricky, it would turn out, was just the beginning—the doorway to the house of mirrors.

On August 2, the day of the return from Wichita Falls, Mary called the JFK Assassination Center in Dallas, a business in a downtown mall that retailed assassination geegaws, conducted "research," and had sponsored the Ricky White press conference. Ricky, Mary was told, was busy with CNN and couldn't come to the phone; they took a message.

A week later, the La Fontaines heard from Gary Baily, president of Matsu Corporation in Midland, Texas. Midland was reputedly the most affluent community per capita in the U.S., as well as the home of Baby Jessica and Ricky White. Matsu (named after the spunky island off mainland China that refused to knuckle under to the regime of Chairman Mao) was comprised, Ray and Mary learned, of a group of young Texas oilmen who had become interested in the tales Ricky had been telling for some time in the West Texas town. Ricky had a young partner of sorts, a fellow Terminex man with a lady-killer reputation, Andy Burke. He and Ricky had been traveling about Texas, investigating some fabulous finds Ricky had supposedly made in his father's footlocker in Paris, Texas. Chief among the alleged finds was a diary kept by Ricky's father, Dallas policeman Roscoe White—a diary containing admissions that Roscoe not only shot President Kennedy from behind a stockade fence on Dealey Plaza (therefore being the "grassy knoll" culprit), but later the same day, killed Officer J. D. Tippit as well. There was an unfortunate glitch, however, in that the diary was no longer in evidence. It had mysteriously disappeared, Ricky claimed, after an FBI visit to his Midland home. In any event, the investigative travels of Ricky and Andy required funding, and who better to hit up for this patriotic fieldwork than the young oil turks abounding in Midland, Texas?

Matsu partner Tim Collier later related:

> The two of them came to my office so often that my secretary came in, shut the door, and whispered, "Do we have a bug problem?" They looked like Ghostbusters in their Terminex uniforms. I was obsessed with this for about a year. Ricky sounded sincere, and if what he said was true he had the key to the biggest mystery in American history. We were young and naïve, and being in Midland, had nothing much better to do. We figured we could spend about as much on this project as it would cost to drill a dry hole.

(Translation: Ricky got into Matsu for six figures.)

After initially meeting with Gary Baily in Ray's Las Colinas office, the La Fontaines met with him again in Midland, this time with Brian Sirgo present. Gary and Brian were the two most active members of Matsu, the corporation they had formed with Tim Collier and others to bankroll Ricky's exploits. Ray's proposal was fairly simple. He wanted to investigate the Ricky White story for a theatrical documentary along the lines of *The Thin Blue Line*. The nonnegotiable bottom line was that the project would be guided by the search for the truth, wherever it might lead; if the story was a hoax, the La Fontaines would have to report it. As Ray and everyone else in the room saw it at the time, though, this was really a kind of technicality. Ray had already had one of his infallible intuitive flashes watching Ricky on TV a couple of weeks earlier. He *saw* that Ricky was telling the truth—that he was sincere, though he might have misinterpreted some clues, as anyone can—and that besides, the young West Texas bug sprayer was just too unimaginative to lie. Gary and Brian, who naturally would have liked to have seen a return for their financial stake in Ricky, were nevertheless as committed to chasing down the truth as the La Fontaines, and readily agreed on the ground rules. To their credit, they never changed their commitment after the depressing facts began to come out.

In the meantime, the Midlanders had been told by the late Larry

Howard of the JFK Assassination Center, with which Matsu had made a publicity deal, that Oliver Stone was planning a movie on the assassination. Larry proposed to sell the Ricky White story to Stone, and, indeed, he and Ricky (and their wives) had gone to California to visit Stone personally. According to Ricky, Stone had instantly said he wanted the story, and told his producer, Alex Ho, to sign the young Texan. It's possible, even given that Ricky claimed it, that that was what happened; but it didn't work out that way.

Ricky has changed his story a couple of times, but its main line goes something like this. Sometime in the early 1980s he found his father's diary in a footlocker. He didn't read it at the time, however. When he did, several years later, he showed the diary to his mother, Geneva, and told the Midland County district attorney's office about the find. The Midland FBI was then notified, and interrogated Ricky. The diary disappeared, he says, after agents visited his home. He implies it left with them. The contacts with Ricky are verified by the Midland D.A. and FBI.

In time Ricky hooked up with Andy Burke, and the pair told the story to the Midland oilmen who were to form Matsu, as well as to a literary agent in San Antonio, Charles Neighbors. Ricky claims that a big book deal was forthcoming, but that he nixed it when they tried to "change the story." Ricky also took his story to the JFK Assassination Center in Dallas, then co-owned by Larry Howard and Gary Shaw. The center persuaded Ricky to drop Burke in favor of a solo act.

Then, in May or June of 1990, Shaw, the late Houston private detective Joe West, and Ricky got to digging on the grounds of an old lake cabin owned by Ricky's family near Lake Whitney. Ricky, the story goes, believed that as a child he'd seen his father, Roscoe, burying something by the cabin. The diggers worked all day and into the night, but found nothing.

Ricky started back toward Midland, but stopped on the road and called his wife, Trisha. She told him his mother, Geneva, had been trying to reach him. He then called Geneva and was told to go search in the attic of his grandfather, Geneva's father, in Paris.

Ricky changed course, heading for Paris and arriving in the middle of the night, but luckily with a flashlight. He started beaming it through the charred remains of the attic (which Benny, Geneva's brother, had set fire to some years earlier) and caught a glimpse of a "glint of metal." It turned out to be a naval gun canister, used on ships to protect small arms, and contained various artifacts associated with Roscoe and Geneva: family photographs, Roscoe's Marine dog tags, a Gregg shorthand book, and typed pieces of paper encased in plastic.

As Ricky explains it, the Gregg volume was a "witness elimination book." Someone had pasted on its pages pictures of people to be bumped off: Jack and Bobby Kennedy, Perry Russo (a witness in Jim Garrison's Clay Shaw trial who placed Oswald together with Shaw and David Ferrie), and other assorted figures. The Kennedys were dead, and not notably "witnesses," whereas witness Russo was still alive—not yet "eliminated," apparently.

The typed pages in plastic—transcripts of three "intelligence cables," according to Ricky and his Assassination Center handlers— became the centerpiece of the press conference that followed on August 2, a few months after the claimed canister-in-the-attic discovery. The purported intelligence cables order Roscoe White to go forth to Dallas, where he is to take care of a threat to "world wide peace," and to hang around long enough afterwards ("hidden within the department") to tidy up any loose ends, if necessary; for "witnesses have eyes, ears and mouth." Like everything else associated with the canister, the painfully hokey cables proved to be hoaxes, though they appear to have been fabricated by someone knowledgeable of intelligence operations. They contain, for example, the insider notation *Re-rifle*. Not too long before the canister was found, one of Ricky's handlers at the JFK Center, Gary Shaw, had appeared on an Austin access TV show expounding his theories about the involvement in the assassination of ZR/RIFLE, an intelligence operation for murdering foreign leaders. Shaw was also the assassination impresario who prior to Ricky had sponsored babushka lady-impersonator Beverly Oliver, and after him, self-professed tramp Chauncy Holt, in their forays into grassy knoll mythologizing.[4]

Whoever may have helped, it's certain the cables were planted in the attic of Ricky's grandfather's house in Paris, Texas sometime after he visited there with his now-discarded partner, Andy Burke; and that Ricky supplied his father's dog tags for placement in the canister, along with pictures of two of his grandparents and the typed cable "transcripts."[5] Andy, who now lives in California, told Mary that he searched the attic on a precanister discovery visit to the house with

Ricky, and that the attic was then empty. His story is supported by Ricky's maternal aunt Ora, and by his paternal aunt Linda Wells, who didn't even like Andy.

More damningly, both Ricky's paternal grandmother and his father's half-sister have said they each gave Ricky a set of dog tags. His grandmother adds that one of the pictures in the canister also came from her house. Thus the canister couldn't have been left in the attic by Ricky's father, Roscoe, who died in 1971. "Unless there are *three* sets of dog tags," says Roscoe's sister Linda, "Ricky put those dog tags in the canister. I gave him a set and my mother gave him a set. That's two." As of 1993, there was only one set of dog tags accounted for—the set found in the canister and held by Matsu in a vault.

But while the flakiness of Ricky's stories soon became evident to the La Fontaines, it didn't necessarily follow, they also discovered, that there was no validity to the possibility that Dallas policeman Roscoe White was in some way connected to the events of November 22, 1963. He *may* have been; his role remains a mystery. The art of Roscoe White interpretation begins, in any case, with the fundamental and necessary step of cutting Ricky out of the picture (perhaps with a retirement trinket for his years of service in bringing the matter to public attention).

His mother, the much ridiculed Geneva, is another matter—though like Ricky, she too manufactured evidence. The mortgage company was moving in on her house (as inept with money as Emma Bovary, Geneva had bankrupted one husband and might have bankrupted two others, if death or divorce hadn't intervened), and she came up with a laughably inept forgery of a "diary" to support Ricky's story that his father's diary contained a coded confession. Geneva's desperate attempt to stave off the bill collectors by trying to profit from the mangled yarns Ricky was blabbing to the world earned her a few thousand dollars from the coproducer of Oliver Stone (more out of compassion than interest), and the immeasurable contempt of the JFK Assassination Center for endangering the credibility of its current conspiracy star, Ricky White, Son of the Assassin. Geneva's obvious forgery had already been lambasted at a Houston press conference.

But for all of Geneva's inconvenient antics, it was she, not Ricky, who was the true witness to whatever real story existed. The following are known facts: Geneva was one of Jack Ruby's bar girls, and is seen hiking up her skirt for the ogling bar owner in a photo published in *Time* in 1988.[6] Her husband, "Rock," Roscoe White, was one of the many Dallas policeman who knew Ruby. In August-September 1957 Roscoe, also a Marine, took the same boat to Japan as Lee Harvey Oswald. Contrary to the claims of amateur sleuths Gary Mack and David Perry of Dallas, the connections between the two did not end there. In November of the same year, both White and Oswald ended up in Subic Bay, the Philippines, and, later, off the coast of Indonesia as part of a secret CIA invasion force planned for that island nation. Roscoe White wrote of the matter to his wife, Geneva, in letters that survive, complete with their naval-vessel postmarks.[7] Oswald talked with Priscilla McMillan about the incident, as she testified to Warren investigators.[8] The "maneuvers" were protracted; the Marines did not return to their original assignments for several months. Did White, Oswald, both, or neither become trained intelligence assets during this clandestine action? Oswald was, as we've wearily seen, an offbeat, unpredictable sort about whom very little can be said for sure; and no military intelligence files can be found for him. White was more conventional in the best sense—cheerful, outgoing, practical, good with his hands—as well as a highly intelligent Marine, as evidenced by his entrance testing.[9] His high scores and aptitude would have made him a likely nominee for intelligence consideration, and his letters show him to have been both a good son and an uncompromising patriot, not someone likely to have refused an intelligence assignment.

In 1959, Oswald defected to the Soviet Union, and stayed for almost three years. Roscoe White, in the meantime, remained in the Marine Corps. He was a superb marksman, and frequently wrote of his duties on the rifle range. One of these included developing a specialty in "surveying target sites." In the fall of 1962, just as Oswald was preparing to move to Dallas for the first time, Roscoe White was obtaining a hardship discharge (as Oswald had done three years previously). His destination: Dallas.

And so it was that Roscoe White and Oswald landed in Dallas within a month or two of each other. Roscoe's first job in Dallas was with American National Insurance, where his employer was later to recall that he didn't show much interest in his work. Oswald in the meantime worked for six months in Dallas, left for New Orleans, made a trip to Mexico City, and returning to Dallas, started working at the Texas School Book Depository eight days after Roscoe White joined the Dallas Police Department.

During his tenure at the DPD, Roscoe White seems to have been "the man who wasn't there." No one, to this day, can explain exactly what he did for the Dallas police. His personnel file contains a few insurance papers, a background check, and nothing else—no assignment, no commendations or reprimands (J. D. Tippit's file is voluminous by comparison). He stayed two years, to October 1965, leaving to take a series of retail and skilled jobs until his untimely death from burns suffered in an explosion in 1971 at age thirty-six. Roscoe left behind his widow, Geneva, two young sons, and a bizarre legacy: a set of photographs that would continue to puzzle assassination researchers until the present day.

Geneva White began to make waves in September 1975 when, as Geneva Dees, she presented herself to Gerald Weatherly of the Dallas County district attorney's office. She had come literally from a mental ward, having just been released from a Dallas hospital. Her mission was to obtain assistance in locating pictures that had belonged to her late husband, Roscoe White. The pictures, Geneva told Weatherly, connected Oswald to the CIA.

For whatever reasons, Gerald Weatherly believed Geneva Dees. He sat down and wrote letters (on the letterhead of his boss, Dallas County D.A. Henry Wade, though he made it clear he was writing as a private citizen) to Sen. Richard Schweicker, Cong. Henry Gonzalez, and Texas Attorney General Waggoner Carr. He stated his purpose clearly: nothing less than the desire to see the investigation into the assassination of President Kennedy reopened. He also told these men that he had done some checking, and found that Mrs. Dees' late husband, Roscoe, had worked for the Dallas police, but learned that there was no record of what division he worked in, or what he did.

One thing Roscoe White did soon became apparent, though. He kept evidence that showed that Dallas police officers had lied to the Warren Commission about the "backyard photographs" of Lee Harvey Oswald. The police had sworn they found two such photos. Roscoe White had a print of yet another, different pose.[10] And he had something else—something that as we've seen (chapter 3) could be construed as evidence that Oswald worked for the CIA. He had a picture of Oswald's Department of Defense ID card.

Geneva made other, more extravagant claims—that she overheard

HENRY WADE
DISTRICT ATTORNEY
DALLAS COUNTY GOVERNMENT CENTER
DALLAS, TEXAS 75202

The Honorable Richard S. Schweicker,
Senate Office Building,
Washington, D.C. 20510:

The Honorable Henry B. Gonzalez, M.C.,
House of Representatives,
Washington, D.C. 20515:

The Honorable Waggoner Carr,
305 Stokes Building,
Austin, Tx 78701:

Re: Possible reopening of investigation of J.F. Kennedy assassination:

Dear Sirs:

Learning from newspapers that each of you urges reopening this investigation -
Mr. Carr saying only as to possible connection between Oswald and the FBI or CIA -
I send you the information herein and enclosed herewith as possibly of interest.

As part of my duties as Assistant District Attorney of Dallas County, Texas, I
sometimes take what we call walk-in complaints, from people who come to this office to file criminal complaints. And yesterday a lady who gave me her name and
address as Mrs. Ben K. Dees (Geneva Ruth Dees), 3405 Bonham Street, Paris, Tx 75460,
phone 214-785-4366, came to me here and told me in substance that she had had, but
had recently been swindled out of possession of, a set of 34 actual photographs of
Lee Harvey Oswald, which she says link Oswald with the CIA. And, as is customary,
she made affidavit to me that this information she'd furnished to me "is true and
correct to the best of my knowledge and belief."

How reliable her story is, I do not know. But I referred her complaint to
the Dallas County, Texas, Grand Jury, 7th Floor, New County Court House, Dallas,
Tx 75202, phone 214-749-8511. At some date not yet set, they will subpoena Mrs.
Dees to testify before them on the matter, and will also attempt to send a form
letter to the possible defendant, Dan Robinson.

I enclose herewith for each of you a xerox copy of the case summary I took from
Mrs. Dees, and of her form affidavit in connection therewith.

I am not acting officially as Assistant District Attorney in giving you this information. Merely as a private person, I think this information may be of interest to you gentlemen. And, again in my private capacity only, I would like to see
the Kennedy-Assassination investigation reopened by Congress or either House thereof.

Yours truly,

Gerald Weatherly

*Undated letter (ca. September 1975) from Gerald Weatherly, assistant D.A. of
Dallas County, to Sen. Richard Schweicker, Cong. Henry Gonzalez, and
Texas Attorney General Waggoner Carr, telling of Geneva White's claims of
having pictures linking Oswald to the CIA. Weatherly says he thinks the
Kennedy assassination investigation should be reopened.*

HENRY WADE
DISTRICT ATTORNEY
DALLAS COUNTY GOVERNMENT CENTER
DALLAS, TEXAS 75202

29 September 1975:

The Honorable Richard S. Schweicker,
Senate Office Building,
Washington, D.C. 20510:

Attention: Mr. David Marston, Administrative Assistant:

The Honorable Henry B. Gonzalez, M.C.,
House of Representatives,
Washington, D.C. 20515:

The Honorable Waggoner Carr,
305 Stokes Building,
Austin, Tx 78701:

Dear Sirs:

Pursuing a telephoned suggestion made to me by Mr. Marson, I today telephoned Mrs.
Dees of Paris, Texas, our complaining witness in our grand jury referal against
Dan Robinson for alleged theft from her of 34 photographs of Lee Harvey Oswald,
which she says link Oswald with the CIA. And, by telephone, she told me this morning:

The pictures were left to her by her deceased former husband, Roscoe A. White, and that
he was on the Police Force of the City of Dallas, Texas, two years - what branch is unknown to her, she says.

Today by phone Miss Slovacek of the Personnel Department of that Police Force, told me,
on consulting, as she said, a card in the records there, that Roscoe A. White "was employed" by and on that Police Force; that he was so employed 10-7-1963 and resigned 10-
18-1965 (thus you see he had been on the force a month and sixteen days before the J.F.
Kennedy assassination, at the time of the assassination, and for nearly two years after
it); but that that card "doesn't say where or on what division or where he was working."

As I was typing this letter, Mr. Marston phoned me, and I told him all the above and
more.

Yours truly,

Gerald Weatherly

---

*A similar letter from Weatherly, dated September 29, 1975, shows that he
checked with the Dallas Police Department and found police had no record of
where Roscoe White worked in the department.*

Roscoe and Ruby discussing the assassination, for example, a statement she made on tape shortly before her death. In light of new evidence discussed previously, the claim is not as wild as it once seemed; there is a better case now for Ruby's involvement. Still, Geneva invented a diary and once said she met mobster Charles Nicoletti while attending a Mary Kay convention in New Orleans; she most likely "overheard" this conversation in the same spirit.

One seemingly bizarre claim has some documentary support, however. She attested to having had numerous electric shock treatments to "erase her memory." Her psychiatric record reveals that Geneva did indeed undergo numerous hospitalizations for shock therapy. The earliest record available to us shows EST on November 22, 1966. The treatments continued periodically for many years. Geneva's psychiatric record also reveals some truth in another of her claims—that a family friend, Philip Jordan, warned her that Roscoe was involved in the assassination, and that this would come out in the House Select Committee investigation. Her psychiatrist noted in January 1977 that Geneva had been visited by a friend, "PJ," who asked if she knew Jack Ruby, and told her she was under surveillance. This followed immediately on the heels of Geneva's interview by HSCA

P.O. Box 357 Mt Home, Arkansas 72653 CA-4-3476
Name White, Geneva Ruth   Age 25   Phone No. FE-1-5455   Date November 15, 1966
Address 219 Glengairn, Dallas, 75234   SMW M   Occupation Housewife   Ref. By Paul Boren M. D.
Charge To Husband: Roscoe Anthony White. 8243 Marquelle, Dallas, Texas 75217

DATE	REMARKS	CHARGED	PAID	BALANCE	DATE	REMARKS	CHARGED	PAID	BALANCE
1966					1966	Balance forwarded			255.00
Nov. 15	Hospital Consultation	25.00		25.00	Dec. 5	HV&EST	20.00		275.00
Nov. 18	HV	10.00		35.00	Dec. 6	HV	10.00		285.00
Nov. 19	HV	10.00		45.00	Dec. 7	HV	10.00		295.00
Nov. 20	HV	10.00		55.00	Dec. 8	HV	10.00		305.00
Nov. 21	HV	10.00		65.00	Dec. 9	HV&Disc.	10.00		315.00
Nov. 22	HV&EST	20.00		85.00	Dec. 19	OV (ck)	25.00	25.00	315.00
Nov. 23	HV&EST	20.00		105.00	1967				
Nov. 25	HV(Pass)	10.00		115.00	Jan. 6	OV (ck)	25.00	25.00	315.00
Nov. 25	HV&EST	20.00		135.00	Jan. 30	INS. Forms: Anxiety Reaction With			
Nov. 26	HV	10.00		145.00		Depressive Symptoms			
Nov. 27	HV	10.00		155.00		OV	25.00	25.00	315.00
Nov. 28	HV&EST	20.00		175.00	May 1	Received on acct.(ck)		5.00	310.00
Nov. 29	HV	10.00		185.00	July 18	Received on acct.(ck)		30.00	280.00
Nov. 30	HV&EST	20.00		205.00	Oct 2	Received on acct.(ck)		5.00	275.00
Dec. 1	HV	10.00		215.00	Oct. 3	Received on acct.(ck)		5.00	270.00
Dec. 2	HV&EST	20.00		235.00	Nov. 17	Received on acct.(ck)		5.00	265.00
Dec. 3	HV (pass)	10.00		245.00	1968				
Dec. 4	HV(pass)	10.00		255.00	Jan. 31	Received on acct.(ck)		10.00	255.00

A billing card from Dr. Pearson shows one of several series of electroshock treatments, this one beginning on November 22, 1966.

investigators. Although Jordan denied making such statements to former assistant Texas attorney general Ned Butler in a 1991 interview, the psychiatric record gives the lie to Jordan's disclaimer in favor of Geneva's account.

Unnecessary to say by now, no doubt, all these odd twists and turns in one introductory spin through the outskirts of Kennediana didn't have the salutary effect on Mary of warning her off from the hypnotic dangers of an obviously bottomless story. She didn't recognize ordinary limits, being (in that way only) a little like the former West Texas president, Ed Roach. It didn't matter that other people wandered into this maze and went mad, like Bishop Pike in the desert, never to be seen again, or surfacing only in monstrous dehumanized form, incapable of ever changing the topic. Mary believed she could solve the Kennedy assassination as she had solved Roach, from the bed, with a phone in her hand.

The amazing thing is that in the end she—and her long-distance coconspirator, Bill Adams—did, almost.

In March of 1992, Mary was back at the Dallas archives going through assassination-related police intelligence files. She was surprised to note that the files continued well into the sixties, and included the interest of the Dallas Police Department in the Jim Garrison investigation. Someone in the DPD had systematically archived each new newspaper or magazine article on the flamboyant New Orleans D.A.'s prosecution of Clay Shaw. The Dallas records also showed a more noteworthy fact. Very early—in February 1967, on the week of David Ferrie's death—the department was assisted by a journalist, Hugh Aynesworth, who shared information with the police intelligence division. It was information that, if not divulged, might have led to a different outcome for the prosecutor. Instead, he was never able to question the one man who by his associations connected Ferrie, Shaw, and Guy Banister. His name was Sergio Arcacha Smith.

From the beginning, there was intense pressure on the media covering the assassination of President Kennedy. The pressure was rationalized by the specter of World War III, which new president Lyndon Johnson hadn't hesitated to invoke in cajoling Chief Justice Earl Warren to serve on a commission that would lay to rest any lingering doubts, either about the identity of the assassin, or that he was a *single* assassin, without any known conspiratorial ties. If it were shown that Russia or Castro's Cuba had a hand in the murder of a U.S. president, Johnson argued, the American people might demand retribution with catastrophic consequences. The press supported the efforts of the commander-in-chief to salve the national wounds and get on with the life of the country. In this task the American media performed admirably, bringing to the grieving nation the awful beauty of the state funeral planned by Jackie Kennedy. Closure came to Camelot with the unforgettable farewell salute of a three-year-old boy.

Some newsmen—Robert McNeil, Seth Kantor, Ike Pappas—were not just reporters of the tragedy, but important witnesses as well. Oswald himself pointed McNeil to a phone in the book depository.[11] Kantor ran into Jack Ruby at Parkland Hospital, where the president lay dying (and where Ruby's mechanic, Donnell Whitter, remained in a coma on an upper floor). Pappas, in Dallas to cover the transfer of Oswald to the county jail, covered a murder instead, as Ruby shot the accused assassin before the reporter's eyes.

But of all the journalists to have been touched by the assassination, perhaps none would be more beholden professionally to this single event than Dan Rather and Hugh Aynesworth. By Rather's account he was near Dealey Plaza at the time of the assassination; it was he who called in the first report of the president's death to his network anchor, Walter Cronkite. Rather was also the only television reporter to view the Zapruder film of the assassination. His report that the president's head jerked violently forward at the moment of the fatal shot (ergo the shot came from behind) was the only news account the American public had for twelve years, until a bootleg copy of the film was finally shown on national television in 1975. As we're all now aware, the film *does* show the president's head moving forward very slightly, and for some infinitesimal fraction of time. If the movement weren't interrupted by a violent snap to the *rear*, it needn't have been a more significant detail than the fact that the president, having already been hit by a bullet through the neck, was starting to slip forward. The news that *wasn't* told by Rather for twelve years was the lunge to the rear, practically crushing the president into the back of the car seat. How could Rather have missed it, or failed to report it? (Little wonder that someone, an exasperated news junkie perhaps, finally clobbered the anchor in an alley somewhere, asking, "What's the frequency, Kenneth?")

Rather's failure to tell the story was entirely apart, it should be added, from the separate question of the validity of scientific explanations that were later offered to account for the president's emphatic backward movement. The fact that there were at least two of these—a neuromuscular reflex and the "jet effect"—suggests that their learned proponents were philosophizing rather than explaining with authority. One or the other explanation may be right, but neither has yet to persuade the opposite camp, despite being based on only the most reputable methodologies of their disciplines.

If Dan Rather was distinguished by his silence in this matter, Hugh Aynesworth's role was marked by his ubiquitous presence on virtually every front of the assassination story. Aynesworth was, for example, one of the *Dallas Morning News* employees who provided an alibi for Jack Ruby, supporting Ruby's claim that he was at the offices of the Dallas newspaper when the president was shot. (Though why the reporter was at the newspaper building instead of out on the motorcade route, as were most reporters on November 22, 1963, is something Aynesworth has never explained, as his old news pal Lonnie Hudkins points out.) Remarkably, Aynesworth was also at the book depository within minutes of the assassination, at the Texas Theater when Oswald was captured, and in the police basement when Ruby shot Oswald.

Aynesworth still takes understandable pride in his whirlwind coverage of events during those assassination days. In a 1992 letter to the editor in *Texas Monthly* shortly after the release of *JFK* (a letter in which he takes clinical note of "Oliver Stone's egomania, paranoia, and absolute distrust of anybody who didn't watch the sixties through a marijuana haze"), the writer informs us that

> I covered the Kennedy assassination for the *Dallas Morning News* and the *Dallas Times Herald*—almost every major happening until 1966. I covered every day of the Garrison extravaganza for *Newsweek* from 1967 to 1969 and various new theories and allegations for the *Washington Times*, where I am currently the Southwest bureau chief.[12]

What Aynesworth omitted from his impressive *Texas Monthly* résumé was that his reporting was even more extensive, for he not only "covered" the Garrison investigation for *Newsweek*[13] but provided undercover information of the details of the investigation to intelligence agents in the Dallas Police Department. His information effectively contributed to the sabotaging of Garrison's efforts.

As we know, of course, by the winter of early 1967, the New Orleans D.A., an American original (some have said American grotesque) had taken up the cause of the Warren Commission critics and opened an investigation of persons in his parish. Whatever may be said now about Garrison's mistakes, and they were legion, the D.A. was on a fertile path. He had zeroed in on the early sixties occupants of the Newman Building at 544 Camp Street, and on participants in the burglary of an arms bunker near Lake Pontchartrain in 1961. There were two men who fit both categories—David Ferrie and a Cuban exile named Sergio Arcacha Smith.

In his own way Arcacha was almost as interesting as Ferrie, though unable to match the latter's baroque appearance and lifestyle. Not only did the Cuban occupy an office at the Camp Street address until early 1962, but he knew Ferrie, Guy Banister, and the man Garrison ultimately prosecuted for conspiracy in the assassination, Clay Shaw. According to CIA documents released in 1977, Shaw was indeed a CIA asset, and Arcacha was the New Orleans delegate to an organization set up by the agency as an umbrella for all Cuban exile organizations, the Cuban Revolutionary Council. Guy Banister, the same documents reveal, was Arcacha's FBI contact.[14] In short, it was Arcacha, and only Arcacha, who linked the three men.

On Friday, February 24, 1967, Garrison made his first attempt to question Arcacha. Ferrie, the primary Garrison target, already knowing of his own imminent indictment, had died of a massive brain hemorrhage just two days earlier. Undeterred, Garrison sent two of his assistants, attorney James Alcock and investigator William Gurvich, to Dallas. Someone else would arrive on their heels: journalist Hugh Aynesworth.

The Dallas police intelligence files contain at least two records documenting Aynesworth's involvement. Both are reports prepared by Detective D. K. Rodgers of the DPD's Criminal Intelligence Section, and submitted to police captain W. F. Dyson.[15] The first report, dated February 27, 1967, tells of the attempts of Alcock to contact and interview Arcacha in Dallas on February 25. Alcock initially called, presumably from New Orleans, on Friday night, the 24th. Arcacha wasn't home, and Alcock asked the wife of the Cuban exile if her husband would consider flying to New Orleans, if he were sent the plane fare, so that he might be interviewed by the Garrison investigators. When she declined for Arcacha, Alcock "stated that he would then come to Dallas and question him [there]."[16]

Early Saturday morning, Alcock called again to inform Arcacha that he wanted to arrange to interview him in Dallas, and that he would call back at 10:00 A.M. For still unknown reasons, Arcacha alerted Dallas police officers E. L. Cunningham and the report author, Rodgers, who went to Arcacha's home "in anticipation to the call."[17] The call never came, however, and the officers left at a quarter to noon. Some five hours after their departure, Alcock finally called—but again unsuccessfully. Whether Arcacha was home or not, Mrs. Arcacha was again manning the phone. Alcock tried again at seven that same Saturday evening, by which time he and Gurvich had checked into a Dallas motel. The Garrison investigator informed Arcacha's wife that he would be calling back yet again, still seeking to arrange for an interview with her husband. Again the reluctant Arcacha called DPD intelligence officers, and again two detectives, Rodgers and C. T. Burnley (who had frequently visited at Oswald's boardinghouse during 1963, according to housekeeper Earlene Roberts), arrived at his house to await the expected call.

This time the Dallas officers were there when the phone rang at 9:15 P.M. Arcacha requested Detective Rodgers to pick it up "to determine who and what the caller wanted." The caller was Alcock, and he wanted Arcacha. Rodgers told Alcock the Cuban didn't want to talk with him, and asked if he had an arrest warrant. If Alcock did, Rogers reportedly told him,

> we would be happy to execute the warrant. Alcock stated that he did not have a warrant and that if [Arcacha] would not talk to him he would forget it and go back to New Orleans. An arrangement was made at that time to meet Alcock at the City Hall with [Arcacha].[18]

Leaving directly for city hall, Rodgers, Burnley, and Arcacha met Alcock and Gurvich in a hallway on the third floor of the downtown building. It was 10:00 P.M. The "group adjourned to the Chief's Conference room," where Gurvich placed a tape recorder on the table. The New Orleans investigators asked to talk to Arcacha alone, and Arcacha, as might be expected by now, balked. The investigators then suggested that they would talk with him in the presence of his attorney. [Arcacha] stated that this was fine, that we would try to contact Bill Alexander and then they could have their conference. Alcock then evidently identified the name of Alexander, because he asked if this were a law partner of Henry Wade, the District Attorney. Since [Arcacha] would not talk to these men, this conference ended.[19]

Alcock's recognition of Alexander's name stymied what was apparently a preplanned trick between the two Dallas detectives and Arcacha—to slip the assistant district attorney of Dallas County into the proceedings, disguised as the Cuban's "attorney," thereby obtaining information of Garrison's investigation. Foiled in this attempt, the Dallas detectives returned Arcacha to his home, where he was given better protection from the Louisiana authorities than Dallasites ordinarily received from the criminals of their city. "A security surveillance," Rodgers' report tells us, "was conducted until midnight."

The next day, Sunday, February 26, reporter Aynesworth made his entrance. Placing a call to the already skittish Arcacha, he explained that

his magazine [*Newsweek*] and Columbia Broadcasting System had information on the inside of Jim Garrison's office in New Orleans and that the news media was building a story to blast Garrison for the handling of this so called conspiracy and other mal practices [*sic*] that have occurred in Garrison's office.[20]

A few days later, on March 3, 1967, another report was generated by Detective Rodgers of the DPD's intelligence unit. It revealed, perhaps more lucidly than any other known document, the extent to which the sixties media cooperated with intelligence groups to destroy the Garrison investigation. "An interview," the report began,

was arranged on Monday, February 27, 1967 for [Arcacha] to discuss the "Conspiracy" case of New Oreans D.A. Garrison with Hugh Aynesworth, a reporter for *Newsweek Magazine*. Aynesworth reported that he has informants in the office of James Garrison and that he had a number of names of witnesses interviewed by Garrison's investigators and names of persons Garrison's investigators are seeking for information. This interview was conducted in the office of the Criminal Intelligence Section.[21]

Aynesworth disclosed that the Garrison investigation "centered around acquaintances of David William Ferrie," whom Arcacha admitted knowing in the interview (claiming, however, that he "did not become to [*sic*] friendly with him because of his queer behavior"). The *Newsweek* writer went on to volunteer his own version of Ferrie's innocence, and told Arcacha that Garrison had obtained the Cuban's unpublished phone number and address from one of his friends, Carlos Bringuier.

More substantively, the intelligence report noted, "Hugh Aynesworth submitted the below listed names as persons interviewed by investigators for District Attorney Jim Garrison." The "below listed names," complete with annotations and addresses, were of nineteen Ferrie associates, primarily "suspected homosexuals." The Dallas intelligence unit wasted no time in checking its indices for the names provided by Aynesworth.[22] Similarly, author Jim DiEugenio (*Destiny Betrayed*) has suggested that Aynesworth passed on Garrison's witness list to Clay Shaw's defense team.

Aynesworth concluded the February 27 meeting on what for the Cuban was surely a chilling note—that Garrison considered him "as important a witness as David William Ferrie would be if he were alive." By this time, of course, Arcacha and Aynesworth both knew that Garrison thought Ferrie to be far more than "a witness." Until his death, Ferrie had been Garrison's prime investigative target.

The extraordinary Rodgers report of March 3, 1967 provides a memorable portrait of Hugh Aynesworth. In the guise of a journalist, Aynesworth covered the Garrison investigation for one of the premier print-news organizations in America. His uniformly vitriolic accounts appeared over a period of years, and there is little question they helped shape the national view of Garrison as a corrupt, out-of-control public official. Behind the scenes, however, Aynesworth was interfering with the D.A.'s investigation—tampering with a witness and doing so in the very offices of a law enforcement intelligence unit. Armed with information supplied by the reporter, and with the protection of the police intelligence unit (and apparently, of an assistant D.A. of Dallas County), Sergio Arcacha Smith was ultimately able to successfully fight extradition to Louisiana.

None of this was revealed on CNN's November 1993 interview of grand-old-journalist Aynesworth on the occasion of the thirtieth anniversary of President Kennedy's death, in the self-congratulatory meeting of authentic assassination reporters held at Southern Methodist University the same week, or in the CBS-*Newsweek* "joint investigation" resulting in a two-hour Special Report hosted by age- ing anchor and one-time mugging victim Dan Rather. Even so, Rather (and *Newsweek,* in its accompanying special issue) had to take melancholy note of the fact that 90 percent of the American public, for some reason, still distrusts the media's assassination conclusions.

Some people never learn, apparently.

By the summer of 1992, the La Fontaines believed they had mate- rial sufficient for a documentary on the new assassination evidence. They made a proposal to PBS affiliate station KHOU in Houston. Executive producer Miriam Korshak agreed to provide postproduc- tion and station sponsorship for the project, and sent a letter to this effect to help with fund-raising. Ray then began the chore of raising money, hitting up corporations, foundations, and even individuals, all to no avail. Kennedy assassination stories, no matter how ground- breaking, were outré for institutions and didn't have enough sex for everyone else. After six months of refusals, including one from Ray's uncle, who suggested, not unreasonably, that he try a different line of work, the La Fontaines gave up.

One day Mary received a dream message. She woke up thinking: "Syndication." Ray took the hint. He dialed the number of an inde- pendent Dallas TV station and asked for local names and numbers of syndication salesmen. The programming director was helpful, reel- ing off the names of several syndicators, including the local Para- mount and MTM salesmen.

The Paramount office asked if they had talked with "Hard Copy." They hadn't.

"Somebody will get back with you," Ray was told.

The following Monday, someone did. It was Linda Bell, soon to be co-executive producer of "Hard Copy." Linda asked Mary what made her think of them. "It's not 'Current Affair,'" she said. They hit it off.

Mary explained what they had, focusing on Oswald's cellmate John Elrod, and suggested a headline—"Oswald Talked." Linda requested a tape of the "ACA" story Ray had produced; he shipped it. The conversations continued over the next couple of weeks, then Linda sent her new supervising producer, Ron Vandor, to Dallas to talk with the La Fontaines in Las Colinas. Vandor, a refugee from television news, told a cautionary tale—he went to "Hard Copy" initially planning to stay a few months, and ended up loving tabloid. With the exit of Peter Brennan (who returned to "Current Affair") the show was changing, Ron said. There was less T&A and more serious journalism. The Elrod story could be a step in this direction.

In the meantime, Mary heard from a New York producer named Johnny Parsons. Parsons at the time was trying to put together a new syndicated program for Tribune Entertainment. It would later run as a pilot called "The Conspiracy Tapes," featuring Gerald Posner in full debunk mode.

Mary and Ray met with Parsons in a motel room in Dallas, where he was still nervously recuperating from a brush with sheriff's deputies in Waco (who had chased him out of town while he tried to film the burned-out Branch Davidian complex) and a woman from Indianapolis named Linda Thompson. Linda, whom Parsons had flown to Waco together with her six-foot-five bodyguard, believed Janet Reno had pulled the switch intentionally on the Branch Davidians and that there were at least twenty-five unexplained deaths associated with Bill Clinton. Vince Foster was only the tip of the iceberg, she maintained. Parsons was more interested in the La Fontaines' story—an Oswald roommate was mild by comparison, he may have figured—but wasn't able to put his deal together prior to the contract Ray finally worked out with Paramount's "Hard Copy."

As matters turned out, the experience with the Paramount show was a great improvement over the first tabloid debacle. "Hard Copy" took the stories seriously and protected their confidentiality. The executives didn't even want to know the whereabouts of the key witnesses (the more people who knew, the more possibilities for a leak) or see the documents on the segments Ray would produce. They knew the La Fontaines had these, and they trusted them to do it their way. Ray also retained domestic and foreign rights on the stories after they would air in November. More significantly, the La Fontaines would keep all the raw footage not used in the programs (thirty-three Beta tapes in all) to produce the one-hour documentary they couldn't find funding for earlier. In essence, "Hard Copy" agreed to serve as corporate funder (unlike the MacArthur Foundation, Exxon, Mobil Oil, and a dozen other aggressively civic minded organizations) for the little matter of telling the truth about the Kennedy assassination to the American public.

A few days after the Paramount contract was signed, the La Fontaines and their old friends the Zimmermans (who by this time had themselves abandoned "A Current Affair" and contracted with "Hard Copy") were winging their way to Memphis to find John Elrod. Later, during weeks of unrelenting retrials of Oswald in the print and television media on the thirtieth anniversary of the assassination, the "Hard Copy" Special Report of Elrod's revelations, and the La Fontaine *Houston Post* story (of Sunday, November 14) on the same topic, constituted the only new counter-Warren evidence presented by the media in the brave new age of Posner.

On Wednesday, November 17, 1993, the day after the Elrod story aired on "Hard Copy," U.S. Army Maj. John Newman, an intelligence officer (and professor of history at the University of Maryland), appeared by invitation before the congressional subcommittee overseeing the release of government agency documents on the assassination of President Kennedy. (Among others in attendance: Gerald Posner.) As he had previously planned, Major Newman presented to chairman John Conyers and other legislators Oswald-related CIA materials that Newman himself had uncovered as a consultant to a recently aired "Frontline" documentary on the accused assassin, as well as a photograph depicting Oswald and David Ferrie at a Civil Air Patrol camp-out. The army major then presented the Elrod documents to Congress, pointing out that the FBI had lied when it said Elrod was not in the Dallas jail "as claimed." Newman also cited the fourteen pages of documents then still being withheld on obscure Ruby mechanic Donnell Whitter for reasons of "national security" (a fact uncovered by yet another Bill Adams FOIA request).[23]

It seems likely that the Elrod revelations—courtesy in large part of "Hard Copy"—will ultimately overshadow the million-dollar-plus joint three-hour PBS/BBC project for "Frontline." If so, it would be an irony the La Fontaines couldn't help but enjoy, and lament, at the same time. One of the major historical events of our fast-closing century was ultimately chronicled not on educational television, or even on a commercial network, but on a tabloid.

The idea of continuing on the tabloid trail wasn't a happy thought for Eugenia. She had attended an expensive Catholic girls' school that had honed her natural gift for the guilt trip into a lethal weapon.

"Don't tell me you're going to do *another* one," she told her father.

"It's in the blood now, kid. Once you start doing tabloids, you can't stop."

"Great. Next it'll be pornos."

"I hadn't thought of that. You might have a point. One step at a time, though."

She left the room. Mary came in with an announcement. The book had arrived, Ray's Catalan masterpiece and work for the ages, his *Tirant lo Blanc,* with the name of the translator, RAY LA FONTAINE, in bigger type than the two original authors. He'd loved the graphic cover concept the moment he laid eyes on it.

By some mysterious necessity, his tribute to the eternal had arrived on the same day the Elrod story would be running on "Hard Copy," November 16. It was a clear sign of something, no doubt, but what, and should he be elated or depressed? Who was he, anyway, the gross tabloideer selling misfortune and lucky charms to the multitude, or the prim Puerto Rican gentleman (who had never been to Puerto Rico, but no matter) spinning antiquated tales for the benefit of a small, deeply disturbed academic audience? What would the record show, after he'd gone to heaven for diligently performing his typing duties and spending only an insignificant amount of time goofing off on the phone, unlike some other people he knew and could name if he wanted to? Would you be able to tell "from the record" what kind of person Ray La Fontaine had been, and did he himself know? Does *any*one, with the possible exception of people like Gerald Posner?

APPENDIX A

Countdown to the Assassination

SEPTEMBER 1959

Just prior to his early discharge from the U.S. Marine Corps and defection to Russia, Lee Harvey Oswald receives a Department of Defense ID card routinely issued to intelligence agents abroad.[1]

SUMMER 1962

The DRE, an anti-Castro Cuban exile group that had functioned autonomously under the CIA umbrella in the 1961 Bay of Pigs invasion, continues operating for the intelligence agency under the code designation AMSPELL, with a large number of members on agency payroll.

Nancy and Robert Perrin arrive in Dallas. They attend a meeting in which Jack Ruby provides money for running guns to Cuba, at least some of which are obtained from the post of an army "colonel" also in attendance.

Lee Harvey Oswald arrives in Fort Worth from Russia with his wife, Marina, and a new baby, June. The Oswalds are visited by urbane CIA asset George de Mohrenschildt, who becomes their benefactor, introducing them to the conservative White Russian Dallas community.

AMSPELL creates an international incident (August 24), firing on a beachfront hotel in Miramar, Cuba, where Fidel Castro is thought to be present. Castro accuses the U.S. of complicity in an attempt on his life, but the incident is a PR coup for AMSPELL. DRE funding is forthcoming from former ambassador William Pawley, now a power in the CIA's JM/WAVE station in Miami, and his friend Clare Boothe Luce. The major aim of AMSPELL's new backers: to embarrass the president.

NOVEMBER 1962

CIA deputy director of plans Richard Helms establishes a direct line of communication with the DRE, effectively bypassing JM/WAVE chief Ted Shackley.

MARCH 1963

Oswald, now employed at Jaggars-Chiles-Stovall in Dallas, is recruited by the FBI for projects related to right-wing subversive groups.

In the same month, a beautiful Cuban exile, Silvia Odio, going on twenty-six, arrives in Dallas, ostensibly to receive treatment from a young Cuban doctor at a state mental hospital near Terrell, Texas. She is befriended by society matron Lucille Connell, who pays her passage. Silvia develops a sideline as an anti-Castro gunrunner.

APRIL 1963

Oswald leaves for New Orleans, where he will make contact with FBI asset Guy Banister.

JUNE 1963

Members of JURE, the Cuban exile group backed by Attorney General Robert Kennedy (and the party of Silvia's father, Amador Odio-Padron), travel from Miami to Dallas to finalize a gun deal set up by Silvia Odio. They do not like the deal and leave empty-handed.

JULY 1963

The FBI raids an anti-Castro arms cache near Lake Pontchartrain, Louisiana. (Eventually an FBI employee discovers Oswald's informant's file, showing the ex-Marine as the informant in the Pontchartrain operation.)

AUGUST 1963

Oswald allegedly makes his first attempt to infiltrate the New Orleans DRE headquarters of Carlos Bringuier, posing as a Castro-hating soldier of fortune with military experience. The penetration attempt occurs on the 5th, according to Bringuier.

On the 9th, Bringuier "discovers" that the anti-Castro American is handing out leaflets for the pro-Castro Fair Play for Cuba Committee (FPCC). A street scuffle ensues. Oswald spends the night in jail for disturbing the peace.

The next day, a Saturday, Oswald asks for an FBI man to visit him in the New Orleans jail. Bureau file clerk William Walter is asked by Agent John Quigley to pull any files on Oswald. Walter finds that Oswald's files are classified "informant-type." In his interview, Oswald tells a series of lies to Quigley about the FPCC.

On the 12th, Oswald's court hearing takes place. Present at the hearing are Bringuier and an exile associate, Agustin Guitart, Silvia Odio's uncle. Oswald pays a ten-dollar fine.

Oswald goes into full PR mode, appearing on television as a FPCC organizer and debating Carlos Bringuier and others on radio. Despite handling himself well, the upshot is negative for the FPCC when he is exposed publicly as a Marxist and former Soviet defector.

SEPTEMBER 1963

Oswald is reported by town residents to have stayed briefly with a Cuban doctor at a state mental hospital near Clinton, Louisana. Oswald is seen in Clinton with David Ferrie and Clay Shaw, using his Department of Defense card as identification.

DRE members (AMSPELL) clash in New York City with members of the FPCC. A young veteran of the Bay of Pigs, Fermin de Goicochea Sanchez, moves from NYC to Dallas to live with his sister and brother-in-law. The brother-in-law is part of the same group of Cuban doctors, practicing at the state mental hospital at Terrell, Texas, associated with Silvia Odio.

Oswald leaves New Orleans on the 24th or 25th, alone, and presumably traveling by bus. He is spotted on a bus in Mexico, heading for Mexico City. Later he appears at the Cuban and Soviet embassies. He is denied a visa to enter Cuba. (Though Oswald was photographed several times, the CIA was never able to produce its surveillance photos of Oswald, leading some to speculate that he was accompanied by others.)

OCTOBER 1963

On the first day of October, John Martino, a mobster and asset of AMSPELL sponsor William Pawley, arrives in Dallas to deliver an anti-Castro talk (based on his recently published book, *I Was Castro's Prisoner*) to Cuban exiles, Birchers, and members of the Catholic Cuban relocation committee. Martino speaks privately with some or all of the Odio sisters, explaining that he is a friend of their imprisoned father, whom he met during his own captivity on the island. Silvia Odio's lover Father Walter Machann delivers the invocation at the Martino speech and then abruptly disappears from public life.

That night, in the early morning hours of the 2nd, a member of the Cuban relocation committee who had attended the Martino talk, Marcella Insua, is visited by three men looking for Silvia Odio, who had moved that day. Two are Cubans. The third, in the car, is an American named "Lee."

On the 3rd, Oswald is seen in Dallas for the first time since he left for New Orleans. He will stay until his death seven weeks later.

In midmonth, a party of AMSPELL military leaders (including Manuel Salvat, who led the attack on Miramar) arrives in Dallas from Miami. Their public purpose for the trip is to raise money for medical relief to Cuban exiles. The fund-raising sessions are attended by right-wing Catholics and Birchers, including retired general Edwin Walker. Spotted at one such anti-Castro gathering is an American described by Silvia Odio as "brilliant and clever": Lee Harvey Oswald.

At the same time that they are holding public meetings in Dallas, Salvat and another of the DRE leaders from Miami, Joaquin Martinez de Pinillos, meet with de Goicochea, who by now has enrolled at the University of Dallas (a small, Catholic, and ultraconservative school), becoming a fellow student of Sarita Odio, Silvia's younger sister. Salvat and Martinez recruit de Goicochea as the DRE's Dallas military representative. His task in this capacity is to acquire heavy arms for the group. Before returning to Miami, Martinez introduces de Goicochea (as the organization's new buyer, "George Perrel") to Dallas gun dealer John Masen. Masen learns from the DRE exiles that the weapons they will need are for a planned second major invasion of Cuba, not another Miramar-style hit-and-run strike.

Meanwhile, ATF agent Frank Ellsworth is conducting his own undercover investigation of John Masen and his gun supplier, whom Ellsworth learns is U.S. Army ordnance officer George Nonte of Fort Hood (a gun expert and the same gunrunning "colonel" described by Nancy Perrin as supplying arms to Jack Ruby's ring). Ellsworth also learns from Masen of a big-time buyer of weapons in town named "George Perrel."

Ellsworth immediately travels to the FBI office at Fort Hood, as well as the office of army intelligence at the post, to report that he thinks he knows who is "stealing them blind"—Nonte. The FBI appears to listen with interest (weapons are being stolen from Fort Hood in "truck load lots," the agents admit) and encourages Ellsworth to continue his investigation in Dallas, trying to nab Masen and Nonte in a sting operation. They do not tell Ellsworth that they already know about the contraband weapons—from Nonte himself, who has been reporting to army intelligence.

On the 24th, Nonte notifies army intelligence of Masen's knowledge of the planned invasion. Army intelligence notifies the FBI on the same day. Nonte is not arrested for his activities. Instead, he is recruited by the FBI to report on the invasion plans.

In Dallas, Oswald enters a notation in his notebook about a meeting with Hosty on November 1.

On the 31st, Nonte travels to Dallas and meets with "George Perrel" and Masen, and examines the DRE-AMSPELL's long shopping list of required weapons, ammunition, and plastic explosives. He learns from "Perrel" that the invasion of Cuba is planned to begin the last week in November.

NOVEMBER 1, 1963

Agent Hosty is directed to begin searching for George Perrel. Hosty goes to the residence of Oswald's wife late that afternoon. Oswald opens his last post office box, giving a false home address and listing his business as "Fair Play for Cuba Committee" and "ACLU." He writes a letter to the Communist party, describing his attendance at a meeting where General Walker spoke.

NOVEMBER 8, 1963

Theodore Shackley, chief of the CIA JM/WAVE station in Miami, sends a secret dispatch to his Langley superiors expressing his displeasure with AMSPELL and its military plans. Unlike Pawley and other DRE fans, Shackley views the DRE as an impractical, undisciplined bunch with a hopelessly flawed (and "romantic") military plan involving too long a supply line for a covert operation. Shackley's dispatch recommends rejection of the plan as well as cutting off funding for the DRE, except for propaganda support for those who are actually enrolled in college. (DRE members were supposed to be "students.")

NOVEMBER 9, 1963 (APPROX.)

Following Shackley's dispatch, word begins to leak to the DRE of the unfavorable recommendations. (They are ostensibly accepted by Langley, but when the bad news is officially broken to the group, on November 19, three days before the assassination, the DRE representative indicates he already knows what Shackley's man is going to say.)

NOVEMBER 12, 1963 (APPROX.)

Oswald delivers a warning note to Hosty's office.

NOVEMBER 14, 1963

The National Guard armory at Terrell, Texas is "burglarized." It is an inside job. The guns taken are "on loan" from Nonte's post, Fort Hood.

NOVEMBER 16, 1963

Oswald reports to the Dallas FBI. (Like the date of his meeting with the New Orleans FBI, it is a Saturday.)

NOVEMBER 17, 1963

In the early morning hours following Oswald's report, the New Orleans FBI receives a Teletype warning of an assassination plot against President Kennedy in Dallas by a "Cuban faction"—a "militant revolutionary group."

NOVEMBER 18, 1963

Still working on his sting, ATF agent Ellsworth awaits a shipment of guns from Nonte through Masen. Ellsworth expects to arrest not only Masen but his Fort Hood big fish, the ordnance officer Nonte. The guns never show, however. A few hours earlier, the FBI and four anonymous members of the Dallas police have staked out the transfer of the weapons from a mystery car to two henchmen of Jack Ruby, Donnell Whitter and Lawrence Miller, who are to deliver the guns to Masen's "customer" Ellsworth. The shipment is intercepted and Ruby's thugs arrested, aborting Ellsworth's sting that would have also arrested Masen and Nonte. (As noted in the text [chapters 1 and 10], the likely informant on the transfer point of the weapons was Lee Harvey Oswald. The FBI's interception of the weapons was the probable response not only to its interest in protecting information sources Masen and Nonte, but to Oswald's tip, on November 16, of an impending assassination attempt during the president's visit to Dallas later in the week. The four Dallas detectives involved in the interception were protected from revealing their identities in court, and are not known to this day. The FBI report of the interception was destroyed by the Bureau.)

NOVEMBER 19, 1963

Shackley's man (unidentified in release) officially breaks the news in Miami to its AMSPELL representative that the DRE's military plans for a "Caribbean operation" against Cuba, which was to have begun in the last week of November, have been rejected. The DRE representative receives the bad news jovially, saying he knew he would hear that. "Meaningful glances" are exchanged between the CIA and DRE reps.

NOVEMBER 20, 1963

A disappointed Frank Ellsworth arrests John Masen on a lesser charge. On the way to the police station, Masen identifies a passing motorcyclist as the "George Perrel" he'd told Ellsworth about, and Perrel is followed to his home address. He turns out to be Fermin de Goicochea Sanchez. The information is relayed by Ellsworth to the FBI, which has been looking for Perrel since November 1. The FBI nevertheless continues "looking" for Perrel for ten more months, not interviewing him until September 1964, when the Warren *Report* is out.

NOVEMBER 21, 1963

Jack Ruby visits a bail bondsman and meets Masen's lawyer on the steps of the Dallas County Courthouse. The lawyer, Pete White, has previously represented Ruby on gun charges.

NOVEMBER 22, 1963

Frank Ellsworth (ATF), Ed J. Coyle (Army Intelligence), and James Hosty (FBI) meet in Ellsworth's office in downtown Dallas to discuss Ellsworth's pursuit of Nonte. Hosty and Coyle do not reveal that Nonte was an FBI and army intelligence informant on a planned Cuban invasion by CIA operation AMSPELL. The meeting breaks up approximately forty-five minutes before the president's caravan reaches Dealey Plaza.

President John F. Kennedy is assassinated at approximately 12:35 P.M. Dallas police officer J. D. Tippit is murdered in Oak Cliff about forty-five minutes later.

Lee Harvey Oswald and Daniel Wayne Douglas are arrested as suspects in the Tippit murder. John Elrod is arrested as a suspect in the assassination of President Kennedy.

Coyle's group, 112th Military Intelligence, notifies the FBI by 3:15 P.M. that Oswald carries an ID of A. J. Hidell. Later, the 112th group signals the U.S. strike force that Oswald is a Communist and agent of Cuba.

Immediately upon announcement of Oswald's capture, AMSPELL

leaders in Miami notify the CIA that they will hold a press conference to link Oswald with Russia. New Orleans DRE propaganda specialist Carlos Bringuier notifies the FBI of Oswald's alleged links to the FPCC and Castro's Cuba.

Ruby henchman Lawrence Miller, arrested in the FBI gun stakeout of November 18, is led into the corridor of the tiny three-cell block where the three suspects in the assassination of President Kennedy and murder of Officer Tippit are held.

Oswald identifies Miller and describes a meeting in a motel where a contract was made and money was paid. He says Miller received money and drove a Thunderbird full of guns. Ruby was also present at the motel. (The car in which Miller was arrested—stashed with weapons for delivery to Masen's "customer" Ellsworth—was a blue, late-model Thunderbird.)

Within hours, Elrod and Douglas are removed from the cellblock. Douglas will never be seen again, even by his own family. He does not attend the funerals of his parents in years to come, and will speak to his only brother only by telephone. John Elrod is questioned around the clock until Ruby shoots Oswald, and is then immediately released. Upon the release, he leaves his job of fourteen years and lives today on a secluded inland island.

Silvia Odio collapses upon hearing of the president's assassination, and has to be hospitalized. Her reputed lover, Father Walter Michael Machann, who had dropped out of sight on October 1 following the public talk by John Martino, also collapses at his mother's home.

Jack Ruby tries to enter the interrogation room where Oswald is being questioned. Later, he carries his gun to a midnight press conference where Oswald is exhibited.

AFTERMATH

NOVEMBER 23, 1963

Dallas police announce the discovery of a (single) photo linking Oswald with a Mannlicher-Carcano rifle and Communist/socialist literature. Rights to the picture, as well as to other crucial evidentiary photographs, will be purchased by Luce publication *Life Magazine.* Journalist Hal Hendriks, later to be identified as a CIA asset, publishes a Scripps-Howard story linking Oswald to an international Communist conspiracy by the FPCC.

NOVEMBER 24, 1963

The Sunday *Dallas Morning News* publishes, in its assassination coverage, a banner story revealing that Oswald met with the FBI November 16. Ruby packs his gun, heads for the Dallas jail, and murders Oswald in view of millions.

NOVEMBER 28, 1963

Silvia Odio confides to her best friend, Lucille Connell, that she knew Oswald from meetings of Cuban exiles, considered him brilliant and clever, and had learned from a source in New Orleans that Oswald should not be trusted—that he was probably trying to infiltrate Cuban groups in Dallas as a "double agent." (During this period Silvia tells essentially the same thing to her psychiatrist, Dr. Burton Einspruch.) Immediately upon hearing what Silvia has to say, Lucille Connell calls the FBI.

DECEMBER 1963

In the first week of December, Manuel Salvat, military director of the DRE, travels from Miami to Central America, according to a CIA report of the same month.

On the 9th, an AP story appears in the *Dallas Morning News* reporting an announcement by Mexico City DRE representative Angel Gonzalez. The story belatedly reports the deaths of three anti-Castro "captains" killed in Cuba in mid-September in clashes with Castro's militia. They are identified as Carlos Roca, Julio Garcia, and Sergio Perez. (A check with a high-ranking Cuban intelligence officer in 1994 indicates that the three men did not die in Cuba, although another rebel leader mentioned by Gonzalez did die in a similar mid-September skirmish. The officer claims that one of the "captains" in the article, Carlos Roca, was seen in Miami a few days after the assassination in the company of a DRE member, and that he then traveled to a CIA-sponsored installation in Nicaragua with the same DRE member, but did not return. The officer speculates that Roca was involved in the assassination and that he died in Nicaragua, after which the date of his death was "backdated" as misinformation.)[2]

On the 18th, Silvia Odio is visited at work by the FBI regarding her statements to Lucille Connell (November 28). She tells the agents her now well known story of a single encounter in her apartment hallway with an American named "Leon" in the company of two JURE Cubans. (JURE, the party of Silvia Odio's father, was a socialist organization, despised by Howard Hunt and others in the CIA, but championed by Bobby Kennedy. As chapter 9 suggests, it is doubtful that Silvia and her siblings adhered to the politics of JURE.) The story is palpably false, as chapter 9 shows, pieced together from a prior real visit from JURE representatives, and probably from a visit by "Lee" on the morning of October 2, 1963 to the house of Marcella Insua.

APRIL 1964

On the 13th, Silvia Odio's psychiatrist confirms her best friend's story, telling Warren Commission counsel Burt Griffin that Silvia knew Oswald, having met him at Cuban exile meetings, including one at her own home. (After talking to Einspruch, Griffin theorized that Oswald met Ruby through Ruby's gunrunning activities and Oswald's infiltration of Cuban groups. Griffin's documented ideas were omitted from the Warren *Report.*)

On the 30th, Father Machann, found in New Orleans, tells the Secret Service that Silvia Odio reported to him in a telephone call made that day that one of the JURE men with "Leon" in her story of a hallway visit was Rogelio Cisneros, another obvious fiction on her part.

JULY 1964

Silvia Odio denies all to the Warren Commission except her false Oswald-in-the-hallway story.

AUGUST 1964

John Elrod goes to the Memphis sheriff's office with "information concerning the murder of Lee Oswald," according to one of the sheriff's sergeants. He reveals what he overheard from Oswald when the latter identified Miller in the Dallas jail on November 22, 1963. The FBI takes over the interview of Elrod and claims he was never arrested in Dallas on the day of the assassination.[3]

SEPTEMBER 1964

The identity of "George Perrel" (known to the FBI since before the assassination) is finally revealed in a Bureau interview dated September 18. The author of the report, Special Agent Wallace R. Heitman, provides a lengthy excuse in FBI-ese explaining why Fermin de Goicochea Sanchez couldn't be interviewed until the month the Warren *Report* ships. (The excuse: Agent Hosty was too busy investigating the Kennedy assassination.)

JUNE 1975

Two months before his death, John Martino reveals to a journalist his participation in the assassination. He identifies his coconspirators as anti-Castro Cubans, and tells the reporter that there was a woman in Dallas "who knew a lot of things" about the assassination, none of which had to do with her famous "Leon"-in-the-hallway invention. She was Silvia Odio, the reporter later realized.

THE EMPIRE STRIKES BACK
1994

Late in the summer of 1994, following a story by the authors in the *Washington Post* ("The Fourth Tramp: Oswald's Lost Cellmate and the Gunrunners of Dallas"), a former FBI official, Dallas SAC Oliver Revell, counterattacked with a letter to the editor of the *Post*. The letter, published August 27, charged that "much of what Ray and Mary La Fontaine report never occurred." According to Revell, who opened his letter with a lengthy summary of his years of experience with the Kennedy assassination (though he had persistently refused the La Fontaines' requests for an interview), the unreliable Elrod was guilty of changing his story: *now* he claimed that Oswald had been his Dallas cellmate, but *back then* he "couldn't identify his cellmate" to the FBI. Revell's clincher was that Elrod told the FBI in 1964 that he had been placed in cell 10 of the Dallas jail, whereas prisoner telephone records "confirm F-2 as Oswald's cell." Revell argued,

"Therefore, it is clear that Elrod, in cell 10, was not in a cell with Oswald and certainly not on the afternoon of Nov. 22, 1963."

One week later, Ray, seizing the chance to get his name in the paper again, responded:

Selective Memory About Oswald

I read with interest the Aug. 27 contribution to your paper ("More Unfounded Theories About Lee Harvey Oswald") by former FBI special agent in charge (Dallas Division) Oliver Revell, written in response to our Outlook article of Aug. 7 ("The Fourth Tramp: Oswald's Lost Cellmate and the Gunrunners of Dallas"). Despite a 33-year career in which he was "involved in the Kennedy assassination investigation since its inception," Revell evidently suffers from a selective grasp of the facts.

Revell suggests that John Elrod changed his story over time—that "miraculously, 30 years later, he [Elrod] now can identify his mystery cellmate as being Lee Harvey Oswald"—and that Elrod never mentioned his cellmate's identity to the FBI in Memphis in August 1964. As our story noted, however, Elrod told members of his family from the day he was released from jail that he had been confined with Oswald, and when he showed up at the Memphis sheriff's office eight months later he was still talking about the accused presidential assassin (and Jack Ruby). He claimed to have information "on the murder of Lee Oswal[d]," as a sheriff's deputy wrote to FBI director J. Edgar Hoover. Whether Elrod told the Memphis bureau agents who were immediately summoned to the sheriff's office that his Dallas cellmate was Oswald, or only that the cellmate knew of a motel room meeting with Ruby, must remain conjectural in view of the fact that the agents insisted in their report—repeatedly—that the cellmate was "unknown." Their report itself is not definitive, however, because it also contained the information that Elrod had not been arrested at all in Dallas the day President Kennedy was murdered.

Revell said, "Had the La Fontaines examined public documents, they would have found that Oswald was never placed in the general jail population. Oswald was placed in cell number F-2, one of three maximum security cells, at approximately 12:20 a.m. on Nov. 23, 1963."

Oswald was indeed placed in cell F-2 but not only on Nov. 23. Telephone logs clearly show he was in F-2 on the day of the assassination, Nov. 22. The logs also show that another prisoner,

Daniel Douglas, was in an adjacent cell on the *same day*. Elrod, moreover, was able to describe—correctly—this Oswald neighbor as a "kid from Tennessee who had stolen a car in Memphis." All of this information was included in our article; all of it was ignored by Revell's response.

Revell clings to the fallacy that John Elrod was placed in a "cell 10," although three decades ago the FBI insisted Elrod was not in *any* cell in Dallas on Nov. 22, 1963. There is no "cell 10" in the Dallas jail, regardless of what the Memphis bureau report claims Elrod said. Elrod was arrested as a suspect in the assassination of President Kennedy after police received reports of a man with a gun near the spot where Elrod was found. Douglas was arrested as a suspect in the murder of Officer J. D. Tippit. According to Dallas Police Sgt. James Chandler, cellblock F (where Oswald, Elrod and Douglas were placed) was reserved for "the most serious felons." Thus the three suspects in the murders of President Kennedy and Officer Tippit were all assigned to the same cramped three-cell block F in accordance with police procedure.

Revell professes alarm at a question posed in our story, "Is it possible that Lee Oswald was the informant who tipped off the FBI about the gun deal of Nov. 18, 1963?" Evidence suggests that Oswald had a special relationship with the FBI. Since former agent Revell has officially denied the existence of Dallas bureau reports on the arrests of Lawrence Miller and Donnell Whitter (despite the fact that FBI agent Joe Abernathy was present at the arrests and later became the prosecution's star witness), the identity of the bureau's informant on the arrests must, at the least, remain an open question.

Revell was accurate in claiming that when the long-lost arrest records of the three tramps "were discovered," his Dallas field office "found and interviewed two of the men and verified the death of the third." He failed only to mention that it was we who made the discovery of the records and that the bureau's seminal detective work consisted of reading our front-page story on the finds in the Houston Post of Feb. 9, 1992.

—Ray La Fontaine

After Ray's answer appeared, FBI headquarters told an editor at the *Post* that Revell's letter was not an official response (Revell had retired before his letter was published) and did not represent the Bureau's position on the incarceration of Oswald.

APPENDIX B

The Case Against Oswald

The case against Lee Harvey Oswald is stronger than most conspiracy theorists will concede. In some ways, indeed, it has grown even stronger since the days a gifted writer named Thomas Thompson wrote for the November 29, 1963 issue of *Life* that "slowly, methodically the police were building their case" with such pieces of evidence as a mail-order rifle purchase, a "long parcel" that Oswald was seen carrying into the book depository (and that he claimed contained curtain rods), a palm print on the murder weapon, and a snapshot "showing him holding a rifle that apparently was identical with the one that killed the President." The most recent introduction of evidence damaging to Oswald came in 1993, with the revitalization of the single-bullet theory by Gerald Posner in *Case Closed.* The arguments he presents in one chapter and an appendix of his book make an extremely strong case, based on computer analysis, that President Kennedy and Texas governor John Connally were hit by the same second bullet, and that the bullet could be traced back to a sixth-floor window in the School Book Depository building. Though the third bullet, which killed the president, can't be so traced (a fact Posner forgets to mention), the overall strength of his position on the ballistics front tempers years of rude chortling by conspiracy theorists about the incredible antics of a "magic" bullet. The ballistics analysis Posner presents (the work of a Bay Area organization, Failure Analysis) is itself part of "the new evidence," recently gathered information that should be considered seriously by any assassination student more interested in arriving at the truth than learning to recite Warren or conspiracy conclusions.

On other fronts, Posner fares less impressively. The former lawyer makes what amounts to a lawyer's brief for his anticonspiratorial position, selecting only points that advance the interests of his side and dismissing troublesome testimony by ignoring it or attacking the character of the witnesses. (The Kennedy assassination is a "case," as his title notes.) These tactics, though vigorously executed and accompanied by much research, are one good reason why lawyers are derided—not causes to make us believe Oswald either acted alone or was the person Posner tells us he was. As the next section will show, the case against Oswald has yet to be made convincingly, despite a thirty-year history of prosecutive case making that was already well under way in late November 1963.

New evidence uncovered in the Dallas police files and elsewhere, or in some cases evidence previously ignored, suggests the following points:

1. Oswald defected to Russia under the auspices of the CIA or military intelligence.

2. He was not "acting alone" upon his return.

3. He was initially (and unwittingly) "run" in Dallas by the CIA, under the capable handling of George de Mohrenschildt.

4. He later entered into a reluctant (this time witting) association as an asset of the FBI, and maintained this relationship at the time of the assassination.

5. Jack Ruby also did not "act alone," and was a paymaster in a little-known gunrunning operation involving stolen military arms, probably connected to armory break-ins in Terrell and Fort Hood, Texas, shortly before the assassination.

6. The weapons trafficking included members of the U.S. Army, paramilitary Minutemen, John Thomas Masen, and the CIA-assisted anti-Castro exile group DRE. (Similar gunrunning cooperatives combining mobster, right-wing, and intelligence elements operated along the "Louisiana corridor," supplying arms for the Secret War against Cuba.)

7. Oswald was involved with Ruby in the same gunrunning operation either as a participant or, more likely, as an informant.

8. The FBI tried to cover its association with Oswald as well as all clues pointing to this association, including records on John Elrod,

evidence of Ruby's gunrunning activities, and the clandestine activities of John Masen, George Nonte, and the DRE.

Despite the subterfuges, no evidence exists that the last U.S. government agency to run Oswald, the FBI, was itself involved in the assassination. The guess here is that with the possible exception of New Orleans maverick contract agent Guy Banister, it wasn't. The Bureau's sins, though noxious, all appear of the accessories-after-the-fact variety, cover-up attempts to hide its relationship with Oswald.

Whether Oswald was a patsy or a guilty coconspirator is another tantalizing question left unanswered. We don't know such things as whether he conspired but wasn't a triggerman, or was perhaps one of two men armed with the two rifles found in the book depository that Friday—Oswald's Mannlicher-Carcano and an unknown Mauser, the gun that was actually left on the sixth floor (see below). Oswald was undeniably "in this" in some way, but was it as conspirator (and with the likes of Jack Ruby) or as a clueless Bobby Fischer trapped in a game that wasn't chess? Did the FBI crimestopper gradually realize there was more than gun dealing afoot—that an assassination was being plotted around him—and did he try at the last moment to warn someone about it? The new evidence overwhelmingly suggests that he did.

We can be reasonably certain (though the evidence doesn't confirm this) that Lee Harvey Oswald remained a good Marxist and Marine to the end. On the morning of November 22, 1963, he removed his wedding band and dropped it for Marina in a Russian teacup—a gesture that if telling also said something about an item he chose *not* to remove: his USMC signet. Oswald walked into that dangerous day wearing his Marine ring and, if it hadn't been taken from him by the Dallas police with his other possessions following his arrest, would have died with it on.

The following summary lists the main points of the case against Oswald, and shows in each instance how, if at all, the new evidence impinges on the official story.

I. THE RIFLE

A. *Oswald ordered a Mannlicher-Carcano rifle under the name A. Hidell.*

SIGNIFICANCE: The mail order initiated a paper trail linking Oswald to the murder weapon.

The U.S. Marine Corps ring and identification bracelet Oswald wore at the time of his arrest. (Courtesy Dallas Municipal Archives and Records Center, City of Dallas, Texas)

RELATED CIRCUMSTANCES: The Mannlicher-Carcano, found in the Texas School Book Depository following the assassination, was ordered under the name A. Hidell on March 12, 1963, the day after agent James Hosty located Oswald on Neely Street in Dallas with the assistance of an informant in the postal inspector's office. The gun was sent parcel post from Klein's Sporting Goods of Chicago to a box rented to Oswald, who supposedly had a photograph of a phony ID card in the name of Hidell in his wallet at the time of his arrest.

NEW EVIDENCE: The identity of the person who picked up the Mannlicher when it arrived by parcel post was missing from the records of the post office, even though the P.O. was required by law to keep it for four years. Moreover, the names of other persons authorized to receive mail at Oswald's box (similarly required to be kept) are also missing—from *both* of his Dallas post office box applications of October 1962 and November 1963. The paper trail is incomplete, obscuring other possible participants in Oswald's postal dealings (e.g., the FBI) and failing to make the vital link between the accused assassin and the assassination weapon.

B. *Oswald kept a rifle at home and stored it in the Ruth Paine garage around the time of the assassination, according to Marina.*

SIGNIFICANCE: Ownership of the rifle associated Oswald with the murder weapon, and storage of the gun in the Paine garage allowed him an easy means of taking it with him on the morning of November 22, 1963.

RELATED CIRCUMSTANCES: There is strong evidence that Oswald had the Mannlicher-Carcano in his possession at one time. It was so testified by Marina Oswald and the de Mohrenschildts, and an Oswald palm print was found on the rifle taken from the TSBD. The Paines, however, never saw the gun. (Of the backyard photos, only one of the three poses is sharp enough to make a determination of the type of rifle in the photograph. This appears to be a Mannlicher-Carcano, but the image is not sharp enough to allow a conclusive determination that it is the Mannlicher found in the book depository.) Marina has repeatedly changed her testimony regarding the gun; Warren counsel Wesley Liebeler wrote that he thought she had been "led" when she testified to Oswald practicing dry runs with the rifle in New Orleans and that "no person alive today" could place that rifle in the Paines' garage where Oswald was said to have retrieved it to assassinate the president.

NEW EVIDENCE: None.

C. *Oswald brought a long package to work with him on the morning of November 22, 1963.*

SIGNIFICANCE: The package, believed from its shape to have contained a hidden rifle, helped place the murder weapon in Oswald's hands on the day of the assassination and strongly suggested a premeditated crime.

RELATED CIRCUMSTANCES: The Commission discounted Oswald's claim that the package contained "curtain rods." The only witnesses to the package, B. W. Frazier and his sister Linnie Mae Randle, testified that the package was shorter than what would have been the broken-down length of the alleged assassination weapon, and would not change their stories under great pressure to do so.[1]

NEW EVIDENCE: Newly released Dallas Police files on the assassination contain photographs of "curtain rods" dusted for fingerprints. No evidence could be found that the photos were ever turned over to the Warren Commission. Carl Day, lieutenant-in-charge of the DPD Crime Scene Search division in 1963, could not recall where the curtain rods had been found. He examined the photos of the dusted rods in October 1993, and although it didn't appear to him that the clearest fingerprint (an apparent right thumbprint) was Oswald's, he could not say conclusively that it was not when comparing it with a photo of Oswald's thumbprint. Since then, the curtain rod photos have been examined informally by three fingerprint experts in other cities with similarly inconclusive results. (Bill Adams later found a report signed by Carl Day stating that the prints are not Oswald's. The other questions remain.)

D. *Oswald's Mannlicher-Carcano was found on the sixth floor of the Texas School Book Depository.*

SIGNIFICANCE: Oswald's Mannlicher, if found on the same floor from which shots were allegedly fired at the president, further linked the ex-Marine to the assassination.

RELATED CIRCUMSTANCES: A Mannlicher-Carcano was found in the book depository on November 22, 1963; but evidence ignored (or distorted) by the Warren Commission suggested that the weapon on the sixth floor was not the Italian Mannlicher, but a *second* rifle found in the depository that day—a German Mauser. The sixth-floor weapon was identified as a Mauser by the two men who found it at 1:22 P.M. on the Friday of the assassination, Deputy Sheriff Eugene Boone and Deputy Constable Seymour Weitzman. Weitzman, a former owner of a sporting goods store who was familiar with guns, signed an affidavit the day after the discovery giving a detailed description. "This rifle," the constable's affidavit affirmed, "was a 7.65 Mauser bolt action equipped with a $^4/_{18}$ scope, a thick leather brownish-black sling on it."[2]

Deputy Sheriff Boone later testified (to Warren counsel Joseph A. Ball) that not only he and Weitzman but Capt. Will Fritz and Lt. Carl Day of the DPD believed the found rifle was a Mauser. "He [Fritz] had knelt down there to look at it, and before he removed it, not knowing what it was, he said that [a Mauser] is what it looks like," the sheriff told Ball. Boone also reported that Day expressed the same opinion. "We were just discussing it back and forth. And he [Day] said it looks like a 7.65 Mauser."[3]

Like his cofinder Constable Weitzman, Boone put his assertions about the sixth-floor rifle into writing, preparing two written reports on November 22, 1963. Each noted: "I saw the rifle, that appeared to be a 7.65 mm. Mauser with a telescopic [sight]. . . ."[4]

The Warren attempt at covering up the sixth-floor finding of a Mauser was blatantly straightforward. The *Report* cited a "speculation," namely that "the rifle found on the sixth floor of the Texas School Book Depository was identified as a 7.65 Mauser by the man who found it, Deputy Constable Seymour Weitzman."[5] As Sylvia Meagher noted in responding to this attempted deception, the

> so-called "speculation" is, of course, a mere statement of known fact [i.e., Weitzman identified the rifle as a Mauser in an affidavit], accepted as fact by the Commission itself. The real speculation—that there was a substitution of rifles to incriminate Oswald—was not confronted explicitly by the *Report*.[6]

The *Report*'s version of the facts of the matter (the "Commission finding") was as follows:

> Weitzman did not handle the rifle and did not examine it at close range. He had little more than a glimpse of it and thought it was a Mauser, a German bolt-action rifle similar in appearance to the Mannlicher-Carcano. Police laboratory technicians subsequently arrived and correctly identified the weapon as a 6.5 Italian rifle.[7]

But that Weitzman "did not handle the rifle" or "examine it at close range" was more Warren blather, as we may surmise from the technical details that the constable (and former sporting goods businessman) was able to supply in his affidavit of November 23, 1963. Sadly, by the time of his deposition to Commission attorney Joseph Ball four months later (on April Fool's Day, 1964), Weitzman appeared to be weary of sparring with Warren interrogators, and of taking the rap for what the *Report* would term a needless "speculation" about a German Mauser. He was ready to admit the error of his ways—he'd only taken a cursory look at the rifle, and could have been—probably *was*—wrong after all. About the scope, for example, he told Ball: "I believe I said it was a Weaver but it wasn't; it turned out to be anything but a Weaver, but that was at a glance." And later: "I believe it was a 2.5 Weaver at the time I looked at it. I didn't look that close at it; it just looked like a 2.5 but it turned out to be a Japanese scope I believe."[8]

While Weitzman folded in the stretch, however, there was Mark

Lane, who refused to be sweetly reasonable. The crusty Warren critic, who too had had a chance to examine the rifle, testified before the Commission two months after the deposition of the deputy constable. "Although I am personally not a rifle expert," Lane began,

> I was able to determine that [the rifle] was an Italian carbine because printed indelibly upon it are the words "Made Italy" and "caliber 6.5." I suggest it is very difficult for a police officer [Weitzman] to pick up a weapon which has printed upon it clearly in English "Made Italy, Cal. 6.5" and then the next day draft an affidavit stating that it was in fact a German Mauser, 7.65 millimeters.[9]

The Mauser flap, though illuminated by such moments of righteous anger, and by the enameled pages of Sylvia Meagher (wasted on HSCA Chief Counsel Robert Blakey, evidently, who claimed as late as 1983—years after the conclusion of his committee's investigation—that he'd never heard of the report of a second rifle in the book depository),[10] lasted a single day in public life. Sometime after midnight on the evening of the assassination, Dallas D.A. Henry Wade was still able to reply, to a reporter who asked the make of the murder weapon, "It's a Mauser, I believe."[11] Then it was over; the Warren media machine kicked into gear, consigning the story of a "second rifle"—the *only* rifle found on the sixth floor—to the status of back-room rumors and discredited testimony,[12] and elevating as official truth the convenient tale of a "correctly identified" *single* rifle, Oswald's own Mannlicher-Carcano. (As the new evidence confirms, the "correctly identified" Mannlicher was found in the building, but on a lower floor.)

NEW EVIDENCE: Former ATF agent Frank Ellsworth, who participated in a *second* search of the book depository conducted after 1:30 P.M. on November 22, 1963, according to a Secret Service document, confirms that the Mannlicher-Carcano was found by a DPD detective on the fourth or fifth floor of the building, "not on the same floor as the cartridges"[13] [i.e., not the sixth floor]. He adds: "I remember we talked about it, and figured that he [Oswald] must have run out from the stairwell [to the lower floor] and dropped it [the Mannlicher] as he was running downstairs." Ellsworth's statements contradict the Warren reconstruction, which indicates that

Oswald's rifle, the Mannlicher, was left on the sixth floor "near the staircase";[14] it was the Mauser that was apparently left upstairs on the floor by the stairs. But if the sixth-floor gun was the Mauser—left, say, either accidentally or intentionally overnight in the book depository by an employee who had shown it earlier to co-workers[15]—what was the Mauser doing at that particular spot, which wasn't a likely "storage" place? The location of the rifle suggested a hurried departure from the sixth floor by a man who didn't want to be seen with a weapon; he threw it down as he was preparing to zoom down the stairs in a mad dash for freedom—that much of the Warren line made sense. But a quickly abandoned Mauser—in addition to a similarly quickly abandoned Mannlicher found near the same stairwell on a lower floor—*didn't* make sense, at least according to the Warren one-gunman theory. The Mauser (which was ignored by Posner) introduced a second gun, and consequently a possible second gunman, into the book despository scenario.

E. *Oswald's palm print was found on the Mannlicher-Carcano.*[16]

SIGNIFICANCE: An Oswald print on the murder weapon would obviously strengthen the circumstantial scenario of Oswald as assassin.

RELATED CIRCUMSTANCES: The FBI lab in Washington, D.C. could not locate the palm print on the Mannlicher, and Bureau agent Vince Drain, who took the rifle to the lab, claimed DPD Crime Scene Search division lieutenant Carl Day did not mention the print.

NEW EVIDENCE: Quibbles over who was right or wrong in discovering the palm print are irrelevant; the prints on the weapon—all of them—were useless as evidence. Day noted in an October 1993 interview, "The prints on the rifle weren't made the day of the assassination—or the day before that, or the day before that. The prints were at least weeks, if not months, old." Thus, the palm print and other prints around the trigger housing[17] don't place the rifle in Oswald's hands on November 22, 1963; they only show that at some time, "at least weeks" prior to the assassination, he handled the disassembled rifle (the palm print is partially covered when the rifle is assembled). It remains to be discovered how the gun was fired on November 22 without fresh prints, but with the old prints left intact.

II. BALLISTICS

A. *Shells found near the sixth-floor window were fired from Oswald's Mannlicher-Carcano.*

SIGNIFICANCE: Like the print on the gun, the shells on the sixth floor would add circumstantial ties to Oswald.

RELATED CIRCUMSTANCES: The match between the shells and the Mannlicher-Carcano is undisputed.

NEW EVIDENCE: None.

B. *President Kennedy and Governor Connally were hit by the same bullet (dubbed the "magic" bullet), fired from a sixth-floor window at the southeast corner of the TSBD.*

SIGNIFICANCE: A single "magic" bullet, striking both Kennedy and Connally, strengthened arguments for a lone gunman.

RELATED CIRCUMSTANCES: Governor Connally testified repeatedly that he was not hit by the first shot. Ultimately this was persuasively explained when sophisticated computer enhancements of the Zapruder film and mathematical models of the trajectory of the shot indicated that Connally and Kennedy were both hit by the same second bullet.

NEW EVIDENCE: A forensic analysis group, Failure Analysis, produced a mathematical model of the trajectory of the magic bullet for the 1992 American Bar Association mock trial of Lee Harvey Oswald in San Francisco. This work (incorporated by Gerald Posner in *Case Closed*) represents the most successful recent effort to overturn a cornerstone of many conspiracy theories—that Kennedy and Connally could not have been hit by the same bullet.

C. *The magic bullet, supposedly Commission Exhibit 399, was fired from Oswald's Mannlicher-Carcano (as were bullet fragments found in the presidential limousine).*

SIGNIFICANCE: If the magic bullet was CE 399, it would support the argument that Oswald was a lone gunman.

RELATED CIRCUMSTANCES: Ballistics testing indicates that the bullet tagged CE 399 came from Oswald's Mannlicher. A so-called magic bullet has now been shown, moreover, through the work of Failure Analysis, to have been both fired from the sixth floor of the TSBD and indeed "magic," i.e., capable of hitting both President Kennedy and Governor Connally (see B above). What has yet to be definitively established is that CE 399 was in fact the same as a magic bullet, or that it caused the wounds of either Kennedy or Connally (see D below).

NEW EVIDENCE: None. The ballistics testing of CE 399 was conclusive.

D. *The magic bullet was found in the stretcher of Texas governor John Connally.*

SIGNIFICANCE: This fact, if proven, would support a link between Oswald and the wounding of Connally, as well as the lone-gunman magic bullet scenario. The magic bullet, purportedly shot from the rear and wounding first Kennedy and then Connally, could only have ended its spree lodged in the governor's body (or conceivably on his stretcher), not the president's.

RELATED CIRCUMSTANCES: A bullet, tagged CE 399, was claimed to have been found on Connally's stretcher. As Sylvia Meagher established in her meticulous analysis of 1967 ("The Governor's Wounds, the Single-Missile Hypothesis, and the Stretcher Bullet," *Accessories After the Fact,* 165-77), no evidence could be found that CE 399 was ever in Connally's body or on his stretcher. Following the bullet's chain of possession, she notes that the Secret Service agent

> who took custody of the stretcher bullet at the hospital returned to Washington with the Presidential party. He gave the bullet to his superior, Chief James J. Rowley; Rowley gave it to an FBI agent. In June 1964 the Commission requested the FBI to establish the chain of possession of the stretcher bullet; but the engineer, the chief of personnel at [Parkland] hospital, the Secret Service agent, and Chief Rowley were unable to make a positive identification of the stretcher bullet (CE 399) as the bullet found on the day of the assassination.[18]

NEW EVIDENCE: Recently released tapes of the telephone

conversations of President Lyndon Johnson show that he was told
by FBI director J. Edgar Hoover within a week of the assassination
that the bullet tagged as CE 399 was found on the *president's*
stretcher, and was dislodged as emergency procedures were performed.[19] As noted above, if CE 399 came from the president's
stretcher, it could not have been the same bullet as the magic bullet, which could *only* have lodged in Governor Connally. Though
the director's newly released remarks do not provide definitive
proof of the bullet's origination, they do offer strong validation
of Sylvia Meagher's skepticism regarding CE 399.

In sum, the ballistics evidence suggests the following:

1. A single "magic" bullet (the second shot fired), traceable to a
sixth-floor window of the TSBD, struck both President Kennedy and
Governor Connally, per the findings of Failure Analysis, repeated in
Posner's *Case Closed.*

2. The fatal head shot may or may not have come from the same
location (it isn't similarly traceable).

3. The Connally "stretcher bullet" tagged as CE 399, though known
to have been fired from the Mannlicher-Carcano, is not the same as
the magic bullet. All indications, beginning with its notoriously pris-
tine appearance and including the litany of suspicious circumstances
noted three decades ago by Sylvia Meagher, point us to more possible
mischief, e.g., the dropping of the bullet (fired from the Mannlicher
after the assassination), as "insurance" evidence of Oswald's guilt, or
the possibility that the bullet came from the president's wounds.

III. THE BACKYARD PHOTOS

*The Dallas police found two snapshots showing Oswald with the rifle used
to kill the president and the pistol used to kill Officer Tippit among his possessions in the Paine garage.*

SIGNIFICANCE: The image of Oswald on a 1964 *Life* cover, holding up a rifle identified as the assassination weapon, wearing (on
the hip, like Billy the Kid) a pistol identified as the gun used to kill
Officer Tippit, and smirkingly displaying a couple of crazed-left newspapers, was "the most damning evidence of all," as Thomas Thompson had written in an earlier issue of the magazine. But was the
picture "real"? On the night before his death, Oswald had reportedly

claimed to Capt. Will Fritz of the DPD that the Neely Street back-yard photos (two poses, labeled Commission Exhibits 133-A and 133-B, were known to Warren investigators) showed his head, but on someone else's body. As Fritz testified, Oswald

> said the picture was not his, that the face was his face, but that this picture had been made by superimposing his face, the other part of the picture was not him at all and that he had never seen the picture before. . . . He further stated that since he had been photographed here at City Hall and that people had been taking his picture while being transferred from my office to the jail door that someone had been able to get a picture of his face and that with that, they had made this picture . . . [and] that in time, he would be able to show that it was not his picture and that it had been made by someone else.[20]

Had the photos been tampered with in order to create an incriminating image of the accused assassin? If so, such an act in itself would indicate the existence of a conspiracy, as the HSCA *Report* of 1979 noted:

> If the backyard photographs are valid, they are highly incriminating of Oswald because they apparently link him with the murder weapon. If they are fakes, how they were produced poses far-reaching questions in the area of conspiracy. "Fake" backyard photographs would indicate a degree of conspiratorial sophistication that would almost necessarily raise the possibility that a highly organized group had conspired to kill the President and make Oswald a "patsy."[21]

RELATED CIRCUMSTANCES: In addition to long-running arguments over whether the backyard photos are fake or genuine, an unexpected fuzziness exists over how the photos were discovered. The DPD officers who found the snapshot-sized 133-A and 133-B pictures (allegedly in the garage of Michael and Ruth Paine) could not agree, when questioned under oath shortly afterwards, whether they did so on the morning or afternoon of the day following the assassination—an unusual circumstance for a period of time so etched in many people's minds. There were also inconsistencies on such basic matters as who found the photos and how many negatives were uncovered. (Only one negative was turned over to the Warren Commission.) A third backyard pose, though now known to have

been in the hands of the Dallas police, U.S. Secret Service, and FBI
as early as November 1963, did not reach assassination investigators
until twelve years later, in 1975, when it was provided to the HSCA
by Geneva Dees, wife of former Dallas policeman Roscoe White.
Unlike the smaller 133-A (the "*Life* cover" shot) and 133-B photos,
the third backyard pose, labeled 133-C, was an 8x10 enlargement.

NEW EVIDENCE: a) As noted in chapter 8, Michael Paine says
today (and presumably would have before, had anyone asked him)
that he saw one of the backyard photographs back in April 1963,
shown to him by Oswald himself. Surprisingly, ex-wife Ruth Paine
knew nothing of this matter and was "astonished to learn" of
Michael's claim when "Frontline" producers informed her of it in
1993.[22] Though Kennedy photo analysts will probably continue to
pursue their forgery arguments on technical grounds, credible testimony that a genuine backyard photo existed prior to the assassination would severely undercut conspiracy scenarios based on the
photos.

b) February 1992 finds in the Dallas archives included, in addition
to tramp arrest records, a mysterious matted version of an Oswald
backyard photo (*Houston Post,* February 9 and July 26, 1992).[23]
Oswald does not appear in this print. In his place is a white silhouette
of a human figure holding an apparent rifle and newspapers. The silhouette (clearly Oswald's) is an example of matting, a darkroom
technique that normally serves as an intermediate step in the combining of photographic images. It is this type of darkroom manipulation that has long been postulated by some photo analysts as the
probable means of attempting to frame Oswald by "inserting" his
incriminating image into a backyard background.

A key facet of the matte print is the fact that the silhouette is obviously designed to accommodate only the Oswald pose in the backyard photo catalogued as CE 133-C. As in 133-C (and only 133-C), the
Oswald silhouette holds newspapers aloft in the right hand and the
rifle high in the left hand at a nearly upright angle. It was this same
133-C pose that was withheld from Warren investigators, surfacing
only in the mid-1970s, when the former Geneva White presented
the print, obtained from her late husband, Roscoe, to the HSCA. As
would become apparent after the matte print's 1992 discovery, however, the 133-C photo was indeed known to the FBI, Secret Service,
and Dallas police within days of the assassination.

Shortly after the *Houston Post* initially reported the existence of the Oswald matte, a former Dallas police detective, Bobby G. Brown, admitted his direct involvement in the staging and darkroom manipulation of the unusual photo. Brown did not deny that the matting was intended to accommodate a cutout of Oswald's image—to allow, that is, the insertion of Oswald into an empty backyard. He insisted, however, that the darkroom manipulation had an innocent purpose.

According to the former detective, who in 1963 served as photographer with the Crime Scene Search division of the DPD, Dallas police captain J. Will Fritz, chief of the homicide and robbery bureau, contacted him soon after the assassination on behalf of the Secret Service to request a "re-enactment" of a backyard snapshot of Oswald.

Brown then met Secret Service agent Forrest Sorrels and his men, as well as Fritz and other Dallas homicide personnel, at the backyard of Oswald's former Neely Street address in Oak Cliff on the morning of Friday, November 29. It was on these grounds that Marina had supposedly taken the shots of Lee provocatively brandishing his weapons and left-wing paraphernalia. The purpose of the November 29 session, said Brown, was to confirm that the Neely backyard was the same as that in the two snapshots (133-A and 133-B) allegedly found by Dallas police detectives Richard Stovall, Guy F. Rose, and other officers in the Paine garage on November 23. To this end, Brown produced pictures of the backyard with and without a human figure, using himself to duplicate the stance of Oswald.

The group of Secret Service agents and police officers asked Brown to pose for the re-enactment, he claimed, because he "was the youngest" of the men present. Their request required the photographer to instruct a Secret Service agent how to use his Graflex camera. The agents in turn instructed Brown how to stand, telling him "what hand to hold the rifle in, how to hold the newspapers, and so on." These posing instructions were based on a backyard photo of Oswald provided either by Secret Service agent Sorrels or Dallas police captain Fritz. As evidenced by the pose adopted by Brown and published by the Warren Commission (rifle in the left hand, newspapers high in the right) the photo in the lawmen's possession that day could only have been the picture later designated as CE 133-C, not either of the smaller snapshots known as 133-A and 133-B.

Later, Brown said, the same 133-C photo was brought to him at the Dallas police crime lab by the FBI, allowing him to make the matte

Oswald backyard pictures in Roscoe White's possession: 133-A and 133-C.
The latter was not shown to the Warren Commission. (Courtesy Matsu Corporation)

Detective Bobby G. Brown, DPD Crime Scene Search division, in pose of back-yard photo 133-C. The fact that Brown simulated this pose shows that Dallas police and the Secret Service (who accompanied Brown in this "re-enactment") were aware of the photo within days of the assassination, though it did not surface until Geneva White presented the picture to HSCA investigators in the mid-seventies. (Courtesy Dallas Municipal Archives and Records Center, City of Dallas, Texas)

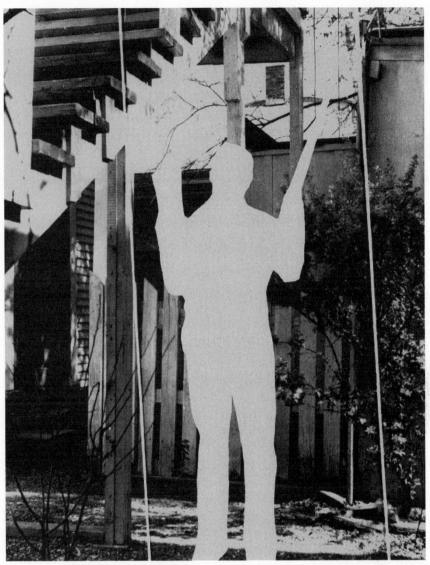

Matted photograph combining silhouette of Lee Harvey Oswald from 133-C pose with a later photo of backyard at 214 Neely Street. This photo is one of two similar shots uncovered by the authors in the Dallas police files. Former Dallas detective Bobby G. Brown claims to have made the composite photos shortly after his "re-enactment," though today he can't explain how or why he did so. (Courtesy Dallas Municipal Archives and Records Center, City of Dallas, Texas)

print of Oswald. As Brown explained it, he created the white silhouette by cutting Oswald out of this photo and shooting the result
against a white background. His reason for constructing this matte
was "just to show him [Oswald] in that backyard," Brown stated.
"That part [making the matte] was my own idea. I just did it to be
doing something."

But Brown's description of the making of the matte print appears
oddly confused. Cutting Oswald from a photograph—in this case, a
copy of 133-C—and shooting the cutout "against a white background" would ultimately have reproduced the identical background
of 133-C. The matte print, however, shows the backyard photographed in the Secret Service-sponsored re-enactment on November 29, not the seasonally different background of the "true" Oswald
backyard photos (shot eight months earlier, on March 31, 1963)—
133-A, 133-B, and 133-C.

The detective's explanation of two vertical white lines on either
side of the silhouette was similarly inadequate. These lines, he
claimed, were "cut lines . . . where it [Oswald's image] was cut out, I
guess." A far more likely possibility is that the two vertical lines were
produced by an acetate overlay. In a typical step for creating such
composite images, an acetate sheet with a cutout of the figure to be
inserted—here, Oswald—would be placed over the picture of the
empty backyard and shot with a copy camera. This procedure
(demonstrated in Stone's *JFK*) could leave "tracks" from the edges of
the overlay in the form of thin white lines similar to those in the silhouette print.

Brown's admissions have clearly raised more questions than they
have answered.[24]

How, for example, did the Secret Service—or FBI—acquire the
mysterious 133-C within a week of the assassination? (It wouldn't
have been from Dallas detectives Stovall or Rose, unless one or the
other perjured himself when he swore that the search of the Paine
garage had produced only *two* snapshots.)[25]

And having acquired the 133-C photo, why didn't the federal agencies, or the Dallas police, turn it over to the Warren Commission?
What was it about the picture that made *it* the one chosen for "re-
enactment" and not the other two supposedly available photos, 133-
A and 133-B? Why did 133-C then disappear between late 1963 and
1975? And did Brown himself, then or now, know the whole story?

Brown says he doesn't have the answers, and the other principals involved can't answer either. Fritz died in 1984, and Sorrels, who planned the motorcade route for Kennedy's visit to Dallas and rode in the lead car, died in 1993.

Even so, "the fog in the backyard photo mystery may be lifting somewhat with the discovery of 'Oswald's ghost'—the silhouette print," Hershel Womack, a photo expert and major researcher of the Waggoner Carr Collection of Kennedy materials at Texas Tech University, told Mary in a 1992 interview for the *Houston Post*. "The fact that the matte photograph was worked up from the precise backyard photo that was withheld from the Warren Commission makes me suspect that the 'ghost' photo, the withheld 133-C photo, and Brown's demonstration photo may all have been part of the same trial series. Once the 'practice' was over and the actual forgery completed, the incriminating materials were discarded—or so they thought."

Womack added: "The photographic panel of the House Select Committee on Assassinations should be reconvened. The question of whether Oswald was framed by faked photographs needs to be asked one more time."

Berkeley's Paul Hoch, though previously convinced by the House Select Committee that the Oswald backyard photos were genuine, has reached a similar conclusion: "The discoveries in Dallas comprise a message to the press that there are surprises in the files, contrary to the claims of [HSCA counsel] Robert Blakey and others. The complexity of the photograph issue points out the need for an ongoing investigative capability at least on the level of the FBI, and if the FBI is not interested, the need to get the major media interested."[26]

Meanwhile, the apparent interest of the FBI in any aspect of the discovered Oswald matte remains in a precarious state, as the Bureau's Marjorie Poshe of Dallas confirmed to the La Fontaines.

The FBI, the spokesperson noted firmly over the phone, "does not *have*, and does not *need*, the photograph."

IV. THE TEXAS SCHOOL BOOK DEPOSITORY

A. *Oswald was the only person missing from the TSBD when a roll call was made prior to 2:00 P.M. the day of the assassination.*

SIGNIFICANCE: The absence would indicate that Oswald (and only Oswald, among TSBD employees) fled the scene of the crime. It was on the basis of this supposedly unique absence that Dallas police captain and chief of homicide J. Will Fritz identified Oswald as a prime suspect.

RELATED CIRCUMSTANCES: Even the Dallas Police Department's own list of TSBD employees, which is not complete, shows that *four* employees did not return to the book depository until three in the afternoon (or later) on November 22. This is contrary to what Captain Fritz told his men when he arrived at police headquarters around 2 P.M. that day, and to what newsman Dan Rather was still telling the nation thirty years later ("CBS Special Report: The Final Chapter," November 19, 1993).

NEW EVIDENCE: None.

B. *Howard Brennan identified Oswald as the assassin in the window.*

SIGNIFICANCE: A "smoking gun" eyewitness of Oswald's guilt would be better than circumstantial evidence.

RELATED CIRCUMSTANCES: In fact, Brennan first could not identify Oswald, changing his mind twice before finally settling on a positive identification. (Suspected Oswald "lookalikes," moreover, had been reportedly spotted in Dallas and elsewhere.)

NEW EVIDENCE: None.

V. OFFICER J. D. TIPPIT

Oswald murdered Dallas police officer J. D. Tippit.

SIGNIFICANCE: Oswald's alleged murder of Officer Tippit raised the probability that he also murdered President Kennedy, at least in many people's minds. ("If he didn't shoot Kennedy, why did he shoot Tippit?")

RELATED CIRCUMSTANCES: Oswald may have killed Officer Tippit—a possibility not popular among conspiracy theorists—but if so, he needn't also have murdered the president earlier in the day. (A panicked person belatedly discovering he was the designated patsy in an assassination could have blindly shot anyone attempting to apprehend him.) It is also more than possible, however, that Oswald killed neither man. Of three or four

NAME	REF. INT.	ADDRESS
HAROLD DEAN NORMAN	NONE	4858 BEULAH PLACE
CARL EDWARD JONES	NONE	3709 SPRING
BUELL WESLEY FRAZIER	NONE	2439 W. FIFTH
		IRVING, TEXAS
JOE EARL JARMAN	NONE	3942 ATLANTA
DOROTHY GARNER	NONE	911 ROYAL
		FORNEY, TEXAS
JANE BERRY	NONE	3126 LEMMON, APT. 2
BETTY FOSTER	NONE	5723 MARQUETTA
MRS. ELSIE DORMAN	NONE	1233 E. LOUISIANA
MRS. OLIVER HOPSON	NONE	4717 WAVERLY
BETTY THORNTON	NONE	3807 ROLINDA
SANDRA STYLER	NONE	2102 GRAUWYLER
		IRVING, TEXAS
MRS. R.A. REID	NONE	1914 ELMWOOD
GENEVA L. HINE	NONE	2305 OAKDALE ROAD
MARTHA REED	NONE	338 W. TENTH
SARA STANTON	NONE	227 N. EWING
MRS. ROBERT E. SANDERS	NONE	4226 DELMAR
HERBERT LESTER JUNKER	NONE	1709 LINDY LANE
		IRVING, TEXAS
L.R. VILES	NONE	3210 ST. CROIX
		CH-7-3854

(Left building approximately
12:15 pm, was across the
street when shots were fired
returned to building at 3:10 pm)

MRS. A.D. DICKERSON	NONE	7310 BRIERFIELD DRIVE
		GA-4-4792
MARG LEE WILLIAMS	NONE	3718 INWOOD ROAD
		LA-8-1775
MRS. HERMAN M. CLAY	NONE	6934 CASA LOMA
		DA-1-2761
GEORGIA RUTH HENDRIX	NONE	2011 N. PRAIRIE
		TA-3-2615
PEGGY BIGLER HAWKINS	NONE	2719 CUMBERLAND DRIVE
		MESQUITE, TEXAS, BR-9-3525

The below listed employees of SUBJECT organization left the building
at 12:15 pm, and were standing across the street. They observed the
assassination of President JOHN F. KENNEDY, and returned at 2:55 pm.

MRS. WILLIAM V. PARKER	NONE	5916 ELLSWORTH
		TA-3-7600
DOLORES P. KOONAS	NONE	825 ARPEGE
		FR-4-7251
VIRGIE RACKLEY	NONE	BOX 573, FERRIS, TEXAS
		544-3827

INDEXED
DAT
S

2965-14A

*List of Texas School Book Depository employees on November 22, 1963. The
list shows that four employees (L. R. Viles, Mrs. William Parker, Dolores
Koonas, and Virgie Rackley) were still out of the building at 2:55 P.M. or
later.*

witnesses at the scene of Officer Tippit's death, only two saw the actual shooting; both said the shooter was not Oswald. None of the descriptions of the killer (or his clothing) squared with Oswald's appearance, and the one witness said by the Warren Commission to have identified Oswald did not do so.[27] As has long been known, moreover, the ballistics "evidence" in the Tippit shooting is highly suspicious—not only failing to implicate Oswald, but hinting of shady doings by police eager to "prove" him the murderer. The shells supposedly found at the scene, though fired from Oswald's revolver (which at the time of ballistics testing was in the hands of the police), did not match the bullets removed from Officer Tippit's body. And the shells did not have the initials marked on them by the officers who retrieved them at the scene, or by the officer who received them in the police property room. Finally, if we can believe housekeeper Earlene Roberts' assertion that Oswald left the boardinghouse three or four minutes after one, he did not have enough time to cover, on foot (without running at a fast jog, which no one claimed to see him doing), the mile between the boardinghouse and the murder scene. The shooting of Officer Tippit was called in, on his own car radio, at 1:16 P.M.

NEW EVIDENCE: None.

VI. A DISCONNECTED MAN

A. *Oswald was not an informant for a U.S. government agency.*

SIGNIFICANCE: The anticonspiracy Warren version of the assassination required a disconnected Oswald, a loner without affiliations except perhaps to obvious Communist fronts. Such an Oswald, by definition, could not be a government agent, a consideration that probably played no small part in promoting the original lone-nut thesis (and its successful 1993 revival in Gerald Posner's *Case Closed*).

RELATED CIRCUMSTANCES: The FBI practiced a series of deceptions apparently intended to obliterate any traces of its association with Oswald. The obliterations included the Hoover agency's destructive "testing" of the former Marine's mysteriously acquired DD Form 1173 card. The implications of this Department of Defense ID were not communicated to Warren investigators. Similarly, the Oswald-Guy Banister Camp Street connection was papered over in a dissembling report, the Oswald notation of a November 1, 1963 meeting with FBI agent James Hosty was initially omitted from the evidence, an Oswald note to the same agent was intentionally destroyed, Oswald's New Orleans (and probably Dallas) informant file disappeared, and the FBI denied its November 16 meeting with him, among other Bureau misdeeds. No evidence exists that a U.S. government agency suspected of employing Oswald was itself involved in the assassination.

NEW EVIDENCE: The DoD ID (the same card carried by known CIA contract agent Francis Gary Powers), examined in some detail in chapter 3, ultimately suggests an agent's role for Oswald in his Russian defection adventure, probably as CIA contract operative. (Military regulations did not provide for the issuance of such a card to Oswald; it was, however, routinely issued to overseas civilian government employees.) Oswald also carried the card when he visited Clinton, Louisiana in the fall of 1963, showing it to a voter registrar there (chapter 6). At the time Oswald was in the company of David Ferrie and either Clay Shaw, a paid asset of the CIA, or Guy Banister, an FBI contact. The evidence is now overwhelming that Oswald was an informant on weapons and Cuban exiles for the J. Edgar Hoover Bureau. Specifically, New Orleans SA Warren deBrueys and Dallas agent James Hosty became Oswald's runners following the ex-Marine's return from Russia. An entry in Oswald's notebook, recovered from his room at 1026 N. Beckley and subsequently covered up by the FBI, has never been satisfactorily explained as anything but his record of a meeting with Hosty (chapter 8). The Marxist-leaning Oswald's compatible FBI "assignments" consisted of tracking right-wing gunrunning activities, including, surprisingly, those of maverick ex-agent and Cuban-exile collaborator Banister. Finally, new evidence described in this book supports former FBI employee William Walter's claim that Oswald was an FBI informant on the DRE arms cache in Louisiana July 31, 1963.

B. *Oswald was held in an isolated cell after he was arrested in Dallas, and provided no information of value to the authorities related to the assassination.*

SIGNIFICANCE: The Warren portrait of a disconnected Oswald was advanced by the sounds of silence—notably, the lack of audiotapes or transcripts of police interrogations of Oswald during the

final forty-eight hours of his life. If Oswald "talked" during this critical period, the lone-nut (or two lone-nut, counting Ruby) scenario
could be jeopardized.

RELATED CIRCUMSTANCES: Both Oswald and Daniel Wayne
Douglas signed phone logs from cellblock F on the third shift of
November 22, 1963. The logs established that Oswald was placed
with at least one other prisoner.

NEW EVIDENCE: As noted in chapter 1, at least two other prisoners were placed in cellblock F while Oswald was held there on
November 22, 1963: Daniel Wayne Douglas and John Franklin Elrod.
Hard evidence exists that both of these men occupied the cell or cellblock (three small cells, with Oswald's, F-2, in the middle). Douglas
placed a phone call on November 22 soon after the "third shift"
began in the Dallas jail, and listed his cell as F-1 or F-4 (the numeral
isn't clear, but the *F* is) on the phone log. The third shift began at
3:00 P.M. Douglas's arrest record, found with those of the three
tramps and John Franklin Elrod in February 1992, showed he was
nineteen and had been arrested after officers investigating the Tippit shooting noticed him lurking in the police station. He told them
he had stolen a car in Memphis, and wanted to turn himself in. Both
John Elrod and his brother Lindy, neither of whom were shown the
Douglas arrest record or even told of its existence, said that John
was put in a cell with Oswald and a "kid from Tennessee who had
stolen a car in Memphis." This description perfectly matches the
arrest description of Daniel Douglas contained in his long-missing
arrest report. That John Elrod was indeed put in a cell with Oswald
was also corroborated to Lindy by Dallas policeman H. R. Arnold.
This policeman, a personal friend of the Elrods (both of whom knew
him by an unlisted nickname, "Hap," to which he still answers today),
called Lindy to notify him of John's incarceration, and again to notify
him that John was ready for release. Arnold further told Lindy that
John was "in the cell with Oswald about four hours," Lindy states.
(Today Arnold claims he cannot remember either of the Elrods.)

A Warren Commission affidavit executed by jailer G. R. Hill states
that Oswald was first placed in a cell at 12:30 A.M. November 23. The
Hill statement is false, however. The phone log shows that following
Oswald's arrest, he, like Douglas, made a phone call during the third
shift of the previous day, November 22; and (again like Douglas) his
cell address is listed in the log as being in the three-cell F block. The

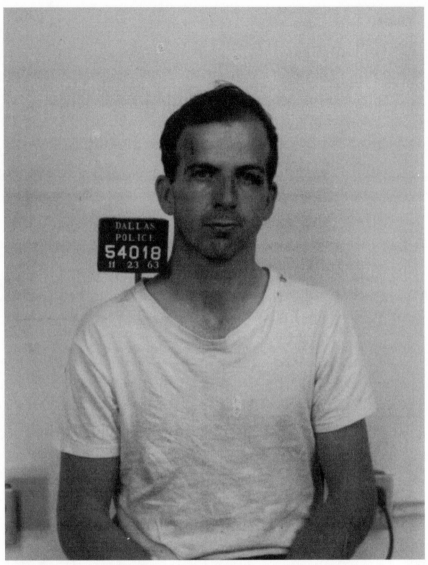

Only known color photo of Lee Harvey Oswald, taken the day before his death. (Courtesy Dallas Municipal Archives and Records Center, City of Dallas, Texas)

Platoon 3rd	PRISONERS TELEPHONE CONTACT FORM			Date 11-22-63
Prisoner's Name	Cell	Contact Yes	No	Officer's Name
Edger Cox	A1	✓		paul
Harold Lane	A-22	✓		Sanders
Ed Lane	A-3	✓		Ryure
woodrow noble	A9	✓		paul
Nichols	#16	✓		Davis
Thomas Miller	C2	✓		Lister
Juan Ivey	A-13	✓		Carl
Jessie Way	H-6	✓		Lister
3Rd. PLATOON 11-22-63				
→ Daniel Douglas	F-1	✓		Hollymon
Ray Joiner	A-15	✓		CRJ
Gene Joiner	A-15	✓		CRJ
Gary Joiner	A-15	✓		CRJ
Bobby Joiner	A-15	✓		CRJ
Johnny Roberson	B-11	✓		Hollymon

Dallas city jail phone log for November 22, 1963, "3rd Platoon" (i.e., third shift, beginning at 3:00 P.M.). The log shows that Daniel Wayne Douglas made a call and was in cellblock F (cell F-1) on the afternoon of President Kennedy's assassination. This cellblock contained only three cells.

Platoon __3 Rd.__   PRISONERS TELEPHONE CONTACT FORM   Date __11-22-63__

Prisoner's Name	Cell	Contact Yes	No	Officer's Name
James Reed	B-13	✓		Walugman
Teddy Watson	A-4	✓		Reid
Chas. H. Elkes	A-8	✓		Walugman
Jack Alford	A-6	✓		JRH
Lewis Johnson	B-5	✓		JRH
Curlee Jones	B-2	✓		JRH
James Hunter	B-2	✓		JRH
Antonio Garcia	A-3	✓		JRH
James Allbrook	A-7	✓		JRH
T. W. Rogers	A-5	✓		JRH
Walter Goodman	A-13	✓		JRH
Paul Harris	A-13	✓		JRH
Leroy Curries	E-4	✓		Reid
Edward D Robinson	E-6	✓		Robinson
Lee H. Oswald	F-2		✓	Bellyfield

CE 2187   C.D. 1444 PAGE 1 OF ENCL. 3

Another sheet of the same phone log, this one showing Lee Harvey Oswald as an occupant of the same cellblock (F) as Daniel Douglas (in cell F-2, which connected to both of the other cells of the block). Elrod, who did not make a phone call that day, does not appear on the log.

log not only refutes the jailer's later statement, but provides independent corroboration that (as Elrod said) Oswald and Douglas occupied the same cell area at least part of the time during the third platoon, from 3:00 to 11:00 P.M., on the day of the assassination. Additionally, jail supervisor Ret. Lt. Thurber Lord confirmed that Hill's statement was false, and that Oswald was in a cell when Lord arrived at the jail at 6:30 P.M. November 22. Lord says Oswald was alone in the cell when he arrived. This supports Elrod's claim that he was removed to another cell sometime on the afternoon of November 22.

While Elrod was in the cell with Oswald, a man with a "smashed up" face was led into the cellblock "where Elrod and his cellmate could observe him," according to the 1964 FBI report of Memphis agents Norman L. Casey and Francis B. Cole. The wording of the report, though ambiguous, suggests that the injured inmate was brought into the corridor outside Elrod's cell for the specific purpose of being identified by Oswald. Such a purpose would conform to the physical layout of the corridor, which was not a central hallway but a brief cul-de-sac off the main corridor and running only the length of the three cells of cellblock F. (Thus Oswald could *only* have seen the injured man from his cell if the inmate had been deliberately steered away from the main corridor and brought into the cellblock cul-de-sac. Perhaps the FBI was earnestly conducting an assassination investigation at this point, not realizing yet the complications regarding Oswald.)

Oswald was indeed able to "identify" the man with the battered face, stating (as Elrod reported to the Memphis agents) that he had seen the man at a motel-room meeting where money had changed hands, and that at the time the man (then uninjured) was driving a Thunderbird filled with guns. More importantly, Oswald also said Jack Ruby was one of the parties at the meeting. As we now know, the injured man, Lawrence Reginald Miller, received his injuries when the car in which he was a passenger, a blue Thunderbird laden with stolen military weapons, crashed into a utility pole after a high-speed police chase. Ruby's auto mechanic, Donnell Darius Whitter, was driving the Thunderbird when it was wrecked. Fourteen pages of documents on the otherwise insignificant Ruby mechanic were withheld from public release by the FBI, purportedly for reasons of national security related to the protection of the president. There is no way Oswald or Elrod could have invented the "Ruby connection" from newspaper accounts of the Miller-Whitter arrest.[28]

C. *Oswald did not know Jack Ruby, the man who murdered him.*

SIGNIFICANCE: If Oswald knew Ruby, a conspiracy to assassinate President Kennedy, and to eliminate traces of this conspiracy by silencing Oswald, is a virtual certainty.

RELATED CIRCUMSTANCES: A preassassination connection between Oswald and Ruby has been widely suspected since the day Ruby shot Oswald, and "supported" with numerous anecdotal tales of claimed sightings of the two men together. Ruby's entrance into the Dallas police station basement, where the murder of Oswald occurred on November 24, 1963, has never been satisfactorily explained.

NEW EVIDENCE: As we saw in chapter 1, the 1992 discovery by Bill Adams of a 1964 Memphis FBI report on John Elrod altered the Oswald-Ruby preassassination landscape, providing for the first time documentary support of a connection between the two men. We know now that Oswald himself spoke of Jack Ruby's presence at a Dallas motel-room meeting where the ex-Marine was present shortly before the assassination. It was Elrod's knowledge that Oswald spoke of Ruby, the man he wasn't supposed to have known, and that he was subsequently murdered by the bar owner even within the "protection" of the Dallas police station, that drove the frightened cook from Dallas forever.

Notes

CHAPTER 1

1. FBI file Nos. DL 44-1639, ME 44-1165, Aug. 11, 1964; report of interview with John Franklin Elrod, same date.

2. Elrod was described that day, in a letter from Shelby County sergeant Alton C. Gilless, Jr., to FBI director J. Edgar Hoover, as a man who "stated he had information concerning the murder of Lee Oswald." The letter was discovered via FOIA by Bill Adams in 1993.

3. The injured inmate was probably brought into the corridor outside the cell for the express purpose of having Elrod's cellmate identify him (see Appendix B, section VI, B).

4. One Dallas arrest on John Elrod's FBI record (for theft, dated Nov. 15, 1962) probably referred to another man, identified on the record as "James F. O. Elrod." The 1962 theft charge was "no billed."

5. U.S. Secret Service materials regarding John Thomas Masen's alleged sales of illegal weapons to Manuel Rodriguez, a member of the militant anti-Castro organization Alpha 66, were declassified Dec. 23, 1975.

6. FBI file No. 105-125147, Teletype, Oct. 25, 1963.

7. A memo (May 8, 1964) from Secret Service agent D. J. Brennan, Jr., to W. C. Sullivan notes: "Ellsworth discussed the arrest of an arms dealer [John Thomas Masen] in Dallas and indicated that the dealer is a member of the 'Minutemen' and may be associated with the 'John Birch Society.' He indicated that he furnished this information to the Bureau." (The FBI did nothing with the information, as we'll see in chapter 10.)

8. Only Miller was jailed, as will be seen. Whitter, whose injuries were more life threatening, was taken to Parkland Hospital, then transferred to a medical facility in Fort Worth.

9. Albert Bolden, a Secret Service agent, claimed after the assassination that the Service had not provided enough protection for President Kennedy. Former military intelligence officer Richard Case Nagell made unsubstantiated allegations, reported in books by Jim Garrison (*On the Trail of the Assassins*) and Richard Russell (*The Man Who Knew Too Much*), that he had prior knowledge of a planned conspiracy to murder the president.

10. After thirty years, information on the two low-level operators is hard to come by, and some has yet to be released. Miller's arrest report on the day of the car crash noted previous arrests for burglary and theft, vagrancy, DWI, and narcotics violations. He was picked up on West Commerce for possession of "40 grains of marijuana," according to a Dallas newspaper article of June 1, 1955. The National Crime Information Center (NCIC) computer (purged five years after an individual's death) draws a blank on Miller, who died in 1973 at age forty-three. DPD microfilm records show him to have a long series of violations, but police clerks are "unable to find the jacket" containing his November 18 arrest record. For Whitter, NCIC records reveal more than thirty arrests in a thirty-year span, ending with his death in Temple, Texas in 1991. Only half of Whitter's DPD arrest record is currently available (the other half contains "more information than can be provided").

11. Stevenson letter, Apr. 17, 1964, Waggoner Carr Collection, Southwest Collections, Texas Tech University.

12. Cunningham memo, Apr. 5, 1964, Waggoner Carr Collection, Southwest Collections, Texas Tech University.

13. Ruby's remarks were included in a sixteen-page handwritten note that he gave to another prisoner sometime after the Warren *Report* was issued (September 1964), and that also contained this statement: "To start off with, don't believe the Warren Report, *that was put out to make me look innocent,* in that it would throw the Americans and all the European countries off guard" (emphasis added). Cited by Seth Kantor, *The Ruby Cover-Up* (New York: Zebra Books, 1978), 238-40.

14. A *Dallas Times Herald* story ("Officer Says He Saw Ruby," Dec. 8, 1963) contained several lines near the end evidently touching on Elrod's incarceration. According to the unbylined article, "a 31-year-old man who gave a Knight Street address," and who on the day of the assassination had been arrested near a railroad track in an area where a man had been seen carrying a rifle, was "still in jail—but no longer as a suspect in the killing." The

"investigative charges were dropped Monday morning" [three days after the assassination], the article explained, but the man was being "held on 'city charges.'" Though the man was not identified in the news story, his arrest and description fit Elrod, who was then thirty-one and had "a Knight Street address." The article, apparently based on an erroneous or altered police ledger, was wrong about the duration of Elrod's stay in jail; both John and Lindy Elrod (who picked up his brother at the police station) insist today that the incarceration lasted no more than several days (as John told the FBI in Memphis). If, however, John Elrod was in fact kept in jail more than two weeks (as the *Times Herald* reported) the question would become why he was treated differently from the "tramps" who were arrested on the same day as Elrod. Had he seen—or heard—something during his incarceration that required "special attention," perhaps? The article, in other words, even if true (it isn't) would not serve as a deus ex machina extricating the FBI and Dallas police from culpability in the handling of Elrod.

15. An FBI Teletype (901-278-1816) dated two days later, Aug. 13, 1964, from Hoover to Gilless, is the only known response to the Memphis sergeant's letter. Hoover's Teletype assures Gilless that the only Elrod "ARRESTS BY POLICE AND SHERIFF, DALLAS, TEXAS, SINCE MAY SIXTYONE" were charges of "DRIVING WHILE INTOXICATED, INVESTIGATION QUOTE VIOLATION STATE BARB LAW UNQUOTE, AND THEFT." The "LATEST" charge, Hoover's Teletype noted, was the Quitman arrest of "MARCH SIXTYTHREE" (i.e., there was no Dallas arrest of November 1963, hence Elrod had to be lying about any information allegedly acquired at that time "concerning the murder of Lee Oswald"). As indicated earlier, the theft charge probably referred to another man, "James F. O. Elrod."

16. Oct. 15, 1993.

17. Taped interview, July 31, 1993.

18. Thus, from Warren counsel Wesley J. Liebeler's memo (Mar. 11, 1964) to Commission attorneys Leon D. Hubert and Burt W. Griffin: "6.b. Details as to how and when Oswald first became a suspect. (Information so far is that Mr. [Roy] Truly [manager, Texas School Book Depository] notified [DPD Captain Will] Fritz, Fritz checked police records and learned, while checking, that Oswald was presently being held at the City Hall in connection with Tippit murder.) Question remains as to how Truly came to notice that Oswald was missing. . . ."

19. Dallas Police Department "Prisoners Telephone Contact Form," Third Platoon, Nov. 22, 1963, Waggoner Carr Collection, Southwest Collections, Texas Tech University.

20. The FBI knew persons in Elrod's east Arkansas hometown, according to Elrod.

21. An FOIA response from the National Archives to Bill Adams (October 1993) noted that the Whitter information could not be released for the following FBI-directed reason: "The public disclosure of the assassination record would reveal a security or protective procedure currently utilized or reasonably expected to be utilized by the Secret Service or another government agency responsible for protecting government officials, and public disclosure would be so harmful that it outweighs the public interest." In 1994, following publication of the authors' *Washington Post* article of August 7, "The Fourth Tramp: Oswald's Lost Cellmate and the Gunrunners of Dallas," FBI headquarters finally released the fourteen-page Whitter document. (See Appendix B, n. 28.)

CHAPTER 2

1. Wainwright, 309. The descriptions of the Luce managing editors' luncheon and initial *Life* reaction to the assassination are based on Wainwright's account.

2. Ibid., 326.

3. *Life,* Nov. 29, 1963, 39.

4. *Life,* Feb. 21, 1964, 80.

5. *Life,* Dec. 6, 1963, 52F.

6. Ibid.

7. DeLillo, 5.

8. *Life,* Feb. 21, 1964, 71.

9. Ibid., 72.

10. WC VIII 217.

11. Hartogs Exhibit I, cited by Meagher, 244.

12. Posner, 12.

13. *Life,* Feb. 21, 1964, 71.

14. Ibid.

15. *Fort Worth Press,* June 8, 1962.

16. A photograph released by Associated Press showed Oswald and Ferrie at a Civil Air Patrol camp near Alexandria, Louisiana in 1955.

17. DeLillo, 33.

18. *Life,* Feb. 21, 1964, 72.

19. Ibid.

20. Epstein, *Legend* (Slawson and Coleman citation), 44.

21. Simco, unpublished 35-page memo to HSCA (Sept. 29, 1978), 2.

22. Ibid., 3, 10-11; Summers, 127.

23. Epstein, *Legend*, 69.

24. Ibid., 70.

25. Ibid., 71.

26. Ibid., 79.

27. Ibid., 82-83.

28. Ibid., 78-79.

29. Ibid., 83.

30. Though author of the Oswald-did-it-alone *Marina and Lee*, Priscilla McMillan "was sorry for" and "respected" the American defector in Moscow:

> Here was this lonely, frightened boy taking on the bureaucracy of the second most powerful nation on earth, and doing it single-handedly. I wondered if he had any idea what he was doing, for it could be brutal to try to stay if the Russians did not want you—futile and dangerous. I had to admire Lee, ignorant, young, and even tender as he appeared, for persisting in spite of so many discouragements.

She adds in a note:

> I have been asked whether, during my brief time with Oswald, I detected any signs that he was being manipulated by outsiders. . . . He said that it had taken him two years to learn the mechanics [of entering Russia] but it had not been "hard." He refused to name any "person or institution" that had helped him. And he added that he had never met any Communist Party member until his arrival in the U.S.S.R. and that officials there were not "sponsoring" him. (McMillan, 91, 629-30)

31. WC XII 172, (for Sylvia Duran) Mexico City Document.

32. Don Abedian Exhibit I, cited by Marrs, opposite 309.

33. Interview, October 1993.

34. Epstein, *Legend*, 84.

35. Thornley's novel was later published as *The Idle Warriors*.

36. Simco, 8.

37. WC VIII 236.

38. WC VIII 243.

39. WC VIII 237.

40. Ibid.

41. WC VIII 251.

42. WC VIII 250.

43. Epstein, promoting a KGB conspiracy theory in his *Legend* of 1978, addressed the question of Oswald's "trips" from Santa Ana to Los Angeles this way: "The moment Oswald began receiving his correspondence from the Cubans, he began 'putting on a coat and tie' and going with Delgado into Los Angeles, about one and a half hours away by bus" (*Legend*, 88). Despite the Puerto Rican Marine's emphatic insistence (repeated four times to Wesley Liebeler) that Oswald made only one known trip to Los Angeles, Epstein's use of the present participle expanded Oswald's visit to the consulate from a one-time occurrence to a habitual event.

44. Delgado on "Maggie's drawers": WC VIII 235. In 1959, Oswald's last year in the Marines, he scored a 191 on the rifle range (19 points below "sharpshooter"). After the assassination, he was assessed as "slightly above average" by Sgt. James Zahm of the USMC marksmanship unit (WC XI 308). *However, Oswald's roommate Jim Botelho says Oswald never took the 1959 test, and faked the scores in his own records.*

45. WC VIII 249. Lane cites additional instances of FBI "abuses" of Delgado's testimony: "He said . . . they wanted him to exaggerate Oswald's ability with a rifle instead of stating that he was inaccurate. . . . One of them 'kept on badgering me,' he declared" (*Rush to Judgment*, 388).

46. WC VIII 259. This was an approximation, apparently; elsewhere Delgado told Liebeler that he went to Los Angeles "every weekend that I was off, you know, roughly three weekends a month" (WC VIII 251).

47. WC VIII 259.

48. Simco, 11; Botelho, interview, August 1993.

49. Simco, 11; Botelho, interview, August 1993.

50. Simco, 11; Botelho, interview, August 1993.

51. Botelho, interview, August 1993.

CHAPTER 3

1. Though not with equal effect. Epstein's speculations about KGB connections

are not generally taken seriously, and have not been supported by disclosures following the collapse of the Soviet Union.

2. From PRAM NOTICE 3-57 (16 July 1957):

[Paragraph] 3014   IDENTIFICATION CARDS

1. Two different identification cards are prescribed for Marines:

a. DD Form 2MC, a green card insert laminated between two sheets of plastic, is prescribed for issue only to personnel on extended active duty.

b. DD Form 1173, Uniformed Services Identification and Privilege Card, is prescribed to all other personnel.

6. Responsibility for issuance

b. DD Form 1173 will be issued as follows:

(1) On appointment, enlistment, or reenlistment in the Marine Corps Reserve, the card will be issued by the organization effecting the action.

3. As Dennis Vetock expected, a navy directive on the new three-card ID policy had in fact been issued prior to the distribution of the July 1959 manual. A PRAM revision notice of April 7, 1959 was obtained by Ray via FOIA from USMC deputy manpower director J. S. Vitalie in correspondence dated February 18, 1993. The cover letter from deputy director Vitalie noted flatly: "The provisions of enclosure (2) [PRAM NOTICE 5-59 (7 April 1959)], paragraph 3014.5, did not provide for issuance of the DD Form 1173 to Mr. Oswald on September 11, 1959." He added an escape clause: "It is highly conceivable that Headquarters and Headquarters Squadron, Marine Corps Air Station, El Toro, California did not have enclosure (2) by September 11, 1959, due to printing and distribution lag time that would have followed the April 7, 1959 signature date, and they were probably referencing enclosure (1) [PRAM NOTICE 3-57 (16 July 1957)], paragraph 3014.5." Director Vitalie's "highly conceivable" scenario, however, does not account for the fact that *only* Oswald received the DD Form 1173, not the other Marines in his unit (who received red cards per the April PRAM cited below). The La Fontaines had already learned from Vetock, moreover, that the new regulations were included in the July 1959 manual.

From PRAM NOTICE 5-59 (7 April 1959):

[Paragraph] 3014   IDENTIFICATION CARDS

1. Three different identification cards are prescribed for Marines:

a. DD Form 2MC, a green card insert laminated between two sheets of plastic, is prescribed for issue only to members of the Marine Corps and Marine Corps Reserve on active duty for periods in excess of 90 days.

b. DD Form 2MC(RET), a gray card insert laminated between two sheets of plastic, shall be issued to retired members of the Armed Forces who are entitled to retired pay.

c. DD Form 2MC(RES), a red card insert laminated between two sheets of plastic, may be issued to members of the Reserve who are not otherwise entitled to either of the cards prescribed above.

4. Observes Scott: "By 1978, when Blakey became Chief Counsel to the House Committee, prosecutorial accounts of 'La Cosa Nostra,' and the falsified 'history' given the world by [Joseph] Valachi (and his FBI handlers) in 1963, had already been exposed by scholars as falsehoods to support an 'alien-conspiracy' theory or 'alien conspiracy myth' of 'La Cosa Nostra.' We shall have to draw attention to the lawyerly way in which Blakey, clearly aware that some of the historical claims he makes had already been refuted, presented 'alien conspiracy' fictions in such a way as to make them appear, falsely, to be consensually accepted facts" (*Deep Politics*, 71-72).

5. Almost a year later, a fuller story would emerge on the rascally computer marauder. Ned Dolan, Larry Haapanen informed Mary, was more than a retired Marine. An old *Washington Post* story (Sept. 8, 1974, G-6) described Dolan, a candidate for the Maryland legislature, as retired from the Marines and a veteran of seventeen years in the CIA. Later, Dolan became president of Challenge, Inc., a corporation set up to pay the legal bills of another retired CIA agent, David Atlee Phillips (aka "Maurice Bishop"), who had sued, among others, assassination writers Anthony Summers and Gaeton Fonzi. Not long after his nonstop criticism of the La Fontaines' Nov. 22, 1992 *Houston Post* story on the DoD card, Dolan adopted a new CompuServe identity, "Steve Newman." Curious, Mary finally placed a call to Dolan/Newman at his Maryland home. He confirmed that he was indeed retired from the CIA, and that he hadn't revealed this because he had been speaking only as a "retired Marine."

6. WC XIX 269 (Commission Exhibit 1114).

7. Harold J. Berman, "Introduction," in *The Trial of the U2* (Chicago: Translation World Publishers, 1960), ii.

CHAPTER 4

1. Russell, 271.
2. HSCA XII 270.
3. WC IX 237.
4. WC IX 236.
5. WC IX 274.
6. WC IX 237.
7. Numbered 70-315 in HSCA (XII) pagination.

8. HSCA XII 227.

9. HSCA XII 307.

10. HSCA XII 306.

11. HSCA XII 224.

12. HSCA XII 215.

13. HSCA XII 217.

14. HSCA XII 277.

15. HSCA XII 276.

16. HSCA XII 275.

17. HSCA XII 293.

18. HSCA XII 294-95.

19. HSCA XII 75.

20. HSCA XII 76.

21. Ibid.

22. HSCA XII 77.

23. Marrs, 286.

24. HSCA XII 273.

25. HSCA XII 305.

26. Epstein, *Legend,* 178. On the subject of de Mohrenschildt's background, Epstein, who interviewed the Russian on the day of his death *(Assassination Chronicles),* is the most informative; see, e.g., *Legend,* 177-83.

27. For what de Mohrenschildt was up to in Mexico, see Melanson, 77-78.

28. HSCA XII 295.

29. Epstein, *Legend,* 182.

30. Interview, July 1993.

31. HSCA XII 208-9.

32. HSCA XII 209.

33. HSCA XII 209-10.

34. HSCA XII 208.

35. "I personally have always felt that George was a CIA agent," Patrick Russell reportedly said in 1978. "[The baron] traveled abroad regularly, frequently without his wife. And each time upon his return to the States he would undergo debriefing. It has always seemed most plausible to me that he was an agent, that he did have an assignment, that his association with Lee Harvey Oswald went a little deeper than friendship" (Summers, 196).

36. Summers, 198.

37. CIA document 18-522.

38. Epstein, *Assassination Chronicles*, 564.

39. The colonel himself shot another hole in de Mohrenschildt's story when he told interviewer Edward Jay Epstein that "the only time he accompanied de Mohrenschildt to Oswald's [Fort Worth] home, the two were already well acquainted" (Epstein, *Legend*, 176).

40. Epstein, *Assassination Chronicles*, 559.

41. Ibid.

42. HSCA XII 116.

43. HSCA XII 86.

44. HSCA XII 87-88.

45. HSCA XII 90.

46. HSCA XII 92.

47. Epstein, *Legend*, 189.

48. Two kindly ladies who deserved the gratitude of the Oswalds. Mrs. Hall, an Iranian-born dental technician of Russian extraction, helped Marina with her teeth problems and provided her with a place to stay while Lee "relocated" to Dallas; Mrs. Meller, wife of a Russian scholar, similarly opened her house to Marina and June during a later marital crisis.

49. Epstein, *Legend*, 176.

50. Ibid., 183.

51. Ibid., 185.

52. HSCA XII 97.

53. HSCA XII 96.

54. Melanson, 82.

55. Epstein, *Legend*, 196.

56. Melanson, 84.

57. HSCA XII 85.

58. HSCA XII 310.

59. Like the "two Oswalds" (chapter 7), it would turn out there were also two "Bowens," both aliases. "John Bowen" was the assumed name of elderly English "preacher" Albert Alexander Osborne, who reportedly sat on a Laredo-to-Mexico City bus next to Oswald in September 1963 . . . a man whose own *real* name Oswald had used as *his* alias in New Orleans that summer (Russell, 483).

60. Epstein, *Legend*, 209.

61. HSCA XII 128.

62. HSCA XII 128-29.

63. Summers, 200.

64. HSCA XII 136.

65. HSCA XII 122-23.

66. HSCA XII 99.

67. HSCA XII 159.

68. Epstein, *Legend,* 198.

69. HSCA XII 138.

70. HSCA XII 143.

71. HSCA XII 139.

72. HSCA XII 142.

73. Ibid.

74. Ibid.

75. HSCA XII 163.

76. HSCA XII 144.

77. HSCA XII 163.

78. HSCA XII 164.

79. HSCA XII 166-67.

80. Epstein, *Assassination Chronicles,* 558.

81. Palm Beach County associate medical examiner Dr. Gabino Cuevas, Coroner's Inquest (hereafter cited as "Inquest"), Palm Beach County Courthouse (Fifteenth Judicial Circuit), Apr. 5, 1977, transcript, 44.

82. Russell, 280-81.

83. HSCA XII 287.

84. HSCA XII 283.

85. HSCA XII 282.

86. HSCA XII 283.

87. Ibid.

88. HSCA XII 284.

89. HSCA XII 282.

90. HSCA XII 284.

91. Ibid.

92. HSCA XII 285.

93. Ibid.

94. HSCA XII 286.

95. HSCA XII 287.

96. Marrs, 286.

97. "The Missing General," *Gallery,* March 1978, cited by Russell, 280.

98. Cited by Marrs, 287.

99. Marrs, 286.

100. Ibid.

101. Ibid.

102. WC IX 274.

103. Marrs, 285-86.

104. Epstein, *Assassination Chronicles,* 558.

105. Russell, 278-79. As noted previously, the edited version of the 1967 Oltmans interviews had disappeared mysteriously just the previous year (in 1975), according to the Dutchman. At the time of Russell's visit, however, the couple still seemed unaware of this "fact."

106. Cited by Russell, 280.

107. Russell, 279.

108. Epstein, *Assassination Chronicles,* 556.

109. Cited by Marrs, 287.

110. Russell, 281.

111. Cited by Russell, 282.

112. Ibid.

113. Epstein, *Assassination Chronicles,* 558.

114. Ibid., 564.

115. Ibid., 555.

116. Ibid., 555-56.

117. Fonzi, "The Last Investigation," *The Third Decade: A Journal of Research on the John F. Kennedy Assassination,* vol. 1, no. 1 (Fredonia, N.Y.: State University College, November 1984), 11. (See n. 120 below.)

118. The baron found Epstein "very fair and very good" and thought he "was a very intelligent guy," according to Alexandra. Interview, fall 1993.

119. HSCA XII 95.

120. Fonzi, "The Last Investigation," 11. Fonzi's article, originally appearing in *Indian River Country Life* (November 1980), was later expanded into a book. In the book, the quoted passage becomes: "If Gonzalez had lived in Miami, when he awoke the next morning he would have found a horse's head in his bed" (*The Last Investigation,* 185).

121. Fonzi, "The Last Investigation," 11. Book version (slightly revised), 189-90.

122. Fonzi, "The Last Investigation," 11.

123. Russell, 281.

124. Alexandra de Mohrenschildt, Inquest, 51.

125. Lt. Richard Sheets, Inquest, 108.

126. Ibid., 110. The certainty of the lieutenant, who himself reconstructed events and answered jurors' questions, did not prevent conspiracy writers from using his "doubts" to try to suggest a foul cover-up. Thus Marrs: "Although several aspects of DeMohrenschild's death caused chief investigator Capt. Richard Sheets of the Palm Beach County Sheriff's Office to term the shooting 'very strange,' a coroner's jury quickly ruled suicide" (*Crossfire*, 287).

127. Inquest, 76. The cassette therefore provided a benchmark time that allowed the events to be reconstructed to an accuracy of hundredths of a second; it was the Zapruder film of de Mohrenschildt's death.

128. Jerry D. Rose (assisted by Robert Cutler), "Loose Ends in the Death of George DeMohrenschildt," *The Third Decade*, vol. 1, no. 1 (November 1984), 21-28.

129. Anna Viisola, Inquest, 73.

130. Nancy Sands Tilton, Inquest, 67-69.

CHAPTER 5

1. HSCA XII 195.

2. Russell, 259.

3. Ibid., 317.

4. HSCA XII 197.

5. De Mohrenschildt's Warren testimony does not mention direct observation of the contents of the closet. See *Report*, 261.

6. HSCA XII 198-99.

7. HSCA XII 201.

8. HSCA XII 202.

9. HSCA XII 200-201.

10. The German publication was *Deutsche National Zeitung* (Munich), Nov. 29, 1963.

11. Not from FBI interference, according to Jaggars executive Robert Stovall, who called the ex-Marine's performance "inefficient" and "inept" (WC X 173).

12. WC XX 511, cited by Summers (*Conspiracy*, 268), who notes its "date is best fixed between March 23 and April 2" (*Conspiracy*, 587).

13. Though Voebel initially stated he and Oswald had been in the Civil Air Patrol with Ferrie, he "suddenly" could no longer remember the matter, as Summers noted. "The FBI was unmoved by the fact that Voebel had been

scared by a 'crank-type telephone call' and a visit to his home by a strange man. Nor was the Bureau stung into action when another former cadet said Ferrie had scurried around to see him—after the assassination—asking whether any old group photographs of Ferrie's squadron featured Oswald" (*Conspiracy*, 301). Voebel's testimony: WC VIII 14.

14. The photo, first shown on PBS's "Frontline" in November 1993, was taken at a CAP camp near Alexandria, Louisiana in 1955. Despite the extensive evidence that Ferrie and Oswald had indeed been in the same CAP unit together, Gerald Posner argued in 1993 that "CAP records show he [Ferrie] told the truth" [in denying knowledge of Oswald in the Civil Air Patrol], and hinted darkly that the HSCA was derelict in not embracing this special insight: "He [Ferrie] was not even in the Civil Air Patrol when Oswald was a member in 1955. It is not clear why these records were evidently not available to the House Select Committee" (*Case Closed*, 143).

15. Dutz also offered Oswald a loan of $200 until he got settled; Oswald declined (*Legend*, 216).

16. Oswald's relationship with Reily Coffee has been suspicious to various writers over the years. Was the job legitimate or a front, supplying the not-too-industrious Oswald with a stipend while he performed other "real" duties for the FBI (chapter 6)? Most recently, Peter Dale Scott has noted (with documentation): "At least some of Oswald's alleged paychecks from the Reily company are apparently not genuine as transmitted to the Warren Commission; the FBI was aware they had a problem in this area; and they went out of their way to conceal the problem" (*Deep Politics*, 95). Le Blanc's testimony: WC X 214-15.

17. WC XX 512-13 (V. T. Lee, Commission Exhibit 2).

18. WC XX 514-16 (V. T. Lee, Commission Exhibit 3).

19. WC XXII 796-98.

20. WC XX 518 (V. T. Lee, Commission Exhibit 4).

21. WC XX 524 (V. T. Lee, Commission Exhibit 5).

22. Posner, 137, 160.

23. Summers, 286.

24. FBI file No. NO 89-69, Nov. 25, 1963. Despite the deceptive report, Posner claims: "Most ignore that the FBI and Secret Service conducted an extensive investigation in December 1963 to determine whether Oswald was ever at 544 Camp" (*Case Closed*, 138).

25. Summers, 292.

26. Ibid., 295.

27. Ibid.

28. Posner, 137.

29. Ibid., 142.

30. Ibid.

31. WC X 64-66. Scott's observation (about the unemployment con): "Those with either media or protest experience will find it hard to believe that two TV stations would have responded so promptly to a call from Oswald alone, if he were truly an unemployed loner who had just been fired from a coffee factory." He adds: "More likely organizers are the DRE Cubans and their allies" (*Deep Politics*, 84, 327-28).

32. Posner, 142.

33. Ibid., 139, 140, 141. The reference to Delphine's daughter is allegedly culled from a Summers remark to Posner.

34. Interview, October 1993.

35. An internal memo from Wesley J. Liebeler (assistant to Albert E. Jenner) to Leon D. Hubert and Burt W. Griffin (dated Mar. 11, 1964) notes: "One Vance Blalock relates the incident of Oswald's appearance at the headquarters of the Cuban Student Director [*sic*] (CSD), at which time Oswald spoke of training guerillas to oppose the Castro regime. Blalock said that Oswald spoke of guerilla operations of various types, described how easy it would be to derail a train and mentioned that he knew how to blow up bridges, etc." Liebeler's memo continues: "He [Blalock] did seem to remember Oswald mentioning something to him about recently visiting the Casa Nostra (phonetic), 'a Cuban organization in Florida.' Blalock's recollection was vague regarding further details on that matter, as was, apparently, either his knowledge of the exact title of the Mafia (or perhaps it was the misinformation of the FBI agent (Harrigan) that led to this misspelling)."

The term *Cosa Nostra*, allegedly used by Oswald in August 1963 (WC X 77), did not become widely known until Joseph Valachi's testimony in September of that year. Notes Scott: "If Oswald was not being directed by the FBI, how did he come to use a term current within the FBI and (because Valachi had made it up) current nowhere else?" (*Deep Politics*, 252).

36. De Mohrenschildt: "As far as I was concerned, I was delighted. How many times I'd heard her [Marina] call Lee a bore, a fool, a bookworm, how many times she degraded his masculinity and here the loveliest girl of all was in a trance" (HSCA XII 170). Michael Paine was also impressed by Oswald's speaking skills, as he testified to the Commission (Mar. 18, 1964). Describing Oswald's remarks at an ACLU meeting they attended, Paine said that Lee spoke "loud and clear and coherently," and that "that was good speaking . . . it made sense" (WC II 408, cited by McMillan, 521, and Meagher, 243).

37. Interview, October 1993.

38. Ibid.; WC X 38.

39. Once again Scott corrects former HSCA counsel Robert Blakey, whose book (with Richard Billings) stated that state boxing commissioner and anti-Castro crime figure Emile Bruneau paid Oswald's bail at the request of the Murrets, supposedly after Oswald "telephoned the Murrets and arrogantly demanded that they use their influence to get him out of jail" (*The Plot to Kill the President*, 358-59, 364). In fact, it was Bruneau, as Scott points out, who initiated the move to get Oswald out of jail "and then communicated [this fact] to the family, not the other way around" (*Deep Politics*, 83). "We called him [Bruneau], and he told us what had happened . . . [and] a little while after that, he called back and said that everything was all right, that Lee was out," Lillian Murret testified (WC VIII 145, cited by Scott).

40. Re Guitart's presence at trial, see Scott, 252; WC XI 378.

41. Russell, 393.

42. McMillan, 470.

43. Ibid., 472.

44. Ibid., 470.

45. WC XX 526-28 (V. T. Lee, Commission Exhibit 5).

46. McMillan, 471.

47. WC XI 166, cited by McMillan, 471.

48. Harold Weisberg's 1967 perspective:

> If it [INCA] is not connected with the CIA or the USIA, it should be for its function is indistinguishable from that of a government subsidiary or agency. It spreads propaganda, usually not unacceptable to those who find the John Birch perspective attractive. It is [INCA production manager Manuel] Gil who arranged for the Bringuier-Oswald debate that became so effective a propaganda device for the radical right. (Weisberg, 362)

49. Letter from Stuckey to Priscilla McMillan, Jan. 24, 1976. Interestingly, Oswald-did-it-alone author McMillan reveals yet another suspicious FBI "error." The predebate Bureau contact with Stuckey mentioned in the letter "does not appear in FBI reports on its surveillance of Oswald in New Orleans published in the twenty-six Warren Commission volumes," she notes. "Warren Commission Exhibit No. 826, a report filed by Special Agent Milton R. Kaack in October 1963, which summarizes most of Oswald's political activities in New Orleans, states erroneously that Stuckey's first contact with the FBI on the subject of Oswald did not occur until August 30, 1963" [i.e., after the debate] (*Marina and Lee*, 472, 654-55).

50. McMillan, 472-73.

51. As *Spy Saga* author Philip H. Melanson noted: "Oswald held his own in the early part of the program, conducting himself with poise. Ed Butler remembered that Oswald seemed 'very articulate,' especially for a young man twenty-four years old. Butler said that the public image of Oswald as being inarticulate was inaccurate. After listening to an audio tape of the program, the author too was impressed with Oswald's performance" (*Spy Saga*, 67).

CHAPTER 6

1. Interview, October 1993.

2. President Lyndon Johnson, *Recordings of Telephone Conversations Related to JFK Assassination* (Austin: LBJ Library).

3. While some Warren attorneys attempted to investigate possible conspiracy evidence, their inquiries were not followed up by an unresponsive FBI, as noted by Burt Griffin in an interview (October 1993).

4. FBI file No. 105-82555-54.

5. Ibid., New Orleans field office, memo to Dallas (Aug. 13, 1963).

6. Summers, 281.

7. Thus, for example, an early *Houston Post* column by Lonnie Hudkins (December 1963) citing a "rumor" that Oswald was an FBI informant was quickly traced to its source—Hudkins himself, it turned out. The newsman eventually "admitted" that he and Dallas assistant D.A. Bill Alexander were the originators of a story that Oswald had an informant "number" (179) and received $200 a month.

8. Summers, 295.

9. Warren *Report*, 435; FBI file No. 105-82555-30.

10. FBI file No. 105-82555-31.

11. "To order guns by interstate mail is of course an irrational way for a potential assassin to purchase his murder weapons: it lays a paper trail linking the weapon to the purchaser, or at least his post-office box. Conversely, if one is investigating firms known to sell weapons illegally through the mails, a paper trail is precisely what is needed" (Scott, 249). As Scott also notes, Seaport Traders and Klein's were being investigated in 1963 by both the ATF and a subcommittee of the U.S. Senate chaired by Sen. Thomas Dodd.

12. WC VII 527.

13. Section 846.53h of the postal manual describing regulations in effect "at

all postal installations in March 1963" provides that "the third portion of box rental applications, identifying persons other than the applicant authorized to receive mail, must be retained for two years after the box is closed," according to a letter of May 3, 1966 from U.S. Post Office Department Special Services Branch Director Ralph R. Rea (cited by Lane, 412). The Warren *Report* lied on this point, noting: "*In accordance with U.S. Post Office regulations,* the portion of the application listing the names of persons other than the applicant entitled to receive mail was discarded after the box was closed on May 14, 1963" (emphasis added) (Warren *Report*, 575). The regulation was to retain, not discard, this portion of the application, as we've seen.

14. FBI file No. 105-82555-31.

15. See also Appendix B, section I.

16. The fact that the FBI lab in Washington was unable to find the palm print on the rifle (obscured by Lieutenant Day's print dust) led to erroneous speculation that Day had obtained the Oswald palm print elsewhere. One FBI agent, Vince Drain, reportedly suggested that Day had done so as "insurance," confirming Oswald's guilt.

17. "It lifted off pretty well, considering it was a dim print," Posner quotes Day from a 1992 interview (*Case Closed,* 283).

18. WC I 409-10, cited by Meagher, 215. A memo from Warren counsel Burt W. Griffin to fellow Commission attorney W. David Slawson (Apr. 16, 1964) cast Hosty in a similar light. "[ATF agent Frank] Ellsworth," Griffin wrote, "like Agents [Joe] Howlett and [William] Patterson of the Secret Service, expressed his dislike for Agent Hosty. Each of these persons brought up Hosty's name and commented on his own without prompting from me."

19. Hoover, for example, did not believe the Minutemen were much more than a nuisance, calling them "essentially a paper organization with just enough followers over the country so that they can attract a headline." Cited by J. Harry Jones, Jr., *Private Army* (New York: Collier Books, 1969), 112, and Scott, 89.

20. Scott, 87.

21. U.S. Congress, Senate Committee on the Judiciary, *Juvenile Delinquency, Part 15: Interstate Traffic in Mail-Order Firearms, [Dodd] Hearings,* 88th Congress, 2nd sess. (Washington, D.C.: Government Printing Office, 1964), 3642; WC XVII 675, 678; cited by Scott, 249.

22. WC XX 524-25 (V. T. Lee, Commission Exhibit 5).

23. Ibid.

24. FBI file No. 100-16601-18, Special Agent John L. Quigley, memo (Aug. 27, 1963).

25. McMillan, 464.

26. WC XX 264, WC XXII 168 (Commission Exhibit 1145).

27. FBI file No. 100-16601 (Commission Exhibit 826, p. 14).

28. WC XXVI 763, cited by Scott, 262-63.

29. FPCC cards in Oswald's name: FBI file No. 100-16601 (pp. 7-8). Oswald also showed Martello and Quigley a second FPCC card, signed by national chairman V. T. Lee.

30. HSCA *Report,* 222, cited by Scott, 258.

31. Warren *Report,* 180-81; *Dallas Morning News,* Mar. 19, 1978, cited by Scott, 258.

32. Though as Sylvia Meagher showed close to thirty years ago, the case that Oswald himself fabricated the Hidell card is weak (*Accessories After the Fact,* chapter 6).

33. CIA document 1363-501 (Oct. 26, 1967), cited by Summers, 297.

34. Interview, Dec. 31, 1993.

35. Summers, 291.

36. HSCA X 123-36; Summers, 291; Scott, 88.

37. Ties to Marcello: Summers, 309.

38. Scott, 265. The *Digest* "depicted integration as part of the Communist conspiracy," according to William H. Turner, *Power on the Right* (Berkeley: Ramparts Press, 1971), 95.

39. CIA Inspector General's *Report* on the agency's top secret ZR/RIFLE assassination program (obtained by Bill Adams, 1994).

40. Garrison, 106.

41. Ibid., 106-7.

42. Ibid., 232.

43. Ibid.

44. Ibid., 250.

45. Summers, 306-8.

46. Fonzi, 140-41.

47. Garrison, 232.

48. Ibid., 107-8.

49. Summers, 307; Garrison, 108. The application disappeared according to Sciambra.

50. Garrison, 108-9.

51. Summers, 307-8.

52. Posner, 142-48.

53. Ibid., 145. Garrison, writing five years before Posner, notes: "The weather was unexpectedly cool, perhaps an early harbinger of summer's end" (*On the Trail of the Assassins,* 107).

54. Garrison, 106.

55. Summers, 306; Posner, 147. Palmer also told Summers that, as he remembered, the card had a New Orleans address. In this, however, Palmer was mistaken, since only Oswald's (authentic) Selective Service Notice of Classification and Selective Service Registration Certificate indicated a place of residence. Both showed a Fort Worth address. The rest of Oswald's military cards, including the "U.S. Navy ID card" (card No. N [for Navy] 4,271,617, the DD Form 1173 discussed in chapter 3) and the forged Hidell Selective Service card, had no provision for a residence address.

56. Posner, 147.

57. Jim Garrison cites a similar use by Oswald of a "Navy I.D.," though in a vaguer and less substantiated context. The former New Orleans D.A.'s source is C. A. Hamblen, a Dallas Western Union night manager who allegedly claimed Oswald had visited the Western Union office on several occasions to collect money orders sent to him. "According to Hamblen," Garrison tells us, "for identification Oswald showed him a library card and a Navy I.D. card. This was very close to what Oswald routinely carried for identification: a library card and Marine I.D. card" (*On the Trail of the Assassins,* 223). The "correction" by Garrison (who understandably did not know of the Oswald DoD card) is not necessary; the card could well have been, as Hamblen supposedly said, the "Navy" (DD Form 1173) card.

58. Scott has suggested that Banister associate (and employer of Ferrie) Jack Martin was "suspicious" in implicating Ferrie; and that Paulino Sierra Martinez, head of the Junta del Gobierno de Cuba en Exilio, may similarly have been a falsely implicated patsy as part of a "high-level pre-assassination disinformation campaign" (*Deep Politics,* 89, 246-48).

CHAPTER 7

1. Kantor, 251-52.

2. CIA memo No. 431-154B, Dec. 30, 1963.

3. Dallas Police Department file No. INT-2965-58 ("Re: George de Mohrenschildt," report by Bill Murphy for James P. Donovan, completed May 17, 1963).

4. Ibid.

5. Ibid.

6. Ibid.

7. Ibid.

8. FBI file No. DL 105-632, DL 105-1766, Mar. 6, 1964.

9. FBI file No. 100-32965-126, Teletype, Feb. 27, 1964.

10. Ibid.

11. FBI file No. DL 105-632, DL 105-1766, Mar. 6, 1964.

12. Ibid.

13. DPD file No. INT-2965-58.

14. Summers, 218. CIA memo: No. 431-154B.

15. Summers, 218.

16. DPD file No. INT-2965-58.

17. Claflin, 266.

18. Interview, April 1993.

19. Letter from James B. Donovan to John Murchison, Mar. 20, 1962 (obtained by Bill Adams from the Hoover Institute, May 25, 1993).

20. HSCA XII 195.

21. HSCA XII 57, cited by Russell, 318-19.

22. For Kail's alleged connection with Antonio Veciana (and Maurice Bishop), see Fonzi, 150-51, 312-13.

23. HSCA XII 57, cited by Russell, 319.

24. E.g., Summers, 219.

25. Attributed to U.S. Army intelligence officer Roger Pierce in memo to Russell from Bernard Fensterwald, Jr.; Russell, 319.

26. Summers, 219.

27. "Blessing of Antonio Veciana" (see Russell, 330).

28. FBI file No. 105-120807-1, Teletype, May 15, 1963, from SAC, Los Angeles to Director, FBI.

29. FBI file No. LA 105-14523 (p. 6).

30. Ibid., 7.

31. Ibid., 14.

32. Ibid.

33. Ibid., 23.

34. Ibid., 14.

35. Ibid., 23.

36. Ibid., 14.

37. Ibid., 23.

38. Ibid., 6.

39. Ibid., 2.

40. Kantor, 44.

41. Files of Seth Kantor obtained from Bill Adams.

42. Davis was carrying a letter of introduction (the piece of paper that got him into trouble) from New York lawyer Thomas Proctor.

43. Kantor does not list his source for this information, and was incorrect in stating that Davis was jailed in Algiers.

44. FBI file No. 105-120907 (p. 1).

45. WC XIV 336.

46. WC XIV 338.

47. WC XIV 339.

48. Jones, 100 (citing WC XIV).

49. DPD Batchelor Exhibit 5002, booklet entitled "Dallas Police Personnel Assignments," November 1963.

50. WC XIV 341. By the time of her testimony Nancy Perrin had remarried and was Nancy Perrin Rich.

51. WC XIV 343.

52. WC XIV 358.

53. WC XIV 363.

54. WC XIV 364.

55. WC XIV 345.

56. Lane, 296-97.

57. WC XIV 349.

58. Ibid.

59. WC XIV 350.

60. WC XIV 351.

61. Ibid.

62. WC XIV 354.

63. WC XIV 355.

64. Ibid.

65. George Lardner, Jr., "On the Set: Dallas in Wonderland," *Washington Post*, May 19, 1991.

66. Miller was convicted on four counts: that he "unlawfully received, concealed and retained with intent to convert to his own use and gain [five machine guns, type and models specified] . . . the said firearms having heretofore been stolen from Texas National Guard Armory, Terrell, Texas . . . [with the defendant] knowing the firearms to have been stolen"; and that he "knowingly and unlawfully possessed" the specified firearms (Proceedings in the United States District Court for the Northern District of

Texas, Dallas Division, United States of America v. Lawrence Reginald Miller, No. CR-3-225 Criminal, Feb. 10, 1964, pp. 15-18, 140 [verdict]).

67. As Bertha Cheek would testify to Warren counsel Burt Griffin, she had previously met with Ruby in "1957 or 1958" (WC XIII 383).

68. "Assuming . . . that Earlene Roberts and Bertha Cheek provide a link between Oswald and Jack Ruby in a plot to assassinate the President," Burt W. Griffin and Leon D. Hubert wrote in a memo to J. Lee Rankin (Mar. 6, 1964), "the following might be considered. . . . Her [Earlene Roberts] failure to notify the police of Oswald's residence at the N. Beckley address. (Mrs. Johnson apparently called the police from a different address immediately upon seeing Oswald's picture on TV but Roberts who was watching TV at the N. Beckley address, did not)" (Griffin-Hubert memo, 6-8).

69. Ibid., 3-4.

70. Bertha's ownership: WC XIII 384.

71. See Claudia Furiati, *ZR Rifle: The Plot to Kill Kennedy and Castro* (Melbourne [Australia]: Ocean Press, 1994), 123: "The arms at Pontchartrain were supplied with the cooperation of the Mafia. The Louisiana corridor was controlled in Dallas by Jack Ruby, and in Miami by Santos Trafficante . . . [who] was the bridge between the Mafia and the Cuban exiles."

72. Commission Document (CD) 223, 50.

73. Scott, 291.

74. WC XXIV 160 (Commission Exhibit 2002 [DPD Lt. W. F. Dyson, letter to Chief of Police J. E. Curry, Nov. 25, 1963]).

75. While the Warren Commission said Kantor was mistaken, he was later vindicated by the House Select Committee (HSCA *Report*, 620).

76. Ruby bribed his way in with sandwiches, according to the late DPD detective J. W. Finley, who reportedly observed the bar owner in the interrogation room and within a few feet of Oswald. Finley interview by Dr. William Pulte (SMU associate professor of anthropology), "Nov. 22: New story on what Jack Ruby was up to," *The Register*, Nov. 21, 1991.

77. Kantor, 131.

78. Ibid., 132-33.

79. FBI file No. LR 2-13, DL 44-1639, Feb. 3, 1964.

80. FBI file No. DL 44-1639 (p. 1).

81. FBI file No. LR 2-13 (p. 3).

82. FBI file No. DL 44-1639 (p. 1).

83. FBI file No. LR 2-13 (p. 3).

84. Hinckle and Turner, 164-65.

85. Ibid., 165.

86. Nei Sroulevich (producer), *ZR Rifle*. This documentary, by the husband of Brazilian journalist Claudia Furiati, is based on her book by the same title (see n. 71 above).

87. Hinckle and Turner, 165.

CHAPTER 8

1. WC III 100, cited by Meagher, 213.

2. Hubert and Griffin, memo to J. Lee Rankin (Mar. 6, 1964), 9.

3. Hoch's MS: "The Oswald Papers: The FBI Versus the Warren Commission."

4. City of Dallas Archives, receipt signed by James Hosty.

5. HSCA *Report,* 186-87.

6. "The committee [HSCA], though it deemed the incident regretable, found it to be trivial in the context of the entire investigation" (ibid., 190).

7. "In accordance with prior instructions from Oswald, Marina Oswald noted Hosty's license number which she gave to her husband" (Warren *Report,* 327).

8. WC I 48, cited by Meagher, 212.

9. See testimony Warren counsel Albert E. Jenner, Secret Service agent Joe Howlett (WC IX 398); Meagher, 212-14.

10. McMillan, 534.

11. Ibid.

12. Ibid., 534-35.

13. WC I 57 (Marina), WC III 18-19 (Ruth Paine), cited by Meagher, 216.

14. Oswald had made a similar error in his application for the box in New Orleans, listing his address one number off from the actual address of his aunt, Lillian Murret. Thus, if the post office in New Orleans had followed its normal procedure, Oswald's mail carrier would not have verified the information on that application, either. In both the New Orleans box application and the second Dallas one, rules seem to have been bent for Oswald.

15. Indeed, the association was made on the very day of the assassination, in an FBI Teletype to Hoover and the New Orleans field office from Dallas approximately ninety minutes after the Dealey Plaza shooting: "On Nov. one last, Mr. Lee H. Oswald appeared Houston Street Annex, Dallas, secured Box six two two five in name of Lee H. Oswald and showed name of firm as 'Fair Play for Cuba Committee,' 'American Civil Liberties Union.' Showed 'Kind of Business' as 'Non-profit'. . ." (FBI file No. 105-82555).

16. See previous discussion in chapter 6.

17. Perhaps Hosty's anonymous informant in the inspector's office destroyed it, or helpful postal inspector Harry Holmes himself, who provided evidence on the purchase of the alleged murder weapon and lingered with Oswald in the homicide division on November 24 as Jack Ruby made his way to his position in the basement of the DPD. It was Holmes who lied to the Commission about postal regulations.

18. WC XXII 170-71 (Commission Exhibit 1145).

19. WCXX 264, WC XXII 168-69 (Commission Exhibit 1145).

20. Though Oswald had attended an ACLU meeting at SMU with Michael Paine one week earlier, he did not strike Paine then—prior to the apparent November 1 meeting with Hosty—as a likely candidate to join the organization. On the way home from the meeting, "Michael explained what the A.C.L.U. was all about," Priscilla McMillan tells us. "He told Lee that its sole purpose was to defend civil liberties—free speech and other rights of the individual. Lee was amazed that any organization could exist merely to defend a *value*, as Michael put it later, and not to fight for a political objective. Lee remarked firmly that he could never join an organization like that—it wasn't political enough" (*Marina and Lee*, 522).

21. WC I 409-10, cited by Meagher, 215.

22. Robert Oswald: "Marina had recognized this one FBI agent [Hosty] as a man who had come to the Paines' home in Irving, Texas, and perhaps at another location where they might have lived in Dallas or the surrounding territory, and had questioned Lee on these occasions. . . . In or outside of the home . . ." (ibid.).

23. FBI file No. 105-125147-10, airtel, Nov. 15, 1963.

24. This name is also found as *Perilli, Perell,* and *Perrell* in FBI reports. Since the name was an alias known only phonetically, it has been arbitrarily standardized here as *Perrel.*

25. FBI file No. 105-125147, Teletype, Oct. 25, 1963.

CHAPTER 9

1. Sullivan, 90.

2. Ibid.

3. The link between the Odios and the plot on Castro's life via Reynol Gonzalez was initially revealed by assassination researcher Paul Hoch and former CIA employee George O'Toole in *The Saturday Evening Post* ("Dallas: The Cuban Connection," February 1976). HSCA investigator Fonzi

interviewed Antonio Veciana, the Cuban who organized the bazooka plot under the guidance of the CIA's "Maurice Bishop" (thought to be David Atlee Phillip), following Veciana's release from the Atlanta Federal penitentiary. As Fonzi was first to discover, Veciana, like Silvia Odio, claimed to have seen Oswald (in Bishop's company) in Dallas in September 1963. See Fonzi, 110, 117-27.

4. WC XI 380.

5. Griffin, memo to W. David Slawson (Apr. 16, 1964), 3.

6. WC XI 375.

7. Secret Service file No. CO-2-34,030 (Commission Exhibit 2896).

8. The Dallas FBI interview of Rodriguez and Alentado was as interesting for what it omitted as what it included. Left out of the interview report was any mention of Johnny (Juan) Martin, the Uruguayan gun trader who Silvia Odio had already told the Warren Commission (two months earlier) was the reason for Cisneros' trip to Dallas, as he himself verified to the Secret Service. Rodriguez was allowed to say, unchallenged, that the meeting in Silvia's residence was only "for the purpose of organizing the Dallas branch of JURE." As we shall see again, avoidance of gunrunning references in Dallas prior to the publication of the Warren *Report* (it would be printed three weeks after the Dallas FBI interview) was an FBI pattern.

9. FBI file No. DL 100-10461, Sept. 8, 1964 (CD 1546).

10. FBI file No. DL 100-10461, Alentado interview, Sept. 8, 1964 (p. 1) (CD 1546).

11. FBI file No. DL 100-10461, Rodriguez interview, Sept. 8, 1964 (p. 1) (CD 1546).

12. FBI file No. DL 100-10461, Alentado interview, Sept. 8, 1964 (p. 1) (CD 1546).

13. WC XI 371.

14. Ibid., 372.

15. Ibid.

16. Rankin, letter to J. Edgar Hoover (Aug. 23, 1964), cited by Fonzi, 114.

17. Liebeler, memo, cited by Fonzi, 114.

18. Warren *Report*, 324, cited by Meagher, 379.

19. HSCA X 31, cited by Posner, 176.

20. Interestingly, the letter that Silvia produced for the Warren Commission from her father (written in response to a letter she had supposedly written before the assassination about the unsettling visit) referred to the day of the visit as a Wednesday: "Grant me, blondie [Silvia], the additional sacrifice of not going out Wednesdays with your girl friends," he wrote sardonically.

If it was to be an Oswald visit, it had to be a Wednesday (September 25, the only day of that week on which his whereabouts were unaccounted for), as Silvia no doubt knew by the time she presented the letter to the Commission. Amador went on to lecture Silvia to stay home nights. "You are not free—you should avoid everything that might affect your good name. Never accept going out with anyone or to the house of anyone if you are not accompanied by your brothers," etc. Amador still had hopes Silvia could reconcile with her husband, Guillermo ("I am sure that he loves you and adores his children in his way"), who, the doting father wrote, "was criminally indisposed against you by his neurotic mother." As to whether Amador's letter proved what Silvia intended it to—that she wrote her father about the visit prior to the assassination—the late date of his letter, December 25, 1963, leaves the point moot.

21. WC XI 371.

22. FBI report of interview with Annie Odio, July 30, 1964 (pp. 1-2) (Commission Exhibit 2907).

23. Ibid., 2.

24. Chief James J. Rowley (Secret Service), letter to J. Lee Rankin (May 5, 1964), 1-2 (Commission Exhibit 2943).

25. Transcript of taped interview with Col. Robert Castorr and Trudy Castorr, Jan. 30, 1968, by Harold Weisberg (p. 12).

26. Chief James J. Rowley (Secret Service), letter to J. Lee Rankin (May 5, 1964), 5 (Commission Exhibit 2943).

27. Ibid.

28. Ibid.

29. Ibid.

30. Ibid., 6.

31. WC XI 372.

32. In his apparent zeal to protect Silvia as one of his star witnesses to conspiracy, Harold Weisberg quotes her verbatim from the Secret Service report—right up to the mention of Cisneros, at which point Weisberg interposes himself to suppress the tell-tale name. Thus: "'She advised him [Machann] the only information she could provide on the people who visited her was,' *in effect, what she had already said*" (emphasis added) (*Oswald in New Orleans*, 287). Here Weisberg entirely misleads his readers. What she actually told Machann was anything *but* "what she had already said."

33. WC XI 376.

34. The question of whether Liebeler's heart was in the interrogation or mooning over Silvia was raised by Silvia herself later in an interview with Gaeton Fonzi. She remembered having been upset when Liebeler started

joking with her, before taking her deposition, about how he was being teased by the other staffers "for his luck in interviewing the prettiest witness in the case." He "then invited her to dinner on the pretext of having additional questions; afterwards, he invited her to his hotel room." The shocked Silvia supposedly "began wondering how seriously the Warren Commission was taking its investigation." See Fonzi, 115.

35. Griffin, memo to W. David Slawson (Apr. 16, 1964), 1.

36. Dr. Einspruch's assertion to Griffin that he "had great faith in Miss Odio's story of having met Lee Harvey Oswald" was used by *Conspiracy* author Anthony Summers (who omitted the remainder of the paragraph) as validation of Silvia's postassassination claims of a September Oswald encounter in the Crestwood Apartments hallway. As we can see, though, the story that Dr. Einspruch had such faith in was that Silvia had known Oswald before the assassination; she had seen him "at more than one anti-Castro meeting" and provided a picture that was pure Oz: a guy making inflammatory pro-Castro remarks at an anti-Castro gathering.

37. Griffin, memo to W. David Slawson (Apr. 16, 1964), 2.

38. FBI file No. DL 44-1639, Nov. 29, 1963 (Commission Exhibit 3108).

39. Ibid.

40. WC XI 381.

41. FBI file No. DL 100-10461, Sept. 10, 1964 (p. 5) (Commission Exhibit 3147).

42. Griffin, memo to W. David Slawson (Apr. 16, 1964), 2-3.

43. Lucille Connell's report to the FBI of November 29, 1963 has recently resurfaced on the Internet. Taking a new tack, a perturbed Gaeton Fonzi now claims his HSCA investigative notes indicate that the information about prior meetings with Oswald was not told to Mrs. Connell by Silvia, but by one of Silvia's sisters, and that, moreover, the FBI misunderstood what was said. Mrs. Connell herself, however, confirmed to Mary in March 1995 that (as she told the FBI) it was *Silvia* who told her she had met Oswald more than once prior to the assassination.

44. Sullivan, 90-91.

45. The most glaring of Marianne Sullivan's technical errors is her identification of the Warren Commission's "Odum Exhibit" (a CIA surveillance photo of a still-unknown man in Mexico City whom the intelligence agency mistakenly identified shortly after the assassination as Lee Harvey Oswald) as part of the "Odio Exhibit." She compounds the problem by making a lengthy supporting argument that the unknown man is actually Amador Odio-Padron, who, in her mind, "posed" as Oswald in Mexico City. (That Amador was in a Cuban jail at the time doesn't appear to have prevented

this.) Mary pointed out the error to the author, and was told that an errata sheet will be inserted in future books.

46. Sullivan, 19.

47. Ibid., 5.

48. Ibid., 126.

49. Transcript of taped interview with Col. Robert Castorr and Trudy Castorr, Jan. 30, 1968, by Harold Weisberg (Tape 1, p. 10).

50. Ibid., 11.

51. Ibid.

52. Sullivan, 137-38.

53. Ibid., 144-45.

54. Marianne did not exclude the FBI from her assassination suspects. She recalled that Father Machann had spoken to Bureau agents in the committee office (once for some four hours) prior to his disappearance—a fact she tied to Silvia's receipt of "two special delivery letters from Washington, D.C." while Marianne visited her at the hospital on the day after the assassination. ("One of [Silvia's] sisters," perhaps Sarita, delivered the letters to the hospital room.) Noted Faith (according to Marianne):

> "If Father had turned informant to the FBI [prior to the assassination], why was nothing done to halt the murder? Do you think his sudden disappearance was a tactic to insure no slip-ups in some plan?" "Hope," I [Marianne] interrupt, "then that would implicate the FBI, and that is not sensible . . . yet, I wonder." Recalled the official envelope delivered to Sylvia in hiding at the Irving Hospital. (Sullivan, 167)

No preassassination FBI reports of interviews with Father Machann have been released, although he mentioned them to the Secret Service, naming Special Agent Wallace Heitman as his contact.

55. Transcript of taped interview with Col. Robert Castorr and Trudy Castorr, Jan. 30, 1968, by Harold Weisberg (p. 12).

56. Ibid., 12-13.

57. Sullivan, 167.

58. Ibid., 172.

59. Transcript of taped interview with Col. Robert Castorr and Trudy Castorr, Jan. 30, 1968, by Harold Weisberg (p. 11).

60. Sullivan, 173. According to Father Machann's mother, it was Monsignor Thomas Tschoepe who arranged for the priest to enter a nursing home (in New Orleans), and later, Loyola University.

61. Ibid., 265.

62. Ibid., 267.

63. Ibid., 273.

64. Ibid., 280.

65. Ibid., 281.

66. Ibid., 280.

67. Ibid., 127.

68. WC XI 378.

69. Ibid.

70. HSCA record No. 180-10101-10280, agency file No. 013339 (subject: Silvia Odio interview), Jan. 16, 1976.

71. Ibid., 3.

72. Ibid.

73. FBI file No. DL 100-10461, Felix Guillermo Othon Pacho interview, Sept. 8, 1964 (p. 2) (CD 1546).

74. CIA file No. 12395, dispatch, Nov. 8, 1963 (p. 5).

75. FBI file No. 105-133465-2, Sept. 18, 1964 (p. 8). De Goicochea and Salvat were accompanied by another member of the directorate (and CIA operative), Anna Silvera. It is possible that de Goicochea was recruited as early as September 1963, when CIA asset Salvat attended a town-hall debate in New York City. It was at that time that de Goicochea, himself then living in New York, left to attend the University of Dallas.

76. Fermin de Goicochea Sanchez had a connection to Silvia other than through Sarita. His brother-in-law was a "Cuban doctor," Manuel Balbona, a Ph.D. psychologist at the Terrell state mental hospital. Isabelle Collora, a social worker and influential Catholic in the Dallas area (who introduced Marianne Rahmes to the Castorrs) told Mary in March 1995 that a large group of Cuban doctors was employed at Terrell. It included de Goicochea's brother-in-law and a Dr. Cowley. In her Warren Commission interview Silvia testified that she initially came to Dallas to be treated by a Cuban "Dr. Cowley" at Terrell. Interestingly, Oswald too had an alleged link to a Cuban doctor. A number of persons in Clinton, Louisiana believed Oswald may have stayed for a period of time with Dr. Francisco Silva, who was employed at Jackson State Mental Hospital near Clinton. Dr. Silva has been tied by some conspiracy theorists to the DRE arms cache at Lake Pontchartrain.

77. "The Ghosts of November," December 1994, 112.

78. Reached by Mary in April 1994, Silvia Odio was vivacious and charming,

speaking freely about her days in Dallas. "It is strange, Mary," she said at one point, "the more the years pass, the fresher my memory becomes." Despite this admittedly unusual phenomenon, the latest recollections from Silvia do not do much to resolve the contradictions noted above.

She denied being visited by Marianne Rahmes and Faith Leicht on the evening before the assassination, or even having met Marianne, though Silvia acknowledged knowing "of" her as a woman in Father Machann's parish who was "totally obsessed" with the priest.

About the father himself, Silvia added a new turn not mentioned in the Secret Service's report concerning the New Orleans interview of April 30, 1964. When Machann called her that day (at the instigation of Inspector Thomas Kelley, we recall), the priest "betrayed" Silvia by taping the conversation for the Secret Service; he admitted this to her when he called her back a few minutes later, Silvia told Mary. ("I was extremely upset with him for that, and I was estranged from him for a while.") If this is true, the Secret Service may still have a tape of Silvia's claim to Father Machann that one of the men in the "hallway visit" was Rogelio Cisneros.

Silvia also offered a slight variation on another "betrayal" of her—by Lucille Connell. Lucille "was interested in Father Machann too and that was the reason she called the FBI," claimed Silvia. "It was a jealousy thing, because I was young and pretty, and she was fifty-one at the time."

Silvia explained that Father Machann left Dallas shortly after the assassination because he no longer wanted to be a priest. He had been "forced into the priesthood by his family, who were Irish, and he had a nervous collapse, a loss of identity, and the Catholic church sent him to a rest home in New Orleans." There, "in case he was lonely," Silvia put him in touch with her uncle, Agustin Guitart.

She last saw the priest a few years later, she told Mary, when he came to visit her in Miami from West Palm Beach. It was shortly before this time that Marianne Sullivan claimed to have visited the former priest in West Palm and found a note from Silvia in his apartment. Nevertheless, "I would discard that book totally," Silvia advised, referring to Marianne's memoir. Told its title, *Kennedy Ripples*, she laughed—melodiously, of course. "That sounds like her, especially the *Ripples*," Silvia said of the woman she claimed never to have met.

Her final observation: "The problem with these United States is that people have truth in front of them but they don't want to see it, so they have to wait until Oliver Stone does a movie. I don't think the truth will ever be told exactly the way it is." Silvia lives today with her second husband, Mauricio, in Arlington, Virginia. Both are poets writing in Spanish.

CHAPTER 10

1. Interview for television documentary, October 1993.

2. Griffin, memo to W. David Slawson (Apr. 16, 1964).

3. It was the 112th Army MIG, we recall (chapter 6), that was mysteriously able to notify the FBI, less than three hours after the assassination, that Oswald was carrying a phony ID in the name of Hidell.

4. Interview by Larry Haapanen.

5. Hosty had made an indiscreet remark of his own to Revill. It cost him dearly, and may explain why the FBI man was so inclined, even three decades later, to reveal the Dallas police lieutenant's alleged comment of Thursday, November 21, 1963. On the following day, in the shock of learning that the accused assassin of the president was the man in his case file, Oswald (whose note of warning left with Hosty's receptionist earlier in November had been ignored, as we'll see), Hosty blurted to Revill: "We [the FBI] knew that Lee Harvey Oswald was capable of assassinating the president of the United States, but we didn't dream he would do it." Revill carried the report to his chief, Jesse Curry, and it eventually made its way to J. Edgar Hoover and the media. Hoover was outraged, believing Hosty had "done irreparable harm" to the Bureau with the comment, and placed the agent on ninety days' probation, followed by a transfer to Kansas City, suspension without pay, another probation, and a "stop" on all further promotions (Gentry, 545-50).

6. Ellsworth HSCA testimony, 44.

7. Ibid., 48.

8. Ibid., 49.

9. Ibid., 50.

10. Ibid., 50-51.

11. Ibid., 51.

12. Ibid., 55.

13. Ibid., 53.

14. Ibid., 52, 54-55.

15. FBI file No. 105-125147, Teletype, Oct. 25, 1963.

16. Ibid., 1.

17. Ibid., 2.

18. Ibid.

19. FBI file No. 105-125147-7, airtel, Nov. 1, 1963 (pp. 3-4).

20. FBI file No. 105-133465-2, Sept. 18, 1964.

21. Hinckle and Turner, 147.

22. See later references to CIA file No. 12395, dispatch, Nov. 8, 1963. As Hinckle and Turner note more colorfully (p. 147), "Although the DRE was sore at the CIA [for the Bay of Pigs 'betrayal'], it couldn't keep its hands out of the agency's cookie jar."

23. FBI file No. 105-133465-2, Sept. 18, 1964 (p. 8). Martinez and Salvat were accompanied by another member of the directorate (and CIA operative), Anna Silvera.

24. Ibid., 9.

25. FBI file No. 105-125147-7, airtel, Nov. 1, 1963 (p. 2).

26. Ibid.

27. Ibid., 4.

28. The FBI had access to reports of these meetings, and it remains an unanswered question why Special Agent James J. O'Connor of the Miami office, who interviewed Joaquin Martinez after the assassination, did not identify him to Agent Hosty as the same Martinez who was holding clandestine meetings with Masen and Nonte.

29. Hinckle and Turner, 146.

30. Fonzi, 53.

31. Hinckle and Turner, 146-47.

32. CIA file No. 12395, dispatch, Nov. 8, 1963 (p. 5).

33. Ibid., 2.

34. Ibid., 6.

35. Ibid.

36. CIA file No. IN 64959, secret message with name redactions.

37. Another recent CIA release (memo for the record [subject: "Mr. Helms' Conversation with Luis Fernandez Rocha and Jose Maria Lasa of the DRE re their Organization's Relationship with the Agency"], Nov. 13, 1962) indicates that Richard Helms had established a separate channel with the DRE, in effect bypassing JM/WAVE chief Theodore Shackley.

38. An even earlier warning was received on November 10, when Miami police gave the Secret Service and FBI a tape in which white supremacist Joseph Adams Milteer warned that a plot to assassinate Kennedy "from an office building with a high-powered rifle" was already "in the working." (See, e.g., Scott, 49.)

39. FBI San Antonio letterhead memo (Nov. 26, 1963, p. 1).

40. Masen HSCA testimony, 16.

41. CIA dispatch, Sept. 23, 1963. Attachments include memo (subject: "Attempts of the Student Directorate to Purchase Arms and Equipment for Cuban Guerrilla Activities") and three-page equipment purchasing list.

42. Meanwhile, one more FBI Trunk Street curiosity has recently come to light. The Bureau destroyed the only file that would have identified the informant on the arrest of Whitter and Miller. Bill Adams' FOIA request of 1994 to the Dallas FBI field office for the file on the Whitter-Miller investigation was denied. There was no such file, according to the response from Oliver ("Buck") Revell. Using Whitter-Miller trial testimony as proof of the existence of the file, Adams appealed to the Justice Department. He was then told that the file had been "routinely destroyed" in December 1977. Just four months earlier, in August, researcher Mark Allen had written a memo to the House Select Committee suggesting a connection between John Elrod's report to the FBI and the Whitter-Miller incident. The FBI did not provide Adams with a copy of the required report explaining the reason for the destruction. There is no routine destruction of files containing informant information, according to the National Archives. Moreover, as James Lesar of the Washington Assassination Archives and Research Center noted, fourteen years is not a routine holding period for the small number of FBI files occasionally destroyed. The FBI thus nonroutinely destroyed the only file that may have shown that Oswald, who identified Miller to authorities in the Dallas jail, was the informant on the arrest of Whitter and Miller.

43. *Dallas Morning News*, sec. 1, 11.

44. Walter HSCA testimony, 3.

45. Ibid., 10.

46. Ibid., 4-5.

47. Scott, 85; WC XI 352. After the assassination, deBrueys was sent to Dallas to participate in the investigation. He looked into alleged activities of Oswald, including his supposed test-drive of a car in the week prior to the president's murder.

48. Walter HSCA testimony, 49. Another party apparently more concerned with the suppression of Walter's claims than whether they were true or not was the U.S. attorney in New Orleans during the era of the Jim Garrison court case. The main interest of this federal attorney and his aides, Walter testified, was in providing him with an out from having to appear in Garrison's trial: "Their concern seemed to me to be not whether or not what I was saying was fact, but whether or not I was going to cooperate with Garrison in his Clay Shaw trial, and they offered me legal counsel and were going to advise me on my rights of executive privilege" (Walter HSCA testimony, 35).

49. Ibid., 27-28.

50. Ibid., 14.

51. Ibid.

52. Interview, Apr. 28, 1995.

53. Ibid.

54. Curt Gentry told Mary in the fall of 1994 that William Sullivan had revealed to him that he knew "something" about Oswald being an informant for the Bureau. Though Gentry continued to press him for more information on the assassination, Sullivan was still putting him off when he died in a hunting accident. It was during this same period that the high-ranking Hoover aide placed his call to Walter. Walter remarked to Mary that he was under the impression Sullivan was working on a book when he called—as indeed he was, though not as author. The former FBI man was cooperating with Gentry on what would be his widely admired *J. Edgar Hoover: The Man and the Secrets* (1992). Among the book's revelations: the Bureau "destroyed in the hours after Kennedy was assassinated" some "dozens, perhaps even over a hundred" documents concerning threats on the life of the president, "which the FBI had failed to report to either the Secret Service or the Kennedys—and certainly would never mention to the Warren Commission" (Gentry, 547). That the Bureau would have included the Teletype of November 17 in this wholesale destruction of documents immediately after the assassination can hardly come as a surprise.

55. In fact, as Walter reported in April 1995, the FBI took a less circuitous course. One of two agents told him simply, "Mr. Hoover sent us here to shut you up," Walter claims. Later, the president of Patterson State Bank, where Walter served as senior vice-president, received a letter from a "Mr. Hooverson" complaining that the bank should not employ Walter, since he had been known to disclose confidential information, i.e., the warning Teletype of November 17, 1963. Years later, in 1993, Walter discovered that the author of the letter was the next-door neighbor of Special Agent Milton Kaack, Walter's former co-worker at the New Orleans FBI.

56. On Nov. 22, 1963, following the assassination, the FBI director's office sent a Teletype to all field offices "advising them to contact all their informants," Walter told the subcommittee (HSCA testimony, 12).

57. Ibid., 39-40.

58. Nancy Fenner, who claimed to have read the note because it "slipped out" of the envelope (and whom Hosty considered "unreliable" [Summers, 371]), believed that the day of the note's delivery was the first business day after the Veteran's Day holiday (Posner, 214-15).

59. Summers, 371 (citing Hearings on FBI Oversight before House Subcommittee on Civil and Constitutional Rights, Oct. 21, Dec. 11-12, 1975).

60. Ibid.

61. Posner, 217.

62. Summers, 371.

63. Ibid., 372.

64. Fenner House FBI Oversight Subcommittee testimony, 36-59, cited by Gentry, 544.

65. Gentry, 546.

66. Interview, Apr. 28, 1995.

67. Whatever fun the former defector may have extracted from playing ersatz propagandist (a role for which he showed a gifted amateur's flair, as we've seen), it was ultimately the DRE professionals who got the better part of the bargain. Immediately after the assassination, the group resumed the publicity campaign, identifying the apparent murderer of the American president as an FPCC pro-Castro Marxist, probably working in league with Cuban intelligence. By 5:47 EST on the afternoon of November 22, 1963 the CIA was told of the exile group's plans to issue a news release concerning the accused assassin. A Teletype that day from Miami's JM/WAVE station announced that the DRE had information regarding "OSWALD FORMER U.S. MARINE WHO HAD TRAVELED MOSCOW 59 AT WHICH TIME [HE] RENOUNCED AMERICAN CITIZENSHIP AND TURNED PASSPORT OVER TO AMERICAN CONSULATE . . . IN COURSE RADIO DEBATE SUBJ[ECT] CONFESSED HE [WAS A] MARXIST." The agency noted in its Teletype that this information had "not been passed" to the Secret Service or FBI.

68. Summers, 96 (citing interview with Claasen by Earl Golz in *Dallas Morning News*, 1978).

69. The perfect patsy made a wrong turn, apparently; he discovered the fate that had been prepared for him, at least according to one reading of Martino's scenario. Everything seems to have fallen apart at the end, both for Oswald, who took off running, and the anti-Castro Cubans, who, as part of the perfect plot, may have intended to kill him in the book depository, much as Benigno Aquino's "killer" was gunned down on the spot by Ferdinand Marcos's henchmen. The role of Officer Tippit in the desperate endgame remains unknown. He may well have been, as the press portrayed him at the time, an innocent victim. He may also have been, as we learn from Nancy Perrin, one of Ruby's DPD cronies funneling young women into his sleazy business. Tippit's apparent attempt to stop Oswald—barely forty-five minutes after the assassination, based on virtually no description of a suspect, and in an area where he shouldn't have been—is suspicious, Sylvia Meagher tells us (*Accessories After the Fact,* 253-82). Oswald, at any rate, wasn't going quietly.

70. Griffin memo to W. Davis Slawson (Apr. 16, 1964).

71. Cited by Gentry, 548.

72. Ibid.

73. Ibid., 552.

74. HSCA XI 35, cited Gentry, 554-55. The "suggestion" turned out to be a false alarm, supposedly the result of a conspiratorial hoax by a Houston newspaper reporter and Dallas County assistant D.A. Bill Alexander. Nevertheless, consider the reaction, as cited by Gentry: "The committee was stunned. 'If that was true [that Oswald was an FBI informant] and it ever came out and could be established,' Rankin said, 'then you would have people think that there was a conspiracy to accomplish this assassination that nothing the Commission did or anybody could dissipate.'

"BOGGS: 'You are so right.'

"DULLES: 'Oh, terrible.'

"BOGGS: 'The implications of this are fantastic, don't you think so.'

"WARREN: 'Terrific.'

"RANKIN: 'Now it is something that would be very difficult to prove out. . . . I am confident that the FBI will never admit it, and I presume their records will never show it.'"

75. FBI file No. 105-82555-3108 (pp. 13-15); Masen HSCA testimony, 23-24.

76. John Thomas Masen, now in Lewisville, is still in the gun business—mail order, these days. He is not, Ray was told recently by a woman answering the phone, talking to reporters about the assassination.

77. CIA cable, Dec. 4, 1963.

CHAPTER 11

1. Roach, indicted on criminal charges, was removed from his post. The charges were later dropped.

2. The names "Kay Ingram" and "Mr. and Mrs. Taylor" have been changed to protect their privacy.

3. Dallas: Taylor Publishing, 1993.

4. The "babushka lady," an unidentified scarved figure appearing in many Dealey Plaza photographs taken shortly before or after the shooting, "revealed" herself in the 1970s under Gary Shaw's auspices as Beverly Oliver, a nightclub singer turned born-again Christian.

5. A further indication that the cables were hoaxes was the 1975 book by Hugh McDonald, *Appointment in Dallas,* in which a foreign gunman with an author-invented pseudonym "Saul" shot President Kennedy from the Dallas County Records Building. According to Ricky's scenario, Saul was the *actual* code name of the gunman in Roscoe White's diary. The "cables" also

bore a suspicious resemblance to a sequence in the 1973 film *Executive Action*. In the film, which featured an assassination plot by intelligence agents, one of the assassins is depicted receiving orders through coded messages, much like the role Ricky assigned to his father.

6. Numerous family members who say they believe nothing of Geneva's later claims of her husband's involvement in the assassination say she is the bar girl in the *Time* photo.

7. Military travel records and letters show that Oswald and White traveled on the same ship to Japan in August-September 1957, and that White was stationed at Subic Bay, Philippines. (Oswald's travel to the Philippines, where he was stationed at Subic Bay at the same time as White, is not in question though not specified on the travel record.) White's correspondence with Geneva shows him to have been "stationed in the Philippines for a while" and sent (as part of a secret Marine/CIA action) "to Indonesia." Postmarks on White envelopes indicate that he was on a ship heading toward Indonesia at the time of the secret operation.

8. It was at Subic Bay, Oswald reportedly told Priscilla McMillan in Moscow (Nov. 16, 1959), that "he learned to sympathize with local Communists and conceived a hatred for U.S. 'militarist imperialism' for exploiting the Filipino natives" (*Marina and Lee*, 83-84; WC XX 277-85). See also Epstein, *Legend*, 72-77.

9. Geneva's brother, Benjamin Franklin Toland, who joined the Marines with White, reported that "Roscoe made the second highest score in his unit, and was immediately made a group leader" based on his test results (interview, October 1990).

10. See Appendix B, section III.

11. Notes taken during Oswald's interrogation indicate that he apparently believed McNeil to be a "Secret Service agent."

12. "Roar of the Crowd," Letters to the Editor, *Texas Monthly,* January 1992.

13. A *Newsweek* article by Aynesworth ("The JFK 'Conspiracy,'" May 15, 1967) informs us, by way of introduction, that "a veteran reporter" (Aynesworth) was sent to find out what lay behind New Orleans D.A. Jim Garrison's "increasingly notorious investigation." Aynesworth's lead:

> Jim Garrison is right. There has been a conspiracy in New Orleans—but it is a plot of Garrison's own making. It is a scheme to concoct a fantastic "solution" to the death of John F. Kennedy, and to make it stick; in this cause, the district attorney and his staff have been indirect parties to the death of one man [David Ferrie] and have humiliated, harassed and financially gutted several others.

14. See, e.g., Scott, 87; Summers, 297.

15. DPD file No. INT-2965-80, Detective D. K. Rodgers, DPD intelligence reports to Capt. W. F. Dyson (Feb. 27 and Mar. 3, 1967).

16. Rodgers (Feb. 27, 1967), 1.

17. Ibid.

18. Ibid.

19. Ibid.

20. Ibid., 2.

21. Rodgers (Mar. 3, 1967), 1.

22. Ibid., 4-5.

23. As noted in chapter 1, the FBI released the fourteen-page Whitter document in August 1994, following publication of the authors' "The Fourth Tramp: Oswald's Lost Cellmate and the Gunrunners of Dallas" (Aug. 7, 1994). (See chapter 1, n. 21 and Appendix B, n. 28.)

APPENDIX A

1. Oswald was carrying the card when arrested in Dallas following the president's assassination. The FBI obliterated the card, which is now in the National Archives. The Dallas police, however, made a photograph of it in its original state.

2. As a Cuban official, the source of this account, Gen. Fabian Escalante, has a vested interest in blaming anti-Castro Cubans for the assassination, a consideration that should be borne in mind.

3. The arrest record would be discovered by Mary La Fontaine in February 1992, together with that of cellblock mate Daniel Wayne Douglas and the famous (but otherwise irrelevant to the case) "three tramps." The Memphis FBI report on Elrod, revealing what he told the Bureau about Miller, Ruby, and his "unknown cellmate" (so designated by the FBI) Oswald, was discovered that same year by Bill Adams.

APPENDIX B

1. Frazier testified that Oswald told him the package contained curtain rods for an apartment. In an internal memorandum critiquing the evidence against Oswald, Warren Commission counsel Wesley Liebeler thought the distinction of an "apartment" (where Oswald was planning to move) as

opposed to a "room" (where he was currently living) was important.

2. Commission Exhibit 2003 (p. 63), cited by Meagher, 95.

3. WC III 295, cited by Meagher, 96.

4. Decker Exhibit 5323 (p. 508), cited by Meagher, 96.

5. Warren *Report,* 576.

6. Meagher, 95.

7. Warren *Report,* 576.

8. WC VII 109, cited by Meagher, 98-99.

9. WC V 560-61, cited by Meagher, 98.

10. Hurt, 103.

11. Later Wade admitted he made this identification on the basis of secondhand information. On this point Sylvia Meagher noted that the Commission "failed to ask who that person [source of Wade's information] was, a key question so obvious that one cannot escape the impression that it desired to avoid the answer and the possible complications it might have introduced" (*Accessories After the Fact,* 99).

12. Among the overshadowed events: an internal CIA memo of Nov. 25, 1963 noting that the identification of the rifle as a Mannlicher was "in error. It [was] a Mauser" (CIA report 104-40, WC XXIV 829, 831; see Hurt, 102-3). It was also reported that a book depository employee brought a Mauser to work shortly before the assassination. (See n. 15 below.)

13. Telephone interview, February 1993.

14. Warren *Report,* 85.

15. It was reported by Oswald (and supported by other employees) that a day or so before the assassination, an employee of the book depository brought a newly purchased 30.06 Mauser into the building and displayed it to other employees, including Oswald. The Mauser may have been left in the building temporarily (Warren *Report,* 548-56).

16. The DPD's Lt. Carl Day found prints around the trigger housing and under the stock of the rifle on the evening of November 22, 1963. He was never able to identify the prints around the trigger housing as Oswald's, but made a lift of a palm print under the stock. According to Day, he pointed out what remained of the palm print to FBI agent Vince Drain, who came to pick up the rifle and take it to FBI headquarters in Washington while Day was in the midst of his work. "I guess he didn't hear me, but I told him," Day said in an interview in the fall of 1993. Drain has said Day did not tell him of the palm print, and the FBI discovered no trace of it. (The Bureau did find prints of one of its own transporting agents on the Mannlicher.) Day kept his lift of the palm print, and it was later identified as Oswald's. Fifteen years after the assassination, the House Select Committee was able to confirm that

Day's lift came from the rifle. This much was reported in Gerald Posner's book, *Case Closed*, but not that the weeks-old prints Day found were useless as evidence.

17. The "other" prints were recently identified as Oswald's by one of three experts on the PBS television series "Frontline"; the other two could not make such an identification.

18. Meagher, 176.

19. President Lyndon Johnson, *Recordings of Telephone Conversations Related to JFK Assassination* (Austin: LBJ Library).

20. Warren *Report*, 551. Oswald's charges of photographic tampering only became known ten months later, with the release of the *Report* in September 1964. As Sylvia Meagher would note, however, Warren skeptics had been expressing the same doubts about the photographs "on the basis of the shadows and other of its features" virtually from the moment the photos were first shown (*Accessories After the Fact*, 207). The list of questions such critics have raised has only grown over the years. Marina, who supposedly took the backyard photos with a twin-lens Imperial Reflex on Sunday, Mar. 31, 1963, set the tone for later discourse by changing her story on such basic matters as the number of pictures snapped, and making improbable assertions about the manner in which the photos were taken. At first certain that she took only one picture, she later "remembered" a second; meanwhile, it's been known since 1976 that at least *three* backyard poses of Oswald were made. Marina also claimed that (inasmuch as she had no knowledge of picture taking) Oswald had to walk up to her after each shot and cock the camera for her. Yet the photos show him (and the backgrounds) to have "returned" to nearly the same spot, maintaining the continuity of photos taken on a tripod, with an unmoved camera. HSCA investigators, while granting that forged photos would be evidence of a conspiracy to kill the president and incriminate Oswald, concluded in 1979 that the backyard pictures were genuine. The fact that three different poses existed suggested (not unreasonably) an authentic backyard photo spree by a proud revolutionary displaying his wares, as opposed to a forgerer pointlessly triplicating his labors. But on the photo front nothing was conclusive, then or now, and other interpretations remain possible. Summers suggests, for example, either "a private joke" or "an operation designed to discredit the vocal left as a whole" (*Conspiracy*, 69). It was against this already complicated backdrop that Mary added her new find—the Oswald matte print.

21. HSCA VI 139.

22. Interview, September 1993.

23. In the late summer of 1992, Mary uncovered a second Oswald backyard matte photograph in the newly compiled photo inventory book of the DPD

JFK files. The latest matte print does not exhibit parallel acetate lines. It shows the Oswald silhouette of CE 133-C within the Neely Street backyard, but with a slightly different background from any of the known photos.

24. Apparently Brown had more versions of the photo-making story up his sleeve. In October 1992 Mary met Gary Savage and his uncle Rusty Livingston at a JFK forum in Dallas. Savage informed her that he and his uncle (a former colleague of Brown's in the Crime Scene Search division of the DPD at the time of the assassination) had interviewed Brown regarding the matte discovery. According to Brown's reported explanation, the matte started out as a backyard re-enactment in which Brown posed with the rifle in imitation of Oswald. Brown then allegedly "cut himself out of the picture because he didn't want people to see him in that pose." He also told Savage that "they [the La Fontaines] just found some of my cuttings." Mary showed Savage a copy of the matte photo. "Why, that's Oswald," Savage responded, surprised that the matte silhouette was the same as Oswald's in Livingston's copy of the 133-C print. But though admitting Brown had lied to him, Savage went on to publish the same version he recounted from Brown in his 1993 book, *Day One*.

25. In a highly publicized case involving the 1973 murder of a Dallas policeman (which became the basis for the Errol Morris reality film *The Thin Blue Line*), Rose allegedly attempted to coerce homicide suspect Randall Dale Adams into handling the gun used in the killing. Adams was released and Rose was later investigated for perjury in the case.

26. *Houston Post,* July 26, 1992.

27. Helen Markham, said by the Warren *Report* to have identified Oswald, claimed repeatedly that she did not do so. The Warren *Report* insisted otherwise, despite being contradicted by its own evidence volumes. Witness Domingo Benavides testified he could not identify Oswald. Acquilla Clemons said two men were present at the shooting, and a "stocky" man fired the shots.

28. Dallas independent researcher Tricia McGowan has suggested another possible connection between hoodlums Whitter and Miller and the assassination. Mrs. McGowan found a copy of a handwritten report in the Dallas Police files prior to their announced release in 1992. The report is signed "Anderton," presumably Patrolman Kenneth L. Anderton of the headquarters station, second platoon. According to the report, inmate "Robert" Borchgardt called Anderton's office from the fifth floor of the jail on the evening of Dec. 1, 1963. Borchgardt told Anderton that he had obtained information "in jail and on streets" regarding Lawrence Miller and three other men, Elvis Dalrymple, Perry Wydell, and Marvin Frazier. Miller and the three associates, Borchgardt reportedly claimed, "work for a man

named Fred who runs stolen cars and guns to Mexico and brings narcotics back." Borchgardt also told Anderton of a contract Ruby made to kill Oswald, supposedly in satisfaction of a debt owed by Ruby. No further details were contained in Anderton's report. It is virtually certain that Borchgardt was actually Richard Borchgardt, who appeared in a lineup with Oswald on November 22 at about 7:30 P.M. Though Anderton discounted Borchgardt's account, the report's mention of Miller in the context of gun-running provided partial support of the Oswald story related by another man who came in contact with the accused assassin in the city jail—John Elrod.

After the story "The Fourth Tramp" ran in the *Washington Post* August 7, 1994, the fourteen-page Whitter document was released by the FBI to the National Archives. It had been misclassified. It contained thirteen pages of rap sheets and an arrest record on Whitter dated May 1968.

The arrest record provides, perhaps, a clue to the reason why it was mis-classified. The final page shows that four years and one day after Whitter was sentenced to four years in federal institutions on the gun charges, he was arrested again by the Dallas police on "inv. theft, forg." One of the arresting officers was homicide detective J. R. Leavell, a longtime Ruby acquaintance, and the man handcuffed to Oswald as he was led to his death. Leavell has surfaced in Dallas in recent years as a debunker of conspiracy theories. He served a similar purpose when the Elrod story ran in 1992 (and was published in greater detail in August 1994), claiming that Oswald was not even in a cell on November 22. (It is difficult to know how Leavell could know this, since he was busy rounding up "witnesses" and conducting lineups on the afternoon of November 22, nowhere near the jail.)

The FBI needs to explain how the Whitter document came to be mis-classified. A good place to start is with Ferris Rukstuyl, Dallas FBI employee, Leavell pal, and the FBI's headquarters-acknowledged document expert. Leavell needs to explain how, as a homicide detective, he came to pick up a nonviolent, mostly petty thief and pimp like Whitter immediately after his federal release on the November 18 bust.

Bibliography

Bishop, Jim. *The Day Kennedy Was Shot*. New York: Funk & Wagnalls, 1968
Claflin, Edward B. *FK Wants to Know: Memos from the President's Office*. New York: William Morrow & Co., 1991.
Davis, John F. *Mafia Kingfish: Carlos Marcello and the Assassination of John F. Kennedy*. New York: New American Library, 1989.
DeLillo, Don. *Libra*. New York: Penguin Books, 1988.
Epstein, Edward J. *The Assassination Chronicles*. New York: Carroll & Graf, 1992.
—. *Legend: The Secret World of Lee Harvey Oswald*. New York: Reader's Digest Press/McGraw-Hill, 1978.
Fonzi, Gaeton. *The Last Investigation*. New York: Thunder's Mouth Press, 1993.
Garrison, Jim. *On the Trail of the Assassins: My Investigation and Prosecution of the Murder of President Kennedy*. New York: Sheridan Square Press, 1988.
Gentry, Curt. *J. Edgar Hoover: The Man and the Secrets*. New York: NAL/Dutton, 1992.
Hinckle, Warren, and William W. Turner. *Deadly Secrets: The CIA-Mafia War Against Castro and the Assassination of JFK*. New York: Thunder's Mouth Press, 1992.
Hunt, Howard. *Give Us This Day*. New Rochelle, N.Y.: Arlington House, 1973.
Hurt, Henry. *Reasonable Doubt: An Investigation into the Assassination of John F. Kennedy*. New York: Holt, Rinehart and Winston, 1985.
Jones, Penn, Jr. *Forgive My Grief*. Midlothian, Tex.: Midlothian Mirror, 1967.
Kantor, Seth. *The Ruby Cover-up*. New York: Zebra, 1992.
Lane, Mark. *Rush to Judgment*. New York: Thunder's Mouth Press, 1992.
McDonald, Hugh C., as told to Geoffrey Bocca. *Appointment in Dallas: The Final Solution to the Assassination of JFK*. New York: Zebra, 1975.

McMillan, Priscilla. *Marina and Lee*. New York: Harper and Row, 1977.

Manchester, William. *The Death of a President*. New York: Harper and Row, 1967.

Marrs, Jim. *Crossfire: The Plot That Killed Kennedy*. New York: Carroll & Graf, 1989.

Meagher, Sylvia. *Accessories After the Fact: The Warren Commission, the Authorities and the Report*. New York: Random House, Vintage Books, 1992.

Melanson, Philip H. *Spy Saga: Lee Harvey Oswald and U.S. Intelligence*. New York: Praeger, 1990.

Newman, John M. *JFK and Vietnam: Deception, Intrigue and the Struggle of Power.* New York: Warner Books, 1992.

Oglesby, Carl. *The Yankee and Cowboy War.* New York: Berkley Publishing, 1977.

Posner, Gerald. *Case Closed: Lee Harvey Oswald and the Assassination of JFK*. New York: Random House, 1993.

Russell, Dick. *The Man Who Knew Too Much: Richard Case Nogell and the Assassination of JFK*. New York: Carroll and Graf, 1992.

Scott, Peter Dale. *Deep Politics and the Death of JFK*. Berkeley and Los Angeles: University of California Press, 1993.

Scott, Peter Dale, Paul L. Hoch, and Russell Stetler. *The Assassinations: Dallas and Beyond—A Guide to Cover-ups and Assassinations*. New York: Random House, 1976.

Stone, Oliver, and Zachary Sklar. *JFK: The Book of the Film: A Documented Screenplay*. New York: Applause Theatre Book Publications, 1992.

Sullivan, Marianne. *Kennedy Ripples: A True Love Story*. San Clemente, Calif.: Lillian James Publishing, 1994.

Summers, Anthony. *Conspiracy*. New York: Paragon House, 1989.

U.S. Congress. House. Select Committee on Assassinations. *Investigation of the Assassination of President John F. Kennedy: Hearings*. 95th Cong., 2d sess., 1979.

—. *Investigation of the Assassination of President John F. Kennedy: Report*. 95th Cong., 2d sess., 1979.

Wainwright, Loudon. *The Great American Magazine: An Inside History of Life*. New York: Alfred A. Knopf, 1986.

Warren Commission: President's Commission on the Assassination of President John F. Kennedy. *Hearings*. Washington, D.C.: U.S. Government Printing Office, 1964.

Warren Commission. *Report of the Warren Commission: The Assassination of President Kennedy: New York Times Edition*. New York: McGraw-Hill, 1964.

Weisberg, Harold. *Oswald in New Orleans: Case of Conspiracy with the CIA*. New York: Canyon Books, 1967.

Index